Families & Psychosocial Problems

Maureen Leahey, RN, PhD
Team Director, Mental Health Services
Holy Cross Hospital
Adjunct Associate Professor
Faculty of Nursing, University of Calgary
Calgary, Alberta, Canada

Lorraine M. Wright, RN, PhD
Director, Family Nursing Unit
Professor, Faculty of Nursing
University of Calgary
Calgary, Alberta, Canada

Springhouse Corporation
Springhouse, Pennsylvania

Publisher: Keith Lassner

Senior Acquisitions Editor: Susan L. Taddei

Art Director: John Hubbard

Editorial Services Manager: David Moreau

Senior Production Manager: Deborah C. Meiris

Special thanks to the following, who assisted in preparation of this volume: Carol Robertson, Bernadette Glenn, and Jean Robinson.

CHAPTER 3
Reprinted with permission from Walsh, F. (ed.). *Normal Family Processes.* New York: Guilford Press, 1982.

CHAPTER 8
The author wishes to acknowledge the editorial contributions of Mary E. Hagle, MS, RN.

CHAPTER 17
Preparation of this chapter was supported, in part, by NIMH Faculty Development Award #01 MH 1717701.

CHAPTER 20
Excerpts from this chapter have appeared in the *Journal of Strategic and Systemic Therapies,* 1985, vol. 4(1):24-32, Reprinted with permission.

The clinical procedures described and recommended in this publication are based on research and consultation with nursing, medical, and legal authorities. To the best of our knowledge, these procedures reflect currently accepted practice; nevertheless, they can't be considered absolute and universal recommendations. For individual application, all recommendations must be considered in light of the patient's clinical condition and, before administration of new or infrequently used drugs, in light of latest package-insert information. The authors and the publisher disclaim responsibility for any adverse effects resulting directly or indirectly from the suggested procedures, from any undetected errors, or from the reader's misunderstanding of the text.

Printed in the United States of America.

Library of Congress Cataloging-in-Publication Data
Families and psychosocial problems.

(Family nursing series)
Includes bibliographies and index.
1. Family—Mental health. 2. Psychiatric nursing. I. Leahey, Maureen, 1944- . II. Wright, Lorraine M., 1943- . III. Series.
[DNLM: 1. Family—nurses' instruction. 2. Nursing Assessment—methods. 3. Psychiatric Nursing—methods. WY 160 F1978]
RC455.4.F3F357 1987 155.9'24 87-7109
ISBN 0-87434-092-6

To our other "families":

Mum, Jim, Stephen, Dennice, Douglas, and
Adrienne for their love and support.

Maureen Leahey

Fabie, Joanne, Martin, Sheldon, and Wendy for
their love and support and for valuing our
special six-week rituals.

Lorraine M. Wright

ABOUT THE EDITORS

MAUREEN LEAHEY, RN, PhD, is a nurse/family therapist specializing in work with children/adolescents and families with health problems. Dr. Leahey is a chartered psychologist. She is a Team Director and Director of the Family Therapy Institute, Mental Health Services, Holy Cross Hospital; Adjunct Assistant Professor, Department of Psychiatry, Faculty of Medicine; and Adjunct Associate Professor, Faculty of Nursing, University of Calgary. Dr. Leahey maintains a part-time private practice in strategic marital and family therapy and is a consultant. She is a member of the Commission on Accreditation for Family Therapy Education of the American Association for Marriage and Family Therapy.

LORRAINE M. WRIGHT, RN, PhD, is Director, Family Nursing Unit, and Professor, Faculty of Nursing, University of Calgary. Dr. Wright's clinical and research interests include family somatics and systemic therapy; training and supervision of family clinical nurse specialists and family therapists; and split-opinion interventions. She maintains a part-time private practice in marriage and family therapy and is also a family therapy consultant. Dr. Wright is on the Board of the Alberta Foundation for Nursing Research and is a member of the Research Committee of the American Association for Marriage and Family Therapy. She also serves on the editorial board of the International Journal of Family Therapy.

Both editors have taught family nursing and family therapy to nursing and medical students, psychologists, social workers, and residents in family practice, pediatrics, and psychiatry. They have presented papers at national and international conferences in the United States, Canada, Israel, and Europe and have published their work in several journals. They are the co-authors of *Nurses and Families: A Guide to Family Assessment and Intervention* (F.A. Davis Company, Philadelphia, 1984).

CONTENTS

SECTION III: INTERVENING WITH FAMILIES WITH PSYCHOSOCIAL PROBLEMS

PREFACE

Family Nursing Series

Although nurses have always interacted with the families of their patients, today's nurses are not only being encouraged but are also seeking ways to actively help families with health problems.

The Family Nursing Series, which consists of three volumes, focuses on clinically important family health issues. Titles include *Families and Life-Threatening Illness, Families and Chronic Illness,* and *Families and Psychosocial Problems.* Each volume provides an overview of family nursing with assessment and intervention sections on various health problems. Families at various stages of the developmental life cycle (for example, families with young children, families with adolescents, middle-aged families, and aging families) as well as various family forms (for example, single-parent, step-parent, and gay and lesbian families) are presented. Each chapter combines theory, research, and clinical examples to offer practical *how-tos* for assessment and intervention. Additionally, each chapter is organized according to the nursing process with direct access to information about assessment, planning, intervention, and evaluation.

Written for nursing students as well as practicing nurses, the Family Nursing Series provides current clinical information in a practical format. Essential theory is always presented in the context of clinical material, with the emphasis on sound family assessment and intervention. Descriptive case studies illustrate normal and dysfunctional families coping with health issues. Family Nursing Series contributors are authoritative clinicians and educators from a variety of distinguished nursing centers across North America.

Families and Psychosocial Problems

This volume offers an in-depth clinical guide to assessment and intervention with families with psychosocial problems. It offers specific, clear instructions on *how to* assess and intervene effectively.

The first section provides the conceptual base for working with families. To interview families and accurately identify their strengths and problems, a nurse must first have a sound conceptual framework. The chapters in this section deal with different aspects of family nursing and psychosocial issues. Family nursing is defined, discussed, and examined with relevance to family therapy and psychosocial problems.

Reciprocity issues between the family and psychosocial problems are considered as well as the nurse's assumptions about the family's coping abilities. Intercultural issues are dealt with in a chapter on ethnicity, families, and psychosocial problems.

The second section tells *how to* assess families with specific psychosocial problems, such as teenage suicide, depression, chronic mental illness, and attachment problems. Each chapter offers specific questions to use when interviewing families.

The third section goes into depth about issues involved in intervening with families dealing with specific psychosocial problems. It considers various family forms, such as single-parent families and stepfamilies. It focuses on families in various health care settings; for example, community health, hospitals, schools, and outpatient clinics. Each chapter in this section is organized according to the nursing process and includes detailed case examples of families at all stages of the developmental life cycle. Intervention chapters focus on families of infants and child abuse, families of school-aged children with unresolved grief, families of adolescents with bulimia, and aging families with depression. This section deals with such current topical issues as marital violence, sexual abuse, spouse abuse, posttraumatic stress disorder, and alcoholism.

The major difference between this book and other books on family nursing is that its primary emphasis is the application of family assessment and intervention models to deal with *specific* psychosocial problems in *specific* clinical settings with families in *specific* family developmental stages.

ACKNOWLEDGMENTS

We are grateful to our many colleagues and friends who have helped in countless ways to make the Family Nursing Series a reality. They stood by us through the moments of exhilaration and exasperation over the two and a half years of this project.

In particular, we are indebted to:

Susan Taddei, Senior Acquisitions Editor at Springhouse Book Corporation, who first thought of the idea of the series and inspired us to undertake it.

Bernadette Glenn and the staff at Springhouse Book Corporation for their helpfulness in overseeing the technical aspects of the Family Nursing Series.

The 76 authors who contributed 65 chapters in the Family Nursing Series and who have shared their expertise and vision of family nursing.

The secretaries who have graciously assisted us: Lynda Gourlie, Louise Hamilton, Ilona Schiedrowski, and Evy Stadey.

Douglas Leahey, who had confidence in our ability throughout the project. He encouraged and supported us in numerous ways, not least of which was transporting chapters to the courier.

Fabie Duhamel, who patiently listened to the many tales of the various stages of the Family Nursing Series and provided steady support. She was also a very willing, efficient "courier" who transported chapters between us.

Laura Crealy, who graciously took in all our packages from Federal Express.

In the process of editing these books, we have remained friends as well as colleagues and have discovered new dimensions to our friendship. We learned to hone our negotiating skills, oscillate in inspiring and supporting each other, and enjoy punctuating our progress through minicelebrations.

M.L.
L.M.W.

GENOGRAM KEY

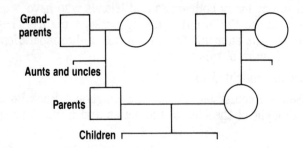

Grand-parents

Aunts and uncles

Parents

Children

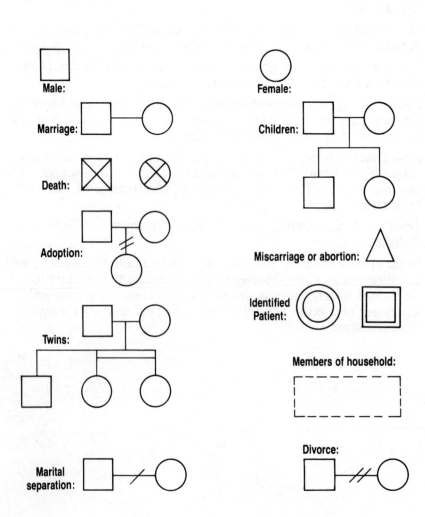

Male:

Female:

Marriage:

Children:

Death:

Adoption:

Miscarriage or abortion:

Twins:

Identified Patient:

Members of household:

Marital separation:

Divorce:

SECTION I

Overview of Families and Psychosocial Problems

1 Psychosocial problems and the family: An overview

Susan L. Jones, RN, CS, PhD
Professor
School of Nursing
Kent State University
Kent, Ohio

OVERVIEW

This chapter presents an overview of family therapy theory and clinical interventions relating to family nursing today. Family therapy is both a philosophy and an orientation to conceptualizing human problems. A case study shows how an individual's psychosocial problems affect the family system and how family system dysfunction impacts on each family member. Distinctions are made between family nursing and family therapy in nursing. The history of family therapy is outlined, followed by an overview of family therapy approaches. Indications and contraindications for family therapy are discussed. The typical phases of treatment, along with the therapy interventions within each phase, are described.

CASE STUDY

Megan O'Connell is a 19-year-old sophomore nursing student from a conflictual Irish family. She is the youngest of five children. Megan's father, Michael, is a domineering man; her mother, Maureen, is quiet but handles her husband in a passive-aggressive manner. Maureen and Michael disagree on most things—particularly childrearing practices. Michael thinks that Maureen is too lenient with the children, and she thinks that he will "correct" and "redo" her discipline of them.

During her first year in college, Megan did very well. She received A's and B's and enjoyed living in the dorm. Because the college was only 40 miles from her home, she visited often. She spent the first summer at home and worked at a fast food restaurant.

When she returned in the fall, Megan was quieter than before. She had difficulty concentrating on school and her grades slipped. She spent much time daydreaming and talking to herself. Rather than fail in school, she dropped out and returned to her family's home to live. This heightened Megan's withdrawn and isolated behavior. Megan was diagnosed as schizophrenic and hospitalized six weeks later.

The preceding case study is true; only the names and a few details have been changed. It poses this question: How is the family affected by the psychosocial problems of each family member; and how does each person's psychosocial problems affect the family? This chapter will demonstrate the reciprocity between families and psychosocial problems and will show how family systems nursing combines family therapy concepts with systems theory to assess and intervene.

The idea of focusing on the family of a child with psychosocial problems such as Megan O'Connell is hardly a new one in nursing (Smoyak, 1975). Nurses—perhaps more than other health care professionals—have traditionally obtained a complete family history as part of a nursing assessment, and they have always included the family in the treatment plan. Since each family member's psychosocial problems affect the entire family, and since the family as a system impacts on the psychosocial problems of each individual member, nurses must consider the family as the patient (Jones, 1980).

PSYCHOSOCIAL PROBLEMS AND THE FAMILY: AN ISSUE OF RECIPROCITY

Interest in the family of the patient experiencing psychosocial problems has, over the years, produced a redefinition of the family as the patient (Jones, 1980). This focus on the entire family system rather than on one individual member is the key to the family therapy approach. Thus, an individual's psychosocial symptoms are not considered purely intrapsychic in origin, but instead represent a family system or family distress. The individual's symptoms are by-products of family struggles and the distressed individual is simply the family's "symptom bearer." Conversely, the individual's psychosocial symptoms affect the family system, creating a "feedback loop" between each family member and the family as a system. Changes in the family system and the individual affect each other reciprocally.

Family therapy interventions are tools for understanding whatever individual behavior patterns arise from the feedback into the family system. The interventions focus on correcting dysfunctional patterns of interaction within the family, with a secondary interest in revealing these patterns' origins and development. Therapy's primary interest is not to discover the "cause" of the problems, but rather to break the dysfunctional "feedback loop" that exists between one (or more) individual family member(s) and the family as a system (Gurman and Kniskern, 1981).

When individual dysfunction is viewed as a by-product of family dysfunction, no single family member can be blamed for the ineffective functioning of the family. All individuals remain responsible for their own behavior; however, the family view of dysfunction emphasizes the ways that each individual influences the family system's effectiveness. Thus, individual mental health is a reflection of family mental health. Family mental health, in turn, measures the family's overall system effectiveness—particularly in terms of decision-making and problem-solving (Sedgewick, 1981).

Once she views the family as a total unit, it becomes obvious to the psychiatric nurse that "dysfunctional" behavior in one family member is linked to the "normal" behavior in another family member. The "normality" of one feeds upon the "abnormality" of another. When one family member's functioning begins to improve, another family member often becomes more dysfunctional. The following example illustrates this:

During her hospitalization and subsequent outpatient therapy, Megan O'Connell improved and she began to attend a local community college part-time while still living at home. As she improved, however, Mr. and Mrs. O'Connell's marriage deteriorated. It can be hypothesized that Megan's illness had been holding her parents' marriage together. The marital couple had nothing to talk about besides Megan's illness and the crisis that it had created.

This situation shows how attempts by the "identified patient" within the family to recover from illness can reshuffle a family's rules and relationships. Such changes threaten other family members, producing illness in one of them.

Ferreira (1967) said that one family member's "psychosis" may be only an enlarged version of the family's system of myths. The individual, therefore, is not psychotic; rather, there is a "family psychosis." The abnormality of one individual may have been written off as "moodiness," "laziness," or the like. But as the myth develops, the abnormality intensifies and enlarges until family members conclude that the family member is "psychotic," when in fact the dysfunction exists within the family system rather than in the individual family member.

Family therapy is a conceptual orientation to human problems rather than a technique; it conceptualizes problems on an organizational level. The individual is not the patient; the family is the patient. Megan merely bears the symptom for her schizophrenic family. Therefore, treatment for the family should occur on a family organizational level rather than on an individual level. Megan will be treated with her family, and the entire family will be the unit of treatment.

Therapy focuses on interactions among family members rather than on events, individuals, or single elements (Jones, 1980). Clarification of communication and interaction during the family therapy sessions helps decrease dysfunctional interactional patterns. As a consequence of the decrease in dysfunction in the family system, Megan's behavior appears more normal; she no longer has to bear the family pathology.

Family systems theory and family therapy assume that a linear causal model is useless for studying or treating human interaction on an organizational level. The focus is not on Megan's individual behavior. Rather, individuals are considered to behave according to a family "pattern." For example, Megan's family argues in the same interactional pattern regardless of the content of the argument; it does not matter if the subject is sex, money, or discipline. Family therapists have referred to these interactional patterns as family rules, quid pro quo, double bind, or pseudomutuality.

Helping families recognize and break these patterns is the essence of family therapy. Just as the pattern is primary and cannot be reduced to smaller elements, it is impossible to isolate Megan, her diagnosis, or her hospitalization from the interactional pattern of the family.

FAMILY THERAPY VERSUS FAMILY NURSING

Family therapy, as a philosophy and a conceptual orientation, assumes that psychosocial problems of individuals within families arise out of and feed back into the family system. The family member who expresses the psychiatric pathology is simply the symptom bearer for the family. Family therapy interventions are meant to change dysfunctional patterns of interaction within the family. When the dysfunctional communication patterns become functional, the individual no longer needs to be a symptom bearer, and thus the psychiatric pathology subsides.

Family nursing, on the other hand, focuses on the family and crosses all clinical nursing specialties. Unlike family therapy, it focuses on the *individual's illness*, with the patient viewed *within a family context.* In family nursing, the individual patient is recognized as being ill; the illness may be acute or chronic, and the patient may be of any age group. Care may be given by a nurse from any clinical specialty area. The course of the illness, however, is shaped by the family's reaction to it and the family must be considered when planning interventions.

Public health nurses have historically been family-focused because they provide care in the home. More recently, a family focus has emerged in maternity and pediatric nursing (Ham and Chamings, 1983), with a focus on fathers and the effect that a new birth or sick child has on the family. Most aspects of medical-surgical nursing focus on the family (Roberts, 1976). All crises involving health and health care are almost always conceptualized with a family focus (Hall and Weaver, 1974). Gerontological nursing has become family-focused (D'Affliti and

Weitz, 1974), and so has care for the terminally ill (MacVicar, 1980; Freel, 1980). In fact, the family has become an important element in all clinical nursing specialties. The focus on the patient—in any illness, in any clinical specialty—within the family context is the essence of family nursing.

However, with the increasing recognition of the reciprocity between family dynamics and illness (i.e., the family's reaction to the illness impacts on the patient and the patient's illness impacts on the family) a new level of family nursing has evolved: family systems nursing. Two levels of family nursing are emerging: the family as context and the family as the unit of care.

The Historical Development of Family Therapy

Before the advent of family therapy, clinicians (including nurses) avoided and even discouraged contact with their patients' relatives (Nichols, 1984). At the time, this prejudice merely reflected current psychoanalytic theory. The most influential approaches to psychotherapy in 1950 were Freud's psychoanalysis and Rogers' client-centered therapy. Both therapies presumed that psychological problems arise from unhealthy interactions with others early in life. In both approaches, the preferred intervention was treatment through a private relationship between patient and therapist.

Freud believed that neurotic conflicts are spawned in early interactions between children and their families. He sought to isolate the family from treatment in hopes of liberating the patient from the family's pathological influences. The family was considered an "infectious disease" to be kept out of the "psychoanalytic operating room" (Nichols, 1984). Freud also discovered that the less he revealed of his own personality, the more his patients reacted to him as though he were a significant figure from their lives; this was called a "transference" reaction. Gradually, Freud fostered and analyzed the transference, which became a cornerstone of psychoanalysis and other dynamic therapies.

Carl Rogers also believed that psychological problems stem from destructive early interactions with others. Each of us, Rogers said, is born with a tendency toward self-actualization; to him, that was the basic premise of all human psychology. Left to our own devices, he said, we will follow our own best interests. However, our healthy instinct toward self-actualization becomes warped when we seek the affection and approval of other people. These others respond to us in terms of their own needs; thus our need for self-fulfillment collides with the need for approval. As a result, we learn to deny the anger, anxiety, and other feelings that may result from our seeking approval. Rogers' therapy was designed to help patients rediscover their own feelings, urges, and self-actualizing tendencies. The Rogerian therapist listens carefully and sympathetically, communicating understanding, warmth, and respect for the patient (Nichols, 1984).

The client-centered therapist, like the psychoanalyst, maintains absolute privacy in the therapeutic relationship; in this way, he avoids any situation in which the patient's feelings and impulses might be denied or distorted to win approval. Involvement of other persons in therapy, it was feared, might destroy the "transference" relationship.

The family approach to therapy dates from the early 1950s, when several therapists, unknown to each other, began seeing families for treatment—usually in response to symptoms manifested by one member (Nichols, 1984). What evolved, however, went beyond the practice of merely obtaining information from the family about the patient, toward refocusing of attention from the individual to the relational dynamics between family members. The therapist's goal became positive change for the entire family.

Therapists broke away from the established ideas about individual pathology and change for several reasons. In one sense, they did so spontaneously. Sometimes family treatment resulted when a therapist brought the family members together to help explain something the patient said. The family might initially be interviewed only for information, but when the therapist saw what was happening between family members, he was forced to consider a new etiology of human problems. Alternatively, the therapist may have noticed that when his patient changed, another family member would develop emotional problems; thus, the individual's recovery did not always benefit each member of the family or the family as a whole. At times, apparently, the treatment of one individual was actually undermined by the family. Such observations forced therapists to reconsider the family's role in the treatment of pathology.

The development of family therapy was also accelerated by the vast amount of research done in the 1950s and 1960s on links between family dynamics and schizophrenia. Such terms as "double bind" and "homeostasis" were coined to describe family functioning through a systems approach. Many of the early subjects of family therapy were families with a member who—like Megan—was diagnosed as schizophrenic. Theoretical and research ideas that had roots in the 1950s blossomed and grew into specific frameworks of family interrelationships in the 1960s, when the field of family therapy truly began. Family therapy journals were established and a variety of clinicians—including nurses—took interest in learning about and conducting family therapy sessions.

Family Therapy in Nursing

Seeing the family-as-client has been a principle of public health nursing for over 50 years (Tinkham and Voorhies, 1977). Indeed, the family has always been one of nursing's concerns, though not a primary concern. The act of caring for patients in their home, in the context of their families, allowed nurses to view the family as a whole and to treat it as such. Many nurses did so, but only because of their own sensitivity and initiative (Leavitt, 1982).

In a 1932 interview in the *New York World Telegraph*, Lillian Wald, an early leader in nursing, described the first years of her visiting nurse service (begun in 1892) and the concept of family nursing at the time: "We went into the home not just as nurses but as friends and teachers. Our nurses were to go into the home, not to tell the mother how to do things, but to get busy and to do things with her" (Ford, 1979).

Although nursing has been family-focused for years, only in recent years (Jones and Dimond, 1982) has family therapy as defined here become prevalent. Family therapy interventions utilized in nursing have been discussed for over 15 years now, and the increasing interest by nurses in this field was manifested in 1975 by the appearance of a family therapy text (Smoyak, 1975). Since that time, several family nursing and family therapy nursing texts have been completed (Clements and Buchanan, 1982; Clements and Roberts, 1983; Wright and Leahey, 1984) and family therapy is now an integral part of both undergraduate and graduate nursing education.

FAMILY THERAPY APPROACHES

Since the 1950s, many distinct approaches to family therapy have been outlined (Jones and Dimond, 1982). All, however, share the belief that family therapy should promote a change within the family system. Most approaches assume that problems stem from the family system of rules and roles. In an attempt to organize the field, several classifications have been developed to identify the various approaches. Five classifications of the field will be presented here.

In 1970, the Group for the Advancement of Psychiatry (GAP) attempted to organize the field. This group surveyed individuals who identified themselves as family therapists and, based upon the results, family therapists were classified on a continuum to indicate their theoretical orientation. The continuum ranged from A (therapists with a primary focus on individual system) to Z (therapists with a primary focus on family systems). Although the GAP categorization was rudimentary, it stimulated a series of other attempts to classify the theoretical orientations of family therapists.

Beels and Ferber (1973), for instance, observed family therapy sessions on-site to construct their classification. In posing the question "How do therapists present themselves to clients?" they found two categorizations: conductors—those therapists with vigorous personalities; and reactors—those who follow the direction of the families.

As a reaction to the "anti-theory" orientation of the 1960s, Guerin (1976) classified therapists according to his own perception of their theoretical orientations. He first classified them into two groups—psychoanalytic and systems orientations—and then subdivided them into individual, group, experiential, and Ackerman-approach categories.

Jones (1980) delineated the approaches of seven family therapy frameworks, categorizing them according to their theoretical and clinical orientations. The seven are: integrative, psychoanalytic, multigenerational, structural, interactional, social network, and behavioral. The same outline for presentation was used to describe each approach (i.e., therapeutic unit, major concepts, goal of therapy, and treatment process) so that systematic comparisons could be made.

Nichols (1984) compared eight family therapy approaches in a systematic manner. The comparisons are similar to Jones' (1980) and include psychoanalytic, group, experiential, behavioral, extended family systems, communication, strategic, and structural. An important family therapy approach, missing in the previous classifications, is the systemic (Milan) approach. This approach, like others, defines schizophrenia as a peculiar pattern of communication inseparable from the other patterns of communication in the family (Palazzoli et al., 1978). One difficulty in classifying the family therapy field today is that different terms are used to identify the same approach.

FAMILY NURSING EDUCATION VERSUS FAMILY THERAPY IN NURSING PROGRAMS

Family nursing education is part of nearly every undergraduate and graduate nursing program today. A few graduate programs in nursing focus exclusively on family nursing. As mentioned previously, family nursing is not unique to any one clinical specialty area but cuts across all of them. There are no stated minimal educational requirements for the practice of family nursing, since it is an essential component of a basic nursing education program.

Family therapy in nursing education, by contrast, consists of advanced and specialized skills in the area of psychiatric and mental health nursing. The American Nurses' Association's division of psychiatric and mental health nursing practice asserts that a minimum of a master's degree is prerequisite for the development of the skills and expertise required to be an effective family therapist (Calhoun, 1982).

The ANA recognizes that many nurses with varied backgrounds are adequately prepared to offer informal counseling services to patients and families. However, this informal counseling differs from the practice of psychotherapy, which consists of a structured, formal contractual agreement between the therapist and client (ANA Standards of Practice, 1983). Family therapy falls within the more structured psychotherapy context, and thus the nurse/family therapist must have a minimum of a master's degree in psychiatric/mental health nursing. Graduate programs in psychiatric mental health nursing usually provide at least one semester of family therapy, which provides the nurse with the minimum requirements to conduct family therapy.

The family therapy course in nursing demands clinical experience with supervised instruction. Therapy is a personal encounter with a family, and the therapist can learn only by doing it (Calhoun, 1982). The best way to learn family therapy is by having live supervision provided by a qualified nurse therapist. Videotape supervision assists with the development of perceptual and conceptual skills. Case discussion alone is the least useful method of developing skills in family therapy (Wright and Leahey, 1984).

INDICATIONS AND CONTRAINDICATIONS FOR FAMILY THERAPY

Treatment is usually indicated when either the nurse therapist evaluates and/or the family indicates that the family system has a psychosocial problem.

When the identified patient is a child, the practice in child guidance clinics has been to involve at least one of the parents. A more thorough approach, however, is indicated when the child appears to be the "symptom bearer" of a more general family problem, such as marital conflict, as was the case with Megan O'Connell. Bowen (1978), as well as the interactional family therapists (Berger, 1978; Sluzki and Ransom, 1976; Watzlawick and Weakland, 1977), suggest that whenever a child shows emotional difficulties before puberty, family treatment is indicated, since the child's symptoms will often be related to marital conflict.

Family therapy becomes the treatment of choice when individual therapy fails. The lack of improvement may stem from dysfunctional communication between family members. If the patient spends a good deal of time talking about a family member he probably needs family therapy. A common example of this is when one spouse spends all of the therapy time talking about the other.

If one family member's (the identified patient) improved functioning causes another member's dysfunction, this too calls for family therapy. A family evaluation frequently shows that when the family homeostasis, or balance, has been upset, another family member must become dysfunctional to maintain the balance. For example, Megan's mother psychologically needed to take care of Megan. Mrs. O'Connell's ambivalence made it difficult for Megan to go back to school, and this resulted in a major increase in the dysfuntion of the marital system in that family.

The need for family therapy also arises when the identified patient is an inpatient and close to discharge. Research (Gurman and Kniskern, 1981) has shown that a patient's improvement during hospitalization often reverses when he returns home unless family members have been involved in the treatment. This was the case with Megan. Until both parents became involved in the discharge planning, their subtle resistance to Megan's returning home kept surfacing. Without family treatment, the patient will return to the same dysfunctional patterns associated with the symptoms that first brought her into treatment.

On the other hand, what circumstances contraindicate family treatment? Some family therapists choose family therapy wherever psychotherapy is indicated. The only exceptions to this rule might be the limited ability of the therapist to work with the entire family, or the unwilliness of the family system to make necessary changes.

Not all disturbed families, however, will necessarily benefit from therapy that involves all family members. In some cases, it may be too late to reverse the family's fragmentation. In others, it may be too difficult to establish a therapeutic relationship with the family because key members are unavailable. In still other cases, one family member may be so severely disturbed and disruptive that the family approach is unworkable. For example, he may be paranoid, manic, or agitated. In the O'Connell case, a few sessions were held without Megan because of her psychosis and her inability to sit through an hour session.

Many nurse therapists believe that family therapy is always indicated unless the patient's symptoms are clearly not linked to the family system. A nurse therapist may have to conduct several sessions with a client—inpatient or outpatient—before she decides whether it would be beneficial or not to involve other family members. In other situations, the nurse therapist may know immediately. And in still other situations, the nurse therapist may follow the approach of Bowen (1978) in which a family-focused approach is taken but only one or two family members are seen in therapy as an inpatient or outpatient.

Phases of Treatment

As in most forms of treatment, the family therapy process can be divided into phases. Understanding each phase of treatment is essential to understanding the process of family therapy. Following are the four phases:

The first contact. Family therapy begins with the family's first contact with the therapist or agency. At this time, one family member will have his own opinion about the type of assistance that is needed for one family member or the family as a whole. The person contacting the agency is usually the person who has taken responsibility for dealing with family problems. Before a first interview is scheduled, a nurse should obtain basic family information. Such information helps the therapist decide whether to have individual or family treatment sessions. A checklist of information has been found useful (Jones, 1984):

• Basic demographic information for all family members (ages, sex, and names of members living in the home and children living outside the home).
• Who is the "identified patient" within the family and what is the problem?
• Has the patient been previously involved in therapy? If so, with whom and for how long? Were other family members involved? Has the patient been hospitalized? When and for what length of time?
• How are the other family members involved with the problem of the patient?
• Who is willing to attend therapy sessions?

Freeman (1981) outlines six problems that family members often present as reasons for family therapy. Each of these problems reflects a family system dysfunction and each indicates how the family has developed over time as a homeostatic entity:

• Personal problem: An adult family member is concerned about himself and complains of anxiety, depression, or fear.
• Parent-child problem: There is conflict between a parent and one or more of the children.
• Child problem: A child is experiencing difficulty or is "acting out."
• Sibling problem: Siblings are in conflict with each other and the adults do not know what to do.
• Extended family problem: A member of the extended family has a psychosocial problem or his behavior is a problem to the family.
• Husband-wife problem: Marital conflict exists between spouses.

The decision about who should attend the first interview depends upon the type of problem. If the initiator of the contact defines the problem as his alone and indicates a desire to work individually, then it may be necessary to work on that basis at first. Nevertheless, if changes in the individual begin to affect the family system, other family members should become involved. When there is a parent-child problem, both parents should participate at once in the therapy process along with the child. If the problem involves a member of the extended family, the therapeutic structure will have to broaden to include several family members (Freeman, 1981).

If the patient is hospitalized, the nurse's initial contact with the patient is usually on an individual basis. Again, however, if the nurse and treatment team suspect a family problem, they must involve the family in therapy. As in the case with outpatients, the family subsystem most closely associated with the problem must be involved. In an inpatient setting, it often helps to observe the interactions between the patient and family members. Observations during visiting hours are particularly helpful.

The initial interview. The first session with the family will determine the course and direction of treatment. During this session, the family will decide whether to continue treatment, so the nurse should first address the family's anxiety. If the family has not yet defined the problem as being a family one, then the members may be anxious and uncertain. They may be confused about their reason for being there— particularly if they believe the problem lies only with the identified patient. How the family's anxiety and fears are handled during this session will determine whether the family decides to work as a unit.

Before the initial session is over, each family member must define the problem from his viewpoint. The therapist must make sure the identi- fied patient does not become the scapegoat; at the same time, she should not be overly zealous in insisting that the problem is a family one. Refocusing the discussion to other members, however, can protect the patient. A good barometer of the family's function or dysfunction is how congruently each member defines the problem. In most instances, the less the congruence between definitions, the more dysfunctional the family's patterns of interaction.

The initial session ends with a short discussion of who will partici- pate in subsequent sessions, how often the sessions will be held, and so forth. Spending the last few moments in such a discussion provides closure for the session.

The middle phase of therapy. The therapy process is anchored by the middle phase; the majority of therapeutic work is accomplished by the family at this time. At this time, the family will learn to identify communication patterns, coalitions, issues, and concerns. Since the issues change as the therapy process proceeds, less attention will be focused on the patient and more on the broader conflicts within the family.

The goal of therapy at this stage is to help the family restructure communication patterns to promote more functional interactions. One goal is to increase the members' autonomy so that they can exercise greater independence in their behavior. Several family therapists (Bowen, 1978; Satir, 1967) refer to this process as "differentiation of self." Greater independence allows the rigid family patterns to relax and enables family members to listen to each other more effectively. Each one may begin to receive feedback, perhaps for the first time, about other family members' reactions to their behavior. While some interaction patterns may be highly resistant to change, the therapist's overall objective is to teach the family how to accept change, and how to achieve its potentially positive benefits.

Termination of therapy. No family leaves treatment problem-free, nor will all members have progressed to the same point by termination. Nevertheless, therapy does not continue forever. When the family begins to effectively handle its problems as they arise, a readiness for termination may emerge. A formal termination session will allow the family the opportunity to share their overall experience in the therapy process and provide closure for the therapy. It is helpful for the family members to evaluate their success in handling old problems and their ability to cope with new concerns.

During a termination session, each family member can discuss what he considers the most and least beneficial aspects of therapy. Again, individual family members are often surprised by other family members' responses. The nurse-therapist at this stage should encourage family members to focus on the family in general so that they can understand the primary communication patterns. The last item on the agenda is to invite the family to return if they feel they need help.

CONCLUSIONS

In summary, family therapy is both a philosophy and an orientation to conceptualizing human problems. It is based on the tenet that an individual's psychosocial problems affect the family and that the family is a system affecting each family member. In this chapter, an overview of family therapy in terms of theoretical orientation was presented. Distinctions between family therapy and family nursing were made. Although the patient's family has always been central in nursing, only within the last few years has nursing, through family therapy, considered the *family to be the patient.* Nursing is in an ideal position to offer family assessments and interventions that assist patients on an individual and family systems level.

REFERENCES

Beels, C., and Ferber, A. "What Family Therapists Do," in *The Book of Family Therapy.* Edited by Ferber, A., et al. New York: Houghlin Mifflin, 1973.

Berger, M. *Beyond the Double Bind: Communication and Family Systems, Theories, and Techniques with Schizophrenics.* New York: Brunner-Mazel, 1978.

Bowen, M. *Family Therapy in Clinical Practice.* New York: Jason Aronson, 1978.

Calhoun, G.W. "The Nurse as Therapist," in *Family Therapy: A Nursing Perspective.* Edited by Clements, I.W. and Buchanan, D.M. New York: John Wiley & Sons, 1982.

Clements, I.M., and Buchanan, D.M., eds. *Family Therapy: A Nursing Perspective.* New York: John Wiley & Sons, 1982.

Clements, I.M., and Roberts, F.B., eds. *Family Health: A Theoretical Approach to Nursing Care.* New York: John Wiley & Sons, 1983.

D'Afflitti, J.B., and Weitz, G.W. "Rehabilitating the Stroke Patient Through Patient–Family Groups," *International Journal of Group Psychotherapy* 25(3):323–32, 1974.

Ferreira, A.J. "Psychosis and Family Myth," *American Journal of Psychotherapy* 21:186–97, 1967.

Ford, L. "The Development of Family Nursing," in *Family Healthcare,* vol. 1. Edited by Hymovich, D. and Barnard, M.U. New York: McGraw-Hill Book Co., 1979.

Freeman, D. *Techniques of Family Therapy.* New York: Jason Aronson, 1981.

Freel, M.I. "The Hospice Movement," in *Current Issues in Nursing.* Edited by McCloskey, J.C., and Grace, H.K. Boston: Blackwell Scientific Publications, 1981.

Green, R.G., and Kolevzon, M.S. "Three Approaches to Family Therapy: A Study of Convergence and Divergency," *Journal of Marital and Family Therapy* 8:39, 1982.

Group for the Advancement of Psychiatry (GAP). *Treatment of Families in Conflict.* New York: Science House, 1970.

Guerin, P. "Family Therapy: The First Twenty-Five Years," in *Family Therapy.* Edited by Guerin, P. New York: Gardner Press, 1976.

Gurman, A. *Questions and Answers in the Practice of Family Therapy.* New York: Brunner-Mazel, 1981.

Gurman, A., and Kniskern, D. *Handbook of Family Therapy.* New York: Brunner-Mazel, 1981.

Haley, J. *Problem Solving Therapy.* San Francisco: Jossey-Bass, 1976.

Hall, J.E., and Weaver, B.R. *Nursing of Families in Crisis.* Philadelphia: J.B. Lippincott Co., 1974.

Ham, I.M., and Chamings, P.A. "Family Nursing: Historical Perspectives," in *Family Health: A Theoretical Approach to Nursing Care.* Edited by Clements, I.W. and Roberts, F.B. New York: John Wiley & Sons, 1983.

Jones, S.L. *Family Therapy: A Comparison of Approaches.* Bowie, Md.: Robert J. Brady Co., 1980.

Jones, S.L. "Family Therapy," in *The American Handbook of Psychiatric Nursing.* Edited by Lego, S. Philadelphia: J.B. Lippincott Co., 1984.

Jones, S.L., and Dimond, M. "Family Theory and Family Therapy Models: Comparative Review with Implications for Nursing Practice," *Journal of Psychosocial Nursing* 20:12, 1982.

Leavitt, M. *Families at Risk: Primary Prevention in Nursing Practice.* Boston: Little, Brown & Co., 1982.

MacVicar, M.G. "A Conceptual Framework for Family-Centered Cancer Care," in *Current Perspectives in Nursing: Social Issues and Trends,* vol. 2. Edited by Flynn, B.C., and Miller, M.H. St. Louis: C.V. Mosby Co., 1980.

Nichols, M. *Family Therapy: Concepts and Methods.* New York: Gardner Press, 1984.

Palazzoli, M.S., et al. *Paradox and Counterparadox.* New York: Jason Aronson, 1978.

Roberts, S.L. *Behavioral Concepts and the Critically Ill Patient.* Englewood Cliffs, N.J.: Prentice Hall, 1976.

Satir, V. *Conjoint Family Therapy.* Palo Alto, Calif.: Science and Behavior Books, 1967.

Sedgewick, R. *Family Mental Health.* St. Louis: C.V. Mosby Co., 1981.

Sluzki, C.E., and Ransom, D.C., eds. *Double Bind: The Foundation of the Communication Approach to the Family.* New York: Grune & Stratton, 1976.

Smoyak, S., ed. *The Psychiatric Nurse as a Family Therapist.* New York: John Wiley & Sons, 1975.

Smoyak, S. "Homes: A Natural Environment for Family Therapy," in *Distributive Nursing Practice: A Systems Approach to Community Health.* Edited by Hall, J., and Weaver, B. Philadelphia: J.B. Lippincott Co., 1977.

Tinkham, C., and Voorhies, E. *Community Health Nursing: Evolution and Process,* 2nd ed. East Norwalk, Conn.: Appleton-Century-Crofts, 1977.

Watzlawick, P., et al. *Pragmatics of Human Communication.* New York: W.W. Norton & Co., 1967.

Watzlawick, P., and Weakland, J.H., eds. *The Interactional View: Studies at the Mental Research Institute, Palo Alto 1967–1974.* New York: W.W. Norton & Co., 1977.

Weeks, G., and L'Abate, L. *Paradoxical Psychotherapy.* New York: Brunner-Mazel, 1982.

Wright, L.M., and Leahey, M. *Nurses and Families: A Guide to Family Assessment and Intervention.* Philadelphia: F.A. Davis Co., 1984.

2 Families and psychosocial problems: Assumptions, assessment, and intervention

Lorraine M. Wright, RN, PhD
Director, Family Nursing Unit
Professor, Faculty of Nursing
The University of Calgary
Calgary, Alberta, Canada

Maureen Leahey, RN, PhD
Team Director, Mental Health Services
Director, Family Therapy Institute
Holy Cross Hospital
Calgary, Alberta, Canada

OVERVIEW

This chapter presents certain basic assumptions about families and psychosocial problems. Guidelines for a systemic family assessment are outlined and examples of circular descriptive questions are given. To help nurses maximize change, both general and specific interventions are described.

INTRODUCTION

Despite significant advances in psychosocial/mental health nursing during the past 20 years, present nursing research offers little help in clarifying and/ or verifying this progress. Therefore, nursing assessment of and intervention with patients with psychosocial problems remains wide-ranging, with little confirmation of any one approach; the nurse's own beliefs or assumptions about human nature, the nature of psychosocial problems, and the means of fostering therapeutic change are therefore important determinants of assessment and intervention strategies.

The assumptions described in this chapter are based on current knowledge and research, and on the authors' clinical experience with psychosocial patients and their families. Assessment and intervention guidelines follow a discussion of relevant general assumptions.

BASIC ASSUMPTIONS ABOUT FAMILIES AND PSYCHOSOCIAL PROBLEMS

Psychosocial problems frequently engender fear, misunderstanding, and blame within families. Strong cultural, societal, and religious beliefs and values often influence family members' understanding of such problems. Indeed, such beliefs prompt many people to try to solve a psychosocial problem themselves more so than they would with problems arising from a chronic or life-threatening illness. The authors believe the following assumptions are the most important considerations in nursing families with psychosocial problems.

Assumption #1: Psychosocial Problems in Families Are Best Understood and Treated from a Circular Rather Than a Linear Perspective

In the authors' estimation, this assumption is the most crucial element in family nursing for psychosocial problems, because it forms the foundation for effective assessment and intervention.

Each family member, it is assumed, contributes to adaptive as well as maladaptive interactions. However, only interactions *over time* allow specific patterns to be formed and identified (Hinde, 1976). These long-term series of interactions are commonly called family *relationships*, and they are significantly different from interactions among groups with no common history (e.g. employment groups, therapy groups).

To describe a relationship, one must note not just the interactions that occur within it, but also their content, quality (Hinde, 1976), and the patterns they form over time. This can be done by obtaining information about absolute and relative frequencies—when they occur with respect to each other—and how they affect each other.

Tomm (1981, p. 85) differentiates between linear and circular interactional patterns:

> One major difference between linear and circular patterns lies in the overall structure of the connections between elements of the pattern. Linear patterns are limited to sequences (e.g. ABCA... or AB, BC, CA). A less obvious but more significant difference lies in the relative importance usually given to *time* and *meaning* when making the connections or links in the pattern. Linearity is heavily rooted in a framework of a continuous progression of time... Circularity... is more heavily dependent on a framework of reciprocal relationships based on meaning.

In clinical nursing practice, this assumption affects the nurse's style of questioning during a family assessment. Linear questions usually identify individual characteristics or events (e.g., "How long have you had a problem with your drinking?"), while circular questions explore relationships or differences (e.g., "Who in your family is most confident you can overcome your problem with drinking?") (Selvini-Palazzoli et al, 1980; Tomm, 1981). Bateson (1979, p. 99) proposed that "information consists of differences that make a difference."

> Differences between perceptions/objects/events/ideas/etc. are regarded as the basic source of all information and consequent knowledge. On closer examination, one can see that such relationships are always reciprocal or circular. If she is shorter than he, then he is taller than she. If she is dominant, then he is submissive. If one member of the family is defined as being bad, then the others are being defined as being good. Even at a very simple level, a circular orientation allows implicit information to become more explicit and offers alternative points of view. A linear orientation on the other hand is narrow and restrictive and tends to mask important data (Tomm, 1981, p. 93).

White (1986) has applied the concept of circularity or reciprocity to family dynamics by describing the relationship between the problem and the family as one of "relative influence." In therapy, he wants to know how much the problem influences the lives of family members. At the same time, he asks how the family members influence the problem—that is, how well they can manage the problem. Linear and circular questions that might be asked during a family assessment are highlighted later in this chapter.

Assumption #2: Families Experiencing Psychosocial Problems Need to Discover Their Own Problem-Solving Abilities

Frequently, families of individuals with psychosocial problems express hopelessness, fatigue, and inadequacy in the face of their problems. A nurse who believes that the family unit *can* solve its own problems will not try to solve the problems for them. By the same token, a nurse who feels responsible for solving a family's problems can inadvertently enhance that family's sense of hopelessness and inadequacy and foster dependence. Nurses can avoid the "responsibility trap" by not becoming overly invested in any particular outcome. For example, if the presenting (psychosocial) problem involves a young teenager who frequently runs away from home, the nurse should resist the temptation to decide on a "best" outcome—that is, to decide whether the child should live somewhere else, with the parents, or have closer supervision when away from home. Any of these outcomes may be reasonable, but a nurse who invests too heavily in one outcome will not help the family explore a variety of alternatives and resolve the problem as *they* deem best.

Alcoholism, for instance, poses a particular nursing challenge in this area. The family and the community usually pressure the nurse to help the family member stop drinking. In such a case, however, the nurse should help family members search for alternative behavioral, cognitive, and affective responses to the problem and to gain confidence that they can discover their own solutions.

Assumption #3: Family Members' Ability to Change Depends Upon Their Ability to Alter Their Perception of the Problem

A family assessment should always ascertain all family members' *perceptions* of the problem. Nurses must test the validity of those individual outlooks and be prepared to offer the family another epistemology. Family members usually build subjective interpretations around problems and base that interpretation on personal beliefs. Normally, family members need help to move from a linear perspective of the problem to a circular one. The nurse can help them only by avoiding linear thinking about family dynamics.

Avoiding linear conceptualization of psychosocial problems means not thinking that any single family member's view is "correct" or "right." By not searching for an "ultimate truth," the nurse can invite each family member's perceptions and provide an *alternate* truth, or perception of reality, that, ideally, will enable the family to solve its own problems. In the authors' experience, when these assumptions are applied, psychosocial problems are usually redefined as interpersonal or relationship problems. In many cases finding out what a family member *thinks* about a relationship may be more important in problem resolution than the interactions that actually occur within that relationship (Hinde, 1976).

How nurses perceive and conceptualize a problem determines how they will intervene.

> Viewing problem behavior not in isolation but in relation to its immediate context—the behavior of other family members—means more than just a specific change of viewpoint, important as that is. This change exemplifies a general shift in epistemology from a search for linear cause and effect change to a cybernetic or systems viewpoint—the understanding and explanation of any selected bit of behavior in terms of its place in a wider, ongoing, organized system of behavior, involving feedback and reciprocal reinforcement throughout (Fisch et al, 1982, pp. 8-9).

The authors' clinical nursing practice with families with psychosocial problems is currently based on a systems/cybernetics/communication theoretical foundation using the Calgary Family Assessment Model (CFAM) (Wright and Leahey, 1984) as an assessment framework. Interventions are based primarily on a systemic/strategic model (Selvini-Palazzoli et al, 1980; Tomm, 1984a and b; Haley, 1977, Fisch et al, 1982). Some of these interventions will be highlighted in the intervention section of this chapter. A nurse who does not conceptualize a patient's psychosocial problem from a systems/cybernetics perspective will develop interventions based on a completely *different* conception of "reality," one based on different theoretical assumptions.

Assumption #4: Families' Understanding of Psychosocial Problems Does Not Itself Lead to Change

Changes or improvements in psychosocial problems rarely occur through improved family understanding of the problem alone; rather, changes in behavior will precede understanding. From a systems perspective, problems are solved as family interactional patterns change, whether or not this is accompanied by insight.

Historically, psychosocial nursing has tried to understand the "why" of a problem first. Thus, many well-intentioned psychosocial nurses spend many hours compiling masses of historical data that will explain that elusive "why." The patient and/or family will even encourage the nurse in this quest and cooperate freely. For example, family members often ask such questions as, "Why is my wife so depressed?" or "Why do I keep washing my hands so frequently?" or "Why is my young son schizophrenic?" However, finding the "why" is not a precondition for change; rather, it steers nurses away from any effective pursuit of change. The prerequisite for change is understanding not the *why* of a situation but rather the *what*. Therefore, rather than ask: "Why is my client so depressed," the nurse should ask: "What effect does the family have on my client's depression?" "What" questions are much more useful in paving the way for interventions. Nurses should reject the search for causes (linear models) and try instead to understand what can be done immediately to effect change (systems/cybernetic models).

Assumption #5: A Therapeutic Context for Change Must Be Created for Families with Psychosocial Problems

For a family to change, members must find a context that will facilitate change. That context might have to be created. Psychosocial family nursing assessments and interventions must always consider the important variable of context. Nurses must recognize their position in the health care delivery system vis-à-vis the family. Specifically, the nurse needs to know what other professionals are involved with the family and in what roles. Also, how does the nurse's role differ from that of the others? How are the family and the nurse influenced by and influencing the context they are in?

Coppersmith (1983) has analyzed the place of family therapy in the homeostasis of larger systems. She suggests that larger systems (e.g.

the hospital, mental health agency, or public service delivery system) impose "rules" upon families that serve to maintain the larger system's homeostasis. The first rule is the "rule" of linear blame. That is, institutions often blame families for difficulties, label them "resistant," and make treatment referrals designed to "cure" the family. This process resembles what happens when a family sends an identified patient to be "cured."

A second "rule" identified by Coppersmith is the "rule" of overinvolvement. Because members of some larger systems, such as hospital staff, become intensely involved in a psychiatric patient or family member's life, they often go beyond the immediate concerns. The end result is that they usurp the family's own resources. This discourages family members from articulating their perceived needs. The intimacy created by the family assessment process can also establish the nurse as just another irritant in the family's predicament; this is another reason why nurses should carefully assess the larger context in which family and staff find themselves. In some cases, more serious problems arise from the interaction of the family with health care professionals than from circumstances within the family itself. Interventions directed toward the family-professional system should therefore precede addressing problems at the family system level.

Coppersmith's third rule is that of undefined leadership. Families often find themselves enmeshed in a larger system, such as an outpatient mental health clinic, where they receive conflicting advice about their problem (e.g. bulimia). This situation occurs because no single clinic or educational program has definitive decision-making power regarding those families. "In short order, client families may find themselves in a situation quite similar to that of a child whose parents cannot agree" (Coppersmith, 1983, p. 221).

Finally, there is the rule of dysfunctional triads, which states that unacknowledged or unresolved conflicts between larger systems, or between families and larger systems, result from dysfunctional triads that prohibit healthy behavior. For example, a family may wish to send a rebellious adolescent to an outdoor living skills program. The nurse and the program director, however, may not agree on what the treatment goals should be or when intervention should begin. The family thus finds itself in a situation where conflicts in the larger system force them to take sides.

Once the family's relationship to the suprasystems has been assessed, interventions can be directed to the appropriate system level. Change occurs more readily when there is respect for context.

Assumption #6: Psychosocial Problems or Symptoms May Serve a Positive Family Function

The Milan associates (Selvini-Palazzoli et al, 1980; Tomm, 1984a and b) by their landmark contributions to systemic thinking, have compelled family clinicians to rethink their views about psychosocial problems and their symptoms. Traditionally, mental health clinicians have viewed psychosocial problems as something that families want to get rid of; they assumed, therefore, that families who did not pursue change were unmotivated, resistant, or unprepared. However, the work of the Milan associates has taught family clinicians that psychosocial problems often serve positive family functions. A situation might appear "problematic," but it may also be helping the family avoid a worse dilemma.

For example, an adolescent in a single-parent family refused to mix with her peers, remained at home constantly, and did not want to work or go to school. The mother, preoccupied with the task of raising three children, and overwhelmed by financial concerns, job dissatisfaction, and a minimal social network, perceived the daughter's problem as one of low self-esteem, antisocial behavior, and depression. Yet, by staying at home, the daughter provided her mother with valuable companionship and emotional support. The mother would even ask her daughter's advice about her boyfriends and whether she should reunite with the daughter's father. This example illustrates the circular or recursive nature of many psychosocial problems, that is, that each behavior simultaneously causes and effects all other behaviors. The daughter's problems would not have existed unless the mother maintained them, and the mother's ability to cope depended on the daughter's problem. The daughter's depression and antisocial behavior was probably helping to avoid a more serious depression with the mother.

This type of systemic conceptualization has profound implications for nursing. Once the connection between *symptom* and *system* has been established, intervention can be directed toward the system and not just toward the symptom—in short, all family members influencing and influenced by the symptom can be involved in treatment.

Assumption #7: Outcome is More Positive if Psychosocial Problems are Treated from an Ecosystemic Perspective

The goal of psychosocial family nursing is to improve family functioning so that families can solve their own problems. There is increasing evidence to recommend taking a broader systemic view when working with individuals with psychosocial problems. For instance, traditional management of schizophrenia involves frequent hospitalizations, pharmacotherapy, and individual psychotherapy. However, a research study by Falloon and coworkers (1985) has demonstrated the relative efficacy of the family approach in preventing schizophrenic morbidity. These researchers assumed that environmental stress contributes to the clinical morbidity of established schizophrenias treated with optimal neuroleptic drugs. Over a 2-year period, they compared a family-based approach aimed at enhancing the identified patient/client family's problem-solving capacity to a similarly intense patient-oriented approach. After 9 months of treatment, the family-managed patients experienced fewer exacerbations of schizophrenia, less severe schizophrenic psychopathology, fewer hospital admissions, and a trend toward lower deficit symptoms and reduced neuroleptic dosage. This influential study supports the superior efficacy of a family approach in reducing the clinical morbidity of schizophrenia.

Research also supports the concept of family intervention in managing marital problems. Gurman and Kniskern's (1981) extensive review of marital therapy outcome research indicated that marital problems are more often resolved successfully when both spouses, rather than either one individually, are treated. In a further review of outcome research, the same investigators determined that families tend to remain in treatment and not terminate therapy prematurely when fathers are involved.

To think and work systemically does not mean that all patients with psychosocial problems must be seen in a family context. However, it is much more difficult to resolve psychosocial problems through work with individuals alone, because the nurse is limited to a single perspective on the problem. When other family members are present, their ideas and perspectives can expand the nurse's base for assessment and choice of intervention alternatives.

FAMILY NURSING ASSESSMENT

Family assessment is the evaluation of relationships and behaviors among all members of a family. Thus, the family nurse focuses on relationships rather than on individual members' behaviors. Numerous family assessment models and concepts have been described in recent nursing texts (Jones, 1980; Friedman, 1981; Clements and Buchanan, 1982; Wright and Leahey, 1984).

Guidelines for Systemic Assessment

The authors rely primarily on a systemic model of interviewing (Selvini-Palazzoli et al, 1980; Tomm, 1984b) developed by four Italian psychiatrists. This model was first developed in work with families of patients with anorexia nervosa and later refined though work with schizophrenic young adults. Three fundamental guidelines—hypothesizing, circularity, and neutrality—provide the context for a systemic interview (Selvini-Palazzoli et al, 1980). A fourth guideline, strategizing, has been proposed by Tomm (1987). All four of these principles are interrelated.

A nurse's basic assumptions about families with psychosocial problems can take the form of hypotheses, which can then help her organize information about a particular family. Before meeting the family for the first time, the nurse should write down her hypotheses about the family and the presenting problem in its relational context. The hypotheses might be parameters or variables already suggested by specific family assessment models, but they can also be based on the nurse's own experience with similar families, problems, symptoms, or situations (Fleuridas et al., 1986). Guidelines for developing hypotheses are given in Table-2.1.

Table 2.1   Guidelines for Designing Hypotheses

- Choose hypotheses that are useful.
- Generate the most helpful explorations of the family's behaviors for the particular time.
- Understand that there are no "right" or "true" explanations.
- Include all family components to make the hypothesis as systemic as possible.
- Relate the hypothesis to the family's presenting concerns so the interview can proceed along the lines most relevant to the family.
- Make the hypothesis different from the family's to introduce new information into the system and avoid being entrapped with the family in their solutions.
- Be as quick to discard unconfirmed or unhelpful hypotheses as to generate new ones.

Adapted from Fleuridas, et al., 1986.

The nurse who uses circular questioning bases her assessment on information about *relationships* (Selvini-Palazzoli et al, 1980). Examples of circular questions that can be used in assessment are discussed in the next section of this chapter. Neutrality, the third guideline, is the nurse's ability to respond without judgment or blame to descriptions of relationships. For example, if a family states that a psychosocial problem (e.g. depression) is genetic in origin, the nurse's reaction should be as neutral as possible. This does *not* mean that she must accept the declared connection. Information about the assigned meaning of family beliefs about psychosocial problems will greatly assist the nurse in intervening. Intervention is only necessary, however, if particular beliefs interfere with or block the family's problem-solving ability.

The fourth interviewing guideline, strategizing, refers to the nurse's clinical decision-making—that is, evaluating the effects of past actions, designing new plans, anticipating the possible consequences of future actions, and deciding how to proceed (Tomm, 1987).

Assessment Questions

Linear descriptive vs. circular descriptive. Assessment questions can function as a recursive loop between nurse and family. Some questions *inform* the nurse and enhance understanding of the family system, while others *effect change* (Tomm, 1985; Tomm, 1987). In this context, linear assessment questions generally inform the nurse, while circular descriptive questions are meant to effect change. The important difference between these kinds of questions is their *intent.* Linear descriptive questions are *investigative;* they explore a family member's perception of a problem. For example, when ascertaining family members' perceptions of their daughter's anorexia nervosa, the nurse would begin with linear descriptive questions: "When did you notice that your daughter's eating habits were different from those of other family members?" "What do you think caused your daughter to stop eating as she normally would?" These questions, while informing the nurse of the history of the young woman's eating patterns, also help illuminate family perceptions or beliefs about eating patterns.

From investigative assessment questions, the nurse moves to more explanatory questioning. To the family just described, the nurse might ask, "Who in the family is most worried about Mavis's anorexia?" ("Mother is because she thinks Mavis is going to get sick if she doesn't start eating more.") "How does Mother show that she's the one worrying the most?" ("Because she keeps checking with the rest of us if we've seen Mavis eat anything and wants us to report to her if we have.") "What does your father do when your mother is so worried?" ("He is not around as much these days. He's working long hours at his office.") The authors have found both explanatory and investigative questions to be useful in gathering information; but the *effect* on families of these two types of descriptive questions can also be quite significant. Linear descriptive questions, for instance, tend to have a liberating effect (Tomm, 1987).

The difference between linear and circular descriptive questions is that circular descriptive questions help discover valuable information because they seek out relationships between individuals, events, ideas, or beliefs. Linear descriptive questions do not.

In psychosocial problems, it is important to assess the family's set of beliefs, since the meaning a family assigns to a psychosocial problem may determine the nursing intervention. A family that attributes a son's enuresis to an organic problem will be managed differently from a family that presumes a psychological origin. Matters become even more complicated and challenging when different family members hold different beliefs about etiology. In one family, for example, the parents were asked, "Do you think your son's enuresis is of an organic or a psychological nature?" The father responded "organic" while the mother responded "psychological." Therein lay many obstacles to the family's attempts to resolve the problem on its own. The nurse's assignment in such a case is to offer the family an alternate "reality" or epistemology of the problem that would enable them to generate their own solutions. To do this, the nurse has to understand the problem in its larger relational context. Thorough assessment revealed that the parents were contemplating separation but would not separate as long as their son was having difficulties. Therefore, the nurse offered an alternate "reality," that is, that the son had found a way to keep the family together; his enuresis reduced the tension between the parents and delayed separation. This nurse's insight gave the family a new perspective on the problem. The parents admitted that they did not want to separate but could not resolve their marital problems on their own. Surprisingly, their son was less worried about the separation than he was about his parents' fights and the possibility that his father and mother might physically abuse each other. When the nurse told the son that "someone wetting his pants was perhaps better than someone hitting and hurting someone else," he agreed. The parents spontaneously decided to obtain therapy in order to reduce marital tension. Within a month after they began therapy, their son's enuresis subsided from four to six times a week to once or twice a week.

Circular descriptive questions also help assign relative value to the advice that a family receives from extended family members, friends, and community resources. Useful questions might include, "What's the best advice that friends have given you with regard to your son's problem?" "What is the worst advice?" "What advice have you tried?" When the family with the enuretic son was asked to describe the worst advice they had received, they responded, "Our family physician told us that each time our son wet the bed to put his nose in the wet sheets and have him smell them and then change them." They said they agreed to having their son change his own sheets, but adamantly disagreed with such a punitive measure as having their son smell his own urine. Circular questions yield valuable information not only about specific advice, but about the types of guidance a family values and from whom. It also indicates what advice the family has tried to follow, its relative success, and what advice the nurse should avoid.

Following an assessment with descriptive linear and circular questions, the nurse is ready to start developing an intervention strategy. If assessment reveals that family functioning and/or problem-solving is blocked (e.g., because of opposing views on problem etiology), then family intervention is indicated.

FAMILY NURSING INTERVENTIONS

Family nursing interventions can help families who are experiencing psychosocial problems. This section presents interventions—based upon family research and clinical practice—that seem the most essential and useful in resolving psychosocial problems.

Interventive Questioning

Interventive questions are intended to actively effect change. Nurses conducting systemic interviews should remember, though, that knowledge of when, how, and to what purpose to pose questions within the framework of a particular model is more important than simply choosing one type of question over another (Lipchik and DeShazer, 1986).

Linear strategic questions vs. circular reflexive questions. Interventive questions are predominantly of two types: linear strategic and circular reflexive questions (Tomm, 1987). The effect of these questions on families is quite distinct. Strategic questions are constraining, while reflexive questions are generative; the latter introduce new cognitive connections, paving the way for new or different family behaviors.

The following two interventive questions, for example, might be asked of the family of a young adult who has been hospitalized for an acute schizophrenic reaction: "Don't you think you're putting even more pressure on your son when you continually tell him to stop acting crazy?" This particular question is strategic and linear and takes a confrontational, blaming stance. It also sends a strong directive to the parents that *they* need to change their behavior if they want their son to improve. In comparison, a circular reflexive question would be: "If you become even more insistent that your son stop some of his disturbing behaviors, do you think it is more or less likely he will continue these behaviors?" This question is more reflexive and is intended to mobilize the parents to *reflect* on their actions without, however, implying that they should consider their behavior inappropriate or counterproductive. These questions are also intended to allow family members to choose their own position and are consequently more respectful of the family's autonomy. The linear strategic form of questioning implies that the nurse knows what is best for the family; it also implies that she has become too purposive and invested in a particular outcome. Strategic questions are intended to correct behavior; reflexive questions are intended to facilitate behavioral change.

One type of reflexive question, the *future-oriented question,* is useful in nursing families with psychosocial problems. Frequently, such families are so mired in their troubles that they cannot project or speculate about the future; thus their problem-solving efforts or alternatives are limited. By asking reflexive questions about their future, the nurse can prompt family members to speculate on it (Tomm, 1987). Future-oriented questions for the family of a child with school phobia might include: "What are you worried will happen if your child remains out of school for 6 months?" and "What's the worst thing that can happen?" Such questions help families discuss and affirm or disaffirm catastrophic expectations. A similar strategy was employed with the family of a young woman with bulimia. The parents were asked, "How much longer do you think it will be before your daughter can give up her bulimia?" The daughter was asked the same question, and surprised her parents by saying, "I'll probably give it up when I move out of the house next year." Future-oriented questions introduce not only the critical variable of time, but also the important message that perhaps problems are controllable rather than, as is often believed, that they "just occurred," and will have to "just stay." The connection of time and symptoms can draw forth family beliefs about how long symptoms will occur.

Another type of future-oriented question stimulates discussion about family goals; for instance, a teenaged son might be asked, "How much longer do you think you will have to remain in the hospital before you can return to live with your mother?" The mother might be asked, "How long do you think your son will have to remain in the hospital?" The answers to these questions can be enlightening (in the case just described, the son said 6 months, while his mother said 1 or 2), and may allow the presenting problem to be understood in a larger systems context. In this case, the hospital nursing staff also believed that it would be some months before this child could return to live with his mother. Upon further questioning, the son said that his mother "needed a man," the first indication that he viewed hospitalization as a "holiday" from the job of providing emotional support to his mother.

Frequently, interventive questions *alone* can create a context for and effect change with families who have psychosocial problems.

Offer an Opinion

Nurses frequently offer opinions, assessment, conceptions, or beliefs about psychosocial problems without regarding them as interventions. However, the authors believe that strategically placed opinions can serve as very powerful and useful interventions. The following have been found to be most beneficial in clinical practice.

Commending family and individual strengths. The authors routinely end their interviews by commending families on strengths observed during the session. Families coping with psychosocial problems frequently label themselves as failures because they cannot resolve their problems. In addition, these families often say that extended family members, friends, and even health care professionals have implied or told them directly that they have failed to fulfill their responsibilities, and that that is why they have problems. Commonly, these families have not been complimented on their strengths or made aware of them for some time. The immediate and long-term positive reactions to such commendations indicate that they are effective interventions.

In one case, a family whose adopted son's behavioral and emotional problems had kept them involved with health care professionals for the past 10 years was told by the nurse interviewer that they were the best family for this boy, because many other families would not have been as sensitive to his needs and would probably have given up years ago. The parents both became tearful and said that this was the first positive statement made to them as parents in many years. An interesting turn of events followed: for many years the parents had been told to be more firm with their son and raise their expectations of him, but they had always been unwilling or unable to do so. Subsequent to interviews with the parents (the son refused to come to the sessions), during which they had been commended for their parenting, the father said that he had talked with his son and told him to cut his long hair and look for a job. To the parents' surprise, their son complied. When they were asked how they could demand such a thing, they said that being told that they were suitable parents had increased their confidence as parents and allowed them to follow through on their actions. They no longer felt unable to manage their son and therefore approached him more firmly. This clinical case exemplifies that reaffirming family competence frees members to behave more spontaneously and to solve problems. The very behavior that professionals requested of these parents for years was now implemented without active direction. In other words, the context for change was created, allowing the family to discover its own solutions.

Commended families also appear dramatically more receptive to new opinions or assignments. The more professionals that family members have seen, the less confident they are about their own skills. Inadvertently, professionals can foster low self-esteem within families and increase dependence on external resources.

Advice and information. Families find advice and information about psychosocial problems valuable. Frequently, information about developmental (e.g. adolescents' needs for privacy and the importance of peer support), medical (e.g. the physiological effects of bulimic binging and purging), and family interactional issues (e.g. how a husband's withdrawal can precipitate a wife's nagging behavior, which precipitates withdrawal, and so on) can free a family to resolve its own problems.

Systemic opinion or reframe. When a presenting problem is redefined as serving a positive family function (Assumption #6), it can be reinterpreted as a solution to another hypothetical or implied problem that could occur were the symptom not present (Tomm, 1984b). Thus the symptomatic behavior is systemically reframed by connecting it to other behaviors in the system. Connections should be based on assessment information derived through circular questioning. When offering a systemic reframe to a family, a nurse should delineate the recursiveness of the symptom, stressing that it serves a positive function for the system at the same time as the system serves a function by contributing and maintaining the symptom. At the Family Nursing Unit, University of Calgary (Wright et al, 1985), the dilemma of a family with the presenting problem of the mother's alcohol abuse was systemically reframed by a nurse who pointed out that the mother's drinking served the positive function of holding this family together because it kept everyone worried about her. Had that worry not been present, family members might have become estranged, as they had been in the past. At the same time, the family "helped" the mother drink by plotting to limit her drinking and by intensely monitoring her drinking.

Split opinion. It often helps to offer a family two or more different and opposing views, one indicating change and another suggesting no change. For a split opinion intervention to be effective, the nurse, during the course of the interview, must show no preference for any particular point of view.

A nurse offered the following split-opinion to a couple at the end of an interview: "My opinion of your situation is divided—part of me believes that the intense competition or symmetry between the two of you spices up your marriage and allows you to express and debate your ideas. Since you do not have many common interests, I would fear that if you were not as competitive you might find your marriage boring and stale, with nothing left to keep you together. However, another part of me thinks that if this competition does not end, your marriage will. Your marriage is in jeopardy as long as each of you holds so firmly to your own ideas; you must learn how to compromise and negotiate. My opinion is split; I will have to leave it with you."

Redefining the context. Redefining the context in which family nursing is provided can have a powerful impact on treatment. A family that objects to attending "family therapy" sessions might be more amenable to treatment if the nurse has labeled them "developmental sessions" (Wright and Watson, 1982). The nature of the work between the nurse and the family does not change; rather, a new context or "name" makes treatment more palatable and promotes change.

Devise Rituals

Families engage in many daily (e.g. bedtime reading) and yearly (e.g. Thanksgiving dinner at Grandma's) rituals. Family therapy can suggest new rituals that are not or have not been observed by the family. Rituals are best introduced when there is a counterproductive level of confusion. Frequently, the confusion is caused by the simultaneous presentation of incompatible injunctions. Rituals serve to provide clarity in the family system.

When parents cannot agree on parenting practices for their children and chaos and confusion reign, the introduction of an odd day–even day ritual (Selvini-Palazzoli et al, 1980) can help. The mother becomes responsible for the children on Mondays, Wednesdays, and Fridays, and the father is given childcare authority on Tuesdays, Thursdays, and Saturdays. On Sundays, they should behave spontaneously. On their "off" days, parents are asked to observe, without comment, their partner's parenting. This strategy isolates contradictory behaviors by prescribing sequence (Tomm, 1984b).

Prescribe Behavioral Tasks

Myriad behavioral tasks can help families improve their functioning when faced with psychosocial problems. Such tasks can be straightforward; for instance, a nurse might instruct parents to read a book on parenting adolescents or ask a family to monitor the number of times they remind a child to eat. Tasks can also be complex and creative. For example, the mother of three alcohol-abusing adult children could be less predictable and responsible toward them to provoke them to more responsible behavior. The mother was assigned the behavioral task of going home and turning all the chairs in the house upside down and writing on the mirrors with lipstick (Wright et al, 1985). She found the task amusing and enjoyable, and the young adults responded by paying more attention to her.

CONCLUSIONS

Treating the family as a unit has gained prominence in nursing management of psychosocial problems. Techniques have evolved from various assumptions about families and psychosocial problems, as well as from family research and clinical practice. Experience demonstrates that family involvement enhances compliance, provides social support, and sustains motivation for health promoting behavior (Barbarin and Tirado, 1985). Family involvement can lead to symptom reduction and overall improvement in family functioning. Nurses are in a key position to help families discover and rediscover their abilities to solve their own psychosocial problems.

REFERENCES

Bateson, G. *Mind and Nature: A Necessary Unit.* New York: Dutton, 1979.

Barbarin, O.A., and Tirado, M. "Enmeshment, Family Process, and Successful Treatment of Obesity," *Family Relations* 34:115–21, 1985.

Brodsky, C.M. "Sociocultural and Interactional Influences on Somatization," *Psychosomatics* 25:673–80, 1984.

Clements, I.M., and Buchanan, D.M. *Family Therapy: A Nursing Perspective.* New York: John Wiley & Sons, 1982.

Coppersmith, E. "The Place of Family Therapy in the Homeostasis of Larger Systems," in *Group and Family Therapy: An Overview.* Edited by Wolberg, R., and Wolberg M. New York: Brunner-Mazel, 1983.

Falloon, I.R.H., et al. "Family Management in the Prevention of Morbidity of Schizophrenia," *Archives of General Psychiatry* 42:887–96, 1985.

Fisch, R., et al. *The Tactics of Change: Doing Therapy Briefly.* San Francisco: Jossey-Bass, 1982.

Fleuridas, C., et al. "The Evolution of Circular Questions: Training Family Therapists," *Journal of Marital and Family Therapy* 12(2):113–27, 1986.

Friedman, M. *Family Nursing: Theory and Assessment.* East Norwalk, Conn.: Appleton-Century-Crofts, 1981.

Glenn, M.L. *On Diagnosis: A Systemic Approach.* New York: Brunner-Mazel, 1984.

Gurman, A.S., and Kniskern, D.P. "Family Therapy Outcome Research Knowns and Unknowns," in *Handbook of Family Therapy.* Edited by Gurman, A.S., and Kniskern, D.P. New York: Brunner-Mazel, 1981.

Haley, J. *Problem-Solving Therapy.* San Francisco: Jossey-Bass, 1977.

Hinde, R.A. "On Describing Relationships," *Journal of Child Psychology and Psychiatry* 17:1–19, 1976.

Jones, S.L. *Family Therapy: A Comparison of Approaches.* Bowie, Md.: Robert J. Brady Co., 1980.

Lipchik, E., and deShazer, S. "The Purposeful Interview," *Journal of Strategic and Systemic Therapies* 5:88-99, 1986.

Selvini-Palazzoli, M., et al. "Hypothesizing, Circularity, Neutrality: Three Guidelines for the Conductor of the Session," *Family Process* 19:3–12, 1980.

Selvini-Palazzoli, M., et al. "A Ritualized Prescription in Family Therapy: Odd Days and Even Days," *Journal of Marriage & Family Counseling* 4(3):3–9, 1978.

Tomm, K. "Circular Interviewing: A Multifaceted Clinical Tool," in *Applications of Systemic Family Therapy: The Milan Approach.* Campbell, D., and Draper, R. London: Grune & Stratton, 1985a.

Tomm, K. "Circularity: A Preferred Orientation for Family Assessment," in *Questions and Answers in the Practice of Family Therapy.* Edited by Gurman, A.S. New York: Brunner-Mazel, 84–87, 1981.

Tomm, K. "Interventive Interviewing: Part I. Strategizing as a Fourth Guideline for the Therapist," *Family Process* 26:3-13, 1987.

Tomm, K. "The Milan Approach to Family Therapy: A Tentative Report," in *Treating Families with Special Needs.* Edited by Freeman, D.S., and Trute, B. Ottawa: The Canadian Association of Social Workers, 1981.

Tomm, K. "One Perspective on the Milan Systemic Approach: Part I. Overview of Development, Theory, and Practice," *Journal of Marital and Family Therapy* 10(2):113–25, 1984a.

Tomm, K. "One Perspective on the Milan Systemic Approach: Part II. Description of Session Format, Interviewing Style and Interventions," *Journal of Marital and Family Therapy* 10(3):253–71, 1984b.

Tomm, K. "Reflexive Questioning: A Generative Mode of Enquiry," Unpublished manuscript. Calgary, Alberta: University of Calgary, 1985b.

Watson, W.L., and Wright, L.M. "The Elderly and Their Families: An Interactional View," in *Families with Handicapped Members.* Edited by Hansen, J.C., and Coppersmith, E.I. Rockville, Md.: Aspen Systems Corp., 1984.

Watzlawick, P., et al. *Pragmatics of Human Communication.* New York: W.W. Norton & Co., 1967.

White, M. "Negative Explanation, Restraint, and Double Description: A Template for Family Therapy," *Family Process* 25:169–84, 1986.

Wright, L.M., and Bell, J. "Nurses, Families and Illness: A New Combination," in *Treating Families with Special Needs.* Edited by Freeman, D., and Trute, B. Ottawa: The Canadian Association of Social Workers, 1981.

Wright, L.M., and Leahey, M. *Nurses and Families: A Guide to Family Assessment and Intervention.* Philadelphia: F.A. Davis Co., 1984.

Wright, L.M., and Watson, W.L. "What's in a Name: Redefining Family Therapy," in *Questions and Answers in the Practice of Family Therapy,* vol. 2. Edited by Gurman, A. New York: Brunner-Mazel, 27–30, 1982.

Wright, L.M., et al. "Family Nursing Unit: Clinical Preparation at the Master's Level," *Canadian Nurse* 81(5):26–29, May 1985.

Wright, L.M., et al. "Treatment of a Non-Drinking Family Member in an Alcoholic Family System by a Family Nursing Training Team," *Family Systems Medicine* 3(3):291–300, 1985.

3 Ethnicity, families, and psychosocial problems

Monica McGoldrick, MSW
University of Medicine and Dentistry
New Jersey—Rutgers Medical School
Community Mental Health Center
Piscataway, New Jersey

OVERVIEW

This chapter provides a framework for understanding ethnicity, human behavior, and mental health. Attention is given to understanding families' help-seeking behavior in an ethnic context. Clinical examples of four major ethnic groups: Jewish, Irish American, Italian American, and black American illustrate the impact of ethnicity on family mental health nursing.

ETHNICITY AND HUMAN BEHAVIOR

Human behavior springs from an interplay of intrapsychic, interpersonal, familial, socioeconomic, and cultural forces. Of these, the mental health field has focused on the intrapsychic influences—the study of factors within the personality that shape life experiences and behavior. The study of cultural influences on the emotional functioning of human beings has been left primarily to anthropologists. And even they have preferred to explore these influences in distant and fragile non-Western cultures, rather than exploring the great ethnic diversity of assumptions about illness, health, normality, and pathology among Americans.

Greeley (1969, p. 5), commenting on this tendency of our culture, has said:

> I suspect that the historians of the future will be astonished that American sociologists, the product of the gathering of the nations, could stand in the midst of such an astonishing social phenomenon and take it so much for granted that they would not bother to study it. They will find it especially astonishing in light of the fact that ethnic differences, even in the second half of the 20th century, proved far more important than differences in philosophy or economic system. Most who would not die for a premise or dogma or a division

of labor would more or less cheerfully die for a difference rooted in ethnic origins.

When mental health professionals have considered culture, they too have been more absorbed in making international cross-cultural comparisons than in studying the ethnic groups in our own culture (Carpenter and Strauss, 1974; Giordano and Giordano, 1977; Kiev, 1972). Only recently have we begun to consider ethnic differences when developing therapeutic models (McGoldrick et al., 1982; McGoldrick, in press; Sluzki and Schnitman, 1982). (The National Institute of Mental Health has, for instance, established a task force on ethnic and minority groups.) Ethnicity is a relatively new concept. The term refers to characteristics of historically unique subgroups, each of which possesses an autonomous structure within the larger culture. Ethnicity has been defined as a sense of "commonality or community derived from networks of family experiences" (Feinstein, 1974). It is a fundamental determinant of values, perceptions, needs, modes of expression, behavior, and identity. This definition implicitly includes all ethnic and racial groups. From a clinical point of view, however, ethnicity is more than race, religion, or geographical origin. (This is not to minimize the significant aspects of race or the special problems of racism.) Ethnicity involves conscious and unconscious processes that fulfill a deep psychological need for identity and a sense of historical continuity. It is transmitted by an emotional language within the family and reinforced by the surrounding community (Giordano and Giordano, 1977). Ethnicity is a profound and abiding aspect of human experience.

Ethnicity is a complex and rapidly changing phenomenon in American society. (Unfortunately, we have a difficult time keeping track of this complex factor, since even the United States Census records include ethnic identification only for foreign-born immigrants and their children. Later generations are not designated ethnically.) Ethnic differences obviously diminish through intermarriage and common experiences in our culture. Some values and traditions prove maladaptive; they may be recognized as such and be set aside, though usually with great difficulty. However, there is increasing evidence that some ethnic values persist for many generations after immigration (Greeley, 1969, 1978), and play a significant role in family life and personal development (Lieberman, 1974).

The United States has had more ethnic diversity than any other nation in history, but the fact that this country is a nation of immigrants has hindered rather than helped our ability to tolerate differences. We have talked about the melting pot and blinded ourselves to its inherent diversity. The desire to obscure cultural variations and develop homogeneous "norms" dominates our culture. This has led to stress and conflict which is always most evident in the cultural group with the least "seniority."

Ethnicity is deeply rooted in the family, through which it is transmitted. Billingsley (1976, p. 13) has discussed the community and family strengths that have enabled black people to survive in a hostile environment for more than 300 years. He describes the link between ethnicity and family:

> Ethnicity and family life are two concepts which...go hand in hand. They are so intertwined that it is very difficult indeed to observe the one or even to reflect on it seriously without coming to grips with the other. So when we think of Italians and certain other Southern Europeans, we think of large families; we think of the English and certain Northern Europeans in compact nuclear families. When we think of Black families we think of strong extended families, and when we think of Chinese families we must encompass aggregations so large that they often encompass whole communities.[1]

Common sense tells us that we experience life on the basis of our own cultural values and assumptions, most of which are beyond our awareness. Unless confronted by others whose values differ from our own, we inevitably see the world through our own "cultural filters" and often persist in our established views despite clear information to the contrary (Watzlawick, 1976).

ETHNICITY AND MENTAL HEALTH

It seems natural that an interest in families should lead to an interest in ethnicity, and vice versa, but this area has been largely ignored in clinical teaching and research. Just as there is a paucity of material on the impact of ethnicity in individual psychotherapy, very little has appeared in the family therapy literature on the subject. In addition to the comparative value analysis by Spiegel and Papajohn (Spiegel, 1971; Papajohn and Spiegel, 1975), a few articles have appeared on black Americans (Boyd, 1980; Foley, 1975; McAdoo, 1977), Jewish Americans (Zuk, 1978), Irish Americans (McGoldrick and Pearce, 1981), and Slovak Americans (Stein, 1978). There are also a few collections in the sociological literature (Glazer and Moynihan, 1975; Mindel and Halberstein, 1976), but, unfortunately, even these sources rarely become part of the knowledge base of family clinicians.

While a few family therapists have recognized the importance of culture, the major models of family therapy make little reference to ethnic differences in the application of their methods. Minuchin, Montalvo, and their coworkers (1967) focused on the multiproblem families and developed specific techniques to deal with poor black and Hispanic families. But the other major family models (Bowen systems, strategic,

---

[1]In fact, the Chinese consider the family to include all the generations of the family from the beginning of time into the distant future (Shon and Ja, 1982).

communications), while emphasizing the importance of the family context, do not make explicit reference to ethnic differences.

Very few family training programs integrate material on ethnic differences in any systematic way. The most prominent exception is the pioneering work of Spiegel in viewing families in their ethnic context. Spiegel and Papajohn (1975) analyzed the cultural values of Mexican Americans, Puerto Ricans, Greek Americans, and Italian Americans in their book *Transactions in Families*.[2] Their schema, based on Kluckhohn's work on value orientations (Kluckhohn and Strodtbeck, 1961), provides a comprehensive framework for considering the therapeutic problems of families at various stages of acculturation.

There has been very little systematic integration of material on ethnicity in the training of mental health professionals (Giordano and Giordano, 1977; Pinto, 1976; Sanua, 1975). In fact, the education of most mental health professionals contains hardly a reference to it. Even clinics established specifically to serve ethnic populations often have no one on staff who speaks the client group's native language. Foreign psychiatric residents are trained to offer therapy on the most subtle aspects of psychosocial adjustment in our culture without any mention being made of the major experiential gaps that may exist between them and their patients.

Understanding Help-Seeking in its Ethnic Context

Defining the word "normal" is extremely difficult. "Normality" describes at best only an approximation of what may be acceptable in a given social and historical context. One may err not only by labeling the normal behavior of a given ethnic group as "pathology," but also by labeling dysfunctional behavior for that group as "normal."

Problems (whether physical or mental) can be neither diagnosed nor treated without some understanding of the frame of reference or the norms of the person seeking help. As Kleinman, a prominent physician-researcher, has observed:

> How we communicate about our health problems, the manner in which we present our symptoms, when and to whom we go for care, how long we remain in care, and how we evaluate that care are all affected by cultural beliefs. Illness behavior is a normative experience governed by cultural rules; we learn "approved" ways of being ill...And doctors' explanations and activities, as those of their patients, are culture-specific (Kleinman et al., 1978, p. 252).

[2]Spiegel conducts a program in ethnicity training at Cambridge City Hospital in Boston. Recently a few other training programs, including the Family Practice Residency at the University of California in San Francisco and the Psychiatry Residency at Bronx Psychiatric Hospital, have also started to develop seminars on ethnocultural differences.

Culture may even determine whether a symptom is labeled a problem. For example, the absence of stuttering among certain groups of American Indians is associated with their less stringent demands for fluent speech (Eisenberg, 1977). In fact, their language has no word for stuttering. Thus, it appears that the diagnosis may help to create the problem.

Such wide differences in symptoms among ethnic groups question the usefulness of the present diagnostic nomenclature (Fantl and Shiro, 1959; Opler and Singer, 1956; Singer and Opler, 1956).

In addition, a patient's "illness" (the experience of being ill) is very different from the course of his "disease" (a physically identifiable dysfunction) (Stoeckle et al., 1964) and is strongly influenced by cultural beliefs. Patients vary markedly in their use of the health care system. Although estimates show that more than 90% of the population experience some physical symptoms of illness at any given time, the vast majority (70% to 80%) of those who believe themselves ill manage their problems outside the formal health care system (Zola, 1972). Of those who do seek professional attention, only about 50% are found to have any diagnosable disease (Kleinman et al., 1978).

Until now, the medical model, with its emphasis on "diagnosing" and "curing" disease, has been the major influence on the psychotherapeutic system. This leads to a systematic inattention to "illness"—that is, to the patient's or family's perception of what is wrong—and is partly responsible for noncompliance, dissatisfaction with clinical care, and treatment failure.

Although using a systemic, contextual model of helping makes sense, taking such a view has been difficult. The subject of ethnicity often evokes deep feelings, and discussion frequently becomes polarized or judgmental. According to Greeley (1969), using presumed common origin to define "we" and "they" touches something basic and primordial in the human psyche.

Indeed, human beings tend to fear, and therefore to reject, what they cannot understand. The ancient Greeks called all non-Greeks "barbarians," considering them to be without culture. The Russian word for a German is "nemetz," which means "one who is mute," thus reflecting the belief that those who are not understood cannot speak at all. We often label that which is different as "bad" or "crazy." Thus, in more modern usage, the German may label the Italian "hysterical," while the Italian may label the German "obsessive-compulsive."

For therapists, it is difficult to remain open to this wide range of cultural possibilities. We seem to find ambiguity threatening and close down emotionally when confronted with too much of it. Understanding our own ethnic biases is the best insurance against such rigidity. This insight is hard to achieve, however, since it requires stepping outside our belief systems. We must accept the fact, for instance, that not all cultures value the pursuit of insight or truth, or "getting ahead," or sharing problems and feelings. By exploring our ethnic assumptions, we are forced to question our primary therapeutic techniques. It is no wonder we are threatened.

But we need to learn how much the world differs from our assumptions about it. For example, seeking help depends a great deal on one's attitude toward the "helper." Italians tend to rely primarily on the family and turn to an outsider for help only as a last resort (Gambino, 1974; Rotuno and McGoldrick, 1982; Zborowski, 1969; Zola, 1966). Black Americans have long mistrusted the help they receive from traditional middle-class institutions (Hines and Boyd, 1982; McAdoo, 1977). Puerto Ricans (Preto, 1982) and Chinese (Kleinman, 1975) are likely to somatize stress and may seek medical rather than mental health services. Norwegians, too, often convert emotional tensions into more culturally acceptable physical symptoms. As a result, Norwegians are more likely to seek out a surgeon than a psychotherapist (Midelfort and Midelfort, 1982). Likewise, Iranians often view medication and vitamins as a necessary part of treating any symptom, regardless of its origin (Jalali, 1982). Thus, a substantial minority of potential patients experience troubles and cures somatically, and strongly doubt the value of psychotherapy.

Almost all of us have multiple belief systems to which we turn when we need help. We use not only the established medical or psychotherapeutic system, but also turn to religion, self-help groups, alcohol, yoga, chiropractors, and so on. We use remedies our mothers taught us and those suggested by our friends. Many factors influence our preferred reliance on one system or another at any given time.

While there is little research on the attitudes of different ethnic groups toward family therapy, studies of ethnic differences in response to physical illness have clear implications for family therapy practice (Sanua, 1960; Zborowski, 1969; Zola, 1966).

In Zborowski's (1969) classic study of physically ill Jewish, Italian, Irish, and White Anglo-Saxon Protestant (WASP) patients, the Jewish and Italian patients tended to complain about their pain, while the Irish and WASP did not. When describing their pain experience, the WASPs and Jews were precise, while the Irish and Italians were conspicuously imprecise. The Italian patients dramatized their pain, and the Irish blocked or denied theirs. When the researchers looked at patients' expected solutions, the results again showed striking differences. The Italians worried about the effects the pain might have on their immediate circumstances (work, finances, family); but once the pain was relieved, they quickly forgot their suffering. While the Italians wanted an immediate remedy to stop the pain, the Jewish patients found this unacceptable. Jewish patients rejected medication that stopped the pain immediately becaue they felt it would not treat the real source of their problem. They also worried about the long-range effects of drugs on their general health. Instead, they sought a full explanation of the meaning of their pain and of its relief. The Irish patients, by contrast, did not expect a cure for their ailments at all. They were fatalistic and tended not to complain of, or even mention, their pain. Rather, they viewed pain as the result of their own sinfulness and held themselves responsible. WASP patients, on the other hand, were optimistic, future-oriented, and confident in the ability of science to cure disease. Operating on the "work ethic," they also sought to control their pain by their own efforts.

Emotional expressiveness can lead to misunderstanding in American culture in general, which tends to be less expressive overall than many of the minority groups within it. "Americanized" medical personnel in Zborowski's (1969) study distrusted the uninhibited display of suffering exhibited by Jewish and Italian patients and saw these patients' reactions as exaggerated. Another researcher found that doctors frequently labeled their Italian patients as having "psychiatric problems," although there was no evidence that psychosocial problems occurred more frequently among them (Zola, 1963). Any group whose characteristic response to illness varies too widely from the dominant cultural norm is likely to be labeled "abnormal." By the same token, one would suppose that Jewish and Italian medical staff would have difficulty understanding the silence of Irish and WASP patients.

Differences in style of interaction may also be misinterpreted. A high level of interaction is expected in Jewish, Italian, and Greek families. But WASP, Irish, and Scandinavian families have much less intense interactions and usually deal with problems by distancing. Intermarriage creates obvious difficulties. Therapeutic problems can develop when a therapist from an ethnic group that values distance faces a family with an intense level of interaction. The therapist may get confused, interpret the intensity as a problem, and try inappropriately to control it. On the other hand, a therapist from an intensely interacting culture may try to increase the emotional involvement of a family from a reserved culture and be frustrated by their lack of response.

Therapists with the same background as their clients may also have difficulties and "blind spots." For example, an Italian therapist may be reluctant to intrude on Italian family "secrets," knowing how strong their family loyalties are. An Irish therapist, on the other hand, may hesitate to question an Irish family about issues that are not "proper," because the therapist shares the family's inhibitions and sees their reticence as "normal."

Problems with an Ethnic Perspective

The negative consequences of emphasizing ethnicity must also be recognized. Overly strict adherence to particular customs, under the supposition that they have a universal value, can make an ethnic group resist change and thereby impede its own development. In fact, values that were functional in another place and time often become dysfunctional in modern America. Ethnocentrism, clannishness, prejudice, fear, and distrust of outsiders can prevent cooperation, reinforce exclusivity, and deepen intergroup conflicts (Giordano and Giordano, 1977; Kolm, 1973). However, the solution to these problems lies not in eradicating cultural differences, but in cultivating them as a source of cultural enrichment.

Every culture generates characteristic problems for itself. These problems are often the consequences of cultural traits that are conspicuous strengths in other contexts. For example, WASP optimism leads to confidence and flexibility in taking the initiative, an obvious strength when there are opportunities for initiative. But the one-sided preference for cheerfulness also leads to an inability to cope with tragedy or engage in mourning (Magill and Pearce, 1982). Historically, WASPs may have had more good fortune than most other peoples. But optimism becomes a vulnerability in times of tragedy. They possess few philosophical or expressive tools to manage situations in which optimism, rationality, and a belief in the efficacy of individuality are insufficient. The WASP strengths of independence and individual initiative work well in some situations, but WASPs may feel lost when reliance on the group is the only way to ensure survival.

Strengthening a client's sense of positive cultural identity is often an important aspect of therapy. This may require resolving conflicts within the family, between the family and the community, or in the wider context in which the family is imbedded. Families may at times use their ethnic customs or religious values selectively to justify an emotional position within the family or against outsiders (Friedman, 1980). Family members may need coaching to distinguish between deeply held convictions and values asserted for emotional reasons.

Describing ethnic patterns sometimes necessitates using cultural stereotypes. There are obvious disadvantages to this apprach, and we view these paradigms only as frameworks within which to expand clinical sensitivity and effectiveness. We use our paradigms not as "truths," but rather as maps which, while they cover only limited aspects of the terrain, may nevertheless provide guidelines to an explorer seeking a path. By no means do we wish to encourage negative labeling or stereotyping of anyone. As Zola (1979, p. 76) has aptly stated, "The danger of training anyone in the details of a particular ethnic group is that it will ultimately squeeze people into unreal categories, and reify their culture as we have rigidified diagnoses."

Some authors argue that such generalizations do more harm then good (Stein, 1979). In our view, developing a relatively simple paradigm is the most realistic way to begin expanding one's knowledge. We think the solution to the problem lies in maintaining openness to new experiences once one has a framework, not in avoiding a framework because it is not pristinely accurate or complete. We believe that negative stereotyping is less of a risk than is trivializing or ignoring a client's characteristics.

Appreciation of cultural variability leads to a radically new conceptual model of clinical intervention. This model requires clinicians to struggle consciously against their own subjectivity and to recognize the limitations of any single belief system in their work. We do not mean that culture is the only, or even the most important, contextual factor to be considered in assessing problems and behavior. Social class and economic factors are also extremely important. In addition, the impact of gender on personality (Silverstein, 1981), development (Carter and McGoldrick, 1980; Gluck et al., 1980), and illness behavior (Mechanic, 1978), though largely ignored until recently, cannot be overestimated.

It would require many volumes to consider any single ethnic group in depth. Most groups are themselves combinations of a multitude of cultural groups. Puerto Rican culture, for example, is a product of many diverse influences, including Spanish, African, and Caribbean Indian. Shon (1979) has suggested that the differences among Asian cultures are even greater than those among the more familiar European cultures.

Many factors influence the extent to which traditional ethnic patterns will surface in any particular family:
• The reasons for immigration—what the family sought and what it left behind (religious or political persecution, poverty, wish for adventure, etc.).
• The length of time since immigration and the impact of generational acculturation conflicts on the family.
• The family's place of residence—whether or not the family lives or has lived in an ethnic neighborhood.
• The order of migration—whether one family member migrated alone or whether a large portion of the family, community, or nation came together.
• The socioeconomic status, education, and upward mobility of family members.

- The political and religious ties to the ethnic group.
- The language spoken by family members.
- The extent of family intermarriage with or connection to other ethnic groups.
- The family members' attitudes toward the ethnic group and its values.

All families in this country have at one time experienced the complex stresses of immigration and migration; these may be "buried" or forgotten, but they may still subtly influence a family's outlook. Also, under the pressure of accommodating the new situation, many immigrant groups have been forced to abandon much of their ethnic heritage (Greeley, 1979; Hines and Boyd, 1982), and thus have lost a part of their identity. The effects of this "cutting off" on the family may be all the more powerful for being hidden.

If the first generation was older at the time of immigration, or lives in an ethnic neighborhood in this country, its conflicts of acculturation may be postponed. The next generation, particularly in adolescence, is likely to reject the "ethnic" values of the parents and to strive to become "Americanized" (Sluzki, 1979). The third or fourth generations are usually freer to reclaim some of the aspects of their identities that were sacrificed in the previous generations because of the need to assimilate. To understand ethnic norms, one must maintain a developmental perspective on both variations in family life cycle patterns and the impact that immigration has on families over succeeding generations (Carter and McGoldrick, 1980; Falicov, 1980; Sluzki, 1979).

The extensive geographical and class mobility in American culture, while cutting some individuals off from their heritage, increases their contact with other ethnic groups. The high rate of interethnic marriage means that many Americans will learn about ethnic differences from marriage partners. But, at best, most Americans will probably come to understand only three or four groups in the course of a lifetime. No therapist, obviously, can become an expert on all ethnic groups. But clinicians must develop an attitude of openness to cultural variability and to the relativity of their own values.

Overviews of Major Ethnic Groups

The following pages highlight some of the differences in family patterns and attitudes toward therapy found in several of America's largest ethnic groups. The reader is reminded that the suggestions are meant only as guidelines and not as "truths" about any particular group.

Jewish families. There are about 5.5 million Jews living in the United States (half of the world's Jewish population). Of these, 35% live in New York City, and another 45% live in nine other major American cities

(Goren, 1980). The following comments refer primarily to American Jews of Eastern European background, the largest Jewish group in this country. Obviously, German Jews, Sephardic Jews, and other Jewish groups have different characteristics, influenced by the countries in which their families lived for centuries before migrating to the United States.

Jewish families have a very strong family orientation and will accept a family definition of their problems more readily than many other groups. Marriage and children play a central role in Jewish family life. As Zborowski and Herzog (1952, p. 290) stated in their classic study of Eastern European Jews:

> Marriage is both the climax and the threshold (of family life). From birth on, every step is directed with an eye to the "Khupa" (marriage canopy), and if that goal is missed, life itself seems to be lost. Once attained, however, marriage is merely the background for the great goal, the great achievement, the great gratification: children.

Parents in Jewish families usually have democratic relationships with their children (Zuk, 1978) and less rigid generational boundaries than most other groups (Herz and Rosen, 1982). They place a high value on verbal explanations and reasoning in child rearing. For a non-Jewish therapist, the parents' desire to reason out issues may seem unnecessary, but within a Jewish context it is extremely important. Parents take great pride in their children's verbal skill, intelligence, and ability to think things out logically.

Jewish families are more likely than other ethnic groups to seek and be receptive to psychotherapy. They value talk, insight, and the recognition of complex levels of meaning. They value the gaining of wisdom, and have a long tradition of consulting with a wise person, or several wise people, while always remaining the final judge of the opinions they hear. This contrasts markedly with, for example, the Irish, for whom the priest is always the final judge. The development of psychotherapy has been strongly influenced by these Jewish values. The first problem in therapy may come when the patient questions the therapist's credentials. Although the therapist may perceive this as confrontation or criticism, it may instead reflect the high value Jews place on education and success, as well as their need to be sure they are receiving the best care.

Jewish verbal skill and willingness to talk about troubles and feelings are important assets, but can also lead to problems (Herz and Rosen, 1982; Zuk, 1978). Families may become so preoccupied with the need to analyze and understand their experience that they become immobilized. The Jewish ability to verbalize thoughts and feelings may also lead the therapist to presume that they possess a greater confidence and sophistication than they actually do. Jewish patients frequently wish to appear intellectual and psychologically aware, and this may make their articulation a difficulty as well as a strength in therapy. The need to appear insightful, interesting, and successful can, in the extreme, make them unable to experience anything without first knowing what they are accomplishing. The solutions offered by traditional therapy at times compound these problems. In such situations, the therapist needs to find ways around the tendency to talk or analyze, such as structural techniques (Aponte, 1981; Minuchin, 1974) or those of strategic therapy (Selvini-Palazzoli et al., 1978; Watzlawick et al., 1974; Weakland et al., 1974). However, therapists should be warned against applying simplistic solutions. Jewish clients generally prefer more complex, sophisticated interventions. Behavior modification techniques, for example, might be very useful, but may be viewed as superficial, covering up the "real" problem, which, they fear, will resurface elsewhere.

The Jewish tradition of valuing education and learning dates back many centuries and has produced an unprecedented culture of artistic and intellectual achievements. Jews lived so often under oppression that they came to value those strengths that could not be taken from them, but that could be transferred from one context to another if they were forced to flee from their homes.

Jewish families generally show much more concern for their children's emotional, intellectual, and physical well-being throughout all stages of their development than do other groups. The non-Jewish therapist may fail to appreciate the meaning of Jewish concern for children's success and upward mobility (Sanua, 1967; Strodtbeck, 1958). Raising successful children is a major responsibility of the parents, particularly the mother. Underachievement or more serious problems are often felt to reflect not only on the family, but also on the ethnic group as a whole. Parents are expected to make great sacrifices for their children, and when children grow up they are expected to repay their parents in "naches," a special pleasure one gets only from the success and happiness of one's children. Non-Jewish therapists may be puzzled by the extent of parental upset when their children do not provide them with such rewards. An obvious contrasting value can be seen in WASPs, who raise their children to be independent and to leave home. While WASPs expect their children to be productive and a credit to the family, they do not expect to experience personal pleasure in their children's accomplishments.

Jewish mothers, at times a harshly stereotyped group, reflect many of the positive aspects of Jewish culture. Mothers have been the ones primarily responsible for the education and development of children.

Their success in this realm is overwhelming, as generations of successful Jewish doctors, lawyers, artists, businessmen, and other professionals attest. But until recently they could not fulfill their own dreams for themselves. Their intensity was turned primarily toward their children. The recent opportunities for women to succeed have offered Jewish women, who had already internalized the values of success and education, a chance to flourish in their own right. Their success reveals the potential that until now has been invested in their children, especially their male children.

Jewish families show a strong concern for the ebb and flow of life at all stages. They place great importance on life cycle rituals, which reflects their awareness of the complexity of the transitions at all of life's phases. For example, Jewish mourning rituals have several phases. The burial occurs as soon as possible after the death, followed by a week of "sitting shiva," when friends and extended family come to share in the mourning. After a year has passed, family members again gather for the "unveiling," which marks the end of the mourning period, although yearly prayers are still said after this. The emphasis placed on the bar or bas mitzvah, which marks the transition of children into adulthood, reflects the value of the transition to serious adult learning and work experiences in Jewish culture. The therapist should recognize the underlying power of these transitions for Jewish families and help them refocus their energies on the important underlying values if they get stuck on the more superficial aspects of the rituals (Friedman, 1980).

Non-Jewish therapists might easily misunderstand the meaning of suffering in Jewish families. Suffering is viewed as a form of work, as even a magical way to deal with adversity. It is a part of their heritage, to be experienced and shared rather than overcome. This attitude contrasts sharply with that of the Irish, who believe they should suffer alone and in silence, and that of WASPs, who believe suffering is to be overcome by personal fortitude, hard work, and good intentions.

Conflicts and hostility are usually expressed directly in Jewish families. In fact, a therapist from a more restrained culture (e.g., WASP, Irish, Scandinavian) may be uncomfortable with the intensity of Jewish criticism and verbal aggression (Herz and Rosen, 1982). Conflicts or cutoffs with the extended family often occur over money or loyalty and may at times be extremely bitter. In a fair number of families, a child's marriage to a non-Jew can also precipitate a cutoff. Preservation of the Jewish heritage (though not necessarily religious practices) is crucial to their sense of identity. Intermarriage, which occurs frequently, especially among Jewish males, creates great sadness and pain for parents. There is considerable pressure for Jews to identify with the group, and if a family member rejects his or her cultural background, it may be a serious issue for others in the family. These problems are naturally more prominent in the Northeast than elsewhere in the United States, where the percentage of Jews is much smaller and the patterns less pronounced (Sanua, 1978).

Jewish families have a number of strengths that are important in therapy. One is their humor—their ability to make fun of their own situation—which offers a release and perspective on themselves and their foibles. Generally, they also have an openness to new ideas and new ways (they are foremost among American ethnic groups in their willingness to explore new ideas). Further strengths are their belief in philanthropy and good works and their esteem for family and extended family relationships. While Jews may at times feel deeply ambivalent about their own ethnicity, their cultural ties are a profound part of their heritage and their identity, perhaps more so than for other groups. This may stem from their 4,000-year history of living as foreigners in other cultures, always under the threat of expulsion or persecution. Bringing them back in touch with their cultural roots may be a particularly rich experience for them.

Irish-American families. The comments here refer primarily to the almost 15 million Americans of Irish-Catholic background, many of whose families have by now been in this country for four or five generations. This group's culture has remained relatively homogeneous for almost 2,000 years. Irish Catholics began to migrate here in large numbers in the 1840s, primarily because of the potato famines and oppressive conditions in Ireland. Irish Protestants, who are a separate group, have been migrating here since before the American Revolution. They do not think of themselves as Irish in any meaningful sense; they have the lowest rate of endogamous marriage of any American ethic group and have virtually lost their sense of ethnicity (Fallows, 1979).

The Catholic Irish tend to assume that any misfortune is the result of their sins. They believe that problems are private matters between individuals and God. They are, therefore, unlikely to seek or expect help for their problems (McGoldrick et al., 1982; McGoldrick and Pearce, 1981; Sanua, 1960; Zborowski, 1969; Zola, 1966). If they do seek help, the Irish are apt to equate therapy with Catholic confession—an occasion in which they tell their "sins" and receive a "penance." They are embarrassed to come to therapy, and usually only do so at the suggestion of a third party; for example, a school, a hospital, or a court.

While the Irish rarely seek help for neurotic disorders, they have extremely high rates of psychosis and addiction, primarily alcoholism (Malzberg, 1963; McGoldrick et al., 1982; McGoldrick and Pearce, 1981; Murphy, 1975; Rabkin and Struening, 1976; Roberts and Myers, 1954). By contrast, Jews, who value therapy as a "solution" to personal problems, are overrepresented in "neurotic disorders" and underrepresented in hospital admissions for all psychoses and addictive disorders (Malzberg, 1973; Rabkin and Struening, 1976; Rinder, 1963; Roberts and Myers, 1954).

While the Irish have, in some ways, the most highly developed skill with words of any culture, they may be at a loss to describe their own inner feelings, whether of love, sadness, or anger. They differ in this respect from Jews, who enjoy and find meaning in giving expression to all their experiences. Language and poetry have always been highly valued by the Irish and closely associated with their love of dreaming and fantasy. For many centuries the Irish existed under wretched circumstances, and they used words to enrich a dismal reality. The poet was always the most highly valued member of their culture, and even today writers are the only members of Irish society exempted from taxes.

Humor is the greatest resource of the Irish for dealing with life's problems, and wit and satire have long been their most powerful means of attack. Hostility and resentments could (and still can) be dealt with only indirectly in the family, through sarcasm or innuendo. As a result, feelings have often built up until, finally, family members silently cut one another off. Hostility was (and is) only permitted against the outgroup and then only for a just and moral cause, such as religion or politics. These values create many difficulties for the therapist trying to understand Irish family patterns. As is reflected in the mystifying character of much Irish literature, the most important things are usually left unspoken or referred to only by allusion. Within the family, feelings are often so hidden that it is hard for anyone to know exactly what is going on.

The Irish have a much greater tolerance for nonrealistic thinking than other groups do (Wylan and Mintz, 1976). In contrast to WASPs and Jews, for example, who value the pursuit of truth, clarification of their feelings does not necessarily make the Irish feel better. Thus, therapy aimed at opening up family feelings will often be unsuccessful. As a rule, structured therapy, focused specifically on the presenting problem, will be the least threatening and most helpful to Irish clients. Suggestions that open communication but also preserve individual privacy, such as Bowen therapy, will be preferable to therapy that brings the entire family drama into the therapy session. The strategic techniques of the Palo Alto and the Milan groups would also be helpful, since they emphasize change without forcing clients to spell out all their feelings or make changes in front of the therapist.

Characteristically, the Irish mother plays a central role in the family. She has been seen as morally superior to her husband, who is traditionally a more shadowy figure, a man who found his companionship in the pub. She directed life in the home and socialized through the Church. Her children were raised to be respectful and well-behaved. Discipline was traditionally strict and enforced with threats such as: "It's a mortal sin; you'll go to hell." Families do not praise their children for fear of giving them a "swelled head." They consider it important to keep up appearances and not to "make a scene."

Church authority was the major unifier for the Irish, and even came before the family (Italians have had the opposite priorities). Irish Catholics have traditionally viewed their lives moralistically, following the rules of the Church without question. This has changed in recent years of course (Wills, 1971), but the underlying rigidity often remains. In working with the Irish, a therapist must understand how they feel about religion, since the values of the Church often have a strong bearing on their problems. Even those who have left the Church may harbor intense feelings about religious issues.

In contrast to those of Jewish, Italian, black, and other American ethnic groups, extended family relationships among the Irish are seldom close. Families may convene for "duty visits" on holidays and they may act jovial and "clannish," but family members do not rely on one another for support. The emotional isolation seen in Irish relationships frequently determines symptom development and has important implications for therapy. For example, large family sessions that draw on the resources of the whole family may be productive for some groups, but it is usually inadvisable for the Irish because it greatly raises anxiety. Meeting with smaller subgroups of the family, at least in the initial stages of opening up family communication, is often more fruitful.

Trying to talk the Irish out of their need to suffer is usually futile. Unlike Jews, for whom the experience of sharing suffering has meaning, the Irish believe they must suffer alone. Certain strategies, such as prescribing their guilt and suffering within restricted time intervals (see McGoldrick, in press; McGoldrick and Pearce, 1981), may help them curtail it. But they are unlikely to give up suffering altogether. In fact, to do so would make them feel vulnerable, because they believe that eventually they will have to pay for their sins.

The therapist working with an Irish family must be content with limited changes. The Irish may not wish to move beyond the initial presenting problem, and the therapist should not pressure them into further work. Attempting to get spouses to deal with marital issues after a child-focused problem has been solved, for example, may make them feel guilty and incompetent. It is better to reinforce whatever changes the family members do make and to let them return for therapy later if they wish. Even if the nurse-therapist sees emotional blocks in the family that are still causing pain, she should not push. Because Irish families offer little immediate feedback about their therapeutic progress, the therapist may be surprised to learn that they have continued therapeutic work on their own. Irish patients' deep sense of personal responsibility is, in fact, their greatest resource in therapy. They often continue efforts started in therapy, though they may not openly admit either the fault or the resolve to remedy it.

Italian-American families. Poverty and hopes of a better life led to a wave of Italian immigration to the United States in the late 19th and early 20th centuries. Today they are the fifth largest American ethnic group. Since southern Italians compose by far the largest percentage of Italian-Americans (80%), the comments here will be limited to this group. Northern Italians are a more industrialized people, culturally distinct from their southern countrymen (Nelli, 1980).

While all cultures value the family, Italians give it higher priority than other groups. Family life is their primary orientation; it is one's greatest resource and protection against trouble. For this reason, family intervention would seem to be the treatment of choice. Italians tend to distrust outsiders, however, and gaining the family's acceptance is the first hurdle in dealing with them. The therapist must not take this group's mistrust personally. Everyone outside the family is mistrusted until proven otherwise.

The characteristic difficulties for Italian families relate to differentiation and/or separation from the family. The family provides such an intense and wide network of support that breaking away from it constitutes a major problem. This tendency lies in direct contrast to American core values, which emphasize independence, individualism, and personal achievement over affiliation.

Anyone who tries to break the close bonds of an Italian family collides with Italian cultural norms. Therapy with Italian families involves not so much helping them deal with a particular emotional issue as it does facilitating the renegotiation of system boundaries that have somehow rigidified. Within the family context itself, all emotions are viewed as understandable. Italians do not disallow feelings, as some cultural groups do, although there are clear rules for behavior that are based primarily on how such behavior affects the family.

Historically, the family in Italy provided an anchor amidst the constant tides of foreigners, changing governments, and natural disasters (floods, volcanos, and famines). Through the centuries, Italians learned to define themselves not by an association with Italy, but by their association with their families first and with their immediate neighbors, or "paisani," second. Allegiance to the family surpassed all other loyalties, and separation from the family was tantamount to spiritual death. Education and occupation were secondary to the security, affection, and sense of relatedness the family had to offer.

Italians have learned to squeeze the most out of the present moment. They have a tremendous capacity for the intense enjoyment of eating, celebrating, fighting, and loving. They take great pleasure in festivals and fiestas, and prize church rituals for their pageantry, spectacle, and value in fostering family celebrations and rites of passage.

The relatively low utilization of mental health facilities by Italians reflects their tendency to turn first to the family for support. While the enmeshment of Italian families certainly creates difficulties for them, it also provides much that families in less supportive cultural environments lack. They have one of the strongest informal community networks of any ethnic group (Fitzpatrick, 1975), and are less likely to leave the neighborhood to get ahead. When they do break away, it is often very stressful for both the individual and their families. When cut off from the family, Italians are much more likely to become symptomatic (Rotuno and McGoldrick, 1982; Stein, 1971). For example, a study of Italian-American patients in Boston revealed that rates of schizophrenia and manic-depressive disorders varied inversely with the number of Italians living in their particular neighborhood (Mintz and Schwartz, 1976).

There is virtually no such thing as a separate nuclear family unit in Italian culture. "La famiglia" includes, first, all blood relatives and all relatives by marriage. Beyond this there are the "comparaggio" or godparents, an important kinship network established in conjunction with rites of passage, and then the "gumbares" (old friends and neighbors). Close and intense contacts are maintained with a wide circle of family and friends. It is not unusual for siblings and parents to maintain daily contact throughout their lives. Even if they move apart, frequent telephone calls keep the family bond alive.

Therapists working with Italian-American families need to learn the whereabouts of and level of contact with members of the extended family. They are often in the same neighborhood, if not on the same block or even in the same building. This contrasts sharply with the habits of WASPs, who raise their children to be independent and self-sufficient above all else, and who think themselves failures if their children do not leave home on schedule. Italians raise their children to be mutually supportive and to contribute to the family. Separation from the family is not expected.

In the Italian household, the father tends to be the undisputed leader, and he is often authoritarian and rigid in laying down rules and guidelines for behavior. A kind of benevolent despot, he takes his responsibility to provide for his family very seriously. Any situation that erodes his authority is likely to have a pronounced negative impact on the Italian father. Since it is in the nature of adolescents to question parental authority, the adolescence of his children may be particularly difficult for him.

The Italian mother, on the other hand, is the heart of the home. While yielding authority to the father, she traditionally assumes total control of the family's affective realm. She is the family's emotional sustenance. Her life centers on domestic activities, and she receives her primary pleasure from nurturing and servicing her family. Her personal needs are expected to take second place to those of her husband. In exchange, she is offered protection and security from all outside pressure or threat. Neither partner is likely to perceive this as a problem, although to an outsider it may appear to reinforce an extreme degree of dependence. The mutual support and complementarity of roles between husband and wife relate to their obligations to the entire family of at least three generations, and not to marital intimacy.

Sons and daughters have markedly different roles in Italian families. Though both can leave home when they marry, sons receive considerably greater latitude prior to marriage. A bit of acting out is expected, even subtly encouraged, as a measure of manliness. Proficiency in the sexual domain is important, not only to fulfill the masculine image, but also to exemplify a sense of mastery in interpersonal relations, which is a core Italian value. Although social skills are considered important for females as well, their behavior is subject to closer scrutiny. They are much more restricted socially; in particular, they are taught to eschew personal achievement in favor of respect and service to their parents. Traditionally, Italian males have been trained to control themselves emotionally—to be cautious and understated in their emotional reactions, especially with outsiders. This has nothing to do with embarrassment about expressing feelings, as it does with WASP or Irish males. Rather, it reflects the historical need to protect oneself against dangerous exposure to outsiders. Women, on the other hand, are allowed to express their emotions freely, but are kept out of "men's business."

Italians tend to dramatize their experiences. Similarly, they may exaggerate their symptoms (Zborowski, 1969; Zola, 1966), and are characteristically colorful and dramatic in their talk. Their expressiveness may be overpowering to a therapist from a more restrained culture, one in which, for example, powerful expressions of hostility would be interpreted literally. For Italians, words express the emotion of the moment and are not taken so seriously. A non-Italian therapist may also find it difficult to deal with family "secrets." While Italian families may appear to talk openly and engagingly, even in the initial contact, sharing real family secrets is an entirely different matter. The existence of the secret may be puzzling to the therapist, since otherwise the family seems to talk openly about all kinds of issues, including sex, death, hostility, and/or antisocial behavior. Often the content of the secret itself is not important; its purpose may simply be to mark and preserve the boundaires of the system—thus clarifying who is inside and who is not. Therapists must deal delicately with secrets, remembering the sense of betrayal families will feel if their boundaries are crossed.

Therapists may also be frustrated by the Italian family's demand for immediate solutions. If a therapist assumes that change occurs through long evaluation and discussion of problems, Italian families will be difficult to help. If, on the other hand, the therapist focuses on mobilizing the family's own natural supports (as noted, this is the preferred Italian solution) and does not try to replace this orientation with one that puts therapy first, there is a much better chance of constructive intervention.

Black American families. There were an estimated 24 million black Americans in the United States in the mid-1970s, making them the nation's largest ethnic group (Holt, 1980). It would be a serious mistake to assume that blacks are an ethnic group like any other, or that their problems can be solved the way those of other immigrant groups can. However degrading the life conditions of early white immigrant groups, whites were not brought here as slaves. The combination of the slavery experience and the difference in skin color has put blacks at an extreme disadvantage in acculturating to American society. The ongoing impact of racism and discrimination is a continuing and pervasive aspect of the lives of black families, and it cannot be overestimated in dealing with them therapeutically.[3]

Much has been written about the characteristics of black family structure and the socioeconomic forces behind these family patterns. In the author's opinion, much useless debate has been generated about the "pathological" nature of black families.

Initially, blacks are likely to view therapy within the context of their other traditional dealings with white institutions. Since white institutions have been basically "foreign" to blacks, a certain level of mistrust and alienation should be taken for granted. In the early stages of therapy, black families may keep their distance, participate in the situations with some reluctance, and offer minimal information. This may at times resemble the inarticulateness characteristic of the Irish, who are uncomfortable, embarrassed, and guilt-ridden about their feelings.

[3] For a more detailed discussion of black Americans and family therapy, see Hines and Boyd (1982), Boyd (1980), Pinderhughes (1982), Allen (1978a, and 1978b), and Staples and Mirande (1980), to name a few of the most important.

By contrast, blacks are likely to be realistic, emotionally aware, and comfortable with the full range of their feelings (Sanua, 1960). Their withholding or reticence has more to do with the specific context of therapy than with discomfort about their feelings or about communication in general.

Religion has been the major formal institution in our society available to blacks for support. It is both a social and a personal resource, and it has been a major source of status and community support for black families. Most blacks will turn to religion as a solution to their problems before they think of therapy. A therapist must always check out the role that religion plays in the family's life, as it may be a powerful spiritual and emotional resource.

While it is true that females head more black families than white families, and that these numbers are increasing, the two-parent family remains the norm among black families. In our time of changing family roles and a changing status of women, black families may actually have achieved a better balance in sex roles than white families have. There seems to be more role flexibility between black spouses, and black fathers seem to take a bigger part in housekeeping, child-rearing activities, and the nurturing of children than white fathers (Allen, 1978b; Axelson, 1970; Kunkell and Kennard, 1971; Lewis, 1975). Some research suggests that black women are more likely to enjoy sex and to take the initiative sexually, and that they are less likely than white women to find sex a source of marital tension (Allen, 1978a; Lewis, 1975; Rainwater, 1966; Scanzoni, 1971). Much more research needs to be done on these and many other aspects of black family patterns, but it is possible that in spite of the severe disadvantages of black families in our culture, they may be closer to accomplishing the shifts in male-female characteristics and relationships that many families have been striving for in recent years (Gluck et al., 1980).

Like the Irish, women in black families tend to be strong and independent, and their sphere of activity often goes beyond the home to work situations and community activities. Given the economic and social pressures on their families, black women have often had to work to help support the family.

Black families develop strong kinship networks that serve as their major resource in times of trouble. Among lower-class blacks, economic factors often militate against the establishment and maintenance of nuclear family units. These stresses make blacks more vulnerable to illness and death than whites (black males have a mortality rate twice that of white males). Often, extended households are the most stable and enduring form of family unit (Allen, 1978b; Stack, 1974). Kinship networks that may include both family and close friends frequently

share resources, household tasks, and housing in a system characterized by mutual obligation (Stack, 1974).

Research shows clearly that blacks are more likely than whites to
have babies out of wedlock (Furstenberg, 1970; Rainwater, 1966).
Abortion and formal adoption are less frequent than they are in white
families. Blacks rely on family and friends for necessary support with
premarital pregnancies (Furstenberg, 1970; Himes, 1964; Pope, 1969),
and children born in these circumstances are accepted readily into
the system.

Black families regard children as extremely important. There are a
number of differences in their child-rearing practices. Early studies
indicated that black parents were more lenient in weaning and feeding
children, but more strict in toilet training (Davis & Havighurst, 1946).
Recent evidence suggests that, over time, black and white child rearing
practices have become more alike (Allen 1978a, 1978b; Radin and
Kamii, 1965; Scanzoni, 1971). Black families tend to deemphasize sex
differences in their socialization of children. Other adults often assume
child care responsibilities if a mother cannot handle them. Extended
kin in black families generally take a more active role in the socialization of children than those in white families do (Aschenbrenner, 1973;
Ladner, 1971; Stack, 1974).

Disciplining of children is often strict and direct, a pragmatic practice
necessary for survival and one that may be misjudged by therapists
not familiar with black culture. Because they rarely have the support of
larger social structures, black families have great difficulty protecting
their children against prejudice, crime, or drugs. When black adolescents
rebel, they are much more likely than whites to associate with peers
who are engaged in serious antisocial behavior. They have fewer non-
dangerous options for acting out adolescent rebellion, and their families
have very few societal supports to protect them from antisocial influences. In therapy, the therapist must consider the realistic pressures on
black youths, even when their families have ample financial resources.

When social pressures have led to underorganization of the family
(Aponte, 1976), children may either take on adult roles prematurely or
fail to develop the discipline necessary for adult functioning. In such
situations, "talking" therapy is unlikely to be effective or acceptable for
black families. Structural therapy to strengthen family organization
and add to its flexibility is probably the most effective model (Aponte,
1976, 1981; Minuchin et al., 1967; Minuchin, 1974).

Initially, the therapist needs to help the family deal with its incipient
crisis and promote positive links with whatever resources or institutions are, or should be, available. Beyond this, strengthening the family's
sense of ethnic identity and connectedness may be a crucial part of

therapy. As Boyd (1980) has pointed out, genograms can provide clear and useful pictures of black family structure. As Boyd suggests, their genograms are often "sloppy," if they are complete at all. Genograms should be taken only after the family's trust has been won, and not in the initial sessions. Understanding and supporting the family's network can be elemental in fostering their ability to mobilize resources and gain confidence.

CONCLUSIONS

The descriptions offered here of ethnic differences in the definition of "normality" and in responses to therapy will not be, the author hopes, interpreted as rigid stereotypes but, rather, as pointers for thought and future research. Ideally, by appreciating the profound impact of ethnicity on human values, clinicians will become more sophisticated in their research and in the development of models of family functioning and therapy.

REFERENCES

Allen, W.R. "The Search for Applicable Theories of Black Family Life," *Journal of Marriage and the Family* 40:117–27, 1978a.

Allen, W.R. "Black Family Research in the United States: A Review, Assessment and Extension," *Journal of Comparative Family Studies* 9:166–88, 1978b.

Aponte, H.J. "Underorganization in the Poor Family," in *Family Therapy.* Edited by Guerin, P.J. New York: Gardner Press, 1976.

Aponte, H.J. "Structural Family Therapy," in *Handbook of Family Therapy.* Edited by Gurman, A., and Kniskern, D. New York: Brunner-Mazel, 1981.

Aschenbrenner, J. "Extended Families Among Black Americans," *Journal of Comparative Family Studies* 4:257–68, 1973.

Axelson, L.J. "The Working Wife: Differences in Perception Among Negro and White Males," *Journal of Marriage and the Family* 32:457–64, 1970.

Billingsley, A. "The Family and Cultural Pleuralism," Address at Baltimore Conference on Ethnicity and Social Welfare. New York: Institute on Pluralism and Group Identity, 1976.

Boyd, N. "Family Therapy with Black Families," in *Minority Mental Health.* Edited by Corchin, S., and Jones, E. New York: Holt, Rinehart & Winston, 1980.

Carpenter, W., and Strauss, J. "Cross-Cultural Evaluation of Schneider's First-Rank Symptoms of Schizophrenia: A Report from the International Pilot Study of Schizophrenia," *American Journal of Psychiatry* 131:204–10, 1974.

Carter, E.A., and McGoldrick, M., eds. *The Family Life Cycle: A Framework for Family Therapy.* New York: Gardner Press, 1980.

Davis, A., and Havighurst, R. "Social Class and Color Differences in Child Rearing," *American Sociological Review* 11:698–710, 1946.

Eisenberg, L. "Psychiatry and Society: A Sociobiologic Synthesis," *New England Journal of Medicine* 296:903–10, 1977.

Falicov, C. "Cultural Variations in the Family Life Cycle," in *The Family Life Cycle: A Framework for Family Therapy.* Edited by Carter, E.A., and McGoldrick, M. New York: Gardner Press, 1980.

Fallows, M.A. *Irish Americans: Identity and Assimilation.* Englewood Cliffs, N.J.: Prentice-Hall, 1979.

Fantl, B., and Shiro, J. "Cultural Variables in the Behavior Pattern of Symptom Formation of 15 Irish and 15 Italian Schizophrenics," *International Journal of Social Psychiatry,* 4:245–53, 1959.

Feinstein, O. "Why Ethnicity?" in *Immigrants and Migrants: The Detroit Ethnic Experience.* Edited by Hartman, D. Detroit: Wayne State University, 1974.

Fitzpatrick, J. "The Role of White Ethnic Communities in the Urban Adjustment of Newcomers," Working Paper No. 2. New York: Institute on Pluralism and Group Identity, 1975.

Foley, V.C. "Family Therapy with Black Disadvantaged Families: Some Observations on Roles, Communication, and Technique," *Journal of Marriage and Family Counseling* 1:57–65, 1975.

Friedman, E. "Systems and Ceremonies," in *The Family Life Cycle: A Framework for Family Therapy.* Edited by Carter, E.A., and McGoldrick, M. New York: Gardner Press, 1980.

Furstenberg, F. "Premarital Pregnancy Among Black Teenagers," *Transaction* 52–55, 1970.

Gambino, R. *Blood of My Blood: The Dilemma of Italian-Americans*. Garden City, N.Y.: Doubleday, 1974.

Giordano, J., and Giordano, G.P. *The Ethno-Cultural Factor in Mental Health: A Literature Review and Bibliography*. New York: Institute on Pluralism and Group Identity, 1977.

Glazer, N., and Moynihan, D., eds. *Ethnicity: Therapy and Experience*. Cambridge, Mass.: Harvard University Press, 1975.

Gluck, N.R., et al. "Women in Families," in *The Family Life Cycle: A Framework for Family Therapy*. Edited by Carter, E.A., and McGoldrick, M. New York: Gardner Press, 1980.

Goren, A. "Jews," in *Harvard Encyclopedia of American Ethnic Groups*. Edited by Thernstrom, S. Cambridge, Mass.: Harvard University Press, 1980.

Greeley, A.M. *The American Catholic*. New York: Basic Books, 1978.

Greeley, A.M. "Creativity in the Irish Family: The Cost of Immigration," *International Journal of Family Therapy* 1:295–303, 1979.

Greeley, A.M. *Why Can't They Be Like Us?* New York: Institute of Human Relations Press, 1969.

Herz, F., and Rosen, E. "Family Therapy with Jewish Americans," in *Ethnicity and Family Therapy*. Edited by McGoldrick, M., et al. New York: Guilford Press, 1982.

Himes, J. "Some Reactions to a Hypothetical Premarital Pregnancy by 100 Negro College Women," *Marriage and Family Living* 26:344–49, 1964.

Hines, P., and Boyd, N. "The Black American Family," in *Ethnicity and Family Therapy*. Edited by McGoldrick, M., et al. New York: Guilford Press, 1982.

Holt, T.C. "Afro-Americans," in *Harvard Encyclopedia of American Ethnic Groups*. Edited by Thernstrom, S. Cambridge, Mass.: Harvard University Press, 1980.

Jalali, B. "Family Therapy with Iranian American Families," in *Ethnicity and Family Therapy*. Edited by McGoldrick, M., et al. New York: Guilford Press, 1982.

Kiev, A. *Transcultural Psychiatry*. New York: Free Press, 1972.

Kleinman, A.M. "Explanatory Models in Health Care Relationships," in *Health of the Family (National Council for International Health Symposium)*. Washington, D.C.: National Council for International Health, 1975.

Kleinman, A.M., et al. "Culture, Illness, and Care: Clinical Lessons from Anthropologic and Cross-Culture Research," *Annals of Internal Medicine* 88:251–58, 1978.

Kluckhohn, F.R., and Strodtbeck, F.L. *Variations in Value Orientations*. New York: Harper & Row, 1961.

Kolm, R. *Ethnicity and Society: A Theoretical Analysis and its Implications for the United States*. Rockville, Md.: National Institute for Mental Health, 1973.

Kunkell, P., and Kennard, S. *Spout Spring: A Black Community*. Chicago: Rand McNally, 1971.

Ladner, J. *Tomorrow's Tomorrow*. Garden City, N.Y.: Doubleday, 1971.

Lewis, D. "The Black Family: Socialization and Sex Roles," *Phylon* 36:221–37, 1975.

Lieberman, M. "Adaptational Patterns in the Middle Aged and Elderly: The Role of Ethnicity," Paper presented at the Conference of the Gerontological Society, Portland, Ore., 1974.

Magill, D., and Pearce, J.K. "Family Therapy with White Anglo-Saxon Protestant Families," in *Ethnicity and Family Therapy.* Edited by McGoldrick, M., et al. New York: Guilford Press, 1982.

Malzberg, B. "Mental Disease Among the Irish-Born and Native White of Irish Parentage in New York State, 1949–1951," *Mental Hygiene* 47:284–95, 1963.

Malzberg, B. "Mental Disease Among Jews in New York State," *Acta Psychiatrica Scandinavica* 49:245–51, 1973.

McAdoo, H. "Family Therapy in the Black Community," *American Journal of Orthopsychiatry* 47:75–79, 1977.

McGoldrick, M. "Clinical Issues in Family Therapy with Irish Americans," in *Culture and Health Care.* Edited by Sluski, C., and Schnitman, D. (in press).

McGoldrick, M. "Irish Americans in Family Therapy," in *Ethnicity and Family Therapy.* Edited by McGoldrick, M., et al. New York: Guilford Press, 1982.

McGoldrick, M., and Pearce, J.K. "Family Therapy with Irish Americans," *Family Process* 20, 1981.

McGoldrick, M., et al., eds. *Ethnicity and Family Therapy.* New York: Guilford Press, 1982.

Mechanic, D. "Sex, Illness, Illness Behavior and the Use of Health Services," *Social Science and Medicine* 12b:207–14, 1978.

Midelfort, F.C., and Midelfort, C. "Family Therapy with Norwegian Families," in *Ethnicity and Family Therapy.* Edited by McGoldrick, M., et al. New York: Guilford Press, 1982.

Mindel, C., and Halberstein, R., eds. *Ethnic Families in America.* New York: Elsevier, 1976.

Mintz, N., and Schwartz, D. "Urban Ecology and Psychosis: Community Factors in the Incidence of Schizophrenia and Manic Depression Among Italians in Greater Boston," *International Journal of Social Psychiatry* 10:101–18, 1976.

Minuchin, S. *Families and Family Therapy.* Cambridge, Mass.: Harvard University Press, 1974.

Minuchin, S., et al. *Families of the Slums.* New York: Basic Books, 1967.

Murphy, H.B.M. "Alcoholism and Schizophrenia in the Irish: A Review," *Transcultural Psychiatric Research* 12:116–39, 1975.

Nelli, H.S. "Italians," in *Harvard Encyclopedia of American Ethnic Groups.* Edited by Thernstrom, S. Cambridge, Mass.: Harvard University Press, 1980.

Opler, M.K., and Singer, J.L. "Ethnic Differences in Behavior and Psychopathology: Italian and Irish," *International Journal of Social Psychiatry* 1:11–17, 1956.

Papajohn, J., and Spiegel, J. *Transactions in Families.* San Francisco: Jossey-Bass, 1975.

Pinderhughes, E. "Afro Americans and the Victim System," in *Ethnicity and Family Therapy.* Edited by McGoldrick, M., et al. New York: Guilford Press, 1982.

Pinto, T. "Ethnicity and Professional Education: A Survey of Curriculum Content," Unpublished manuscript. New York: Institute on Pluralism and Group Identity, 1976.

Pope, H. "Negro–White Differences in Decisions Regarding Illegimate Children," *Journal of Marriage and the Family* 31:756–64, 1969.

Preto, N.G. "Family Therapy with Puerto Rican Families," in *Ethnicity and Family Therapy.* Edited by McGoldrick, M., et al. New York: Guilford Press, 1982.

Rabkin, J., and Struening, E. *Ethnicity, Social Class and Mental Illness in New York City.* New York: Institute on Pluralism and Group Identity, 1976.

Radin, N., and Kamii, C. "The Child Rearing Attitudes of Disadvantaged Negro Mothers and Some Educational Implications," *Journal of Negro Education* 34:138–46, 1965.

Rainwater, L. "Some Aspects of Lower Class Sexual Behavior," *Journal of Social Issues* 22:96–108, 1966.

Rinder, I. "Mental Health of American Jewish Urbanites: A Review of the Literature and Predictions," *International Journal of Social Psychiatry* 9:214–20, 1963.

Roberts, B., and Myers, J.K. "Religion, National Origin, Immigration and Mental Illness," *American Journal of Psychiatry* 110:759–64, 1954.

Rotuno, M., and McGoldrick, M. "Family Therapy with Italian Americans," in *Ethnicity and Family Therapy.* Edited by McGoldrick, M., et al. New York: Guilford Press, 1982.

Sanua, V. "The Contemporary Jewish Family: A Review of the Social Science Literature," in *Serving the Jewish Family.* Edited by Bubis, G. New York: Ktav Press, 1978.

Sanua, V. "Evaluation of Psychotherapy with Different Socioeconomic and Ethnic Groups: A Need for Rethinking in the Training of Therapists," Paper presented at the Annual Conference of the New York Society of Clinical Psychology, New York, 1975.

Sanua, V. "Intermarriage and Psychological Adjustment," in *Marriage Counseling: Psychology, Ideology, Science.* Edited by Silverman, H. Chicago: Charles C. Thomas, 1967.

Sanua, V. "Sociocultural Factors in Responses of Stressful Life Situations: The Behavior of Aged Amputees as an Example," *Journal of Health and Human Behavior* 1:17–24, 1960.

Scanzoni, J. *The Black Family in Modern Society.* Boston: Allyn & Bacon, 1971.

Selvini-Palazzoli, M., et al. *Paradox and Counterparadox.* New York: Jason Aronson, 1978.

Shon, S. "Asian American Families," Paper presented at The World of Family Therapy Symposium, San Francisco, 1979.

Shon, S., and Ja, D. "The Asian American Family," in *Ethnicity and Family Therapy.* Edited by McGoldrick, M., et al. New York: Guilford Press, 1982.

Silverstein, O. "Fusion," Paper presented at Conference on Mothers and Daughters, New York, 1981.

Singer, J., and Opler, M.K. "Contrasting Patterns of Fantasy and Motility in Irish and Italian Schizophrenics," *Journal of Abnormal and Social Psychiatry* 53:42–47, 1956.

Sluzki, C. "Migration and Family Conflict," *Family Process* 18(4):379–90, 1979.

Sluzki, C., and Schnitman, D., eds. *Culture and Health Care,* 1982.

Spiegel, J. *Transactions: The Interplay Between Individual, Family, and Society,* New York: Science House, 1971.

Stack, C. *All Our Kin: Strategies for Survival in a Black Community.* New York: Harper & Row, 1974.

Staples, R., and Mirande, A. "Racial and Cultural Variations Among American Families: A Decennial Review of the Literature on Minority Families," *Journal of Marriage and the Family* 42:887–903, 1980.

Stein, H.F. "The Salience of Ethno-Psychology for Medical Education and Practice," *Social Science and Medicine* 13b:199–210, 1979.

Stein, H.F. "The Slovak-American 'Swaddling Ethos': Homeostat for Family Dynamics and Cultural Persistence," *Family Process* 17:31–46, 1978.

Stein, R.F. *Disturbed Youth and Ethnic Family Patterns.* Albany, N.Y.: State University of New York Press, 1971.

Stoeckle, J., et al. "The Quantity and Significance of Psychological Distress in Medical Patients," *Journal of Chronic Disease* 17:959–70, 1964.

Strodtbeck, F.L. "Family Interaction, Values, and Achievement," in *The Jews: Social Patterns of an American Group.* Edited by Sklare, M. New York: Random House, 1958.

Watzlawick, P. *How Real is Real?* New York: Random House, 1976.

Watzlawick, P., et al. *Change: Principles of Problem Formation and Problem Resolution.* New York: W.W. Norton & Co., 1974.

Weakland, J., et al. "Brief Therapy: Focused Problem Resolution," *Family Process* 13:213–20, 1974.

Wills, G. *Bare Ruined Choirs.* Garden City, N.Y.: Doubleday, 1971.

Wylan, L., and Mintz, N. "Ethnic Differences in Family Attitudes Toward Psychotic Manifestations with Implications for Treatment Programmes," *International Journal of Social Psychiatry* 22:86–95, 1976.

Zborowski, M. *People in Pain.* San Francisco: Jossey-Bass, 1969.

Zborowski, M., and Herzog, E. *Life Is with People.* New York: Schocken Books, 1952.

Zola, I.K. "The Concept of Trouble and Sources of Medical Assistance," *Social Science and Medicine* 6:673–79, 1972.

Zola, I.K. "Culture and Symptoms: An Analysis of Patients' Presenting Complaints," *American Sociological Review* 5:141–55, 1966.

Zola, I.K. "Oh Where, Oh Where Has Ethnicity Gone?" in *Ethnicity and Aging.* Edited by Gelfand, D.E., and Kutzik, A.J. New York: Springer Publishing Co., 1979.

Zola, I.K. "Problems of Communications, Diagnosis and Patient Care: The Interplay of Patient, Physician and Clinical Organization," *Journal of Medical Education* 38:829–38, 1963.

Zuk, G.H. "A Therapist's Perspective on Jewish Family Values," *Journal of Marriage and Family Counseling* 4:101–11, 1978.

SECTION II

Assessing Families with Psychosocial Problems

4 Assessing families with problems attaching to twin infants

Beverly Anderson RN, MSN
Assistant Professor
Faculty of Nursing
University of Calgary
Calgary, Alberta, Canada

Arnette Anderson, RN, MSN
Associate Professor
Faculty of Nursing
University of Alberta
Edmonton, Alberta, Canada

OVERVIEW

This chapter explores the process and problems of attaching to twin infants, emphasizing the psychosocial factors and supportive networks that influence attachment. Case studies and a nursing plan to help families attach to their twins and complete the transition to parenthood are also provided.

NURSING PROCESS

Assessment

The health problem: The twin birth. The twin birth rate is gradually increasing according to the United States Bureau of the Census. Between 1972 and 1980 live twin births increased from 59,122 to 68,339 (statistics based on 100% of births in selected states, and 50% samples in others). Cassill (1984, p. 37) cited some of the speculative reasons for this increase: "First, there is a slight rise in the birth rate overall; secondly, women are having children later in their child-bearing years, which increases their chances of having twins; third, there is evidence that as women come off long-term use of the pill and become pregnant within the first two or three months, they more often have twins; and the fourth reason for the rise in twinning is related to uses of fertility drugs."

Families with twins must establish two relationships simultaneously, taking into consideration each infant's uniqueness and interaction style. Klaus and Kennell (1982) suggest that mothers have great difficulty bonding optimally to two infants. Nurses are in a position to support this most crucial element in human development—attachment. As Brazelton states, "If we train cadres of people for these supportive roles, we must understand the ingredients of attachment in order to help them, because each mother-child dyad is unique and has individual needs of its own." (Klaus and Kennell, 1982, p. 12). Knowledge of the dynamics of interaction would enable caregivers to design programs to promote not only healthy interactions but also intervention programs to detect early interactional problems and pave the way for immediate professional intervention in developmental difficulties.

The nurse cannot assume that all parents are experts about child rearing. Much developmental disturbance in young children can be traced to stressful parent-child interactions and inappropriate child rearing practices (Jarrett, 1982; Taylor, 1980). Nurses themselves must learn more about mothers' attitudes toward raising twins so that their special concerns can be addressed.

Conceptual model for interaction. An important precursor of mother-twin attachment stems is successful—that is, reciprocal and synchronous—mother-twin interaction. To enhance healthy interaction, nurses must examine both maternal and infant capabilities in terms of the relationship between them. Barnard's parent-infant interaction process model has been adapted to accommodate the challenge of interacting with two infants simultaneously, and points out the psychosocial and environmental factors that enhance attachment. The model (Figure 4.1) has four main foci:
- Infants' capabilities for interaction
- Reciprocal interaction
- Mother's characteristics
- Physical and social-emotional support systems.

Infants' interactional capacities. Infants have a remarkable capacity for reciprocal interaction with a maternal figure. Neonates can recognize their mother's voice (DeCasper and Fifer, 1980; Mills and Melhuish, 1974) and clearly prefer a real face to a drawn one (Lewis, 1973). Mc-Call (1979) reports that newborns can see a human face approximately 7 to 15 inches away. Newborns also recognize their mother's smell, and turn consistently to their mother's breast pad rather than that of another mother at the same stage of nursing (MacFarlane, 1975). Newborns also move in rhythm with the mother's voice (Condor and Sander, 1974).

Figure 4.1   A Model of Maternal-Twin Interaction

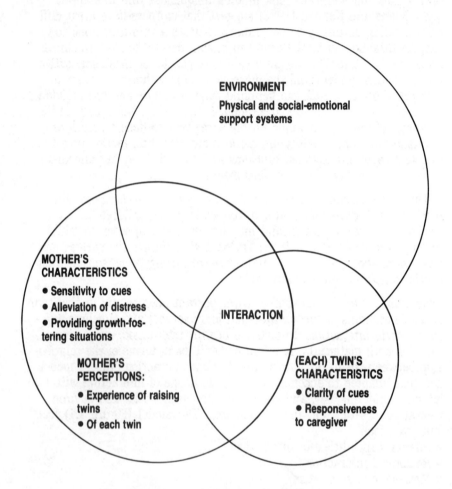

Source: Adapted from "The Child Health Assessment Interaction Model," in *Nursing Child Assessment Satellite Training Project Learning Resource Manual.* Edited by Barnard, K. Seattle: University of Washington, 1978, p. 19.

Emotional discrimination begins at 4 to 5 months of age; studied infants preferred joyful facial expressions to angry or neutral ones (La Barbera et al., 1976; Wilcox and Clayton, 1968).

Brazelton (1973) says that neonates are unique individuals who can cope with shape and organize their environment. Using his Neonatal Behavioral Assessment Scale, Brazelton has documented that babies can decrease their responses to repeated disturbing visual, auditory, and tactile stimuli. The first few unpleasant stimuli might elicit a startle reaction, but most infants quiet very quickly. Also, babies can console themselves when upset by sucking their fist or attending to visual or auditory stimuli.

Infants as young as 14 days can communicate with subtle nonverbal cues (La Barbera et al., 1976); Givens (1978) recognized the significance of this nonverbal language in mother-infant relationships. By reviewing videotapes, Givens described the specific nonverbal cues characteristic of infants at 1, 4, 8 and 12 months while their mothers were feeding them or teaching them an assigned task. These nonverbal cues indicated readiness to eat; alertness or tiredness; interest in engaging or disengaging mother in dialogue; satiety; and responsiveness to mother's social play or games.

Not only can infants send clear cues, they can also respond reciprocally to their mothers' signals. A young infant will attend to the mother's presence by maintaining eye contact, vocalizing, and listening to the mother's voice, among other means.

Reciprocal interaction. A rewarding and satisfying interaction must be both synchronous and reciprocal. Interactionists define attachment as an affectional relationship developed over the first year through reciprocal mother-infant interaction. Mothers have an important role to play in this reciprocal system; they must respond to their infants' cues, alleviate infants' distress, and create growth-fostering situations (Barnard, 1978a). In reciprocal interactions, "The behavior of one of the individuals triggers a response in the other person. This response in turn acts as a stimulus for the other person and leads to further development of the behavior into a more complex pattern" (Tulman, 1981, p. 13). For example, a mother who ignores her infant's satiety cues and continues to feed the infant every last ounce of milk is not displaying reciprocal interaction. Neither is the infant who is unresponsive to his mother's attempts to engage him in social play. Therefore, both mother and infant are responsible for responding to cues and for actively maintaining a healthy interaction.

Maternal characteristics. The psychosocial aspect of the mother-twin interactional model—that is, mother's age, social class, educational level, perceptions of each twin, and thoughts on raising twins—is also important. Barnard (1978a) has noted that psychosocial factors such as insufficient social support, unrealistic developmental expectations, lack of knowledge about infant growth and development, and high level of stress can all affect maternal sensitivity to a twin infant.

Support system. A family's supportive network, including the father's involvement in child care, also helps determine mother-twin interaction. As Barnard (1978a, p. 18) states, "We are forced to pay attention to the matrix of circumstances, attitudes, behaviors, affect, perceptions and stimulation that interact to form the quality of the child's environment and to influence the comfort of parents in their role."

Graphically, the previously described interaction model can be represented by three interlocking circles (Figure 4.1); the largest circle represents the supportive environment, the next largest one the mother's characteristics and perceptions of her twins, and the smallest the infants themselves. The interaction component of the model is reflected in the overlapping of the circles and should be assessed through the Feeding scale developed by Barnard and colleagues. The mothers' and twins' characteristics and supportive network are assessed through a specially devised interview guide. The resulting model offers nurses direction in assessing how a family integrates mutiple births into its system by studying how the parent, child, and environment each influence the quality of attachment within the system.

Nursing Child Assessment Feeding Scale. The Nursing Child Assessment Feeding Scale (NCAFS) is a 76-item behavorial scale that helps the nurse determine a parent's role in child development, the effect of the child on the parent, their degree of "fit," and their developing attachment (Barnard, 1978b, p. 17-18). Specifically, the scale encourages nurses to observe such behaviors as the positioning of the infant during feeding, distress cues, and the mother's verbalizations. Nurses wishing to use this scale can take a training course offered through the University of Washington by local instructors in various cities in the United States and Canada.

Transition to parenthood. The birth of twins produces family delights and difficulties. All new families face unexpected similar developmental tasks: integrating infant(s) into the family unit, accommodating new parenting and grandparenting roles, and maintaining the marital bond (Wright and Leahey, 1984). All of these tasks produce family-wide changes. La Rossa and La Rossa in their 1981 study of the transition to parenthood depict some of the changes necessitated by singleton births. Their findings suggest that an infant requires continuous coverage, meaning a scarcity of free time. This often leads to husband-wife conflict over the allocation of that time; the research shows that husbands and wives move toward a traditional division of labor during the transition to parenthood, with the mother taking charge of the baby and the father filling a "helping" role, rather than "sharing" parental responsibilities. The mother orchestrates and implements child care; if the father participates, he does so under her direction. This study produced a decidedly maternal view of parenting: fathers were more likely to treat infants as objects while mothers were more sensitive to their infant's capabilities. These results led the researchers to hypothesize that mothers found the relationships with their infants more pleasurable than did fathers.

Unfortunately, there is no comprehensive longitudinal research on father-infant attachment behaviors during the child's first year. Research on older infants suggests that they attach to their fathers as well as they do to their mothers (Jones, 1985). Other research has indicated that the father's role with singletons focuses on play activities while the mother's role consists of caretaking. Corter (1982) corroborates these findings, with one exception: he noted that every father of twins was involved in some caretaking activity, while only 13% of the fathers of singletons were. The remaining 87% of singleton fathers either played with their infants or had no interaction at all. The fact that there is a twin infant for each parent may account for the father's assumption of a caretaking role. However, there remains a notable lack of research examining the father's role with twins.

Do families with infant twins develop in the same way that families with singleton infants do? What basic processes facilitate the integration of twin infants into a family system? What are the delights and difficulties that families of twins encounter as they proceed through the developmental sequence of the child-bearing years? The authors, in a longitudinal study of twin infants and their mothers funded by the Alberta Foundation for Nursing Research, explored some of these basic issues. Ten mothers of twins were interviewed in the family context when the twins were 1 month, 4 months, 8 months, and 1 year old. Specifically, their perceptions of three factors—raising twins, the twins themselves, and their physical and social-emotional support system—were examined.

Briefly, the findings indicated that mothers of 1-month-old twins developed an incipient attachment to their infants by differentiating them physically and polarizing their personality characteristics. Twins' personalities were often described as opposites; both active and passive characteristics emerged from the data. Mothers identified their children's personality differences through their different feeding and crying behaviors and their environmental awareness. Auditory, visual, and tactile senses enabled most mothers to develop a beginning relationship with the twins. From the mothers' perspective, all fathers participated in infant care activities; in fact, some fathers were more involved than others. Two types of fatherly parenting styles emerged: the coparent and the helper. Coparent fathers did everything but breast feed; helpers assisted in caretaking under the mother's direction.

These families underwent many lifestyle changes. All mothers became temporarily homebound; half the families complained that their homes—and in some cases their cars—were too small after the birth of the twins; little physical or emotional energy went into the spousal relationship as the twins became the foci of the families' lives; in the case of second-time parents, there was little time for other children (Anderson and Anderson, 1986).

Planning

Nurses must have well-defined plans for facilitating families' attachments to their individual twins, helping couples adjust to parenthood, and teaching families how to recognize and use supportive networks.

Research indicates that the transition to parenthood can negatively influence a couple's existing social support system. Role changes associated with the new mother's decision to remain at home can separate parents from significant work-related associates. In light of these findings, Gottelieb (1981, p. 224) suggests that a nurse "plan interventions that would assist new parents into reorienting themselves to those members of their social networks who can provide support for the parenting role."

In some cases, health care professionals must teach families how to use supportive networks. Curran (1983) states that healthy families can admit problems and freely seek help when necessary. Some, however, cling to old mores and feel that families who cannot handle problems behind closed doors are weak and unhealthy. Nurses often find themselves dealing with families who cannot seek help as a unit, or with the "super-mom syndrome."

After the birth of twins, family members need to balance the new infants' needs with their own. Briggs (1979) considers it impossible to accomplish this task without some external support, and research indicates that children benefit if their families have a good support network. (Crnic et al., 1983; Crockenberg, 1981). The same study showed that a good outside support system is the best predictor of secure maternal infant attachment, and that irritable infants receive less attention from mothers with inadequate support networks.

Some authors suggest that nurses assess not only mother-infant attachment during the planning stage, but also encourage parents to discuss the pleasures they derive from interacting with their children. In a healthy situation, the joys of parenthood should outweigh the trials. Parents who respond only to their infants' crying and dirty diapers, and who think only of their own loss of sleep, risk unsuccessful attachment (Bolton, 1983; Briggs, 1979; Emde, 1980).

Mothers of twins face the difficult task of establishing individual relationships with two infants at the same developmental stage but having different characteristics. The mother may try to respond by stressing their similarities and treating them identically. The following case studies illustrate various types of difficulty in establishing unique relationships with twin infants.

CASE STUDY: JOAN AND BILL

Joan and Bill are first-time parents of identical twin boys, Ron and Don. Referral to the community health nurse was made because of feeding problems and the 1-month-old infants' incessant crying. The areas assessed are indicated in Table 4.1.

Table 4.1   Nursing Process: Joan and Bill

Areas Assessed and Sample Questions	Nursing Diagnoses	Plan
Family's perceptions of the twinship		
• How do you tell your twins apart? • In what ways are the twins most different? • In what ways are the twins most similar? • How did you choose names for your twins? In doing so, how did the family assign the names to each twin? • How do you get to know each twin?	Inability to differentiate between the twins.	• Explore the twins' physical and personality differences. • Discuss normal infant capabilities and behaviors. • Observe for parental enforcement of similarity: names, clothing, reactions to infant behaviors. • Determine each infant's sleeping and feeding patterns. • Determine if parents can differentiate individual twin's cries.
Acceptance of twins as individuals		
• Is it possible to develop a special relationship with each twin? If so, how do you do this? • Do you prefer that others stress the twin's similarities or their differences?	Maternal justice conflict.	• Determine whether the family has a unique relationship with each twin. —note if family reacts differently to each twin's behavior. • Determine whether the family values individuality or sameness. • Discuss with the parents their influence on the development of individuality in twins. • Refer the family to appropriate literature on the twinning bond.
Feeding interaction		
The Nursing Child Assessment Feeding Scale was used to assess feeding interaction in some depth.	Unreciprocal and asynchronous feeding interaction.	• Help mother realize the infants' capabilities. —infants can see, hear and display preferences for the human face, voice and touch. —infants display negative cues when they need to disengage from an interaction.

(continued)

Table 4.1 Nursing Process: Joan and Bill *(continued)*

Areas Assessed and Sample Questions	Nursing Diagnoses	Plan
Feeding interaction (continued)		• Help the mother position the infants so that *en face* interaction is possible. 　—have mother experiment with the various holds for simultaneous breast feeding (criss-cross position, football hold, parallel hold and the front "V" hold) • Explore the mother's feelings on separate feedings, bottle vs. breast feedings. • Encourage mother to touch and talk to the infants during the feeding. • Praise mother's feeding techniques appropriately.

Assessment

During the initial assessment of Joan's attachment to her twins, the nurse noted that Joan differentiated the boys solely on the basis of physical characteristics; she refused to examine behavioral differences. The new mother resented any mention of personality differences in the twins because she did not want the children compared. In addition, she felt defeated, and complained that "The first month particularly was kind of frustrating because they don't respond to you very much. I guess that's one thing that you're waiting for or looking for is some sort of sign of recognition or some feedback from them. But they're pretty selfish, they just want their demands met and then they'll go back to bed and they don't seem to really care who does it...."

Joan was concerned about getting the twins on identical feeding and sleeping schedules. In her words, "One might be wanting to go to bed and the other one's still playful, and I try to keep them together as much as I can. When one goes to bed I work like the dickens to get the other one to bed too so they're waking up at the same time. Keeping that under control is difficult."

Feeding times also proved difficult, because Joan tried to breast feed both infants simultaneously. Ron was an eager feeder but Don had difficulty latching onto the breast; he had a poor sucking reflex and demonstrated distress during feeding. Another problem was Joan's habit of positioning Don so that eye-to-eye contact was impossible. She could not respond appropriately to his distress cues, and maternal verbal and tactile stimulation during the feeding was minimal.

Joan perceived Ron and Don's crying to be a problem. She did not want to spoil her children or show favoritism by picking one up when both were crying. In short, Joan felt obligated to give equal time and attention to each infant. "I can't pick one up and comfort him and leave the other one to cry," She said, "I can't decide which one should be picked up and which one should be left, so I end up usually just leaving them both. I try to comfort them as best I can without actually holding them. That's difficult."

CASE STUDY: MAXINE AND ROD

Maxine and Rod are first-time parents of fraternal male twins. Both parents were delighted about the birth and the grandparents were ecstatic. Before the birth, Maxine worked in a full-time managerial position; Rod presently holds a financially secure management position. At first glance, this couple seemed to have few concerns; however, assessment revealed concrete issues in the transition to parenthood that made community nursing intervention desirable (Table 4.2).

Table 4.2   Nursing Process: Maxine and Rod

Areas Assessed and Sample Questions	Nursing Diagnoses	Plan
• Family's perceptions of raising twins —Tell me what a typical day is like for you. —What are some of the pleasures of raising twins? —What are some of the most difficult things you have to handle while raising the twins? —How confident do you feel about parenting twins? —How satisfied do you feel about the role of mother-hood/fatherhood? —How has the birth of your twins changed your lives? What has changed the most for you?	• Decreased rest for mother. • Lack of outside social and intellectual stimulation for mother. • Expressed ambivalence about parenthood. • Inadequate time for parents as a couple.	• Reinforce to mother the importance of keeping twin infants on a daily routine and feeding schedule. • Reinforce the importance of resting when the twins are napping. • Encourage mother to express her feelings of being cut off from the world, girlfriends, and job. Explore some diversional activities with her. • Help parents understand and accept their feelings of ambivalence about parenthood by reinforcing the universality of their reactions. Promote the pleasures and joys of parenthood by taking a pleasure inventory with the family. • Help couple explore ways to balance the infants' demands for time with their time as a couple.

Assessment

Asked how she spent her days during the first month after delivery, Maxine described a merry-go-round of endless feedings and sleepless nights. Because the infants were premature, feedings were on demand and one feeding led into another. She stated that, "Some days they feed 2 hours apart, so as soon as you set one down then you're feeding the other. So the day is pretty much spent feeding and settling them." At times Maxine resented this constant feeding: "I was ready to pitch them in the crib this morning; it seemed like I was feeding them from 5:30 a.m. until noon without a break," she said.

It was a particular challenge because Maxine was largely deprived of sleep; 3 to 4 hours was all she could get in one period. She would grab naps in the morning when the infants slept or sleep in the evening when her husband came home. However, as the infants approached 4 months of age, she reported that life was normalizing. The infants were sleeping through the night and were on scheduled feedings. At 4 months, however, the infants began demanding to be entertained.

Maxine complained of feeling housebound. Such spontaneous activities as running out for a carton of milk or having coffee with a girlfriend were severely curtailed. Planned outings were out of the question because of the extra effort involved. And Maxine worried about babysitters' abilities to care for two infants.

Because Maxine had pursued a successful career prior to the twins' birth, she felt a strong need for outside social and intellectual stimulation. She described herself as a "vessel full of energy and creativity" who was constantly siphoned off by the twins. She commented, "You've got to have something poured into the cup to keep up the energy and creativity that makes you a person." She enjoyed seeing the infants grow, but she felt a need to keep growing herself.

During the first postpartum months, couples usually have little time for one another. Infants become the focus of their lives, leaving little physical or emotional energy for the couple relationship. Maxine talked about her and Rod's intimate candlelight dinners prior to the twins' birth, and about the way the infants had virtually become the table's centerpiece. She says, "Now we call it candlelight and whine," because whenever they sit down for dinner the twins start to cry; consequently, they prop up the infants in seats on the table. She says, "Somehow, babies crying by candlelight is not conducive to intimate talk. Besides, we are both exhausted."

As the couple assumed the parenting role, their perceptions of one another changed. Maxine described this by saying, "We are looking at each other in a completely different light, particularly because we are adjusting to this new role. I see him as a father first and husband second, and I'm sure he's seeing me much the same way, and I think we're going to have to work at getting that switched around again because he still is my husband first."

CASE STUDY

Because parenting twins can be draining, the family may need outside support and resources to help manage daily stresses (Table 4.3).

Assessment

Audrey, David, and their children had recently moved into a new area from eastern Canada and found themselves without nearby family or friends. The family consisted of 4- and 9-year-old boys and a set of month-old identical twin boys. Although Audrey had been excited about having twins, David had dreaded the financial consequences. A quiet man, David worked long hours mainly on evening shifts; although he was home most mornings he did not want to care for the twins or do housework. Consequently, Jim, the 9-year-old, helped his mother by feeding, bathing, and consoling the infants after school and on weekends. Robert, the 4-year-old, felt left out and became jealous of his brothers. Whenever his mother attempted to care for the twins he intercepted her and said, "Pick me up Mom." Although neighbors offered to help, Audrey found the situation hard to accept. She felt that a mother ought to be able to care for the children on her own.

Table 4.3 Nursing Process: Audrey, David, and the Children

Areas Assessed and Sample Questions	Nursing Diagnoses	Plan
• Family perceptions of physical and social-emotional support —Who helps you the most with raising your twins? How do they help? What type of support is most helpful? What is least helpful? —To whom would you go if you had any concerns related to raising the twins? Would they be able to help? —What part does your husband play in raising the twins? Your other children?	• Maternal inability to accept outside help. • Inadequate support system in family's immediate environment. • Sibling rivalry (exhibited by 4-year-old).	• Explore with the mother her perceived need to be a "supermom." • Help family recognize and make use of outside sources of support (e.g., hiring outside help to give the mother some relief from the twins). —encourage father to become more involved with the children's care —seek out information and resources from the local Twin and Triplet Club. • Encourage the family to make Robert feel important by: —setting aside a special time each day for him —having the father take him to the zoo or plan some other special activity —giving him some small responsibility in the infants' care; praising him for helping —paying attention to him when strangers or visitors make a fuss over his twin brothers.

CONCLUSIONS

Nurses can play a key role in helping parents of twins adjust to their new roles, attach to two infants simultaneously, and fulfill their needs for new sources of support. This double dose of new parenthood is easier to take if nurses offer concrete, relevant information based on theories of parenting and attachment.

REFERENCES

Anderson, A., and Anderson, B. "Maternal-Twin Interaction During the First Month of Life," Invited address at the Parents of Multiple Births National Convention, Edmonton, Alberta, 1986.

Barnard, K. *Nursing Child Assessment Satellite Training Project Learning Resource Manual.* Seattle: University of Washington, 1978a.

Barnard K. *Nursing Child Assessment Feeding Scales.* Seattle: University of Washington, 1978b.

Bolton, F. *When Bonding Fails.* Beverly Hills, Calif.: Sage Publications, 1983.

Brazelton, T. "Neonatal Behavioral Assessment Scales," *Clinics in Developmental Medicine.* Philadelphia: Spastics International Medical Publications (Lippincott), 1973.

Briggs, E. "Transition to Parenthood," *Maternal-Child Nursing Journal* 8(2):69–83, 1979.

Cassill, K. *Twins: Nature's Amazing Mystery.* New York: Atheneum, 1984.

Condor, W., and Sander, L. "Neonate Movement Is Synchronized with Adult Speech: Interactional Participation and Language Acquisition," *Science* 183:99–101, 1974.

Corter, C. "Parenting, Prematurity and Multiple Births," Invited address at the Child Development Conference. Kitchener-Waterloo, Ontario: University of Waterloo, 1982.

Crnic, K., et al. "Effects of Stress and Social Support on Mothers and Premature and Full-Term Infants," *Child Development* 54:209–17, 1983.

Crockenberg, S. "Infant Irritability, Mother Responsiveness, and Social Support Influences on the Security of Infant–Mother Attachment," *Child Development* 52:857–65, 1981.

Curran, D. *Traits of a Healthy Family.* Minneapolis: Winston Press, 1983.

De Casper, A., and Fifer, W. "Of Human Bonding: Newborns Prefer Their Mother's Voice," *Science* 208:1174–76, 1980.

Emde, R. "Emotional Availability: A Reciprocal Reward System for Infants and Parents with Implications for Prevention of Psychosocial Disorders," in *Parent–Infant Relationships.* Edited by Taylor, P. New York: Grune & Stratton, 1980.

Givens, D. "Social Expressivity During the First Year of Life," *Sign Language Studies* 20:257–74, 1978.

Gottlieb, B. "Preventive Interventions Involving Social Networks and Social Support," in *Social Networks and Social Support.* Edited by Gottlieb, B. Beverly Hills, Calif.: Sage Publications, 1981.

Jarrett, G. "Childbearing Patterns of Young Mothers: Expectations, Knowledge, and Practices," *Maternal Child Nursing* 7:119–24, 1982.

Jones, L.C. "Father–Infant Relationships in the First Year of Life," in *Dimensions of Fatherhood.* Edited by Hanson, S., and Bozett, F. Beverly Hills, Calif.: Sage Publications, 1985.

Klaus, H.M., and Kennell, J. *Parent–Infant Bonding,* 2nd ed. St. Louis: C.V. Mosby Co., 1982.

La Barbera, J., et al. "Four- and Six-Month-Old Infants' Visual Responses to Joy, Anger, and Neutral Expressions," *Child Development* 47:535–38, 1976.

La Rossa, R., and La Rossa, M. *Transition to Parenthood—How Infants Change Families.* Beverly Hills, Calif.: Sage Publications, 1981.

Lewis, M. "Infants' Responses to Facial Stimuli During the First Year of Life," in *Research and Commentary.* Edited by Stone, L., et al. New York: Basic Books, 1973.

MacFarlane, A. "Olfaction in the Development of Social Preferences in Human Neonate," *Parent-Infant Interaction-Cibia Foundation Symposium* 33:103–17, 1975.

McCall, R. *Infants.* London: Harvard University Press, 1979.

Mills, M., and Melhuish, E. "Recognition of Mother's Voice in Early Infancy," *Nature* 252:123–25, 1974.

Taylor, P., ed. *Parent–Infant Relationships.* New York: Grune & Stratton, 1980.

Tulman, L. "Theories of Maternal Attachment," *Advances in Nursing Science* 3(4):13, 1981.

U.S. Department of Health and Human Services. *Vital Statistics of the United States,* vol. 1. Washington, D.C., 1976-84.

Wilcox, B., and Clayton, F. "Infant Visual Fixation on Motion Pictures of the Human Face," *Journal of Experimental Psychology* 6:22–32, 1968.

Wright, L., and Leahey, M. *Nurses and Families: A Guide to Family Assessment and Intervention.* Philadelphia: F.A. Davis Co., 1984.

5 Assessing families with a suicidal teenager

Sharon M. Valente, RN, MN, CS, FAAN
Adjunct Assistant Professor
University of Southern California
Clinical Specialist in Mental Health in Private
 Practice
Los Angeles, California

OVERVIEW

This chapter describes several theories and models relating to suicide and guides the nurse in assessing risk factors, warnings, or clues that a teenager may attempt suicide. Family assessment includes evaluating the suicide risk of all family members as well as gauging the family's strengths, resources, coping strategies, and communication skills. Nurses can use crisis intervention and psychotherapy to work with adolescents and families who face a moderate suicide risk; they may decide to refer chronically suicidal adolescents (or those requiring hospitalization, drug treatment, or long-term therapy) to specialists in family or individual suicide therapy. Nurses also plan strategies to reduce the risk of a suicide attempt, to facilitate rapport and collaboration, to encourage constructive coping strategies, and to educate families about stressors that may trigger a teenager's suicide attempt. These steps of crisis intervention are effective in hospital, clinic, school, community, and home settings where nurses practice. A case study illustrates the steps of the nurse's assessment.

NURSING PROCESS

Assessment

The health problem: Teenage suicide. Suicide is defined as a self-intended, self-inflicted death. This means the individual's motives, intentions, and actions are very important. Parasuicide, a British term, is used to describe self-destructive acts or behaviors which are intentional, nonfatal, self-destructive, and prompted by suicide wishes. Suicide always implies death, while common examples of parasuicide include wrist slashing, drug overdoses, and self-poisoning; as a rule, the person survives, having also planned his rescue or discovery. Of course, the more likely an attempt is to cause death, the higher the suicide risk. One example of a highly lethal suicide attempt that did not cause death is the 17-year-old high school senior who stepped to the podium at graduation announcing, "This is the American way," and then shot himself with a gun.

Adolescents who imagine, attempt, or succeed at suicide are often responding to significant feelings of loss and pain—many say they do not want to die but want relief from suffering. They feel excessively stressed, hesitant to communicate their distress to family or others, and feel that life is not worth living. For these adolescents, suicide offers an escape from an intolerable reality, an escape from an environment where they feel unloved and unable to cope. Most adolescents hope someone will discover their distress and suicidal plans. Many wait silently for someone to extend a helping hand.

When suicide thoughts and plans go unnoticed or undiscovered, the teen feels ignored, and ultimately, he may become the 1 out of 10 teens with a specific suicide plan who will die. Suicidologists disagree about the factors that lead a teen to choose suicide as a coping strategy, but they agree that warning signs precede most suicidal acts. Suicidal adolescents are ambivalent about life; they simultaneously wish to live but also want to escape their pain and suffering. This ambivalence encourages teens to transmit mixed messages about suicide—they mix serious threats with joking comments. Because they want help from adults but fear ridicule, they may make light of their terror. Most suicidal adolescents drop hints about their self-destructive thoughts; some exhibit behavioral clues such as depression; others give away prized possessions. More direct cries for help include suicide attempts, suicide threats, and withdrawal. Threats such as, "I'm going to be gone; you'll be better off without me," "Don't worry about me—nothing matters anymore," or "I wonder what it would feel like to jump or be shot," are often warning clues to suicide. Such messages are often communicated ambivalently to more than one person in the family or at school. The adolescent may hide the urgency of this message behind a facade of denial, levity, or contradictions. Other messages may be so covert that the nurse must search for suicide warnings behind general distress signals such as drug abuse, forgetting to complete homework, truancy, misbehavior, or isolation. Typically, the warning, "I'm depressed; life just isn't worth it anymore," may be implied either by behavior or words.

Teenage suicide: Statistics. Suicide ranks as the second most common cause of death in adolescents. For every adolescent who dies by suicide, experts estimate that at least 10 others deliberately attempt suicide. Despite the well-known underreporting of suicide to protect family image, the adolescent suicide rate has tripled in the last two decades (Shaffer and Fisher, 1981; Holinger, 1981). Some experts believe the number would be even higher if suicides were reported accurately and if automobile fatalities prompted by suicidal wishes were included; they conclude that adolescent suicide has reached epidemic proportions. Maris (1985) agrees that adolescent suicide is an important problem but finds that the case for an "epidemic" has been overstated. For certain age, sex, and ethnic groups, the rates of suicide are much higher than average. Compared with males aged 15 to 19, who have the highest rate among teens, even higher suicide rates are found among white males age 20 to 29; white males over 40; and among black, Hispanic, and certain Native American tribes as well as Eskimos in the Yukon, who have a high rate of adolescent and young adult suicide. Statistics indicate that for black teens and young adults, the first suicide attempt is often lethal; for other groups, 20% to 60% of those who commit suicide have made at least one prior attempt. Other studies correlate suicide method with age and ethnicity (McIntosh, 1982).

Black males typically use guns or knives as a suicide method, Asians use knives, and female adolescents prefer drug overdoses. Males die by suicide about three times as often as females do. Statistics, however, describe average group behavior; they do not describe clearly what any individual will do.

Need for family involvement. In the past decade, adolescent suicide has been defined as a family problem; the family is in a position to prevent suicide, and adolescent suicide is best understood within a family context. While psychoanalytic literature has traditionally claimed that early childhood trauma or disturbed parent-child interaction causes suicide attempts, other investigators emphasize current family interaction as the contributing factor (Tishler et al., 1981; Hatton and Valente, 1984; Kerfoot, 1980). The teen's suicidal threats often indicate that the family itself is in distress, that family communication has broken down, that the teen believes that suicidal thoughts are a way to keep a family united, or that another family member is suicidal. Some teens use suicide to draw attention to family tensions or to ward off such frightening events as separation, divorce, relocation, or death. In these cases, the suicidal thoughts may offer a new problem that might "magically" hold the family together and prevent separation or loss. In families where children learn to cope with problems through secrecy and self-destruction, suicide may become the way "this family handles problems."

Some adolescents mimic role models who demonstrate various self-destructive behaviors; other adolescents have a relative who committed suicide. Tishler's (1981) study of 108 adolescent suicide attempters identifies the various motives for their actions: 51% problems with parents, 30% problems with opposite sex, 30% problems with school, and 16% problems with siblings. In addition to having depressive symptoms that also served as *suicide clues,* such as fatigue, insomnia, crying, sadness, or weight loss, 22% of these teens described feelings of loss or reactions to a death prior to the suicide attempt (Tishler et al., 1981). The classic teenage suicide attempter was a 14-year-old white female who overdosed with Tylenol (acetaminophen) one week after a painful breakup with a boyfriend; she also had a history of emotional problems prior to the suicide attempt. The frequency of problems with siblings, parents, or a suicidal family member highlight the importance of family assessment.

Risk factors. Common risk factors in adolescent suicide include depression (Tishler et al., 1981), parental suicide, death of a parent before the child was 5 years old (Tishler et al., 1981), self-poisoning after age 5 (Kerfoot, 1980), suicide attempts, a history of child abuse or incest, and loss (see Table 5.1). Other factors include parental divorce or separation, schizophrenia, alcoholism and substance abuse, isolation, withdrawal, and preoccupation with death in writing or artwork (Hatton and Valente 1984). Rofes (1983) states that another risk factor may be the adolescent's discovery of homosexual tendencies. Rofes (1983) provides case histories of adolescents who said that the social stigma attached to their "coming out" as a gay man or lesbian provoked their suicide attempts. The connections between the stigma and alienation surrounding homosexuality and suicide need to be clarified by further research. Roesler and Deisher highlighted the fact that 31% of young men making a suicide attempt had done so because of the stigma attached to being gay (Roesler and Deisher, 1972).

Some adolescents seem to be more vulnerable to self-destructive and suicidal coping strategies than others. Farber (1977) reported factors such as predisposition to depression, role models of suicide, and disturbed grief reactions in families where suicide was a repeated pattern. A nurse needs to understand how the family influences suicide, but she must also avoid blaming the family for the suicide and not allow the family to scapegoat any member as the "cause" of the suicide.

Table 5.1   Risk Factors for Suicide

• Suicide Attempts	• Incest
• Suicide of Parent or Relative	• Child Abuse
• Death of Parent	• Schizophrenia
• Divorce of Parents	• Isolation, Withdrawal
• Preoccupation with Death	• Alcoholism
• Problems with Relationships and Homosexuality	• Drug Abuse

Source: Rofes, 1983.

Theory and models of teenage suicide. The major theoretical models used to explain suicide do not explain teenage suicide in the context of the family or social network (see Table 5.2). A more helpful perspective emphasizes the adolescent's current disturbed interaction with family, school, and peers. This perspective relies heavily on coping, systems, and family theory. Shneidman (1981) focuses on this quality of disturbed interaction when he describes suicide as a dyadic event reflecting a disturbed interaction between the suicidal individual and a significant other.

Table 5.2 Major Theories of Suicide

Theory	Major Themes
Biological	Depression, which accounts for 15% to 20% of adult suicides, is linked to biological imbalance. Research explores the link between suicide and blood cortisol, 5HIAA and other chemicals.
Psychoanalytic	Suicide is primarily an intrapsychic phenomenon caused by early childhood trauma, anger, or death wishes turned inward to destroy the self.
Sociological	Suicide primarily reflects disrupted ties with society, alienation, or attraction to pro-suicide norms within society which advocate suicide and result in Anomic or Altruistic Suicide (Durkheim, 1951).
Relationship/Interpersonal Family	Suicide is primarily a disturbed relationship between the person, significant other, and the environment. The person suicides because a dyad (Shneidman, 1981) or a family bond is broken. Examples include suicide after death of a loved one, divorce, breakup, abandonment, and messages from family that say, "You should be dead" (Shneidman, 1981; Richman, 1985; Hatton and Valente, 1984).
Crisis	Suicide results from a crisis or disruption of equilibrium; it is an acute, time-limited disruption with severe symptoms and painful feelings of being unable to cope (Schneidman, 1980). Crisis intervention is effective as suicide prevention during a crisis.
Developmental	Adolescent suicide results when teens cannot cope with the intense stress or turmoil of adolescent tasks of establishing identity, relationships, intimacy, career, or sexuality. Teens who are denied employment, approval for sexual gratification, and a place in society consider themselves useless and disenfranchised and may believe life is worthless.

Family therapy emphasizes the disturbed interaction between adolescents and their families. Suicidal behaviors in one individual may trigger the same tendencies in other family members, so the nurse should routinely assess suicidal ideas among all family members. Assessment of the teenager's support network is important for the same reasons. For teens who are separated from their families, family theory also tries to explore how the teen has interpreted and internalized the family messages about self-esteem, deliberate self-harm, and coping with suicidal thoughts.

Family theory (Richman, 1985) suggests that one individual's symptoms may signal a family problem and that intervention with the family may mobilize coping resources while reducing distress. Intervention strategies that ignore family dynamics may be limited or ineffective. In addition, this theory emphasizes the impact of family rules, values, or messages that encourage suicide (Kerfoot, 1980). Suicidal adolescents often believe the family wishes they were dead; sometimes this perspective is accurate, and sometimes it is not.

By contrast, traditional psychoanalytic theory views suicide as an affective and cognitive disruption within the individual which may stem from early childhood trauma. Assessment and intervention are aimed at discovering death wishes and instincts hidden from the patient's conscious awareness. Psychoanalysts may work primarily with the adolescent and may greatly limit interactions with the family. Some families complain of being "on the outside" of this therapy relationship. Family members want to understand and help the adolescent, but they find the therapist distant and reluctant to divulge information. Following a suicide attempt, families often feel bitter and angry because they believe they have been excluded from helping the suicidal teenager. They may blame the therapist and think that "if only" they had been included in the therapy, they might have prevented this crisis (Hatton and Valente, 1984).

Developmental theory, another viewpoint, considers adolescent suicide a response to the intense stressors that accompany normal development. In North America, adolescence is characterized by great change, crisis, pressure, sexuality, and choice. It is a period of rapid reorganization of personality and recognition of the limits of parents. Developmentalists say that adolescents are often impulsive in responding to pressure to make critical choices about college, career, occupation, or to a newly-discovered awareness of their own sexual orientation as heterosexual or gay. During this period, adolescents may overreact to feelings of alienation or of "not fitting in" with their peers; because they are impulsive, teenagers may act out their frustration by attempting suicide. To what extent developmental trauma or individual vulnerability predispose an adolescent to suicide is unclear. Giovachini (1981) summarizes the adolescent's dilemma: they are poorly prepared for their developmental tasks; transitions during adolescence are neither smooth nor gradual; and family stability may be most lacking at the time adolescents must cope with establishing their own identity and sexuality.

Sociological theory looks at the impact of social forces that are outside the control of the individual. In this model, alienation may lead to specific patterns of suicide, but other issues such as race, gender, socio-economic status, powerlessness, and age deserve even greater consideration. Adolescents often blame themselves for failure and ignore the role that race or sexual orientation might play in their problems. For these adolescents, assessment of sociological factors and of their own power to solve their problems can help decrease their confusion and clarify the problem. Although this model helps the nurse understand the adolescent's situation, it does not provide adequate guidelines for intervention. From a sociological model, strategies would include advocacy, empowerment, social change, and social action.

Crisis theory is one of the most useful models for assessment and intervention of acute suicide; nurses find this a practical and effective model of the family and suicidal adolescent in acute distress. In the crisis model, active involvement and assessment begin as soon as the nurse clarifies the current problem and the adolescent's and family's emotional and cognitive reactions to the problem and its symptoms. She should evaluate the family's coping strategies, resources, and significant others relative to the adolescent. A crisis, which is typically resolved in 6 weeks, can provide opportunity for growth, learning, and improved coping because the person and family in crisis are usually willing to depend upon helpers for a short time.

The goals of intervention are to prevent a suicide attempt and to help the family develop efficient coping skills to resolve the crisis. The crisis model is directive, active, and offers a cost-effective model of brief psychotherapy that is useful in a variety of health care settings. Nurses who must often intervene in a suicidal crisis triggered by hospitalization, diagnosis, loss, or threat to health will find the crisis model advantageous. It provides excellent strategies for a concise assessment of a patient's potential suicide and for establishing a no-suicide contract if the nurse has little time to see a client at school, in the emergency room, in the clinic, on the telephone, or before discharge in the hospital. The model does not address the additive effects of multiple crisis (e.g., the effects of facing many problems at once) that adolescents typically experience, and it does not provide adequate strategies for the adolescent who chronically uses suicide as a coping strategy. Adolescents who make a career of suicide attempts often have a long history of moderately lethal attempts; they are a difficult-to-treat, high-risk group that needs other strategies to supplement crisis intervention.

Assessment tools. Nurses can use a variety of tests to measure suicide potential: Beck's Depression Scale (a self-rating scale for children and adults that includes suicide) and the suicide subscale on the MMPI (Minnesota Multiphasic Personality Inventory), a self-administered questionnaire. Beck's Depression Scale asks respondents to complete a self-rating form with questions about suicide. This scale rates depression and can be used to track changes in depression scores; it effectively records a baseline for depression and suicide potential for individual family members. However, none of these tools evaluates family interaction, communication, resources, or coping. Interview and observation provide the most accurate evaluation of suicide potential (Lester, 1974). Unfortunately, most suicide scales have a high degree of error. Many family therapists use an interview to evaluate the family in terms of communication, interaction, support, coping strategies, and areas of conflict or disagreement.

Depression scales can indicate the suicide potential in patients whose depression correlates with suicide. Scales may be less helpful for schizophrenic adolescents who impulsively contemplate suicide in response to voices they hear. These teenagers often lack depressive symptoms. Tishler and coworkers (1981) recommend that the nurse's initial assessment should emphasize mental status; feelings; prior suicide attempts by patient, family, or friends; recent loss; an understanding of the adolescent's self-evaluation of his motivation; goals; interest; stress; coping strategies; concerns about his body and sexuality; and a history of his life stresses.

One simple, easy-to-score questionnaire, the Moos Family Environment Scale, compares and contrasts each member's view of the family in terms of relationship dimensions, personal growth, and system maintenance. This 90-question, true-false form asks simple questions to measure how family members evaluate family behaviors. The areas covered include:

Relationship dimensions
• Cohesion: Each family member's amount of concern and commitment to the family, and the degree of help and support they offer each other.
• Expressiveness: The extent to which open expression of feelings is encouraged.
• Conflict: The extent to which open expression of anger, aggression, and conflictual interactions are characteristic of the family.

Personal growth dimensions
• Independence: The extent to which assertiveness and self-sufficiency are encouraged.
• Achievement orientation: The extent to which activities are cast into an achievement-oriented or competitive framework.

• Intellectual-cultural orientation: The extent to which the family is concerned about political, social, intellectual, and cultural activities.
• Active recreational orientation: The extent of active participation in sports and recreational activities.
• Moral-religious emphasis: The extent to which the family actively discusses and emphasizes ethical and religious values.

System maintenance dimensions
• Organization: The extent to which order and organization are important.
• Control: The extent of the family's hierarchical organization and rigid rules, and extent to which family members give each other orders.

After each member independently completes the questionnaire, the nurse plots each one's patterns on a graph and identifies areas of discrepancy among family members. If several family members say that the family has very low control and encourages expression and conflict—yet the adolescent sees a completely opposite pattern in the same areas—the nurse can stimulate a discussion of these differing views. During the discussion, the family can be supported and encouraged to consider one another's views. The nurse may suggest that the family is entering a new stage of growth, one in which adolescents may view things very differently from parents. Encouraging the family to use discussion as a way to learn how to listen and to respect individual difference is one way to improve family communication and interaction. This scale gives the family a chance to review areas they may have taken for granted and to explore how they can work together more effectively. The scale is particularly helpful when families believe everyone shares the same view; it encourages healthy relationships and offers the family an opportunity to analyze their relationships, personal growth, and maintenance functions. Because this questionnaire highlights areas of health rather than illness, families respond well to answering it to learn more about how they interact.

Planning

Reduce risk of suicide attempt. The nurse's first priority is to determine the potential for a suicide attempt by *any* family member in the next 24 to 48 hours and to evaluate all aspects of a suicide plan. The nurse must arrange for safety measures such as hospitalization or constant supervision by a responsible person or family member, especially if the adolescent has a precise, specific plan to commit suicide in the next 24 to 48 hours. The most effective strategy is to involve both the adolescent and the family in the suicide risk and prevention assessment plan.

The risk of an immediate suicide attempt can be effectively reduced if the teenager agrees to make a no-suicide contract and promises to call a specific crisis center or person for help before doing any accidental or intentional self-harm. The nurse determines when to reassess this emergency risk and prepares a referral for therapy with the teen and family. A referral is indicated for any teenager who has made or planned a lethal suicide attempt, or who needs more support and follow-up than the nurse can provide, or whom the nurse fails to establish a therapeutic relationship with. A referral is also indicated if the adolescent needs hospitalization and the nurse cannot hospitalize patients on her own. A referral is not indicated if the nurse is skilled in therapy and suicide prevention and if the patient and family are coping well and assure her that they will call if symptoms worsen.

Until the teen is evaluated by a therapist, the nurse must continue to monitor any suicide plan or thoughts. Follow-up includes at least one phone call to check on the referral, to ask how the family is managing, and to determine if there is a further need for nursing care. The nurse should follow the patient until the patient is transferred to another therapist; this referral period is a critical time during which suicide attempts could escalate. The nurse should also emphasize the importance of therapy, because the family members often wish to ignore the seriousness of a suicide threat or attempt. They hope that denial will make the problem disappear. Families may also interpret the need for therapy as evidence that they have been "bad" parents or that the adolescent is "crazy." These myths must be dispelled if the adolescent is to view therapy as a suitable resource. Also, a nurse should remind families that someone who is suicidal needs a specialist just as much as someone with a broken leg does; just as the family would not think of treating a broken leg themselves, they should recognize that a broken wish for life also needs special concern and treatment.

Facilitate rapport and collaboration. Cultivate the family's and the adolescent's motivation for working as a team on this problem. Encourage each family member to listen more effectively to the adolescent and to support him. Show family members how they can decrease the teenager's isolation and increase his communication within the family. Each family member can help monitor the teenager's symptoms, provide assessment data for the nurse, and help the family as a whole to understand and respond to the problem.

Encourage constructive coping strategies. Help the family communicate feelings and thoughts, encourage active listening and discourage making immediate judgments or interrupting. Identify resources that the adolescent can use, significant others the adolescent might talk with, and additional coping strategies that could reduce the problem. Teach the family to express their needs and desires; help them offer more positive and specific feedback to the adolescent and to each other. If the adolescent copes with stress by using alcohol or drugs, identify other coping strategies or find ways for the adolescent to drink safely or reduce drinking. If the adolescent drinks at parties, encourage at least one sober family member to be available to drive the adolescent home after the party.

Assess crisis and intervention potential. Evaluate the family's crisis symptoms, resources, supports, and coping strategies. Discuss the teenager's and the family's understanding of their crisis and how they can rally resources and significant others. For instance, if the adolescent becomes most suicidal at 2 a.m., encourage the family to decide whom the teen should awaken when his suicidal thoughts escalate. Identify grandparents and other supportive individuals who can fill in when the immediate family members are fatigued. Teach the adolescent to reduce his suicidal impulses through exercise, music, or talking with a friend. Help the adolescent understand that the family members care for him and want to help him feel better and enjoy life.

Obtain regular consultation. Depending upon the setting, the nurse may consult with a mental health team, a suicide consultant, or other professionals involved in the care of the teen and family. Suicide assessment and intervention usually benefits from multidisciplinary input—others must be alerted to the suicide risk, and they can collaborate in observation, assessment, and support. Coaches, teachers, school counselors, custodians, and cafeteria aides can often provide vital information; they may also be significant others in the teen's life. Another critical source of information comes from peers; they may be concerned about the teenager and want to help.

Provide information to the family about teenage suicide stressors. Educate families about the pressures teenagers experience so that parents do not discount them or fail to hear their teen's distress. Help families recognize the clues to suicide and learn the most important methods of assessment and intervention so that they can identify a potential suicide early, before a tragedy occurs. Acquaint families with suicide prevention resources within the community so that they can refer friends or relatives for training.

Evaluate the delivery of health care services. Changing trends in health care delivery have influenced suicide prevention in three major ways. First, bed shortages and an emphasis on acute care mean that fewer teenagers will be hospitalized after a suicide attempt. Hence, nurses need to explore outpatient strategies for monitoring the high-risk teenager. Having another trusted adult available to help the adolescent relax and talk about suicidal feelings can provide safety during the crisis. When family or friends can offer 24-hour supervision or support, safety can often be ensured without hospitalization.

When bed availability makes it difficult to admit a suicidal patient, the nurse should contact the hospital emergency room to discuss the patient's needs prior to sending him there. Suicidal teens who present themselves for emergency care or admission may hesitate to confide in staff members or to share their acute feelings. Hence, staff may not realize how suicidal this adolescent is. Before referring a suicidal adolescent, nurses should provide their own evaluation, observations, and recommendations for care.

Premature discharge also interferes with teenage suicide prevention. In one case familiar to the author, an adolescent was scheduled for discharge on three different occasions but received no discharge planning. No arrangements were made for food, clothing, or shelter after leaving the hospital. A discharge with no arrangements could only add to this adolescent's suicide risk. Because the nurse identified this adolescent's pattern of using disruptive behavior to provoke early discharge, the hospital staff could recognize and confront this behavior constructively and make adequate discharge plans.

Increased emphasis on outpatient and home care allows the nurse more opportunity to observe the suicidal adolescent in his home. Home visits provide critical information as well as an opportunity for intervention. For example, a home visit may alert the nurse to a depressed family member's suicide risk or reveal family strengths or needs that were previously concealed. Hence, the nurse should make home or school visits whenever possible. Nurses working with ethnic groups other than their own will agree that a home visit helps cement a therapeutic alliance.

Finally, increasing numbers of acute psychiatric patients are being assigned to nursing students who have minimal knowledge and experience with teenage suicide. While this state of affairs gives professional nurses fewer chances to provide direct care, it gives them more opportunities to act as a patient advocate. In that capacity, they can share their assessment of the patient, identify resources in suicide assessment, question the student's treatment plan, and offer collaborative support. Professional psychiatric nurses are also emerging as cost-effective care providers and therapists for suicidal patients. Nurses who care for suicidal patients need to know that some patients will commit suicide despite their best efforts at prevention. Nurses must therefore plan for their own support; they should anticipate their own need to grieve when prevention fails and a patient chooses suicide. Such grief is often painful and may cause the nurse to question her abilities, asking, "Did I do everything that was needed?" The understanding support of her colleagues and mentors can help the nurse during this difficult time.

CASE STUDY

The Lee family has five members—Brian Lee, 41, a businessman; his wife Charlene, 39, a lawyer; and their three children: Brad, 17, Jennifer, 12, and Eli, 8. They reside in an upper-middle-class suburban neighborhood and take part in community and religious activities. The Lees have been concerned about Brad's sullen and moody behavior at home, which contrasts sharply with his behavior among his peers, who say Brad always listens to their problems and offers help. Brad's friends consider his family to be perfect; they say his parents are warm, friendly, and available. Brad has always performed well in school, where he has held student council offices and participates in sports. Classmates agree that Brad has "everything going for him": good grades, a great family, and a great future after graduation.

At home, however, Brad is moody and very private. He complains of never getting his fair share of gifts or possessions, even though he gets more than his brother and sister, according to his parents. Over the past several months, Brad has become even more withdrawn; he has lost interest in sports and schoolwork and has been spending less time with peers. His sleeping and eating patterns have become irregular and disturbed. The Lees insisted that Brad have a physical checkup to locate the cause of his weight loss, insomnia, and unhappiness but no physical cause was found. The Lees are now seeking family or individual counseling at the mental health clinic. They are frustrated; they don't know what is wrong with Brad or what they should do. An elder at church recommended that they consult a nurse therapist. Brad won't talk about his difficulties, however; he just wants everybody "to get off my back and leave me alone." Recently, Charlene found Brad stuporous; she had great difficulty awakening him and wanted to know why. She remains alarmed, even though Brad explained that "It was nothing; I just accidentally took another sleeping pill because I couldn't sleep before my exams."

The Lees asked the nurse at the community health clinic for help in two specific areas. They wanted Brad to be happier and to discuss his problems, and they wanted to resolve his sullen behavior, mood swings, and isolation at home. They were also concerned about Brad's potential for suicide. The Lees eventually entered therapy at the community mental health clinic recommended by their religious elders.

In therapy, the Lees spoke of their concern to use discipline wisely, and emphasized that Brad always played soccer with Dad, was successful at school, and had a close relationship with his mother. Nonethless, he has always been a private person. The Lees talk about their respect for the individual differences in their children. They said they have tried to make Brad happier and easier to live with. They were confused by Brad's behavior at home, since they knew he could be charming with friends and teachers. The Lees were puzzled by Brad's mood changes at home; they asked the nurse if they were overreacting to his sullenness.

The Lees responded well to the initial therapeutic plan, which was intended to ease the family's immediate fears with a suicide evaluation. A no-suicide contract and family meetings were to improve communication and support. Brad was encouraged to think of himself as a family member who had a very important contribution to make and who needed help to express his frustration with the many disruptive experiences in his life. Brad hesitantly agreed to see the nurse individually and to attend family meetings. Because he had difficulty verbalizing feelings, he was encouraged to use painting and other nonverbal methods such as family sculpture, a potent form of communication, to express himself.

In placing Brad's overdose in the context of his family's reactions and his other behavior patterns, the nurse therapist hoped to underscore the importance of the event and emphasize the risks of self-harm. The family debated whether stresses in recent months might have led Brad to demonstrate the distress he could not express in words. The family was asked to recognize that the pressures Brad faced were serious and worthy of concern.

In the course of working with this family, the nurse was able to increase their communication skills. The family agreed to convene before dinner to listen to each other's problems. In these sessions, no one was allowed to interrupt the speaker, all comments had to be supportive, and the task was to learn about the difficulties and successes that each member experienced that day. They learned how to ask about feelings and how to listen actively to each other. When anyone was discouraged or upset, the family was asked to evaluate the distress, identify coping strategies, and expose any potential suicide plan. These strategies, ideally, would teach them to identify the early clues to distress and apply interventions that would reduce suicide lethality. During the process of assessment and intervention, the nurse stressed the idea that each family member was important and respected and that each person had an important contribution to make toward understanding the problem and working on a solution.

In an atmosphere of heightened hope and respect, Brad found the safety he needed to reach out to his family. Both the family and nurse monitored suicidal thoughts. The family established new patterns for sharing concern about stress and providing support. For example, the family's old patterns of blaming each other and requiring each other to be "in complete control" of everything were replaced by active listening. The easy response that, "It isn't as bad as you think," was replaced with, "Tell me more about that; it sounds difficult." Comments such as, "You are sullen and moody," were replaced by such comments as, "I am confused and concerned about you when you spend all evening in your room and don't tell me how you are feeling."

The nurse met weekly with Brad and his family. The family noticed that Brad was beginning to talk more and to tell others when he felt discouraged. At first, Brad shared his feelings only sporadically but his suicidal impulses decreased. Homework assignments from therapy included communication exercises; these encouraged active listening between Brad and his family and called for practice sessions where family members were asked to communicate their needs and concerns. The family agreed to continue therapy until constructive communication patterns (including positive reinforcement, expression of feelings, reduction of blame, increased ability to discuss conflict and different viewpoints) were firmly established. During the initial stage of therapy, Mr. and Mrs. Lee discovered some communication problems of their own and wanted time to work on these as well. Mrs. Lee discovered that she was irritated whenever Brad interrupted her; it made her think that he didn't respect her opinion or think she had anything of value to contribute.

There was no further suicidal behavior during the year of therapy or in the follow-up discussions held at 6 months and 1 year after therapy. Brad and his family continued to improve their communication skills; they increased their abilities to express anger or disappointment, and to respect individual responses to stress and individual needs for privacy.

Evaluation

Outpatient family therapy reduced this family's suicide risk by improving the communication skills of its members, and by increasing external resources and support. The family learned to detect warning signs of suicide and to prevent Brad's self-harm. In this case, Brad and his family agreed to a no-suicide contract. Brad did not present an emergency suicide risk requiring hospitalization or continuous supervision, so outpatient therapy with a nurse therapist who had access to consultation was the treatment of choice. Family assessment and intervention was an effective tool for preventing future suicidal behaviors in all family members, and it taught children and adults alike how to understand and support both Brad and each other. As part of the process, the younger children learned that the family could adapt to individual needs and provide support for them as they grew. They also discovered their own capacity to provide support and understanding for their parents, for Brad, and for themselves.

CONCLUSIONS

Nurses can assess, plan, intervene, and evaluate their work with the suicidal adolescent and family. Most suicidal adolescents demonstrate, either verbally or behaviorally, distress in themselves or their family. Though they may be ambivalent about expressing their suicidal ideas and fears, most of them will exhibit suicide warnings, messages, and clues. Major theorists use psychoanalytic, sociological, biological, developmental, and relationship and crisis concepts to explain suicide. Family theorists stress the importance of assessment and intervention strategies; such strategies help family members work together to understand the problem of suicide and to improve their coping strategies, resources, and relationships with significant others. Immediate distress and suicide risk can be reduced by asking the family and adolescent to agree to a "no-suicide" contract and to begin weekly therapy sessions.

Based on her evaluation of the client's suicide potential, the nurse may decide to manage the patient with a low suicide risk herself; for the acutely suicidal patient, she may prescribe hospitalization or some form of psychotherapy. The nurse should consider referring any patient who has a chronic history of suicide, who needs hospitalization, or who does not form a therapeutic alliance with the nurse. These patients should usually be referred to another therapist who specializes in suicide and can provide long-term therapy. Other patients should be referred if they need services that the nurse cannot provide, such as drug therapy. Unless the nurse is on 24-hour call, patients at risk for a potential lethal suicide attempt on holidays or early morning hours should be referred. Nurses skilled in crisis intervention and family therapy may see adolescents and families in therapy as long as they make a no-suicide contract and will commit to a therapeutic relationship.

Crisis intervention, family assessment, and therapy offer a means for evaluating a suicidal crisis and for decreasing the risk of suicide. If the adolescent is in crisis and uses suicide as a major coping strategy for stress, then he may need more than crisis intervention. Not all suicides can be prevented, of course, but most suicidal adolescents demonstrate a "cry for help" which, if recognized, will enable the nurse to intervene and perhaps save a life.

REFERENCES

Centers for Disease Control. *Suicide Surveillance—Summary: 1970-1980.* Atlanta: U.S. Department of Health and Human Services, 1985.

Durkheim, E. *Suicide: A Study in Sociology.* New York: Free Press, 1978.

Farber, M.L. "Factors Determining the Incidence of Suicide Within Families," *Suicide and Life-Threatening Behavior* 7(1):3–5, 1977.

Giovachini, P.L. *The Urge to Die: Why Young People Commit Suicide.* New York: Macmillan Publishing Co., 1981.

Hatton, C.L., and Valente, S.M. *Suicide: Assessment and Intervention,* 2nd ed. East Norwalk, Conn.: Appleton-Century-Crofts, 1984.

Holinger, P.C. "Self-Destructiveness Among the Young: An Epidemiological Study of Violent Death," *The International Journal of Social Psychiatry* 27(4):277–83, 1981.

Kerfoot, J. "Assessment of the Young Adolescent and the Family," in *Suicide: Assessment and Intervention.* Edited by Hatton, C.L., and Valente, S.M. East Norwalk, Conn.: Appleton-Century-Crofts, 1984.

Kerfoot, M. "Family Context of Adolescent Suicidal Behavior," *Journal of Adolescence* 3:335–46, 1980.

Lester, D. "Demographic Versus Clinical Prediction of Suicidal Behaviors," *The Prediction of Suicide.* Edited by Beck, A.T., et al., 1974.

Maris, R. "The Adolescent Suicide Problem," *Suicide and Life-Threatening Behavior* 15(2):91–109, 1985.

McIntosh, J.L., and Santos, J.F. "Changing Patterns in Methods of Suicide by Race and Sex," *Suicide and Life-Threatening Behavior* 12(4):221–34, 1982.

Moos, R.H. *The Family Environment Scale.* Palo Alto, Calif.: Consulting Psychologists Press, 1974.

Peck, M. "Adolescent Suicide," *Suicide Assessment and Intervention.* Edited by Hatton, C.L., and Valente, S.M. East Norwalk, Conn.: Appleton-Century-Crofts, 1984.

Richman, J. *Families and Suicide.* New York: Springer Publishing Co., 1985.

Rofes, E. *I Thought People Like That Killed Themselves: Lesbians, Gay Men and Suicide.* San Francisco: Grey Fox Press, 1983.

Roesler, R., and Deisher, R. "Youthful Male Homosexuality," *Journal of the American Medical Association* 219(8):1018–23, 1972.

Sal, L., et al. "Relationship of Maternal and Perinatal Conditions to Eventual Adolescent Suicide," *Lancet* 624-27, March 1985.

Shaffer, D., and Fisher, P. "The Epidemiology of Suicide in Children and Young Adolescents," *Journal of the American Academy of Child Psychiatry* 20:545–65, 1981.

Shneidman, E. "Suicide Thoughts and Reflections 1960-1980," *Suicide and Life-Threatening Behavior* 11(4):198–226, 1981.

Tishler, C.L., et al. "Adolescent Suicide Attempts," *Suicide and Life-Threatening Behavior* 11:63–92, 1981.

Valente, S.M. "Suicide in the Hospitalized School-Age Child," *Paedovita,* 1985.

6 Assessing families with depression

Patricia Winstead-Fry, RN, PhD
Professor and Head
Division of Nursing
New York University
New York, New York

OVERVIEW

This chapter presents a brief overview of Bowen's family systems theory and its use in assessment and planning when clients present with depression. The multigenerational nature of depression is highlighted, and symptoms discussed.

THE NURSING PROCESS

Assessment

The health problem: Depression. The term "depression" signifies a variety of moods, ranging from transient sadness to pathological melancholy. Everyone has experienced a period of "blues," or a "bad day," but for some these periods become the prevailing pattern of their lives. Clinically depressed persons consider themselves worthless and experience lowered mood tone, somatic changes, and altered thinking.

Depression is a common phenomenon and is usually diagnosed by the client or the client's family. Close to half a million persons are treated annually for some form of depression (Dressler, 1985). The incidence of depression increases with age, it is thought, as a consequence of personal loss. Recent research suggests, however, that the young are much more susceptible to depression than previously thought (Caplan et al., 1984; Schoenbeck, 1983; Victoroff, 1984).

There are several theories of depression. Freud (1915), in his classic *Mourning and Melancholia,* first documented the relationship between depression and grief. A depressed person presents the same symptoms and alienations as a person who has recently suffered a loss, Freud said, and he made the important connection that loss could be symbolic as well as real. Research by others indicates that persons who experi-

ence more loss have a higher incidence of depression (Warheit, 1979).
Emerging literature suggests a genetic (Weitkamp et al., 1981) and
a biochemical basis for depression, and advances in neurophysiology may
lead to further understanding in this area (Arieti & Bemporad, 1979).
Interpersonal, communication, and family theories also reflect on the
nature of depression. The present chapter focuses on Bowen's family
systems theory of depression and the nursing assessment of depressed
families.

Bowen's family systems theory. Regardless of their theoretical orientation, most clinicians agree with the developmental literature when it
states that children begin to learn who they are while still in the family
context. The messages that parents send to children about their worth,
roles, and accomplishments will set the tone for the young person's
development of a sense of self. Within the family arena, significant
losses may occur—death of a parent, departure from a beloved neighborhood, the loss of a job—all of which will affect the entire family.
Even "positive" events can produce feelings of loss: Marriage, for instance, involves the loss of being single; a promotion may mean the loss
of valued peers. Each family loss can affect the developing child's
sense of self.

In family systems theory, understanding the family requires mapping
at least three generations. The family must be perceived as a network
of interrelationships, with each member inextricably bound to the other.
Symptoms of any type, therefore, will comment on family status.

Assessment within Bowen's family systems theory requires the
development and use of a genogram (see Figure 6.1). A genogram outlines the basic milestones and components of a family's emotional life
over three generations. The top line represents the grandparents, the
second line the parents, and the third line the current generation.
The symbols used most frequently are illustrated on page xii.

Before discussing the Smith family (see Figure 6.1), a review of
Bowen's Family Systems Theory is in order. Bowen (1978) suggests
that two closely-related intrafamilial processes determine how family
members function: Their anxiety level and their level of self-
differentiation reduces chronic anxiety. Self-differentiation is a product
of human evolution which has produced two separate, yet integrated,
systems: the emotional and the intellectual. The emotional system
is associated with the lower brain centers, making it the older of the
two. The newer intellectual system is associated with the cerebral
cortex. The connection between the intellectual and emotional systems
determines the level of self-differentiation.

In some persons, this intellectual/emotional connection is weak. They
cannot distinguish feelings from fact; they live in a feeling-dominated

Figure 6.1   Genogram—The Smith Family

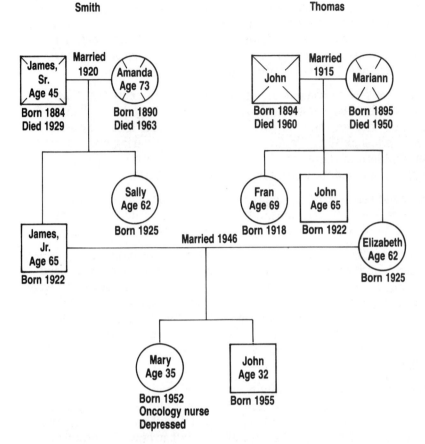

Smith

Thomas

James, Sr.
Age 45
Born 1884
Died 1929

Married 1920

Amanda
Age 73
Born 1890
Died 1963

John
Born 1894
Died 1960

Married 1915

Mariann
Born 1895
Died 1950

Sally
Age 62
Born 1925

Fran
Age 69
Born 1918

John
Age 65
Born 1922

James, Jr.
Age 65
Born 1922

Married 1946

Elizabeth
Age 62
Born 1925

Mary
Age 35
Born 1952
Oncology nurse
Depressed

John
Age 32
Born 1955

world and base their decisions upon what "feels right." Goal-directed behavior is impossible for them. Since they do not understand change over time, they cannot meet their children's needs adequately. Families characterized by low self-differentiation are chronically anxious; their members are emotionally, physically, or socially ill.

Next, there are moderately differentiated families. Members of such systems are characterized by some intellectual input, but their primary goal is to establish comfortable emotional relationships. Such people perceive the world in dichotomous terms; they see only good or bad, love or rejection. Typically, parents with moderate differentiation perceive their children as separate persons, but adopt a rigid approach to child rearing. They cannot adapt their view of the parental role to their child's specific needs. Because they long for comfort, persons at this level tend to over-bond in close relationships, creating anxiety on both sides.

Persons at the next level of differentiation enjoy a healthy balance between their intellectual and emotional systems, thus allowing behavioral spontaneity and flexibility. Children are perceived as unique, and parents offer guidance and example without feeling compelled to control their children absolutely. Relationships are close, but not fused. These people challenge one another to change and grow; comfort is not the only valued aspect of the relationship.

There are few persons at the highest level of differentiation. These people are the "wonder women" or "supermen." They accomplish a great deal because they are free of chronic anxiety. They have well-defined philosophies of life. Decision making and sharing are easier for them. Children in these families are appreciated for their uniqueness and are stimulated to develop individual personalities.

In low-stress situations, undifferentiated families can function as well as differentiated families; although even well-differentiated families can become ill when stress is high, they will recover more quickly.

From a family systems perspective, illness can be physical, emotional, or social. (Excessive alcoholism and gambling, for instance, are social sicknesses.) Illness is a family phenomenon, traceable through multigenerational patterns. (To date, Bowen does not hypothesize that these patterns are genetically based.) Emotional activity and the multigenerational transmission process determine illness levels (Bowen, 1978; Miller and Winstead-Fry, 1982) and the emotional illness which might develop from family interaction.

The nurse using Bowen's family systems approach can use the genogram to asses the course of illness. The nurse must carefully go through the genogram line by line, noting dates of marriages, separations, divorces, births, deaths, as well as relationships. For example, the nurse hearing about a client's sudden death would be very interested in its impact on the rest of the family. The nurse's questions should emerge from her discussions with the client. Her goal is to chart the events that shaped the client family's emotional life. When the genogram is completed, the multigenerational transmission of the depression should become obvious. If the genogram does not result in a clear picture, the nurse should back up and consult a more experienced colleague to ascertain whether some area was missed.

Planning

Planning in Bowen's model begins after the genogram is complete, which usually takes a couple of sessions. The current trend toward decreased hospital stays and other economic considerations should not influence planning. Generally, the family systems therapist does not hospitalize her clients because most hospitals follow the biomedical model of illness in which the illness resides in the individual. Family systems therapists think the illness resides in the system.

CASE STUDY

The Smiths are a family in which depression developed over three generations. Thirty-five-year-old Mary Smith first presented herself at an outpatient clinic complaining of depression. As a nurse, she recognized that her loss of interest in work, chronic tiredness, and insomnia were symptoms of depression. She was an oncology nurse specialist and loved her work; she skied and had an active social life until about 6 months previously. At first she thought she was only "burned out." The hospital where she worked had just completed its accreditation process and she had led one of the teams preparing the report for the accreditation visit. Since she was tired, she took vacation time and went to Colorado to ski. She hated the trip: no one interested her; the food was not appetizing; she could not sleep. As Mary reflected upon these feelings, she realized that, objectively, she should have enjoyed herself. There were many interesting people at the lodge; everyone else enjoyed the food; and the skiing conditions were wonderful. She realized that she simply did not enjoy anything anymore. Somewhat reluctantly, she decided that she was depressed and sought treatment.

Assessment

The nurse therapist who interviewed Mary quickly began constructing her genogram. Like many people, Mary did not know her family's three-generational history offhand and needed to do "homework" to complete it. However, she immediately made several interesting comments about herself and her family. She said that she resembled her father more than her mother, whom she described as "mousey." Her father, she said, was a dynamic and successful surgeon specializing in oncology. She felt that she had let him down when she chose nursing over medicine, but that he supported her decision. Her brother John, a lawyer, was seriously involved with a young woman. Mary dated several men, but was not serious about any of them.

As the family history was pieced together, the Smith and Thomas (her mother's family) families came to life and the multigenerational pattern which culminated in Mary's depression became obvious. James Smith Sr. and his wife Amanda, Mary's paternal grandparents, had emigrated from England at the turn of the century. James Sr. was remembered as a wise, generous man devoted to his wife and family. His children, James Jr. and Sally, who were 7 and 4 years old at the time of his death from brain cancer, had few personal memories of him. Amanda never remarried and devoted herself to raising the children. Financially, the family was well off. James Sr., foreseeing the Depression, had sold his stocks and removed his money from the banks prior to the "crash" of 1929. James Jr. recalls that his behavior became bizarre and frightening prior to his death. Amanda did not allow the children to attend the wake or funeral services but did take them to see the grave twice a year. Visits to James Sr.'s grave became a family ritual and continued until Amanda's death in 1963.

The Thomases, a family of farmers, came to America in the early 1800s and prospered. John and Mary had fond memories of visiting their cousins (not shown on the genogram for reasons of simplifying the presentation) on the family farm. There are numerous photographs of the children with sheep, cows, and other farm animals. Everyone looks happy and connected to one another. Elizabeth, Mary's mother, remembers her parents as quiet, church-going people who loved their children and spent a lot of time with them, enjoying their escapades and successes.

Elizabeth Thomas and James Smith, Jr. met during the Second World War. It was a romantic courtship; the threat of James' being sent overseas made their time together precious. They met at a party and fell in love "at first sight." The only cloud over their courtship was Amanda's insistence that Elizabeth was not "good enough" for her son; James and his mother argued about Amanda's intrusion into his love life. Despite Amanda's opposition, the couple married in 1946 after James' discharge from the Navy. He used the GI bill to complete college and medical school.

The early years of their marriage were happy; they postponed having children until James' studies were completed. A truce was negotiated with Amanda. James visited her—without Elizabeth—every Wednesday evening. Elizabeth did not resent this and thought it better than fighting, although she found Amanda's possessiveness perplexing.

Mary's birth in 1952 was a major family event. James was so excited by his beautiful daughter that he bought a new home; it was one of the few decisions he made without consulting Elizabeth. The home would not have been his wife's choice, since is was too far from her friends and shopping. However, the birth of John in 1955 pleased Elizabeth. She considered him every bit as special as James considered Mary.

James became a respected surgical oncologist, and Elizabeth enjoyed the status and income that accompanied his success. Mary and John were "typical" children, getting into mischief and fights, but were nevertheless the delight of their parents' lives. Mary recalls feeling especially close to her father, while John felt closer to his mother.

The family told wonderful stories of vibrant fun-filled vacations and holidays. Throughout the years, James continued to visit his mother on Wednesday evenings. The only thing that Mary thinks was missing from her childhood was the opportunity to know her paternal grandfather, James Sr.

The genogram offers several clues to the development of Mary's depression. A family systems-oriented nurse looks for recurring behavioral patterns indicating such things as family dysfunction and intra- or intergenerational triangles. (A triangle consists of three persons or two persons and an issue.) These are unconscious, automatic behaviors developed in response to anxiety. The less differentiated the person, the more rigid the triangles.

In Bowen's (1978) view, triangles derive from the basic instability of the dyad—especially a dyad of fairly undifferentiated persons. The undifferentiated person strives for comfortable relationships; conflict and anger must be avoided. The easiest way to accomplish this avoidance is to focus energy and attention upon a third object (person, issue, or thing). Couples can avoid conflict by overinvesting in the child, for instance, or by drinking. Just about anything can become the objective of triangulation, depending upon the family values and culture.

In Mary Smith's family, a triangle existed between James Sr., James Jr., and Amanda (Figure 6.2). It is likely that when James Sr. died, Amanda could not deal with the loss and pain; therefore she pulled James Jr. into the relationship. This development is indicated by her possessiveness when James Jr. wanted to marry and by Mary's statement that the *only* thing missing from her childhood was the opportunity to get to know her paternal grandfather. Mary's comment is especially telling because her grandfather's death preceded her birth. To be so emotionally involved with a person one never met indicates the degree to which James Sr.'s death remained unresolved. Further, James Jr.'s choice of oncology as his area of medical specialization indicates that his father's cancer is reverberating throughout the system.

Figure 6.2   Triangle in Smith Family

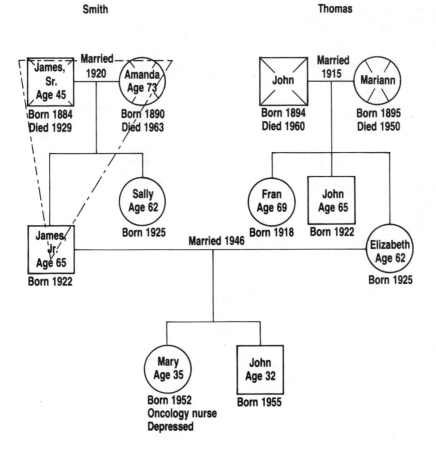

In the present generation, Mary is triangled between her parents. Figure 6.3 shows the two-generational triangle. Mary is her "father's daughter" in a dysfunctional sense. Her choice of oncology as profession shows the strength of her unresolved grief over James Sr.'s death. Her depression indicates the family projection process (Bowen, 1978), or transmission of anxiety from generation to generation. James Sr.'s death triggered anxiety in Amanda, who projected it to James Jr. who passed it on to Mary. The Smith case represents the multigenerational emotional metastasis of cancer through a family.

Figure 6.3 Multigenerational Triangle

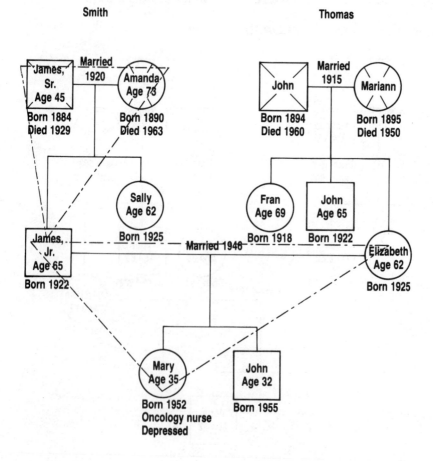

In terms of self-differentiation, the Smith family is in the mid-range. They have strengths and are not chronically ill. The fact that James Jr. supported Mary's decision to become a nurse indicates that he sees her as a separate person. There are, however, indications of fusion in the relationship between Elizabeth and James Jr., a fusion which created anxiety and led to a situation where James focused on Mary and Elizabeth on John.

What led to the development of Mary's depression at this time? Sometimes there is a nodal event, such as a parent's illness or the loss of a friend through moving or promotion. Sometimes the symptoms begin on the anniversary of a death or birth. In Mary's case, symptoms appeared around the anniversary of James Sr.'s death.

This chapter is not intended to elucidate all potential triangles in the Smith family. Rather, it focuses on the maladjustment that seems to have prompted Mary's depression—the triangle between Mary, her mother, and her father. It is the nurse's goal to "bury" James Sr., who remains alive in a metaphoric sense in the lives of James Jr. and Mary. The distance between James Jr., and his wife must be explored and decreased so that Mary can have more freedom. This will also benefit John, who is too close to his mother.

The goal of family therapy is to establish closeness but separation between generations. In James Jr. and Elizabeth's case, they needed to identify the negative feelings separating them so they could move to a more satisfactory marital relationship. James Jr. and Mary needed to examine the role of oncology practice in their lives. It is unlikely that 63-year-old James Jr. will change careers. However, dealing with the loss of his father will help him face retirement in greater peace. It may be that Mary could change specialites when the systemic anxiety about James Sr.'s death subsides.

Norman Paul's (1975) concept of operational mourning might help the Smiths let go of James Sr. The goal of this approach would be to have James Jr. mourn for his father and resolve his feelings of loss. It is somewhat paradoxical that people can often give up healthy relationships more easily than dysfunctional ones. James Jr. should be able to recall personal memories of his father. He might have to talk to members of the extended family and to his sister first, but letting his father go is a feasible goal.

In summary, the Smith family displayed a common reaction to unresolved grief: depression in one member. The depression was a product of multigenerational transmission of the unresolved grief over James Smith Sr.'s death and was expressed by the daughter Mary, who was overly close to her father. The treatment goals were to increase closeness between James Jr. and his wife and decrease the triangling of

Mary. Mary will need to examine her own life desires as she ceases to live out the image presented by the family projection process.

CONCLUSIONS

This chapter has presented the assessment and planning for the treatment of a family member experiencing depression. The etiology of the dysfunction, from a family systems perspective, was outlined. Events over three generations, culminating in the onset of depressive symptoms, were presented and discussed.

REFERENCES

Arieti, S., and Bemporad, J., eds. *Severe and Mild Depression.* New York: Basic Books, 1979.

Bowen, M. *Family Theory in Clinical Practice.* New York: Jason Aronson, 1978.

Caplan, S.L., et al. "Adverse Health Behaviors and Depressive Symptomatology in Adolescents," *Journal of the American Academy of Child Psychiatry* 23:595–601, 1984.

Dressler, W.M. "Epidemiology of Depressive Symptoms in a Black Community: A Comparative Analysis," *Journal of Nervous and Mental Disease* 173:215–55, 1985.

Freud, S. *Mourning and Melancholia.* New York: Alfred A. Knopf, 1930.

Miller, S., and Winstead-Fry, P. *Family Systems Theory in Nursing Practice.* Reston, Va.: Reston Publishing Co., 1982.

Minuchin, S. *Families and Family Therapy.* Cambridge, Mass.: Harvard University Press, 1974.

Minuchin, S., and Fishman, H. *Family Therapy Techniques.* Cambridge, Mass.: Harvard University Press, 1981.

Paul, N., and Paul B. *A Marital Puzzle.* New York: W.W. Norton & Co., 1975.

Schoenbeck, V.J. "Prevalence of Self-Reported Depressive Symptoms in Young Adolescents," *American Journal of Public Health* 73:1281–87, 1983.

Victoroff, V.M. "Depression in the Elderly," *Ohio State Medical Journal* 80:180–83, 1984.

Warheit, G. "Life Events, Coping, Stress and Depressive Symptomatology," *American Journal of Psychiatry* 136:502, 1979.

Weitkamp, L., et al. "Depressive Disorders and HLA: A Gene on Chromosome 6 That Can Affect Behavior," *New England Journal of Medicine* 305:1301, 1981.

7 Assessing families with chronic mental illness

Doris S. Greiner, RN, MSN, CS
Associate Professor
University of Alabama at Birmingham
Birmingham, Alabama

OVERVIEW

Families of the chronically mentally ill are forced to manage high degrees of anxiety. Increased mental illness symptoms require prompt family as well as individual nursing assessment. This chapter describes how to balance family tension with the need to complete a comprehensive assessment. Reasons for involving families in work with a chronically mentally ill member and approaches to family-focused nursing are reviewed. Key procedural points in assessment are discussed. In addition to assessing anxiety in these families, emphasis is also placed on obtaining and using information about development, resources, and problem-solving skills.

NURSING PROCESS

Assessment

The health problem: Chronic mental illness. Before discussing a specific approach to assessing families of the chronically mentally ill, definition and discussion of the problem—or constellation of problems—are in order. The definition of chronic illness adopted by the U.S. Department of Health and Human Services Steering Committee on the Chronically Mentally Ill (1980, pp. 2-11) provides a useful description of the affected population.

> The chronically mentally ill population encompasses persons who suffer certain mental or emotional disorders (organic brain syndrome, schizophrenia, recurrent depressive and manic-depressive disorders, paranoid and other psychoses, plus other disorders that may become chronic) that erode or prevent the development of their functional capacities in relation to (three or more of) such primary aspects of daily life as personal hygiene and self-care, self-direction, interper-

sonal relationships, social transactions, learning, and
recreation, and that erode or prevent the development of their
economic self-sufficiency.
The definition goes on to identify common hospital and community
treatment patterns and states that this population includes "persons
who are or were formerly 'residents' of institutions (public and private
psychiatric hospitals and nursing homes), and persons who are at high
risk of institutionalization because of persistent mental disability."

Goldman (1984) estimates the numbers of chronically mentally ill
people in the United States at 1.7 to 2.4 million. Chronicity in the seriously depressed is estimated at 600,000 to 800,000; psychosis is
estimated to affect 600,000 to 1,250,000 of the elderly. However, not all
individuals experiencing an isolated psychotic episode will become
chronically mentally ill (Goldman, 1984).

Any discussion of the incidence of chronic mental illness should note
that the rates of schizophrenia and manic-depressive illness remain
constant; it is the nation's demographics that are changing. "We will
experience an explosive growth in the number of people who will be
vulnerable to chronic mental illness," particularly as life expectancy
continues to increase (Talbot, 1984, p.9). Talbot also notes that children
make up 4% of the current chronic population, and that 40% to 60%
of them will retain their illnesses into adulthood.

At the time of this national report no estimates of the number of
chronically mentally ill persons living with families were available.
Lamb (1981) cites an estimate that more than half of California's
institutionalized patients live with relatives, suggesting that this figure
is higher than most hypotheses. He wonders if such patients are less
visible than those living in other facilities.

The families of the chronically mentally ill. A major influence on current
attempts to assess family needs in chronic mental illness is the
family's previous experience in the mental health care system. By
definition, most chronic patients have a long history of symptoms and
interventions. Most families' reports allude to three major themes.
First, relatives are seldom involved in planning the ongoing care of the
chronically ill member. (Indeed, many report exceptional difficulty
even getting information about such plans.) Secondly, many therapists
do not appreciate the difficulty of living with a chronically mentally
ill family member. Thirdly, and probably most devastatingly, the family
is often characterized as a causal agent, subjecting relatives to subtle
accusations by professionals. As McFarlane (1983, p. 3) succinctly
states, "By 1950, almost everyone believed that the family drives the
schizophrenic crazy." This situation is the subject of a discussion of the
adverse effects of family therapy in which Terkelsen (1983, p. 191)

states that "when either therapist or family harbor the belief that schizophrenia is caused by personal experience with family members, therapeutic misalliance is bound to follow."

Published evidence of family needs and characteristics in chronic mental illness continues to accumulate (Krauss and Slavinsky, 1982; McFarlane, 1983; Mirabi, 1984; U.S. Department of Health and Human Services, 1980; Talbot, 1984). This is especially true of research in schizophrenia. Brown and colleagues (1972) set the stage for research that continues today. Their findings—including the concept of expressed emotion (EE) which is evidenced by high criticism, excessive attention, overprotectiveness, and prolonged face-to-face contact—have been used to develop contemporary intervention programs. Brown and colleagues estimated that 20% of the families in their study were socially isolated as well as evidencing high EE.

Social isolation is typical of many families of chronic patients and an important consideration in the context of social network research. Another research area, communication deviance (CD), describes the amorphous, fragmented, tangential communication patterns found in some families of schizophrenics. Wynne's (1981) work contributes to this matter and is included in a review of both EE and CD literature.

Family involvement in health care delivery. Low key but direct efforts to involve family members in mental health care delivery have proven helpful. Family members can serve as program and ward monitors in a state hospital (Reiter and Plotkin, 1985); family education about prodromal symptoms in relapse makes early intervention possible and decreases the incidence of hospitalization (Heinrichs and Carpenter, 1985). Stickney and colleagues (1980) report that predischarge scheduling of a family followup appointment and contact with a community mental health nurse can decrease recidivism. They report that families use this follow-up appointment to keep members in treatment without coercion.

Bernheim (1982) describes supportive family counseling similar to many of the research-based approaches described above. Families are educated in an accepting mannner about the illness, treatment options, and the monitoring of an ill family member's behavior. Special care is taken to differentiate this approach from those associated with family therapy.

Nevertheless, a need for increased family involvement in chronic mental therapy remains; the literature in the field is too individually-oriented. Examples of this restricted focus can be found in Krauss and Slavinsky (1982). Likewise, a discussion of chronicity as a challenge to the clinical nurse specialist only generally refers to the family in a subsection on strengthening social support (Godschalx, 1984).

Research-based theories' attempts to delineate the family characteristics and needs that indicate particular interventions have gradually
shifted the thrust of work with the families of the chronically mentally
ill away from its traditional adversarial or avoidance position. Such
work is now information-based, supportive, cooperative, and openly long-
term. Current published work suggests a need for technical refinement
in assessment and intervention, and it advises identification of the
needs of families with special characteristics, especially those with
very young and very old chronically ill members. Finally, the importance of periodic reassessment as families experience life cycle changes
is implied.

Family assessment approaches and theory. This chapter's discussion of
family assessment in chronic mental illness is conceptualized within a
Bowen systems theory framework (Bowen, 1978). This theory has
proven accurate in describing observations of families and family
functioning. Two of its concepts are central to the current discussion:
triangles as the patterned way of handling anxiety within systems, and
self-differentiation (Greiner, 1984).

"The concept of triangles provides a framework for understanding the
microscopic functioning of all emotional systems" (Bowen, 1978, p.
478). When tension increases between two people, a third person or
object may be involved to decrease the anxiety between the original
pair. This involvement can be interactional, or the third party may
simply become the focus of the original pair's attention and concern (so
they don't have to address issues in their own relationship). When
this maneuver works, anxiety among the three decreases, leaving one
member of the triangle more distant from the others. The outside
position can be relatively comfortable, but it can also lead to a disturbing sense of exclusion, at which time the outside person may move
back toward one or both of the other two.

In families, a number of interlocking emotional triangles form
repeated patterns. During periods of high anxiety, the family's usual
triangles are not adequate, and outside individuals and agencies are
sought to help decrease the emotional turmoil. The nurse should
learn to identify these triangles in order to minimize the risk of her
own involvement in a client's unproductive emotional patterns.

Self-differentiation describes the interaction between an individual's
emotional and intellectual functioning. Each person exists at a basically
constant level of differentiation. Those at lower levels function in
automatic ways that are emotionally dictated; their emotional and
intellectual functions are fused, and behavior is directed toward finding
emotional comfort. As differentiation increases, emotional and intellectual functioning become relatively separate. People feel freer to choose

involvement with others, to be intimate, and to separate themselves from patterned emotionality; decisions are based on thought-out positions rather than on emotional comfort. Bowen (1978), however, points out that those at these higher functional levels seem to experience more life problems and recover more slowly from them.

Most families with chronically mentally ill members fit the latter description. Identifying emotional interaction patterns and helping family members think about their experiences is the best way to enhance family functioning.

The higher a family's anxiety level, the less likely any thought could or would be brought to bear on its problems. Therefore, decreasing anxiety and increasing active thought is a first step toward problem identification and resolution. Families with a chronically mentally ill member might display symptoms as indicators of increased systemic anxiety. The chronically mentally ill family member may have, over time, become a messenger for the family system's felt, but unarticulated, needs. Family perceptions of and reactions to anxiety are likely to be either completely unpatterned or ritualistic. The triangle described earlier is one mechanism for recognizing these maladaptive patterns. The professional who can recognize those anxiety patterns without getting caught in them has the opportunity to obtain more useful information about the family, its needs, and its strengths.

Awareness of one's own anxiety is the first step in this recognition process. The overwhelming nature of the family emotions, especially during high stress times, makes intervening or escaping highly appealing alternatives to the caregiver who is not bound to the situation. To stay with such family members and to evaluate their problems requires consistent monitoring of one's own anxiety and observation of its effect on professional decision-making. Common cues of increased anxiety in the nurse are:
• Acceptance of one individual's self-reported point of view as that of every family member.
• Participation in automatic family interactions without recognition until after the fact (for example, talking about, but not to, individual family members in their presence, or using indefinite pronouns).
• Involvement of the health care team in solving problems for the family.
• Blaming, in all its forms.

Knowing how to recognize and manage one's anxiety, and thus making oneself more available to client families, is a prerequisite for effective clinical work. Such self-awareness must be continually developing. In addition, an awareness of the way contact with a particular family has triggered personal anxiety can be valuable in understanding the unit's particular emotional system.

In sum, conceptualization of anxiety in families, in self, and in systems is central to effective family assessment.

Proceeding with the assessment process requires a sound theoretical base for the nurse's own practice. The purpose and context of the assessment give further direction regarding the amount and type of information needed and ways it might be obtained.

In a thoughtful discussion of choice points in making an assessment, Reiss (1980) identifies a number of reasons for initial assessment, including learning the family's strengths or resources; developing long- and short-term prognoses; and establishing a baseline for measuring improvement. The author finds all of these applicable to her practice, whether she is working directly with one or more family member(s).

Reiss also states that theory determines the nurse's phenomenological focus. He expresses his choice points in terms of polarities, an approach the author has used to increase nursing awareness of what information is considered and what is left out.

In the work described here, a consistent attempt is made to see family problems in their developmental context. While the author remains aware of environmental impacts on the family, interventions in this case are directed toward change within the family; therefore, the choice is to focus on the external influence.

The author also finds it useful to primarily work from a pathologic model, but work is directed at enhancing the family's individual and systematic problem-solving competence. This is a pivotal consideration since some intervention for chronic mental illness involves assessment of pathology and at least a consideration of medication. Between the thematic and the behavioral poles, the author's work focuses more on the former. Helping clients think about emotional issues and become aware of subtle patterns in their lives will increase their behavioral choices.

Example of systematic family assessment. The assessment process provides a wealth of information about family needs. This chapter is based upon work with chronically mentally ill clients of a community mental health center. It is in the context of assessing the client's current needs that family assessment is initiated.

In the author's opinion, family assessment should only be undertaken if the nurse has a definite reason for doing so. The nurse working from a family systems theory base should always have specific questions about a client's family system and how it functions. The client information available from records and staff observations facilitates the overall family assessment process. If family members have brought clients to the clinic, they should be included when the client is interviewed about the family.

The author has found it helpful to first talk to the client and then invite waiting family members to join in. When work with the family has not been part of previous client care and/or if no family members are immediately available, careful work with the client often precedes initiation of group contact. The client's concerns and needs are ascertained and the nurse's need to know more about the client's family explained. When this is done in a nonanxious, informative way, many clients will volunteer information and help in arranging further family contact. Emphasizing the need for the nurse to understand *all* of the problems with which the family is contending generally enhances positive family response.

Depending on the client's anxiety level and level of functioning, the nurse should explain the ideas on which the family assessment is based. These include, in order of priority, brief statements concerning the following information:
• Each member of a family is affected by what is happening in the life of each other member.
• When problems generate stress, it is harder for most people to hear and understand each other. Assessment should involve an attempt to reestablish communication.
• Each family has its own effective problem-solving strategies, but they can be lost during times of stress.
• The changes associated with individual growth and development make new demands on other individuals within the system, and on the unit itself. Old problem-solving methods may prove inadequate. Identifying changes within the family is a first step to solving problems. If the client is too anxious to understand and fully participate, the nurse should involve other family members without detailed prior explanation.

New clients and those with long-standing but sporadic disease involvement usually present with increased or exacerbated symptoms. The nurse should immediately help the symptomatic member and the rest of the family cope with the demands directly related to those symptoms. But she should also move quickly beyond identifying symptoms to uncover coping problems and find out whom they primarily affect.

The first information to be obtained is very basic: who is in the family and how are they emotionally and structurally related? A genogram of the identified patient, noting such relationship issues as closeness, distance, conflict, and cutoff simplifies the collection of this data.

Gathering this information leads to the formation of hypotheses about the family's emotional history and its current developmental issues. In all families, increased anxiety can be predicted at identifiable transition times (Carter and McGoldrick, 1980). The degree of disruption experienced by the family being assessed may be so massive that normative evaluation is impossible and the opportunity to intervene with developmental problems is lost.

Four assessment categories. The initial genogram helps the nurse identify client family problems or issues, particularly those centering around the chronic relative's symptoms. From this foundation, the nurse should move to an assessment of family resources and/or strengths.

Family strength or health can be conceptualized in many ways; its organization into categories helps the nurse obtain needed information more efficiently. Four categories that might prove helpful are *developmental achievement, physical health, economic health,* and *social support.* In the first category, the nurse should try to ascertain each family member's strengths in relationship to broad indicators of interpersonal development. In addition, she should note those members' ideas about achievement. For example, an adult child's preparation to leave home may be absolutely counter to family expectations.

In the second category, physical health, the nurse should gather details about both illnesses and treatments and about caretaking. She might ask if anyone in the family has been seriously ill recently. The answer to this question will indicate family members' ideas about seriousness as well as timing. If the answer is yes, ask for more details about the illness and the responsibilities family members take in dealing with it. About medication, ask if anyone other than the identified client takes medication. Then ask for details about prescriptions, over-the-counter medications, and length of time on the drug(s). Questions about whether the ill family member self-administers the medication should follow. A brief investigation of the family behaviors and roles that have developed around illness and health can provide much useful information. Typically, the roles of caretaker and caregiver are reciprocal, and eventually become essential. Imbalance in these roles and/or a move by any family member toward fuller personal functioning will reverberate throughout the system.

Assessment questions about illness and treatment may uncover misinformation that has resulted in unnecessary suffering. Information about medication use can be significant. When treating families of the chronically mentally ill, listen to how and why they cope—medicinally or otherwise—without making judgments about what they should be doing.

The relationship of economic need to family distress can be so complete that many nurses avoid it. Current changes in the financing of health care affect most people and can exacerbate financial worries. Many families of the chronically mentally ill depend on public assistance. Sources of outside help, including hospitalization, are limited. Because they are a significant factor in coping, therefore, economic matters need cooperative efforts from families and professionals.

When assessing economic resources, start by asking questions about current financial arrangements. Responsibility issues related to income will become apparent through this process, as will power issues. Illness often keeps a breadwinner from providing income, creating a situation in which clients often feel powerless.

Although the author's intervention efforts focus on the family system, a client family's "fit" within its larger social context also suggests interventions. In conversations with a client and his family, people or activities involving people are often mentioned. The nurse should ask about friends that family members go to when they need help or anyone in the extended family who would help if necessary. The assessing nurse should not imply that families should take care of themselves, but might ask what rules the family has about asking for help. Intense emotion in isolated families can be decreased by reestablishing neglected familial or non-familial relationships.

Planning

Planning interventions based on the above process begin with three central questions: What can I (the nurse) do to satisfy this family's identified needs; what additional resources are available to the family; and who is responsible for what?

Other vital questions include: What needs are being stated? By whom? Who is affected? Why now? Why here? These questions are important for helping families of the chronically mentally ill because of their often negative experiences with professionals. Identifying needs carefully and respectfully is essential. An initial family assessment also lays groundwork for future reassessments.

To plan effectively, the nurse must identify family members and structure, emotional patterns, developmental stage, and resources. Potential for information-sharing with regard to these categories increases as anxiety decreases. The assessment process itself initiates the intervention.

CASE STUDY

The setting for contact with the family described is a community mental health center. A highly anxious 34-year-old woman was seen by the clinic intake worker and referred to the nurse for assessment and treatment. The woman was brought to the clinic by an older brother who was concerned that she could no longer live alone. Her husband had divorced her the previous year, leaving her with three children and limited financial support. He remarried the following March and in August successfully sued her for custody of the children. The time of referral was October. The brother became involved when he learned that a succession of men were seen entering and leaving his sister's home. She was not seen outside of the home, and neighbors were concerned. The brother went to his sister's home and told her to come live with him. She was anxious, disorganized, and at times furious with her brother for interfering in her life; she accused him of plotting against her. He brought her to the clinic within a few days, because her behavior was uncontrollable and her presence intolerable. The first session with this woman revealed useful family information, which was organized in a genogram format, Figure 7.1.

Though her anxiety was extremely high, the client could focus (with help) on factual information and manifested some problem-solving ability. Her living situation represented an immediate problem, and economic support was a constant dilemma. Her physical health was described as good, though she had lost weight recently and considered herself too thin. The client displayed limited interpersonal skill, although she had established and maintained a marriage for 10 years. For much of her marriage she had also handled parenting responsibilities adequately (by her own description). After the children left, she had apparently become increasingly disorganized.

At the second session, the nurse discussed the need to meet with family members who might assist in immediate and long-term problem-solving. A family session was arranged, and the client's mother, mother's husband, oldest brother, and youngest sister were present. In preparation, the nurse spoke with each of the participants, except the mother's husband, by phone, inviting them to discuss the client, her situation, and its influence on family members.

The family session revealed that the client's mother had few actual responsibilities to and high degrees of anxiety about her two sons, who were not present at the session. Everyone present agreed that these men suffered from serious mental problems. The younger brother was living alone and hearing voices. He was unpredictably cordial or hostile when family members visited. He lived on monthly military disability checks, was in good health, and maintained adequate nutrition. His mother phoned him many times a day. The mother's anxiety became the central focus of intervention in subsequent work with this family.

The client's mother said she was willing to take her daughter back into her own home. The daughter's existence had always been marginal, all family members agreed. She had never lived alone until recently. Before her marriage, she lived with and kept house for the two disturbed brothers.

The mother attended a series of joint sessions with her daughter, who was the identified client. These sessions focused on anxiety reduction and resolution of the problems defined. The theoretical guide was Bowen systems theory. In that context, particularly with the mother, triangular patterns and issues in the family of origin were identified. Validation of the mother's patterns of thinking and being was a constant theme. Her life choices were reviewed and possibilities for redirecting her energies explored.

Interventions with the daughter were directed toward creating a stable living situation in which she could clarify her relationship with her mother and other members of her family of origin. In this context, she could establish consistent and limited contact with her own children. She considered working outside the home, but with little real interest; she thought of herself as a wife and mother. Consequently, she found a mate in the vocational rehabilitation setting to which she was referred.

Figure 7.1   Genogram—The Dyck Family

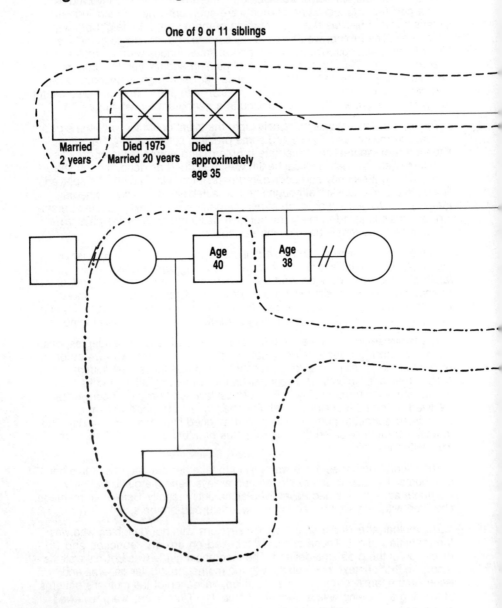

One of 9 or 11 siblings

Married 2 years

Died 1975 Married 20 years

Died approximately age 35

Age 40

Age 38

Legend

Household at time of initial contact with client

Household as family assessment progressed

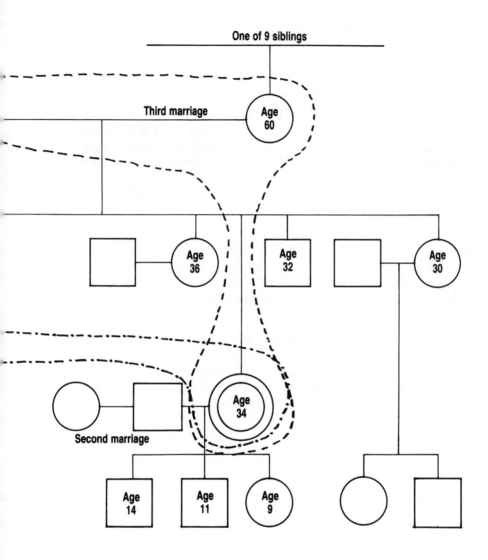

CONCLUSIONS

Understanding the manifestations of anxiety is a prerequisite to assessing the health needs of families of the chronically mentally ill. Helping family members identify and ponder their unique problems is basic to identifying their needs, and to eliciting the information needed for effective care planning.

Bowen systems theory (1978) has been useful in conceptualizing family-wide emotional patterns and in planning for families whose ability to think about emotional issues is limited. The theory can also illuminate personal anxiety reactions of nurses toward client family emotional systems. An awareness of this reactivity in oneself and in the mental health care system can increase a nurse's availability to client families.

In the future the problem of chronic mental illness will increase rather than decrease because of a relatively stable incidence pattern and an increase in the total population. Systematic programs to assist families with a potentially lifelong problem remain in varying stages of development. Family members and nurses have every reason to cooperate on behalf of the symptomatic client.

Assessment approaches must be purposeful and must rely on a theory or model which organizes the information obtained and offers direction for intervention. A nurse should recognize, however, that any single focus will preclude extensive investigation in areas that another professional might find important to assess.

REFERENCES

Anderson, C.M. "A Psychoeducational Program for Families of Patients with Schizophrenia," in *Family Therapy in Schizophrenia*. Edited by McFarlane, W.R. New York: Guilford Press, 1983.

Anderson, C.M., et al. "Expressed Emotion and Social Networks of Parents of Schizophrenic Patients," *British Journal of Psychiatry* 144:247–55, 1984.

Anderson, C.M., et al. "Family Treatment of Adult Schizophrenic Patients: A Research-Based Psychoeducational Approach," *Schizophrenia Bulletin* 6:490–505, 1980.

Beels, C.C., et al. "Measurements of Social Support in Schizophrenia," *Schizophrenia Bulletin* 10:399–411, 1984.

Bernheim, K.F. "Supportive Family Counselling," *Schizophrenia Bulletin* 8:634–40, 1982.

Bowen, M. *Family Therapy in Clinical Practice*. New York: Jason Aronson, 1978.

Brown, G.W., et al. "Influence of Family Life on the Course of Schizophrenic Disorders: A Replication," *British Journal of Psychiatry* 121:241–58, 1972.

Carter, E.A., and McGoldrick, M., eds. *The Family Life Cycle: A Framework for Family Therapy*. New York: Gardner Press, 1980.

Clarkin, J.F., and Glick, I.D. "Recent Developments in Family Therapy: A Review," *Hospital and Community Psychiatry* 33:550–56, 1982.

Ellison, E.S. "Social Networks and the Mental Health Caregiving System: Implications for Psychiatric Nursing Practice," *Journal of Psychosocial Nursing and Mental Health Services* 21:18–24, 1983.

Falloon, I.R., and Liberman, R.P. "Behavioral Family Interventions in the Management of Chronic Schizophrenia," in *Family Therapy in Schizophrenia*. Edited by McFarlane, W.R. New York: Guilford Press, 1983.

Falloon, I.R., et al. *Family Care of Schizophrenia: A Problem-Solving Approach to the Treatment of Mental Illness*. New York: Guilford Press, 1984.

Godschalx, S.M. "The Challenge of Chronicity," in *The Clinical Specialist in Psychiatric Mental Health Nursing: Theory, Research, and Practice*. Edited by Critchely, D.L., and Maurin, J.T. New York: John Wiley & Sons, 1984.

Goldman, H.H. "The Chronically Mentally Ill: Who Are They? Where Are They?" in *The Chronically Mentally Ill: Research and Services*. Edited by Mirabi, M. New York: SP Medical and Scientific Books, 1984.

Greiner, D.S. "Hospitals and Outpatient Clinics," in *Practicing Family Therapy in Diverse Settings*. Edited by Berger, M., and Jurkovic, G.J. San Francisco: Jossey-Bass, 1984.

Haley, J. *Leaving Home*. New York: McGraw-Hill Book Co., 1980.

Heinrichs, D.W., and Carpenter, W.T. "Prospective Study of Prodromal Symptoms in Schizophrenic Relapse," *American Journal of Psychiatry* 142:371–73, 1985.

Johnson, D.L. "The Needs of the Chronically Mentally Ill: As Seen by the Consumer," in *The Chronically Mentally Ill: Research and Services*. Edited by Mirabi, M. New York: SP Medical and Scientific Books, 1984.

Krauss, J.B., and Slavinsky, A.T. *The Chronically Ill Psychiatric Patient and the Community.* Boston: Blackwell Scientific Pubs., 1982.

Lamb, H.R. "What Did We Really Expect from Deinstitutionalization?" *Hospital and Community Psychiatry* 32:105–09, 1981.

Liberman, R.P., et al. "Social Skills Training for Chronic Mental Patients," *Hospital and Community Psychiatry* 36:396–403, 1985.

Madanes, C. *Strategic Family Therapy.* San Francisco: Jossey-Bass, 1981.

Madanes, C. "Strategic Therapy of Schizophrenia," in *Family Therapy in Schizophrenia.* Edited by McFarlane, W.R. New York: Guilford Press, 1983.

McFarlane, W.R. *Family Therapy in Schizophrenia.* New York: Guilford Press, 1983.

Mirabi, M. *The Chronically Mentally Ill: Research and Services.* New York: SP Medical and Scientific Books, 1984.

Reiss, D. "Pathways to Assessing the Family: Some Choice Points and a Sample Route," in *The Family: Evaluation and Treatment.* Edited by Hofling, C. New York: Brunner-Mazel, 1980.

Reiter, M., and Plotkin, A. "Family Members as Monitors in a State Hospital," *Hospital and Community Psychiatry* 36:393–95, 1985.

Selvini-Palazzoli, M.,et al. *Paradox and Counterparadox.* New York: Jason Aronson, 1978.

Stickney, S.K., et al. "The Effect of Referral Procedures on Aftercare Compliance," *Hospital and Community Psychiatry* 31:567–69, 1980.

Talbot, J.A. "The Chronic Mental Health Patient: A National Perspective," in *The Chronically Mentally Ill: Research and Services.* Edited by Mirabi, M. Jamaica, N.Y.: Spectrum Pubs., 1984.

Terkelsen, K.G. "Schizophrenia and the Family: II. Adverse Effects of Family Therapy," *Family Process* 22:191–200, 1983.

U.S. Department of Health and Human Services. *National Plan for the Chronically Mentally Ill.* Washington, D.C.: U.S. Government Printing Office, 1980.

Wright, L.M., and Leahey, M. *Nurses and Families: A Guide to Family Assessment and Intervention.* Philadelphia: F.A. Davis Co., 1984.

Wynne, L.C. "Current Concepts About Schizophrenics and Family Relationships," *Journal of Nervous and Mental Disease* 169:82–89, 1981.

SECTION III

Intervening with Families with Psychosocial Problems

8 Intervening with newly married couples and marital violence

Mark J. Hirschmann, PhD, RN
Assistant Professor
College of Nursing
Wayne State University
Detroit, Michigan

OVERVIEW

Physical violence between a newly married husband and wife can be treated with a structural/strategic form of marital therapy. The following case example demonstrates how the formation of early family relationships and inadequate adjustment to marriage can result in domestic violence. The couple's patterns of interaction and the ambigious boundaries with their families of origin are the focal points for the nurse's interventions. Special attention is given to the identification of marital violence in the health care setting, contraindications for marital therapy, and how to handle confidentiality between husband and wife.

CASE STUDY

Joan and Tom, both 21, were a bright and attractive couple. They had been married for 8 months when they sought treatment at a university marriage and family therapy center. Joan was in her third year of college working on a bachelor's degree, and Tom was nearly finished with technical training in electronics. They were having prolonged arguments that occasionally escalated in Tom hitting Joan. These incidents grew out of unresolved disagreements about their unsatisfactory sexual relationship, their relationship with in-laws, and their leisure time together.

The assessment of the problem included a detailed description of the pattern of conflict that preceded the violence. The couple's preconceived notions about marriage, ambiguous family boundaries, and Tom's and Joan's patterns of interaction were the subjects of the nurse's further assessment. The plan was to block violence-supporting behaviors, promote better resolution of conflict, and reduce the stress associated with the unfulfilled family life cycle tasks (e.g., differentiation from family of origins) of newly married couples. Joan and Tom attended 23 sessions of joint outpatient therapy over 8 months. Using a predominantly structural/strategic approach to marital therapy, the nurse helped Tom and Joan reduce violence in their marriage and grow closer as a couple.

NURSING PROCESS

Assessment

Health problem: Violence between spouses. The incidence of violence between husbands and wives has been estimated at 50% to 60% of the general population; such figures assume that a high rate remain unreported because marital violence is considered unacceptable behavior (Strauss, 1980). It is further estimated that three to four million women are beaten each year in the United States by husbands, ex-husbands, or boyfriends. One of every four suicide attempts by women, and half of all suicide attempts by black women, are triggered by battering. Thirteen percent of all murders in the United States are committed by spouses. (Stark, 1981).

Violence between spouses is a serious problem, and many incidents are untreated. Although couples like Tom and Joan do elect marital therapy, they are the exception; most abuse is identified by observant health care personnel. Greany (1984) hypothesized the ratio of reported to nonreported cases as close to one in 50. As the head nurse of a New York medical center emergency department, Greany encourages her staff to be alert for discrepancies between wounds and the explanations given for them by the patient. Different stages of healing in the same area suggest repeated beatings. Patients making frequent emergency visits for vague symptoms may be asking for help.

Substance abuse is also associated with violence between spouses. Though a person may deny substance abuse, the medical and nursing staff should objectively enter suspicious observations into the record for possible legal action in the future. And, should a patient disclose such abuse in a health care setting, steps should be taken to provide medical and nursing treatment, emotional support, security, referrals, and collection of evidence.

Referrals may include the police and agencies that specialize in abuse victim advocacy and treatment. If the victim and the abusive spouse appear willing to work together, then a nurse or other professional specializing in marriage and family therapy would be an appropriate referral. Some couples approach a therapy situation willing to talk about abuse; however, it is common to see couples begin by describing more socially acceptable problems, such as difficulties with children, or poor communication with the spouse. Once trust has been established, a spouse may talk about violence. Therefore, the nurse should occasionally meet with spouses separately.

Models of therapy for violence between spouses. In assessing the couple, the nurse should approach the information given by the couple with a theory or model of therapy. It is "...the lens of the therapy model which will affect the kind of diagnosis/assessment one will conduct" (Liddle, 1982). Assessment is therefore preceded by training in a theoretical approach to therapy.

There is no shortage of theories about family violence. Gelles and Strauss (1979) attempted to integrate 13 theories into a general sociological theory. Applications of psychotherapeutic theories to marital violence are less abundant. *Cathartic therapy* (Bach and Wyden, 1968) urges the abuser to express aggression in alternative, safe ways. In *rational emotive therapy,* Albert Ellis (1976) conceptualizes anger as an unrealistic response brought on by a person's irrational belief that he must not be frustrated or disappointed with "significant others." Abusive spouses are led to discard irrational beliefs about their spouses and find appropriate ways for expressing their anger. *Behavioral marital therapy* (Margolin, 1979), which is often applied to marital abuse, states that violence is a learned behavior and is maintained, in part, by interactive cues expressed by each spouse during conflictual situations. The goal of behavioral marital therapy is to diminish behaviors that precede aggression and to learn more appropriate behaviors for resolving conflict. In *systems/cognitive therapy* (Bedrosian, 1982), a couple identifies the thoughts and emotions associated with violent behavior. The cognitive therapist then evaluates the problematic beliefs that precipitate violence between the couple and intervenes according to systemic principles. *Structural/strategic therapy* is concerned with the present, not the past. Clinical research with marital violence is non-existent (Bagarozzi and Giddings, 1983), although behavioral marital therapy (Jacobson, 1980) and cognitive therapy (Novaco, 1978) with couples in general are each supported by empirical studies.

Joan and Tom were treated with a structural/strategic form of marital therapy. Significant data were elicited by asking both spouses about their views of their problems and the efforts they had made to solve them (Watzlawick et al., 1974; Haley, 1976). Tom and Joan viewed their problem in the same way. Arguments were common and Tom sometimes hit things, including Joan. To prevent violence, Tom repeatedly pledged not to become violent again, and Joan tried to avoid starting arguments. Significantly, Tom reported that there was no history of violence in his family.

The goal of strategic therapy is to block the undesirable behavior. The couple should be asked to describe in detail their interactions before, during, and after the violence. During this process the therapist should repeatedly say, "What happened next?" The nurse's assessment goal is to identify a pattern of interaction that leads to the violent behavior.

By interviewing Joan and Tom separately and together, it became obvious that their interactional pattern perpetuated violence by allowing frustration to build in the presence of unresolved conflicts. This is the pattern:
• Tom would ask for time or attention.
• Joan would agree, without specifying duration or type.

- Neither one's expectation for a pleasant experience would be met.
- Tom would blame Joan.
- Joan would withdraw.
- Tom would become angry.
- Joan would lock Tom out of the bedroom.
- Tom would threaten or actually knock in the door while he was angry and then leave.
- Tom would return.
- Both would be sorry and promise that it wouldn't happen again.
- Days would pass.
- Tom would ask for time or attention (the cycle repeats).

Based on this cycle, the nurse's interventions would be designed to block the violent sequence of events and develop new and healthier behaviors for coping with conflict.

Assessment of newly married couples. During their lifetimes, 95% of Americans will marry at least once. A couple is most likely to divorce during the first year of marriage. Filled with romanticized expectations and having given little thought to the adjustments required, newly married couples are vulnerable to unanticipated disappointment, tension, and stress. If the couple is amenable to therapeutic intervention, improvements can be made to sustain the marriage during this period.

Although the focus here is on the newly married stage of the family life cycle (Duvall, 1977; Carter and McGoldrick, 1980), a two-dimensional assessment can be applied at any stage. The first dimension organizes the family member relationships into three groups: marital, familial, and extrafamilial. The second dimension separates family adjustment behaviors in terms of expectations, family boundaries, and interactive patterns.

The various relationships of a married couple are complex and interrelated. Grouping marital, familial, and extrafamilial relationships facilitates the nurse's assessment. Within each group of relations, information contributes to the overall picture of the couple's situation.

Marital relations. A newly married couple brings to their marriage two sets of rules for eating, sleeping, relieving tension, spending money, and performing other routine activities. The couple must negotiate their own set of rules.

When Joan and Tom began therapy, Tom's idea of fun was to play golf or go fishing. Joan preferred to shop and go out to dinner. Each could not understand that the likes of one were not necessarily the likes of the other. In their sex life, Tom's only barometer of Joan's pleasure was his own sexual arousal and fulfillment. Joan was not accustomed to helping Tom find ways of meeting her sexual needs. As a result, Joan found their sex life dissatisfying. Tom and Joan had not yet made their own rules as a couple.

Family relations. In a similar sense, the newly-married spouse undergoes a change with its family of origin. The parents no longer play the protective role; the new spouse provides security. After redefining their relationship with their own parents, both spouses must learn to relate to their in-laws.

For example, Joan's mother was deceased and Joan became estranged from her father when she started college. (Joan had been sexually abused by her father between the ages of 9 and 14. Joan was seeing an individual therapist to work through this experience.) The couple was financially dependent on Joan's uncle. His job allowed him to visit two or three times a year and to stay for a week or so. During these visits the uncle drank heavily and made lewd sexual remarks about Joan. The couple wished to stop this intrusion but did not know how.

Extrafamilial relations. In the extrafamilial world of each spouse there are still more changes. Decisions once made easily about work or play are now complicated by the needs of another person. Time spent with friends shifts from single-oriented to couple-oriented activities. In the first year of marriage each couple faces a large number of complicated but seldom anticipated situations. Without love and patience, the relationship can be easily overwhelmed. Tom was often frustrated that Joan could not visit his family or even have fun, since her education demanded more time and effort than his.

Assessment of family life cycle stage adjustments. The information describing each of the three above-mentioned types of relationships can be made more useful by analyzing it in terms of the types of adjustments to be made at each stage of the family life cycle. As a couple gets married, or has a child, or the child leaves home, each family member must set realistic expectations and establish new family boundaries and effective interactive patterns.

Forming realistic expectations. The utopian syndrome (Watzlawick et al., 1974) is a tendency of family members to enter a life cycle stage with unrealistic expectations of happiness and harmony. The couple's expectations of their new marriage and one another provide much data for explaining the frustrations they encounter. With a thorough understanding of the couple's views of the situation, the nurse can help the couple reconsider their expectations. Both Joan and Tom repeatedly frustrated each other by expecting the other to know his or her likes or dislikes without expressing them.

Forming new family boundaries. During the newly married stage of the family lifecycle, boundaries with each spouse's family of origin, in-laws, friends, and each other must be redefined. Each partner must establish distance from the family of origin and intimacy with the new mate. Women who marry before the age of 20 have twice the divorce rate of those who marry in their twenties (Glick and Norton, 1977); this statistic suggests the strain of simultaneously separating from family and forming a marital relationship. "The ideal situation, and one very rarely found, is the one in which the partners have become independent of their families before marriage and at the same time maintain close, caring ties" (McGoldrick, 1983).

The concept of "family boundaries" is a key element of Minuchin's (1974) structural family therapy, and it enables the nurse to conceptualize the structure of the family. Although the nurse needs to have an ideal model of family structure at each life cycle stage, she must also remain aware of the different norms of family behavior associated with various ethnic backgrounds. The ideal model must also allow for the changing role of women in society (Avis, 1985).

While Joan and Tom shared a tolerance for the changing role of women in society, Tom's mother did not. She criticized Joan's education and career plans at least once during each visit. Tom, his father, and four brothers had long ago adapted to the mother's constant criticism by ignoring it. This blurred Tom's father's boundary as parent because he had formed a coalition with his sons against her criticism. Joan entered the situation with the expectation of peaceful relations with her mother-in-law, but she was devastated by the ridicule to which she was subjected. Tom and his father could not stand up to Tom's mother to spare Joan. This breakdown in the boundary around the marriage of Tom's parents and Tom's inability to maintain a boundary between his mother and Joan became a long-term stressor for Tom and Joan.

Forming effective patterns of interaction. The third group of adjustments can be considered a microview of the family boundaries. The boundaries are the summation of numerous interactive patterns (Minuchin, 1974). In particular, the couple needs the skill to resolve most of their marital disagreements, without outside interference.

At the beginning of therapy, Joan would retreat from any discussion of conflict rather than demand that her point of view be heard. In this way, frustration would build with each unresolved issue. One goal of therapy was the enhancement of the couple's ability to sustain an effective dialogue while resolving difficult issues.

Planning

Indications/contraindications for marital therapy. Once the nurse learns of violence in a marriage, she must decide if the couple's situation is appropriate for marital therapy. The couple should meet three conditions: both spouses must express a desire for reconciliation; the abusing spouse must agree to stop using physical force and the victimized spouse must agree to abandon the cues that prompt violent responses from the abusing spouse; and the history of the abuse compiled from talking separately with each spouse must be free of repeated severe beatings or the use of lethal force. If the couple cannot meet any of these criteria, then marital therapy is contraindicated and proper referrals should be made to other treatment programs.

Having decided that marital therapy is appropriate for the couple, the

nurse makes three planning decisions. These include the management
of confidentiality in therapy, the choice of which persons will participate
in therapy, and the establishment of therapeutic goals.

Confidentiality in therapy. Individual meetings with each spouse are
recommended when any type of abuse is revealed or suspected. During
these meetings, the nurse encounters a common dilemma; she wants
to extend confidentiality to each spouse, yet she wants the freedom to
share relevant information revealed by one spouse with the other. To
minimize the potential conflict of interest, the nurse can begin these
meetings with the following ground rules. First, information relating
to the harm of an individual would be shared to protect that individual.
Second, the nurse keeps information confidential only if the client
identifies the information as such before giving it. Third, the client may
retain the information as a secret if therapy progresses well. If therapy
is being hampered by the secret, then the nurse will ask the client to
share the secret with the spouse or family. Fourth, if the client refuses
to share the secret, the nurse reserves the right to withdraw from
the therapeutic relationship. In this way the nurse is not obligated to
continue therapy with a couple in which a spouse has secretly described
domestic violence or other harmful situations. These rules give both
the nurse and the client some control over the flow of information.

Participants in treatment. The potential unit of treatment includes the
couple, their families of origin, and any involved professionals, such
as Joan's individual therapist. As a rule of thumb, the nurse should
interview all family members living in the home.

> From her assessment, the nurse hoped to include the couple's relationship
> with Joan's uncle and Tom's family. However, the uncle was unavailable, and
> Tom and Joan lived alone most of the time. Secondly, the boundary between
> the marriage and Tom's family of origin was considered ambiguous because
> Tom could not restrain his mother's criticism of Joan. By working alone with
> Tom and Joan, the nurse circumscribed a needed boundary around the cou-
> ple.

One factor that demanded attention in the early stage of therapy was
the role of Joan's individual therapist. A firm boundary around the
couple was important. A therapist providing a listening ear to Joan
could disrupt the formation of the interactive patterns between Tom
and Joan. With Joan's permission, the nurse contacted Joan's therapist
and established an agreement that Joan would not discuss marital
issues in their therapy. Joan's therapist would therefore reinforce Joan's
and Tom's marital boundary. Had the individual therapist been less
cooperative, the nurse would have asked her to defer individual treatment during marital therapy.

Goals of treatment. While the nurse may be aware of many problems,
she will best retain the interest of the couple if she works with the
problem most important to them (Haley, 1976).

In the case of Tom and Joan, the primary concern was the violence in their relationship. Tom, Joan, and the nurse made a verbal contract to eliminate the threat of violence in the marriage. The original contract also included the enhancement of sexual satisfaction. Although the nurse was aware of other issues, she chose to keep the goals as simple as possible. Additional problems could be added as the initial ones were resolved.

Intervention

The distinction between different types of interventions can be somewhat arbitrary. Although the nurse uses different interventions—executive, relational, blocking, and building—their identities often blur during the practice of therapy.

Executive interventions. Like most goal-oriented human endeavors, marital therapy needs rules and someone to conduct therapy according to those rules. Groups of people in therapy can find each other intimidating, particularly when the group includes couples and families who are prone to violence. The nurse must remain in charge of the therapy session, enabling the clients to feel safe and secure. Executive interventions regulate such things as who sits where, who speaks, and when they speak. Harmful, rude, and non-therapeutic behaviors are to be prevented by the nurse.

Relational interventions. Additionally, the nurse must personally engage the couple in the process of therapy. In doing this, she empathetically learns the "position" of the client (Fisch et al., 1981) and "joins" with each client (Minuchin, 1974). Active listening and expressions of caring are key ingredients to the therapeutic relationship. The nurse demonstrates an understanding of each spouse's point of view without antagonizing the other spouse. From the trusting context of this relationship, the therapist will ask the couple to do things that they could not do on their own. Though caring for the couple is the dominant theme, the therapeutic plan may call upon the nurse to express disapproval of client behavior to reach the goals of therapy.

Blocking interventions. In working with violence-related problems, the nurse must establish certain ground rules. The nurse seeks a contract with the abusive spouse to abandon all physical force within the marriage. The victim then agrees to leave the home if the spouse becomes violent. Privately, the nurse and the victim identify alternative places to live and obtain support. The victim should know the consequences and procedures for pressing charges against the abuser. This is a necessary form of blocking intervention made early in therapy for the protection of the victim.

There are more subtle forms of blocking interventions designed to disrupt maladaptive behavioral patterns between spouses. For example, there is one theory of spontaneous change which holds that when an accustomed method of family functioning is blocked, the family will adapt new ways of interacting to maintain equilibrium. New rules for interacting emerge, creating "second order" change (Watzlawick et al., 1974). First order change is observable and conscious but is thought to have little effect on the systemic rules governing interactions.

Second order change is the basis for most strategic therapies. The nurse's interventions in such cases are often complex and require specialized training to execute well. The blocking interventions used with Joan and Tom, for example, were relatively straightforward. The nurse followed a five-step procedure:

• The nurse actively listened to each spouse's views, taking pains to understand the details and empathize with each spouse.
• From the information she obtained, the nurse constructed a pattern to show how the behavior of one spouse prompted the behavior of the other. The pattern of abuse (identified in the assessment section above) was repetitive and circular, and neither spouse was blamed.
• The nurse suggested changes in behavior patterns and asked each spouse to work on these changes in the coming week.
• The nurse explained to the couple why it was important to follow these changes.
• The results were evaluated each week. If a spouse did not comply with one of the nurse's suggestions, all three would discuss the spouse's reasons for not complying; the nurse would then construct a more detailed behavior pattern, and suggest more effective changes. Tom and Joan would then develop a healthier way of resolving their conflict.

Joan and Tom made several changes in their conflictual pattern. The first significant change came when Tom began to recognize his rage during an argument. By prearrangement with Joan, Tom would leave the apartment, stating that he needed to calm down. In a few minutes he would return to resume the discussion. From the beginning, Joan avoided the behavior that cued Tom's violence: locking him out of the bedroom. As time went by, Joan realized that she deserved to be treated with more respect by Tom, and she began to identify those times when Tom failed to show her respect. At such times, she would say in a neutral tone of voice, "This discussion is getting too hot." In this way the violent sequence never got started.

Building interventions. The building interventions involve another theory of change. By directly restructuring even a part of the family system's boundaries or interactions, the entire family system can change (Minuchin, 1974).

The nurse helped change Joan's and Tom's pattern of interaction by making it more complex (Haley, 1976); that is, by increasing their behavioral "repertoire" of their relations as a couple. By building on the couple's strengths, the nurse taught them to actively listen to each other's points of view, to propose alternative solutions, to choose the best, and to develop cooperation in carrying out those solutions (Jacobson, 1980; Margolin, 1979). This was done during several sessions, in which the nurse played the role of "director," and extracted the best performances from both spouses.

This type of role playing led Joan and Tom to accomplish several family life cycle tasks. They discussed the steps required to alter the uncle's position in their marriage. This included moving to a less expensive apartment and taking part-time jobs. The couple practiced the words and tone of voice they would use during the "showdown." A similar effort was made to help Tom establish the boundary around his marriage and its interface with his family of origin. Tom practiced asking his mother to respect Joan's feelings. Joan and Tom also used this method to settle their differences on birth control and their expectations of their sexual relationship.

Integration of blocking and building interventions. Joan and Tom were treated with a combination of blocking (strategic) and building (structural) interventions. The decision to block the behavior pattern during conflicts was based on the couple's claims that they could not control the violent behavior. "Unfree" behaviors with cooperative clients can be treated with compliance-based strategic interventions (Tennen et al., 1981; Minuchin and Fishman, 1981). "Free" behaviors, such as self-centered sexual interactions, were changed by building the couple's repertoire of sexual behaviors.

The integration of different types of therapy is controversial. The structural and strategic forms of family therapy are fairly complex, and each is thought to benefit a wide range of problems. Although one may seem to complement the other, the principles for integrating different theoretical approaches are not well documented in the therapy literature. Only therapists with advanced levels of experience and training should try to combine therapeutic orientations.

EVALUATION

Over the course of 8 months and 23 sessions of therapy, Tom's and Joan's self-reported progress indicated that they had eliminated the threat of violence from their marriage and had developed better methods of problem-solving. In the presence of the nurse they could discuss and resolve conflictual issues. They agreed upon a method of birth control and developed mutually satisfying sexual behaviors. After about 5 months of therapy, after finding part-time jobs and taking a less expensive apartment, Tom and Joan asked the uncle to leave during one of his intrusive episodes. Only minor progress was made in helping Joan relax with Tom's mother. However, Joan and Tom developed hand signals with which Joan could tell Tom she had had enough and wanted to go home. Further improvement would have required the participation of Tom's family, but the couple declined to take this step.

At a 20-month follow-up, Tom and Joan had both graduated from school and found jobs in a neighboring state. They continued to avoid the threat of violence. They were making time for each other in their busy schedules and were finding satisfaction fixing up an old house they had recently purchased. Tom's father visited them for an extended period, during which time he and Joan enjoyed getting to know each other better. With this support, Joan felt more comfortable visiting Tom's mother. Like the rest of Tom's family, Joan learned to get along by ignoring the mother's criticism.

CONCLUSIONS

Violence between husbands and wives is a widespread problem. Marital therapy is appropriate for those couples who want to work at staying together. Because the interactive patterns are newly formed and amenable to change, the newly married stage of the family life cycle is well suited for intervention in cases of abuse and other marital problems. Nurses and other health professionals are in a position within the health care system to help identify and treat marital violence in our society.

REFERENCES

Avis, J.M. "The Politics of Functional Family Therapy: A Feminist Critique," *Journal of Marital and Family Therapy* 11:127–38, 1985.

Bach, G.R., and Wyden, R. *The Intimate Enemy.* New York: Morrow, 1968.

Bagarozzi, D.A., and Giddings, C.W. "Conjugal Violence: A Critical Review of Current Research and Clinical Practices," *American Journal of Family Therapy* 11(1):3–15, 1983.

Bedrosian, R.C. "Using Cognitive and Systems Intervention in the Treatment of Marital Violence," in *Clinical Approaches to Family Violence.* Edited by Hansen, J.C., and Barnhill, R.L. Rockville, Md.: Aspen Systems Corp., 1982.

Carter, E.A., and McGoldrick, M., eds. "The Family Life Cycle: An Overview," *The Family Life Cycle: A Framework for Family Therapy.* New York: Gardner Press, 1980.

Duvall, E.M. *Marriage and Family Development.* New York: J.B. Lippincott Co., 1977.

Ellis, A. "Techniques in Handling of Anger in Marriage," *Journal of Marriage and Family Counseling* 2:305–15, 1976.

Fisch, R., et al.*Tactics of Change: Doing Therapy Briefly.* San Francisco: Jossey-Bass, 1981.

Gelles, R.J., and Strauss, M.A. "Determinants of Violence in the Family: Toward a Theoretical Integration," in *Contemporary Theories About the Family: Research-Based Theories.* Edited by Burr, W.R., et al. New York: Free Press, 1979.

Glick, P.C., and Norton, A.J. "Marrying, Divorcing and Living Together in the U.S. Today," *Population Bulletin* (32/5). Washington, D.C.: Population Reference Bureau, 1977.

Greany, G.D. "Is She a Battered Woman? A Guide for Emergency Response," *American Journal of Nursing* 6:725–27, 1984.

Haley, J. *Problem-Solving Therapy: New Strategies for Effective Family Therapy.* San Francisco: Jossey-Bass, 1976.

Jacobson, N.S. "Behavioral Marital Therapy," in *Handbook of Family Therapy.* Edited by Gurman, A.S., and Kniskern, D.P. New York: Brunner-Mazel, 1980.

Liddle, H.A. "Diagnosis/Assessment in Family Therapy: A Comparative Analysis of Six Schools of Thought," in *Family Therapy Collections, vol.3. Diagnosis and Assessment in Family Therapy.* Edited by Kenney, B.P. Rockville, Md.: Aspen Systems Corp., 1982.

Margolin, G. "Conjoint Marital Therapy to Enhance Anger Management and Reduce Spouse Abuse," *American Journal of Family Therapy* 7:13–24, 1979.

McGoldrick, M. "The Joining of Families Through Marriage: The New Couple," in *The Family Life Cycle: A Framework for Family Therapy.* Edited by Carter, E.A., and McGoldrick, M. New York: Gardner Press, 1983.

Minuchin, S. *Families and Family Therapy.* Cambridge, Mass.: Harvard University Press, 1974.

Minuchin, S., and Fishman, H.C. *Family Therapy Techniques.* Cambridge, Mass.: Harvard University Press, 1981.

Novaco, R.W. "Anger and Coping with Stress," *Cognitive Behavior Therapy: Research and Application.* New York: Plenum Press, 1978.

Stark, E.M.A. *Wife Abuse in the Medical Setting: An Introduction for Health Personnel.* Monograph Serial Number 7, April. Rockville, Md.: Clearinghouse on Domestic Violence, 1981.

Strauss, M.A. "Wife Beating: How Common and Why?" *The Social Causes of Husband-Wife Violence.* Minneapolis: University of Minnesota Press, 1980.

Tennen, H., et al. "Reactance Theory and Therapeutic Paradox: A Compliance-Defiance Model," *Psychotherapy: Theory, Practice, and Research* 18(1):14–22, 1981.

Watzlawick, P., et al. *Change: Principles of Problem Formation and Problem Resolution.* New York: W.W. Norton & Co., 1974.

9 Intervening with families of infants and child abuse

Maureen R. Keefe, RN, PhD

Associate Director of Nursing for Research
The Children's Hospital
Assistant Professor
School of Nursing
University of Colorado
Denver, Colorado

OVERVIEW

This chapter presents a young family dealing with the crisis of child abuse. The steps of assessment are outlined and the predisposing factors leading to child abuse are discussed. Several theoretical frameworks are examined in light of their ability to explain the occurrence of child abuse, and the current conceptual trends in this area are described. A nursing framework is used to define the various roles the nurse assumes as she intervenes in a family dealing with child abuse. Finally, family goal evaluation is discussed and identified as an important and integral part of the nursing process.

CASE STUDY

Mary Bronson, a 20-year-old woman, brought her 2-month-old female infant, Angela, into the local health department's well-child clinic for a check-up and immunization. Angela had been seen by the clinic's nurse practitioner once previously, when she was 2 weeks old. At that time, Mary stated that the family was new to the area and that her husband, Roy, 24, had just started medical school. She explained that Angela's birth was not planned and that her husband had hoped for a boy. They had moved to the area just before Angela was born because the school year was starting, and Roy felt that this was his only opportunity to become the physician he had always wanted to be.

Mary was a quiet, soft-spoken woman who did not maintain consistent eye contact. She appeared tender and caring toward her child. Angela had been born 3 weeks early; since Mary chose not to breastfeed, she was frustrated by her lack of contact with the infant during the first 2 weeks after birth, a time when Angela was hospitalized for observation and weight gain. As eager as Mary was to be alone with her daughter, she reported feeling overwhelmed when she brought the child home, and said she missed the support of her family and friends. She stated that her husband was pleased with the baby except when she cried or had "fussy spells" in the evening; she also pointed out that he was so busy with his studies and a part-time job that he did not have time for either her or Angela.

During the latest clinic visit the nurse practitioner noted that Angela was fussy when held and moved about. Her weight gain was adequate, although she remained in the 10th percentile. On physical examination, a swollen area was noted in the mid-region of Angela's left upper arm, and the area was painful upon touch. The nurse also observed that Angela did not move her left arm spontaneously. Upon questioning, Mary said that, a few nights before, she had gone into Angela's room because the infant was crying. She noticed that Angela had rolled over and had her arm caught under her in a "funny" position. Angela showed increased fussiness for the previous 2 days, Mary said, but she was not sure of the cause, since Angela fussed quite a bit anyway.

The nurse practitioner informed Mary that Angela's arm might be broken and that she should be taken to the hospital for an X-ray and observation. At this point, Mary began to cry, and worried out loud about what Roy would say. The nurse phoned the emergency room at the local children's hospital and explained that she would be sending Angela in for evaluation of a possible fractured left humerus due to nonaccidental trauma. Then the nurse informed Mary that Dr. Drummand would be waiting for her at the hospital and that she would also be talking to a social worker about Angela's injury and the surrounding circumstances. The nurse explained that she would contact Mary again soon to follow up on the hospital evaluation.

Angela was admitted to the hospital and a protective service case worker was assigned to evaluate the home situation. During the hospitalization, the unit nurses assessed both mother-child and father-child relationships, and observed interaction processes. It was decided that Angela would be discharged to her parents with close protective services supervision and follow-up. At the time of discharge, the staff nurse referred Mary to the local public nursing service and the lay visitor program attached to the hospital social work department. The court recommended reevaluation of the case in 4 months.

At Angela's 4-month visit to the well-child clinic, she seemed to be achieving normal weight and appeared developmentally normal. She presented as a smiling, sociable baby. Mary was also more sociable and at ease; she seemed better able to reflect on the difficulty of her first few months with Angela. She found the public health nurse an excellent resource for baby care and she enjoyed the lay visitor's adult female companionship. She and Roy had entered marital therapy and had begun to communicate about the concerns and the demands both felt. Roy reported applying for a grant that would alleviate the financial burden he said had weighed heavily on him since Mary first announced her pregnancy. Without referring specifically to Angela's injury, Mary said she knew they needed help, but just didn't know how to ask for it.

NURSING PROCESS

The health problem: Child abuse. C. Henry Kempe and Ray Helfer coined the term "the battered child" in 1961 to focus attention on what they saw as a major national health problem. Their goal was to dispel the complacency that existed within society and the health care profession toward the problem of child abuse. Kempe and Helfer defined the battered child as "any child who received non-accidental physical injury as a result of acts (or omissions) on the part of his parents or guardians" (Kempe and Helfer, 1972).

As knowledge and awareness of the problem has improved, various subtypes of child abuse have been delineated and defined (Schmitt, 1984):
- Physical abuse
- Sexual abuse
- Failure to thrive
- Intentional drugging or poisoning
- Health care neglect
- Safety neglect
- Emotional abuse and neglect
- Physical neglect
- Educational neglect

Incidence. The rate of reported child maltreatment in the United States and its territories is 23.8 of every 1,000 children. More than a million (1,007,658) reports of child maltreatment, involving 1.5 million children, were documented in 1983 by the American Association for Protecting Children (Table 9.1) (AAPC, 1985). This represents an 8.4% increase over the previous year and an increase of 142% since 1976.

Table 9.1 Documented Child Abuse in the United States, 1983 (by type)

Type of Abuse	Percentage of Total
Major physical injury	3.2
Other physical injury	23.7
Sexual maltreatment	8.5
Deprivation of necessities	58.4
Emotional maltreatment	10.1
Other	8.3

The average age of the involved children was 7.1 years.

Impact on the abused child. The consequences of child abuse are both physiological and psychological. The physiological effects include physical impairment, anemia, hearing loss, growth failure, and poor health; psychological consequences usually involve low self-esteem, poor interpersonal skills and limited capacity for enjoyment. Developmental delays, especially in the areas of motor ability, learning, memory, understanding, perception, or speech and language are often observed. (Kempe and Helfer, 1980).

Erickson's developmental framework provides a basis for understanding these delays and personality deficits. Abused children experience an extremely serious impediment to the development of basic trust—the first stage of normal development. Logically, these children have difficulty mastering such later stages as autonomy and initiative (Kempe and Helfer, 1972).

Physical child abuse. Physical child abuse is often the easiest type to identify or detect. Major abuse-related physical injury is concentrated among very young children; 60% of such injuries occur in children under age 4, although such abuse is *most* common in children under 3.

The abusive family. The abusive individual is in most cases an individual with whom the child lives. Eighty-three percent of all abusers are the abused child's caretakers. Forty-seven percent of the reported abusive households were receiving public assistance. Only 50% of the families had both male and female caretakers. Forty-three percent of abusive families were headed by a single female, compared to an incidence of 19% single female household heads in the general population. The average age of the abusers was 31.3 years and 60% were female (AAPC, 1985).

In assessing a family's child abuse potential, the nurse should be aware of certain "high-risk" or predisposing factors. These factors can be broken down into characteristics of the abusive adult, the abused child, and the family. Table 9.2 contains questions helpful for assessing these high-risk factors in the home.

The abusive adult may demonstrate a history of childhood abuse, low self-esteem, rigid child-rearing patterns, inappropriate or unrealistic expectations of the child's behavior, isolation, and mistrust of others. The child may be the product of an unwanted or unplanned pregnancy, may be perceived by the parent as the wrong sex, or as having a difficult temperament. The abused child is more likely to have been born prematurely or to have some type of physical or mental impairment. The family dynamics involved in abuse situations often include marital disharmony; social and kinship isolation; financial difficulty; early, forced marriage; and high levels of general family stress, combined with limited adaptive resources (Caulfield et al., 1977; Kempe and Helfer, 1980; Martin, 1982; Oates, 1982).

Table 9.3 summarizes the subjective and objective findings identified in the literature as most frequently associated with physical child abuse (Helfer and Kempe, 1976; Schmitt, 1980; Solomon, 1980). The nurse noting any of these circumstances during assessment should suspect possible physical child abuse.

Families with young children. Physical child abuse occurs in families in the early childbearing and childrearing stage of family development.

Table 9.2   Home Environment Assessment Guidelines

Use of Outside Resources	• Have parents demonstrated both a willingness and an ability to use others in time of need? • Is outside support available to the parents on a 24-hour basis? • Do parents have out-of-home interests? • Do the parents have positive self-images?
The Spouse	• Can the husband and/or wife realize when the partner needs help? Can he/she provide support when a problem is recognized?
The Crisis	• Are obvious crises—those involving housing, food, in-laws, job, illness—being resolved? • Does someone know the family well enough to recognize immediate and pending crises? • Can that person intervene when a problem is recognized? • Are there obstacles to getting help (e.g, no phone or transportation)?
The Child	• Do the parents see the child as "different"? • Are their expectations of the child realistic? • Do they enjoy the child? • Do they see the child as an individual? • How old is the child?

Table 9.3   Findings Associated with Physical Child Abuse

• Unsatisfactory parental explanation of injury:
  self-inflicted
  sibling-inflicted

• Implausible patient history

• Parental delay in seeking medical assistance

• Child/patient unusually fearful, watchful

• Eyewitness account of abuse

• Signs of parental neglect:
  poor hygiene
  inappropriate dress
  malnutrition

• Incidence of repeated or unmentioned injury:
  abrasions
  burns
  swollen tissues
  hematomas
  dislocations/fractures

• Coma, convulsions, death

Rubin (1975) has identified the following four maternal tasks associated with this developmental stage:
• Seeking safe passage through pregnancy, labor, and delivery for self and child.
• Ensuring acceptance of the child by significant persons in the family.
• Bending in to the unknown child.
• Learning to give of self.

Traditionally, the father's role has been that of provider and indirect caretaker for his wife and children. This practice has been influenced by the economic system and a social bias toward the privacy of the mother-infant bond. However, more and more fathers are discovering the pleasure and challenge of becoming active coparents, while sharing the financial burden with their wives.

Family developmental tasks at this stage begin with the establishment of a couple bond, a step that requires new communication patterns, role negotiation, and decision-making strategies. Preparation for the addition of an infant also includes role shifts, financial adjustments, physical changes, and psychological preparations (Duvall, 1979).

This adaptation and readjustment of the couple bond is vital to the transition to parenthood. For couples whose relationship is one of fusion, the new child will introduce the nuclear family triangle. The baby's presence may threaten the parental relationship's stability by drawing one parent close and making the other feel left out. In many cases, the triangle distances the father from the close mother and child bond (Bradt, 1980).

Theoretical models. An understanding of the origins and underlying mechanisms of child abuse provides a basis for developing appropriate methods of prediction, assessment, intervention, and prevention. Several theoretical models help explain the occurrence of physical child abuse.

Early psychiatric models of child abuse focused upon the individual abusive parent in an attempt to discover an underlying mental illness; these approaches waned, however, for lack of substantive evidence of psychotic disorder or consistent aberrant personality characteristics (Parke, 1982). Later models incorporated the parent-infant dyad, focusing upon developmental aspects of the abnormal interpersonal relationship. In 1976, Helfer proposed what he called the world of abnormal-rearing cycle (WAR), which is characterized by a childhood in which early needs are not met, roles are reversed with the parent, and a disproportionate sense of responsibility is felt for events and others' feelings. For the child growing up in the WAR, there are few choices or opportunities to develop decision-making and problem-solving skills. As social development begins, the WAR child learns that others cannot be trusted; rather, that they are sources of hurt or disappointment. The child subjected to abnormal rearing also fails to learn to differentiate—or grasp the relationship between—feelings and actions. The result is a child with low self-esteem and minimal interpersonal skills, one who is easily discouraged and depressed. By young adulthood, many of these children see "having a family" as a solution to their loneliness, at which point the cycle begins to repeat itself and the world of abnormal rearing is passed from one generation to another. Kempe and Helfer (1980) believe understanding these concepts is essential to breaking this cycle.

Another model which has had a major impact on the study of child abuse development and prevention is the maternal-infant bonding model, which was first delineated and described by Klaus and Kennell (1976). Within this framework, the battered or abused child is a victim of severely disturbed mother-infant bonding. Klaus and Kennell identify the following major behavioral influences affecting the mother's ability to bond to her infant appropriately and hence engage in adequate or effective parenting:
• Mother's care by her own mother
• Mother's genetic endowment
• Cultural practices
• Relations with family and husband
• Previous pregnancy experience
• Planning of and events during pregnancy

Klaus and Kennell also identify alterable variables, areas in which health care professionals can intervene and facilitate bonding—and by doing so, promote adequate maternal parenting. These alterable variables include:
• Behavior of doctors, nurses, and hospital personnel
• Separation of mother and infant during the first days of life
• Hospital practices

Research using this model has demonstrated the impact of early mother-infant contact on a series of affectionate maternal behaviors during the first postpartum day, especially in the cases of young, low-income women. However, many questions remain regarding the theoretical basis of a maternal-infant bonding construct; the relationship between bonding and attachment and the mechanisms that link early contact to such subsequent outcome measures as child abuse are still unknown (Siegel, 1982).

These models, which limit interaction patterns to the dyad and address only the direct effects of one individual on another, have been criticized for being inadequate in their understanding of family social interaction and lacking a full appreciation of the ways in which abusive patterns develop (Parke, 1982). Alternative models of child abuse expand the causal focus from individual analysis of the parent or mother-infant dyad to the social environment. Fig. 9.1 depicts Parke's (1982) interactional model of child abuse.

Figure 9.1   Social Interaction Model of Child Abuse

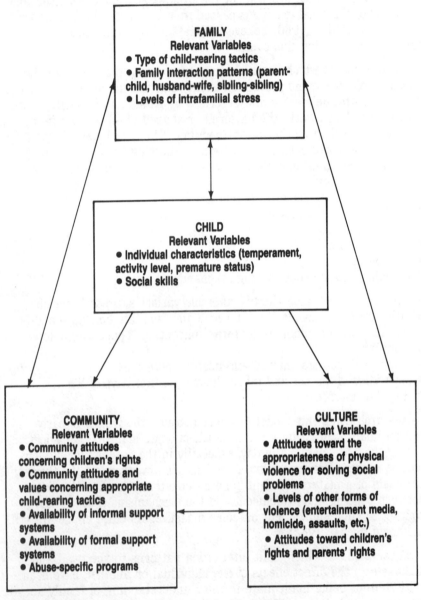

FAMILY
Relevant Variables
• Type of child-rearing tactics
• Family interaction patterns (parent-child, husband-wife, sibling-sibling)
• Levels of intrafamilial stress

CHILD
Relevant Variables
• Individual characteristics (temperament, activity level, premature status)
• Social skills

COMMUNITY
Relevant Variables
• Community attitudes concerning children's rights
• Community attitudes and values concerning appropriate child-rearing tactics
• Availability of informal support systems
• Availability of formal support systems
• Abuse-specific programs

CULTURE
Relevant Variables
• Attitudes toward the appropriateness of physical violence for solving social problems
• Levels of other forms of violence (entertainment media, homicide, assaults, etc.)
• Attitudes toward children's rights and parents' rights

Reprinted with permission from Starr, R.H. *Child Abuse Prediction: Policy Implications.* Cambridge, Mass.: Ballinger Publishing Company, 1982.

In 1981, Millor, a nurse researcher, described a nursing framework for research in child abuse and neglect; her model incorporated the role of the social environment and depicted child abuse as a multifactorial phenomenon. Components within the model include attitudinal input from the community and family, as well as parent-child characteristics; it is the interaction of these components that leads to neglectful or nurturant relationships.

In contrast to the traditional psychiatric emphasis on abnormality, Millor's and Parke's models assume that normal parents are socialized into abusive child care patterns through the combined impact of the cultural, community, and familial influences that comprise the larger social interaction. Within this framework, child abuse becomes one manifestation of a general cultural attitude of violence.

The community, under this scenario, provides educational, monitoring, and support services for the child-rearing family; interfamily influences include traditional child-rearing practices, the amount of stress felt by family members, interaction patterns, and the infant or child's temperament (Parke, 1982; Millor, 1981). Parke emphasizes the importance of two factors in understanding how abuse develops within a family: the parents' prior history and the nature of the parent-child interaction. He argues that, from the social interactional perspective, it is misleading to view child abuse as unidirectional and rooted in the parent's inadequacy. All family members play roles in both eliciting and maintaining abuse patterns. Abuse may result from parent-child interaction or develop through the mediation of another family member. Therefore, the role of the abusing parent in such families is an important factor in determining nursing assessment, intervention, and evaluation.

Planning

Two key elements in nursing abusive families are, first, the formation of a cooperative relationship and, second, the establishment of mutually agreeable goals. Both steps will be particularly challenging if the clients have little past experience with trust or positive relationships.

An effective nursing approach to the abusive family requires a nonjudgmental attitude and an open discussion of areas of concern. Sharing observations and concerns with the parents can lead to discussion, potential courses of action, and appropriate short- and long-term goals. Parents must be informed of the legal requirements to report any questionable injury in a child; they must also be reassured that the matter will be handled confidentially by a child protection agency, not the police, and that the overall goal is merely to help them and their child.

Each family's specific goals and care plan will be unlike any others and will be based on the nurse's assessment and the particulars of the situation. Both the child/victim and the abuser's needs must be addressed (Table 9.4).

Table 9.4 Goals to be Achieved in Child Abuse Intervention

Short-term (Immediate) Goals	Long-term Goals
• Assure safety of child —hospitalization —removal from home —temporary placement • Treat child's injuries or wounds • Comply with required reporting procedures • Refer family to protective service agency • Promote coordination and communication among treatment team and family members	• No recurrence of child abuse or neglect • Improved family dynamics, marital relationship, parent-child interaction • Improved parenting skills and attitudes —self-esteem —expectations —discipline —positive feedback • Reduction in family stress level —financial burdens —other stresses • Increased use of resources (personal support networks, community services)

Consultation and referral. The nurse's role throughout the treatment process will be a varied and vital one. She may encounter an abusing family in any of several roles: as the nurse practitioner assessing the child in an outpatient setting, as the staff nurse treating the child in the emergency room, as the clinical specialist evaluating parent-child interactions on the inpatient unit, as the visiting nurse identifying community resources, or perhaps as the psychiatric nurse providing therapy in a mental health center. Depending upon her role, she may encounter the family at different points in the assessment and intervention process. To maintain continuity of care, complete nurse-to-nurse referrals preceded by sharing of assessments and plans are essential. The extent to which this information can be effectively transmitted will affect the quality of care. Disruption and/or disorganization in the handling of abusive families is likely to lead to quick alienation and distrust in what is often a tentative and fragile nurse-client relationship.

Beyond good nurse-to-nurse communication, the larger health care and child care team must be considered. The interdisciplinary team approach to child abuse management is the accepted model for service delivery to these complex and needy families. The team may include a nurse, physician, social worker, lay visitor, and psychiatrist or psychologist. Communication among team members as well as respect for the unique contributions of each is essential for the achievement of treatment goals. The nurse often becomes a central figure for the parents and for the other team members as a coordinator and conveyor of information.

Intervention

Nursing roles. A study conducted by Gray and colleagues (1979) demonstrated that early intervention, characterized by frequent contact with a primary physician, a public health nurse, mental health workers, or lay health visitors, significantly decreased abnormal parenting practices in a group of families identified as "high risk" for child abuse or neglect.

In another study, the effects of a nursing-led team intervention program, based upon mental health nursing services, were evaluated. This team approach increased the home management, child care, and mother-child interactional skills of mothers who had abused or neglected their children (Carter et al., 1975).

Scharer (1979) has used Peplau's (1956) six distinct nursing subroles as a theoretical basis for understanding the various nursing functions in intervening with a physically abusing family (Table 9.5).

Table 9.5   Using Peplau's (1956) Nursing Subroles to Intervene in Cases of Physical Child Abuse

Subrole	Nursing strategy
Mother-Surrogate	• Establish a trusting relationship with the family • Begin "reparenting" abusive adults • Focus attention on the parent/child in a supportive, accepting manner • Act as a role model of the caring, sensitive parent
Manager	• Coordinate the family's treatment activities • Refer the family to appropriate community resources
Technical Support	• Maintain ongoing assessment of all family members' health needs • Provide necessary physical care to both abused child and family
Teacher	• Educate through role modeling and direct facilitation of problem-solving • Rely on nondirective teaching techniques
Counselor	• Be aware of the family's readiness to begin exploring feelings, insights, past experiences, anxieties, and fears • Provide assistance appropriate to the family's situation (e.g., health care, behavior modification, psychotherapy, referral to other health professionals)
Socializing Agent	• Introduce the family to basic positive social interaction skills • Help family members form friendships, establish a supportive and helpful social network

Source: Scharer (1979).

The first subrole is the mother-surrogate role; it is predicated on the belief that meeting the abusive parents' needs and raising their self-esteem will indirectly benefit the child (Kempe and Helfer, 1972). The second is a managerial subrole, while the third, or technical, sub-role, refers to direct physical care and treatment of the abused child or any other family member. The fourth role, that of teacher, is essential to nursing intervention and is designed to enhance the family's ability to make its own decisions and solve future problems. The fifth subrole, that of counselor or nurse psychotherapist, is based upon a basic trusting relationship developed over time. The sixth nursing subrole, socializing agent, involves developing and facilitating interpersonal relationships (Scharer, 1979).

Often, the community-based nurse plays the pivotal role for the abusive family. The community-based nurse must work closely with the local or county social services departments and child protective services to provide the following types of assistance (Kempe and Helfer, 1980):
- Therapy and counseling for children and parents
- Therapeutic foster care and crisis nursery placements
- Lay therapy
- Entrance into volunteer programs (Big Brother, Big Sister, Foster Grandparents)
- Day care (therapeutic if necessary)
- Parenting education
- Concrete emergency assistance, i.e., groceries, financial assistance, furniture, clothing, appliances.

Obviously such a comprehensive treatment program involves other professionals and paraprofessionals; however, the nurse often remains the key coordinator of services. It is often the nurse who develops a long-term, close relationship with the family and acts as a primary contact and conduit for communication.

Prevention. Child abuse intervention, however, does not end with treating the victims and initiating remedial family therapy. Intervention must also prevent further abuse. For nurses, the obligation extends beyond the individual families with whom they are involved, to the community and society at large. In short, the aim of child abuse intervention is the elimination of child abuse from all families. Meeting this goal requires the development of both prevention programs and mechanisms for early identification of potential abuse situations.

No single program presently exists to achieve this goal. It is more realistic to work toward the development of a range of programs directed at curbing child abuse throughout the developmental cycle. Kempe and Helfer (1972) suggested a set of prevention strategies geared to specific life cycle stages (Table 9.6).

Table 9.6 Proposed Child Abuse Prevention Programs

Life Stage*	Program(s)
Perinatal (birth-3 mos)	• Perinatal coaching/parenting education: Teach parents to "read" the newborn's signals/cries Teach skills necessary for parental communication with the child
Infancy (0-2 yrs)	• Parent-child development service • Home care/visitation • Expanded well-baby care
Preschool (2-5 yrs)	• Parent-child skill development: Interpersonal Cognitive Problem-solving
School Age (5-18 yrs)	• Continuing skill development**: Interpersonal Decision-making
Young Adult (18 + yrs)	• "Refresher" on appropriate interaction with children, peers

*Defined by age of abused child
**Children with a less-than-optimal childhood and inadequate interpersonal and problem-solving skills will require retraining before they reach the stage of having their own children.
Source: Kempe & Helfer, 1980

Campbell and Humphreys (1984) have studied the nurse's role in primary prevention in the following four arenas: the prenatal setting, the hospital, the community, and society at large. The prenatal period is the optimal time for establishing contact with the expectant family. Campbell and Humphreys advise the use of childbirth education classes and prenatal visits to convey information regarding psychological adjustment, the stress of the baby's arrival, newborn care and behavioral expectations, and the need for ongoing childrearing or parenting instruction.

Nursing interventions in the hospital include encouraging contact between mother and newborn, involving parents in their infant's care, and educating, supporting, and reassuring the parent(s). The community nurse should observe and advise families in the home, school, or clinic. Community-based nurses can provide primary preventive care to families at risk for abuse, especially adolescent parents, economically deprived and single parents, stepparents, and parents of handicapped children.

In the society, cultural sanctioning of physical force in child discipline must change. Some progress has been made in the legislative area. Prior to 1964, no effective child abuse reporting laws existed. In 1962, pediatrician C.H. Kempe organized a multidisciplinary conference to publicize the "battered-child syndrome." At this conference a model child abuse statute was developed; 5 years later, it was adopted by every state. Further efforts to eliminate poverty and racism are also needed, because they can lead to family dysfunction and abuse.

Nurses who work with abusive families should know of these two national sources of information and consultation on child abuse:

C. Henry Kempe National Center for the Prevention and Treatment of Child Abuse and Neglect
1205 Oneida Street
Denver, Colorado 80220
(303) 321-3963

American Association for Protecting Children
9725 East Hampden Avenue
Denver, Colorado 80231
(303) 695-0811

Evaluation

Nursing evaluation can greatly assist the family that gets actively involved and asks for input. An established set of short- and long-term goals provides an excellent starting point and evaluation framework. The more specific and concrete the goals, the better they will serve as measures of progress and growth toward the overall goal.

Evaluation must also consider the likelihood that abuse may recur after the child's initial treatment ends. Once again, the questions developed by Kempe and Helfer (1972) in Table 9.2 can determine whether the child will be safe in the home environment.

The abused child's future will depend upon the effort made to coordinate a treatment program that involves the entire family, and upon the prevention of further trauma to the child through nursing and other professional interventions. While hospitalizing the child, separating him from his parents, or placing him in alternate home care may be unavoidable, the psychological trauma of these stresses can be diminished by preventive, anticipatory counseling. Therapeutic intervention focused on remediation of developmental delays, attention to associated medical or educational problems, and healing of psychological scars will decide the outcomes for abused children. Without intervention, these children have little chance of becoming socially well-adjusted and happy adults (Martin, 1982).

CONCLUSIONS

Working with a family in which child abuse has occurred is a challenging personal and professional experience for any nurse. The nurse must first set aside her own feelings and reactions to the client family's crisis before adopting the nonjudgmental and open approach most likely to elicit the cooperation of the family members. She must also understand the dynamics of the events that commonly lead to child abuse.

Most of the literature on child abuse consists either of studies designed to predict predisposing factors or of general consciousness-raising information written for health care professionals and society.

Some guidelines for nursing abusive families have been set forth, but additional intervention strategies and programs to help establish and evaluate short- and long-term outcomes are sorely needed.

Beyond intervening with individual families, nurses must look for ways to prevent child abuse throughout society. Nursing is in an excellent position to develop and integrate lifelong health promotion programs which can break the cycle of family abuse and violence.

REFERENCES

American Association for Protecting Children. *Protecting Children.* American Humane Association, Denver, 1985.

Bradt, J.O. "The Family with Young Children," in *The Family Life Cycle: A Framework for Family Therapy.* Edited by Carter, E.A., and McGoldrick, M.M. New York: Gardner Press, 1980.

Campbell, J., and Humphreys, J., eds. *Nursing Care of Victims of Family Violence.* Reston, Va.: Reston Publishing Co., 1984.

Carter, B.D., et al. "Mental Health Nursing Intervention with Child Abusing and Neglectful Mothers," *Journal of Psychiatric Nursing and Mental Health Services* 13(5):11–15, 1975.

Caulfield, C., et al. "Determining Indicators of Potential for Child Abuse and Neglect: Analytical Problems in Methodological Research," in *Communicating Nursing Research,* vol. 10, *Optimizing Environments for Health: Nursing's Unique Perspective.* Edited by Batey, M.V. Boulder, Colo.: Western Interstate Commission for Higher Education, 1977.

Corey, E.J., et al. "Factors Contributing to Child Abuse," *Nursing Research* 24(4):293–95, 1975.

Disbrow, M.A., et al. "Measuring the Components of Parents' Potential for Child Abuse and Neglect," *Child Abuse and Neglect: International Journal* 1:279–96, 1977.

Duvall, E.M. *Marriage and Family Development,* 5th ed. Philadelphia: J.B. Lippincott Co., 1979.

Ebeling, N.B., and Hill, D.A. *Child Abuse and Neglect: A Guide for Treating the Child and Family.* Boston: PSG Pub. Co., 1983.

Elmer, E. "A Follow-Up Study of Traumatized Children," *Pediatrics* 59(2):273–79, 1977.

Finkelhor, D.,et al. eds.*The Dark Side of Families: Current Family Violence Research.* Beverly Hills, Calif.: Sage Publications, 1983.

Gray, J.D., et al. "Prediction and Prevention of Child Abuse and Neglect," *Seminars in Perinatology* 3(1):85–90, 1979.

Heindl, M.C., ed. *The Nursing Clinics of North America.* Philadelphia: W.B. Saunders Co., 1981.

Helfer, R.E., and Kempe, C.H., eds. *Child Abuse and Neglect: The Family and the Community.* Cambridge, Mass.: Harper & Row Pubs., 1976.

Kempe, C.H., and Helfer, R.E. *Helping the Battered Child and His Family.* Philadelphia: J.B. Lippincott Co., 1972.

Kempe, C.H., and Helfer, R.E., eds. *The Battered Child,* 3rd ed. Chicago: University of Chicago Press, 1980.

Klaus, M.H., and Kennell, J.H. *Parent-Infant Bonding.* St. Louis: C.V. Mosby Co. 1976.

Martin, H.P. "The Clinical Relevance of Prediction and Prevention," in *Child Abuse Prediction.* Edited by Starr, R. Cambridge, Mass.: Ballinger Publishing Co., 1982.

Millor, G.K. "A Theoretical Framework for Nursing Research in Child Abuse and Neglect," *Nursing Research* 30(2):78–83, 1981.

Oates, K.R., ed. *Child Abuse: A Community Concern.* Boston: Butterworths, 1982.

Parke, R.D. "Theoretical Models of Child Abuse: Their Implications for Prediction, Prevention, and Modification," in *Child Abuse Prediction.* Edited by Starr, R. Cambridge, Mass.: Ballinger Publishing Co., 1982.

Peplau, H. "Workrole of the Staff Nurse," "Excerpt from a paper entitled "Therapeutic Functions." Washington, D.C.: Eastern Regional Conference on Psychiatric Nursing, 1956.

Richardson, S. "Abusive Parents and Their Nonabusive Partners," *Communicating Nursing Research,* vol. 13, *Directions for the 1980s.* Boulder, Colo.: Western Interstate Commission for Higher Education, 1980.

Rubin, R. "Maternal Tasks in Pregnancy," *Maternal-Child Nursing Journal* 4(3):143, 1975.

Scharer, K. "Nursing Therapy with Abusive and Neglectful Families," *Journal of Psychiatric Nursing and Mental Health Services* 17(8):12–21, 1979.

Schmitt, B.D. "Child Abuse and Neglect: Types, Epidemiology, and Characteristics," in *Clinical Management of Child Abuse and Neglect.* Edited by Sanger, R., and Bross, D.C. Chicago: Quintessence Publishing Co., 1984.

Schmitt, B.D. "The Child with Non-Accidental Trauma," in *The Battered Child,* 3rd ed. Edited by Kempe, C.H., and Helfer, R.E. Chicago: University of Chicago Press, 1980.

Siegel, E. "A Critical Examination of Maternal-Infant Bonding—Its Potential for the Reduction of Child Abuse and Neglect," in *Child Abuse: A Community Concern.* Edited by Oates, K.R. Boston: Butterworths, 1982.

Solomon, T. "History and Demography of Child Abuse," in *Child Abuse: Commission and Omission.* Edited by Cook, J.V. Toronto: Butterworths, 1980.

Walker, W.F. "Child-Rearing Experiences, Support Systems and Couple Cohesiveness as Antecedent Factors in Parent-Child Interaction in Child Abuse," *Communicating Nursing Research,* vol. 12, *Credibility in Nursing Science.* Boulder, Colo.: Western Interstate Commission for Higher Education, 1979.

10 Intervening with families of preschoolers and incest

Leslie L. Feinauer, RN, PhD
Associate Professor
College of Nursing
University of Utah
Salt Lake City, Utah

OVERVIEW

This chapter describes a family-focused approach to the psychosocial problem of incest. Issues to be aware of in assessment and theoretical models that can be utilized by nurses are presented. Interventions for compliant and noncompliant families are illustrated through two case studies.

CASE STUDY

Laurie, age 4, had been sexually molested by her father and was brought into therapy by her mother. At the time of the assault, the parents were separated and in the process of obtaining a divorce. Laurie and her mother were living with her maternal grandparents.

During a visit, the father had taken Laurie to his mother's home to see his family. When Laurie returned home her mother noticed that the child was nervous and that she cried continuously. She wanted her mother or maternal grandmother to constantly rock her. When her father returned for a subsequent visit, Laurie hid behind a chair and refused to leave with him. The mother refused to let the father take her.

Three days later, Laurie told her mother that her father had hurt her while she was visiting her paternal grandmother. She said that he had placed her on the couch and inserted his finger in her vagina. Laurie also said her father warned her not to tell anyone or he would come and take her away and hurt her mother.

Laurie's mother reported that Laurie's behavior changed dramatically during the 3 months following the assault: she was depressed, anxious, and withdrawn. Laurie returned to using her security blanket; she refused to eat and lost 7 pounds; she engaged in self-injurious behaviors; she had difficulty sleeping; she was afraid to leave the house and did not allow her mother out of her sight; and she was frightened of men.
[This case example was adapted from the work by Becker, Skinner, and Able (1982).]

CASE STUDY

Sara was 13 years old when she was brought to therapy by her older brother, with whom she was living. The brother explained that authorities removed Sara from their parent's home after Sara spoke to a teacher about her sexual involvement with her father.

Physically, Sara appeared to be about 7 or 8 years old. She had a slight build, long stringy hair, and wore no makeup; she looked very solemn, made no eye contact, and spoke in a high-pitched soft voice. She was dressed in baggy, tattered clothing that looked like remnants from charity. Emotionally, Sara was severely depressed, anxious, withdrawn, and phobic. She was anorexic and seemed anxious about her body development.

Since she was 5, Sara's father had insisted on fondling her genitals and engaging her in intercourse at least weekly while her mother was at work. He convinced her that sexual experiences were important for young girls to ensure that they would marry well. He explained that he had taught Sara's older sister in the same manner. If she objected to the sexual activity, he used a combination of bribes and threats to make sure she cooperated.

During Sara's preschool incestuous experiences, she was very angry at her mother for not protecting her. When Sara was 5, she told her mother about her father's activities, but her mother did not believe her. She felt abandoned and alone, and became alienated and distant from her mother. Sara's mother was at home even less often after this revelation and relied on Sara to do more household chores. Sara had a security blanket and wore special "magic" clothes. She didn't sleep or eat. She engaged in dangerous and foolish activities, such as running into the street after a stray kitten and climbing onto the roof of the house and jumping down. Sara was always bruised or injured from falling down, running into something, or hurting herself with one of her father's lawn tools. She became increasingly withdrawn and shy. She spoke to few people and was seldom outside. Children teased her about looking sickly. Sara played with no one except her younger brother, who was intellectually slow.

When Sara started school, she became aware of a world different from the one she had known. Sara's father refused to let her leave the house after school or to have friends whom he did not know. She spent all her time after school at home with her one younger brother. Her father, a janitor at an elementary school, returned home shortly after Sara and her brother finished school in the afternoon. If Sara was not at home, he punished her physically and grounded her.

As Sara grew older, she insisted that she be allowed to visit her older sister, who was married and had an infant daughter. Sara's father agreed that Sara could baby-sit the infant. Later, he visited Sara while she was caring for the young infant. During this time, Sara told her teacher about her father. The school reported the incident to the authorities. Although Sara's mother did not corroborate Sara's charges, an investigation took place and family therapy was mandated. Sara's father was convicted of a felony, lost his job, and was sent to a state hospital for treatment as a sex offender. He presented himself as a "helpless victim of misunderstanding." Although he admitted his sexual involvement, he blamed society and rationalized his acts by saying that his wife was uncaring and cold and that his daughters were warm.

Sara refused to read the daily letters her father wrote to her. He threatened suicide if she did not respond. Her family was angry with her for reporting the incest, and her mother refused to allow her to move back home. Her mother and sister blamed Sara for the incest but were more concerned with and angry over the resulting family chaos.

NURSING PROCESS

Assessment

The health problem: Incest. Sexual abuse is defined as the involvement of dependent, developmentally immature children and adolescents in sexual activities that they neither understand nor agree to. Incest is considered a type of sexual abuse that occurs between family members. Blood relationship is not required; "family" is used in its broad social connotation as well as to describe the actual living arrangement of the involved persons (Kempe and Kempe, 1984). According to Kempe and Kempe (1984), most legal definitions of incestuous sexual abuse of children include the following categories:

Pedophilia (literally, "love of child"): The preference of an adult for prepubertal children to achieve sexual excitement. In pedophilic incest, the fathers have an erotic fascination with children and use their own children as sexual objects, rather than find children unrelated to them. In either case, the child becomes the participant-object of the activity.

Exhibitionism (indecent exposure): The exposure of the genitals by an adult male (including parent or other adult relative). The exhibitionist's purpose is to experience sexual excitement from the encounter (he may masturbate as well as expose himself). Although he may call attention to himself, he does not make any other approach.

Molestation: A rather vague term used to include such behaviors as touching, fondling, or kissing the child, especially on the breasts or genitals, masturbating the child, or making the child fondle or masturbate the parent or other adult. It is not a particularly useful term, because it does not have limits to its definition.

Sexual intercourse (statutory rape) with a child of either sex: Fellatio (oral-genital contact), sodomy (anal-genital contact), or penile-vaginal intercourse may occur without physical violence through seduction, persuasion, bribes, use of authority, or other threats.

Rape: Sexual intercourse or attempted intercourse without the victim's consent. Although rape has occurred in children younger than 6 months, the victims are generally over age 5.

Often the rapist drinks alcohol to remove his inhibitions so that he can act out his fantasies. The rapist usually plans the rape before the event while not under the influence of alcohol or drugs. In male children, the rapist is generally from the neighborhood, or a relative, and the rapes may continue over a prolonged period of time and involve many partners.

According to Kempe and Kempe (1984), official reports suggest that at least 1% or 2% of American women have been a victim of incestuous sexual abuse by her father or stepfather before she reached adulthood; thus between 1 and 2 million women in the United States have been victims of incest. Abuse due to other perpetrators, such as child molesters and rapists unrelated to the children, brings the estimate to well over 4% or 5%. This means that 4 to 5 million women in the United States were victims of sexual abuse as children.

Meiselman (1978) supports this view based on the 1953 Kinsey reports in which about 4% of the women interviewed regarding their sexual histories revealed that they had been approached sexually by an uncle, father, brother, or grandfather prior to adolescence.

In conclusion, while only about 50% of the cases of incest are reported each year, evidence shows that there are at least an equal number of cases which go unreported each year. This chapter will focus on the victims of a father- or stepfather-daughter incest.

Yeates (1978) followed the histories of 54 women who had had incestuous relationships prior to adolescence. Of these, 46 were functioning normally in the community at the time of the study and seemed unaffected by the experience. These women were young and initially pleased with the relationship, and apparently remained emotionally unscathed; however, they were devastated by the social consequences after discovery, which usually occurs in late adolescence or young adulthood. Guilt occurs relatively late, often not until adolescence.

A recent study by Gomes-Schwartz and Horowitz (1985) supports Yeates (1978). These researchers found that only 20% of the preschoolers had problems in emotional, social, and/or intellectual development following an incident of sexual abuse. They based their conclusions on the child's ability to comprehend the sexual nature of the experience. Children who cannot understand the meaning of sexual approaches can rationalize their experience better than those who can understand.

Neither author (Gomes-Schwartz and Horowitz, 1985; Yeates, 1978) addressed the issues of hypersexuality and failure to separate from parents as developmental issues for preschoolers. The most common outcome of the detection and reporting of preschooler incest is removal of the child or father from the family. In either case, loss of a significant parent as well as feelings of responsibility, shame, guilt, and confusion can result. It is difficult for a preschool child to resolve these issues. No less problematic is the confusion the child feels as she learns that behaviors which had brought approval from father and mother are no longer acceptable. She must revise all her relationships and find new ways to get affection, support, comfort, and attention. These same issues will probably arise in adolescence when her sexuality and separation issues surface again.

Families with preschoolers. Couples with preschoolers need to show their children that a strong marital bond exists; this provides the children with security and attachment as they attempt their major tasks of autonomy and initiation. This task is accomplished by preschoolers as they gain mastery over their bodies and begin to separate from their parents. For parents this is a time of turmoil, since they are usually young adults trying simultaneously to establish careers and financial security. Often parents neglect their marital relationship. Their ability to communicate as adults may be pushed into the background as they cultivate their parental roles and strive to communicate with their children.

Children at 2 and 3 are not modest. They are curious about their bodies and proud of them. As they become more aware of themselves and their bodies, especially their genitalia, their parents teach them how to present their bodies in socially acceptable ways. They learn how to approach the world, especially members of the opposite sex. But if a girl is encouraged by her father to be sexy, such training and the child's own developmental tendency will collide.

The gravest damage occurs when a youngster is bound closely to a sexually stimulating parent. If a daughter receives most of her parental affection and attention from a father through sexual activities, there is danger that she will think that she can receive nurturing and affection only through sexual means. She may completely miss the normal development of a nurturing relationship, which should be based on respect for her needs as a developing individual; the lack of this experience can skew all of her future initimate relationships (Kempe and Kempe, 1984). A child who remains sexually preoccupied will have difficulty learning how to seek affection in more appropriate ways. Such children may be totally unacceptable in preschools or day-care facilities because they try to involve others in their sexual interests.

Children must be free to develop erotic interests on their own. They need to experiment and grow outside the highly charged and necessarily frustrating relationships within the family. As they grow, their world widens and they look beyond their mother and father. They observe how others relate to one another and what effect outside events have on themselves and their parents.

Incest: A family problem. Incest is symptomatic of serious problems within the family. In father-daughter incest, a reversal of the mother-daughter roles may exist. The mother may look to her daughter to help save her marriage, at the expense of the daughter's development. The daughter may become the housewife and take care of the home and siblings as well. The mother may not be capable of a mature mothering relationship or able to place her daughter's needs above her own. In such cases, the incestuous relationship develops over time and is emotionally rather than physically coercive.

There are many girls for whom incest is not a gentle seduction, but a threatening, frightening experience. No pretext of affection is made and the girl maintains silence and submits because of beatings or fear of them. Her father or stepfather may be abusive, drunk, or both. Threats of violence may keep her mother and siblings intimidated as well, with everyone afraid to report the man (Meiselman, 1981).

Regardless of the family dynamics and pathology, incest alters the roles and rules within a family. It places the child in an abnormally powerful, yet vulnerable, position. In the father's eyes, the girl takes precedence over her own mother but forfeits the warm, safe role of child. She may be possessed by a jealous father who restricts her from healthier outlets. If she reveals their sexual secrets, she may be discredited, forced from the home, shunned by friends, and cross-examined in court. She may feel responsible for her father's jail term, for the family chaos, and for the divorce, if one occurs.

Other siblings may be indirect victims of the incest. Uninvolved parents, older siblings, grandparents, or other relatives frequently feel guilty because they believe they did not adequately protect the child. Father and brothers of the victim, though not involved, may identify simultaneously with the aggressor and the victim. As in rape, clinical evidence indicates that the young girl's significant support system must be involved in therapy if it is to be successful (Feinauer, 1982). Additionally, family members may express a desire to take revenge on the assailant and may become overzealous in their attempts to gain retribution (Becker et al., 1982). Often this retribution occurs in the court system and results in the incarceration of the father. Unfortunately, the removal of the father from society and the loss of the family's breadwinner is another source of victimization for the victim. Not only is she responsible for tearing the family apart, now she is responsible for taking food out of their mouths as well.

Theoretical models. There are a variety of theoretical approaches to therapy with compliant families in incest cases. One of the most common is a behaviorally oriented program in which desired behaviors are reinforced and undesired or dysfunctional behaviors are ignored. Parents are taught how to help the child, and each positive behavior is noted. They are also helped to handle their own feelings relative to the incident.

Treatment strategies vary in noncompliant families. Many therapists who treat noncompliant families try to alter the family structure by using structural and strategic interventions; the methods of intervention vary with the therapist.

Furniss (1983) uses a treatment approach which focuses on specific issues in the different family dyads using a systems approach. Play therapy and art therapy are usually integrated into work with preschool children and have been developed by Adams-Tucker (1984). Boatmen and colleagues (1981) use a humanistic approach which utilizes individual, couple, dyad, group, and family modalities at different times during therapy. Feinauer (1984) has developed a multiple family treatment program that has proven to be more effective than individual therapy in preliminary studies.

Planning

Obviously, a child who is a victim of incest should receive individual attention to assess and alleviate any trauma resulting from the experience. But unless a therapist resolves the underlying family pathology, the child cannot be assured of protection from sexual abuse in her home. One of the major problems encountered in family therapy is the incestuous father's lack of cooperation in therapy (Meiselman, 1981). Currently, many clinicians prefer to see the fathers, mothers, and victims individually. Some see the individuals first, then parents in marital therapy, and finally the entire family group. The decision about whom to see in therapy is important. If the victim is ever to resolve her feelings toward men and their use or misuse of power, the father must at least once in a safe setting tell his daughter that their sexual involvement was his responsibility and that he was wrong to force or expect her to participate in it. If the family is to remain together, each member must be involved in altering the dynamics that allowed the incest to occur. Since most incestuous families have blurred or non-existent generational boundaries and weak parental subsystems, the marital subsystem should be seen concurrently with the whole family (Feinauer, 1984).

Even when all members of an incestuous family are cooperative, problems may arise. Serious sexual problems will usually exist in the marital relationship. Prior to the incest, the intergenerational boundaries prohibiting sexual expression were violated. If sexual issues are to be dealt with, therapy should focus on family boundaries rather than on the parent's sexual relationship. To include the children in discussion of marital issues confuses the boundaries. Family therapists commonly try to make all members of a family aware that they share responsibility for family problems; this stance, however, may increase the child's sense of guilt. Unless the issue of responsibility for the incest is handled very clearly and carefully, the child may believe she is to blame. The young girl must hear repeatedly from her parents and from the therapist that nothing she may have done justified the parent's incestuous behavior.

Often, because he is uncooperative and/or removed from the family by legal authorities, the father is not available for therapy. In such cases, some therapists have elected to concentrate on the mother-daughter dyad. Browning and Boatmen (1977) reported that decreasing the passivity of the mother was often accomplished by treating chronic depression. Characteristically, the mother is highly dependent and needs help to decrease the negative effects of incest on her family. The preschool child needs the assurance that someone is in charge while the mother gradually becomes more believable in this role.

While it is important to talk openly about the incest and correct any misconceptions about sexuality related to it, it is more important to provide activities that encourage a healthy attitude towards sex. Children learn about themselves in their preschool years by doing and observing. A concept of sexuality must become a natural "good" part of the preschool child with appropriate boundaries, rather than evil, destructive, or exploitive.

Interventions

Regardless of the type of family to be treated, a nurse should have information regarding the interactional system and family history of the individuals involved. The most common assessment tools used during initial interventions include genograms, ecomapping, and information about how previous crisis situations have been handled.

In compliant families, the actual treatment process may be quite simple and straightforward; in noncompliant families, the course of therapy is often difficult and varied. An example of each was presented above. The intervention used and the outcome of each will be discussed in this section.

Compliant families. Compliant families are usually the victims of incest rather than the perpetrators. In these cases, the parents are often separated, or the incest occurs with a relative, such as an uncle or cousin. The parent or parents are usually willing to follow instructions and comply with the therapy suggested. While the approach may be simple, the task of undoing a traumatic and confusing experience may require much time and patience on the part of all those involved. Initially, the child is frightened, anxious, guilty, phobic, and will regress to earlier behaviors. Depression and fear are often manifested in wanting to be rocked, refusing to eat, and various dependent behaviors. For instance, Laurie (Case I) wanted to take her stuffed tiger with her to preschool so that it could beat up her mean daddy if he came. Listening carefully to what the child says and carefully observing her behavior will help determine how the child viewed the incest experience. Often anatomically correct dolls and play therapy can help the child reconstruct the sexual experience accurately. If physical trauma occurred, a physical examination should take place as quickly as possible.

Parents may benefit from books or articles written by parents who have successfully dealt with sexual abuse of a child. Parents often need a "sounding board" so they can express their fears and their feelings of having failed in their parental responsibility (Feinauer, 1982). They may also need to express their feelings of being cheated and betrayed by someone they had trusted. The clinician helps most by listening carefully, reflecting on what the parent said, allowing silence as the parent reflects on the events, and inviting the parent to talk after several minutes.

For this approach to be successful, the child must be allowed to discuss the incident and attempt to make sense of it when she wishes. After the initial discussion of the events and the correction of misconceptions, the parents should not initiate the discussion but must be willing to address it openly and clearly if the child mentions it.

In Case I, Laurie's mother complied with the behavioral therapy provided (based on Patterson's *Living with Children*, 1967). After 12 weeks of directed reinforcement for desired behaviors, concern and support from her mother and maternal grandparents, and open discussion of the incident, Laurie was eating all of her meals, not engaging in self-destructive behaviors, and exhibiting no fear or anxiety. This was true 25 weeks later, when a follow-up visit was made (Becker et al., 1982).

Noncompliant families. In noncompliant families, a variety of interventions have been used with limited success. Most therapists initially attempt the same interventions used with compliant families; if these fail, they use techniques reserved for defiant or noncompliant families. With the exception of determining responsibility for the incest, the approach used to treat these chaotic and dysfunctional families is often paradoxical and indirect.

The basis of strategic or paradoxical intervention is the belief on the part of the therapist that the family will not comply with his instructions but will instead defy the therapy (Papp, 1983). A double message is therefore given to the family. The therapist hopes that the family members will defy the part of the message that restrains them from changing. The therapist must connect each symptom with the positive function it serves in the system, and prescribe each in relation to the other. The consequences of eliminating the symptom are described and discussed. The therapist recommends that the family continue to resolve their dilemma through that symptom. Each message contains within it an implied alternative that points toward the direction of change. This technique must be closely based on the information presented by the family. Additional methods for working with noncompliant clients are discussed by Papp (1983) as she uses it in the Brief Family Therapy Model at the Ackerman Institute, by the Milan Group (Tomm, 1984), and by Wright and Leahey (1984).

In Case II, Sara's noncompliant family came into family therapy after Sara had received individual therapy. The court ordered the father to participate in family therapy while he was in jail. Therapy was the only contact Sara's father had with Sara other than through letters. While traditional direct approaches were tried with limited success in the early therapy sessions, it was not until the clinician adopted a more strategic approach to the father's letter writing that change occurred.

A major objective for therapy was to return a sense of control to Sara. Sara saw the letters written by her father as an intrusion. She was pressured by her mother and sister to respond to the letters and to cheer up her depressed father; after all, he was the one in jail. For Sara, the letters symbolically represented continuing incest.

In therapy, the father was instructed to continue writing his pleading, inadequate, pathetic love letters to his daughter twice a day from the jail. Rather than throwing them away, Sara was to deliver them to her mother, who was to determine if they were letters written to a lover or a daughter. If they were written to a lover, she was to keep them. If they were written to a daughter, however, she was to give them to Sara. Sara could then decide whether to keep and read the letters or reject them. Sara's sister was to be given the letters if the mother could not decide if they were appropriate expressions of affection, and the sister could decide either to read or reject them. If the letters were appropriate for a daughter, the sister was to give them to Sara; if not, the sister was to return them to her mother.

The mother said that the assignment was ridiculous. She thought that the letters were private and intended for Sara; she did not want to be an "eavesdropper." The sister refused to accept any letters from her father that might have sexual overtones, and she told her mother to screen them carefully. Sara indicated that she was sure her mother could not carry out this task. At that point, the mother responded that indeed she could. The father was angry that his letters to Sara would be censored but was hopeful that she might read them.

The father wrote daily letters during the week, all of which the mother determined were appropriate for Sara to read. Sara refused to read them, however. The next week, the father increased the number of letters. Although none of the letters contained explicit sexual or inappropriate affectional references, the mother gave none of them to Sara or her sister. Instead, the mother brought them to therapy. She said that she did not know what to do with the letters, since they were not meant for a lover or a daughter. The letters were coercive and demanding. The daughters and their mother discussed more directly the incest and their roles in it. The mother took a more active role and seemed more animated. She requested that therapy be directed toward the marital relationship, since she had determined that the problems existed between her and her husband rather than with her daughter.

The mother remained in therapy for several months. She decided to divorce her husband. She got a job and became self-sufficient. Sara remained with her brother and his wife. She modeled her sister-in-law's clothes and asked for a pair of blue jeans and some lessons in makeup. Although she had difficulty during her early adolescence with hypersexuality and being compulsively seductive toward men she liked, she addressed these areas as they arose. She is an active high school freshman and has several close school friends of both sexes.

In this case, Sara's early preschool exposure to sexual activity with her father delayed her development. She could not separate from her family and become an autonomous individual. The delay in growth and withdrawal from all social interactions kept Sara from proceeding through normal developmental stages and accomplishing their related tasks. At 13, she was still experiencing and experimenting with preschool, school age, and early adolescent tasks. She was coping with a limited family support system. She had assumed adult roles while in a child's body.

Evaluation

Evaluation of how well the incestuous events and their meaning have been resolved requires some subjective determination by the clients; however, in preschool children, behavior is also an important indication. Their ability to interact spontaneously, the character of their drawings, the type of play in which they participate, the roles and activities they assign themselves and others while "playing house" are all indications of how they feel about themselves.

As said earlier by Kempe and Kempe (1984), the preschool stage of development is essential for the future development of intimate relationships. Children like Sara and Laurie cannot understand the differences between sexual activity and sexual intimacy. More unfortunately, they cannot achieve relationship intimacy. Therapy is usually required before individuals who experience preschool incest can resolve the issues it creates.

CONCLUSIONS

Dealing with the psychosocial problem of incest is both complex and challenging for nurses. However, if an appreciation of incest as a family problem is adopted then more intervention alternatives are available and outcome more successful.

REFERENCES

Adams-Tucker, C. "Early Treatment of Child Incest Victims," *American Journal of Psychotherapy* 38(4):505–16, 1984.

Becker, J., et al. "Treatment of a Four-Year-Old Victim of Incest," *American Journal of Family Therapy* 10(4):41–47, 1982.

Boatmen, B., et al. "Treatment of Child Victims of Incest," *American Journal of Family Therapy* 9(4):43–51, 1981.

Browning, D.H., and Boatmen, B. "Incest: Children at Risk," *American Journal of Psychiatry* 134:69–72, 1977.

Feinauer, L.L. "Multiple Family Therapy for Female Adolescent Incest Victims," in *Structured Family Facilitation Programs.* Edited by Hoopes, M.H., et al. Rockville, Md.: Aspen Systems Corp., 1984.

Feinauer, L.L. "Rape: A Family Crisis," *American Journal of Family Therapy* 10(4):35–39, 1982.

Furniss, T. "Family Process in the Treatment of Intrafamilial Child Sexual Abuse," *Journal of Family Therapy* 5:263–78, 1983.

Gomes-Schwartz, B., and Horowitz, J.M. "7 to 13 Year Olds Especially Vulnerable to Sexual Abuse," *Sexuality Today* 8(10):1, 1985.

Kempe R., and Kempe, H. *The Common Secret.* New York: W.H. Freeman & Co., 1984.

McNaron, R.A., and Morgan, Y. *Voices in the Night: Women Speaking About Incest.* Minneapolis: Cleis Press, 1982.

Meiselman, D.C. *Incest.* San Francisco: Jossey-Bass, 1981.

Papp, P. *Process of Change.* New York: Guilford Press, 1983.

Patterson, G.R. *Living with Children: New Methods for Parents and Teachers,* 3rd ed. Champaign, Ill.: Research Press, 1980.

Sagatun, I.J. "Attributional Effects of Therapy with Incestuous Families," *Journal of Marital and Family Therapy,* 8(1):99-104, 1982.

Schechter, M.D., and Roberge, L. "Sexual Exploitation," in *Child Abuse & Neglect: The Family and the Community.* Edited by Helfer, R.E., and Kempe, C.H. Cambridge, Mass.: Ballinger, 1979.

Tomm, K. "One Perspective on the Milan Systemic Approach: Part II. Description of Session Format, Interviewing Style and Interventions," *Journal of Marital and Family Therapy* 10(3):253–71, 1984.

Wright, L.M., and Leahey, M. *Nurses and Families: A Guide to Family Assessment and Intervention.* Philadelphia: F.A. Davis Co., 1984.

Yeates, A. *Sex Without Shame.* New York: William Morrow, 1978.

Intervening with families of school-aged children with unresolved grief

Joan E. Bowers, RN, EdD
Associate Professor
Psychosocial Nursing
School of Nursing
University of Washington
Seattle, Washington

OVERVIEW

More than two million children under the age of 18 have suffered the death of a parent. These children and their surviving parents are at risk for unresolved grief response. Unfortunately, few families seek counseling after the death of a member; it is often the school-aged child's behavior problems that bring the family to a nurse. This chapter discusses the issues that influence the family grieving process, the stages of therapy, and examples of the nurse's direct and indirect interventions. Evaluation of outcomes and needed areas of research on the family grieving process are also presented.

CASE STUDY

Madge Shannon called the local mental health center. She and her husband, George, were having problems with his niece, 7-year-old Bonnie Brady, who lived with them. The family also included two boys: Bonnie's brother, Steven, age 4, and the Shannons' son, Jimmy, age 2. Mrs. Shannon reported that Bonnie had trouble getting to school on time and was not working up to her potential in school. At home, Bonnie was "telling lies" and not properly caring for her clothes and other possessions. Bonnie's and Steven's parents died 2 years earlier in a single-vehicle auto accident; Mr. Shannon's other family members asked him and his wife to assume guardianship of the Brady children. Mr. Shannon's mother and his older sister Helen promised to help with them. The grief counseling agency that Mrs. Shannon called referred her to the center. She recognized that Bonnie's problems might reflect unresolved grief. The family attended counseling sessions 15 times over a period of 8 months.

Assessment
Assessment of this family included a genogram (see Figure 11.1) and a lengthy family history, including the events surrounding Tim and Jane Brady's fatal accident; current problems with disciplining Bonnie and Steven and information about the Shannons' long-range plans for the children were also examined.

Planning

Treatment plans were developed around managing the children's behavior, which included defining problems, setting limits, and establishing rewards; further assessing marital problems between Madge and George Shannon; and clarifying the Shannons' plans to adopt or to make other arrangements for Bonnie and Steven.

Intervention

The nurse's interventions initially consisted of helping the Shannons develop limits for all three children based on age-appropriate expectations. As treatment progressed, Mrs. Shannon complained about her husband's and his family's unwillingness to share the burden of the Brady children's care. The second phase of treatment focused on the marital couple's unresolved grief issues. Several sessions later, the question of long-range plans, i.e., adoption, was broached. The Shannons resumed their efforts to adopt the children, but movement was slow. Finally, Mr. Shannon asked for a joint session with his older sister, Helen. During this session, Mr. and Mrs. Shannon confronted Helen with her escalating criticisms of their parenting and her reluctance to help with Bonnie and Steven. During this highly emotional encounter, Helen confessed that 3 months before the accident she promised Jane Brady that she would adopt her children should anything happen to her. Because of Helen's husband's physical disability, however, Helen could not keep this promise. Her guilt and depression over this fact were damaging her marriage and job performance. The Shannons, who had resolved much of their own grief since starting treatment, offered Helen support and assurance of her worth.

Evaluation

Helen saw the author once individually after the group sessions ended. Several weeks later, the Shannons returned for a final visit. Both Bonnie and Steven were in school and registered under the name of Shannon. The adoption would be finalized the following week, and a major family celebration was planned to mark the occasion. In a follow-up phone call 3 months later, Mrs. Shannon reported that the minor ups and downs of family life had become manageable and that Bonnie was selected for an accelerated learning group, while Steven was adjusting well in kindergarten.

NURSING PROCESS

Assessment

The health problem: Unresolved grief in children. Census data (Bureau of the Census, 1983) indicate that there were approximately 62.3 million children under age 18 living in the United States in 1983; 3.5%, or slightly more than 2 million, live with a widowed parent. Garmezy (1983) reminds us that few experiences are more traumatizing for a child than a parent's death. The loss itself is highly significant, and the child's environment is radically changed. It is vital that the surviving parent support the child(ren) during the grieving process; unfortunately, the remaining parent may be too grief-stricken to provide enough emotional sustenance to help the child cope with the loss. Thus, for a time, the child loses access to both parents. In addition, the vast

Figure 11.1   Genogram—The Shannon Family

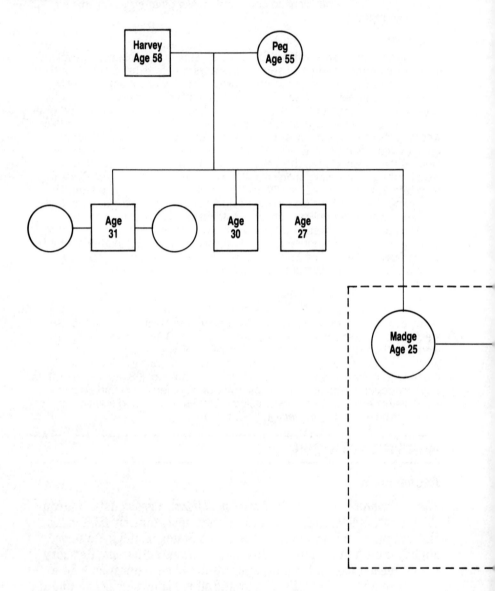

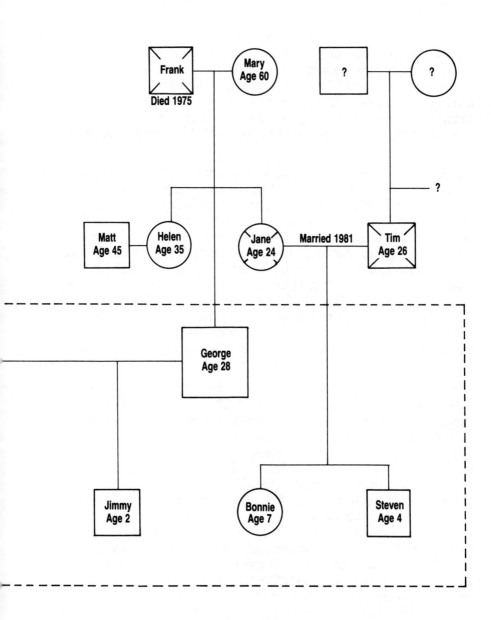

majority of these children live with widowed mothers (a 9 to 1 ratio according to Bureau of the Census 1983 data); thus, many surviving mothers also face the economic problems encountered by women in our society.

The family who knows and trusts a primary care provider at the time of a member's death may comply with a recommendation for grief counseling. Certain predictors of problematic grieving that the health care professional should be aware of are sudden death, particularly as a result of an accident, suicide, or homicide; death of a parent in a young family; indicators of low social support combined with a high level of stress; death following a long illness that has drained the family resources.

Families with school-aged children. This family life cycle stage begins when the first child starts elementary school (Wright and Leahey, 1984). The tasks of this stage focus on the child's development of peer relations and on the parents' adjustment to the child's peer school influences. It is a time of industry and achievement for the child, and the parents need to allow the child to test new relationships, new ideas, and new values. It is a busy period for the family, as well, and some families describe it as a time of decreased satisfaction with marital and parental functioning (Wright and Leahey, 1984). With the death of a parent, the family inevitably experiences some disruption of task accomplishment as the members struggle with their painful loss. In families that suffer from unresolved grief, the child's poor school performance often brings the family to therapy.

A school child's behavior problems after the death of a family member indicate a need for a family assessment. The child's behavior may signal unresolved grieving in the parent(s) and other family members, or it may mean that the adult(s) cannot deal with the child's grief. The adults in the family may feel angry at the child or reject him because they do not understand how children cope with painful events. Extremely disruptive behavior in the child, such as expressions of hatred towards the surviving parent, may indicate confusion and anxiety generated by fantasies about death. The child may be struggling to ask, "What really caused Mom (or Dad) to die?" "Could the same thing happen to me?" "Could the same thing happen to Dad (or Mom)?" "What will happen to me if something does happen to my Dad (or Mom)?" Left alone with these troubling and recurring questions, the child may be unable to concentrate on school work. At home, the emotional distance of the surviving parent or other caretaking adults may prevent the child from resolving his grief and fears.

Theories/models. Lindemann (1965) and Kübler-Ross (1969) provide descriptive models for the assessment of the adult grieving process.

Both of these models include affective, cognitive, and behavioral elements. The assessment of grieving in children necessitates a perspective that clearly focuses on age and on the stage of cognitive development (DeVaul et al., 1979; Garmezy, 1983; Glicken, 1978; Koocher, 1974; Raphael, 1983). In his review of the literature, Garmezy (1983) noted that the systematic study of the relationship between cognitive understanding of death and the coping responses used by bereaved children remains a fruitful area of research.

In his study of 75 nonbereaved children, ages 6 to 15, Koocher (1974) asked several questions about the causes and consequences of death. The children's responses were categorized using Piagetian stages of cognitive development. Responses from the children in the 6- to 8-year-old group were clearly preoperational and included magical thinking, fantasy, and egocentric reasoning. A child in this age group cannot share other people's experiences and might not regard death as permanent. Some of the ways in which the level of cognitive development might influence the child's response to a parent's death are provided by Raphael (1983).

First, the young child is likely to interpret the explanations of the parent's death literally. For example, if the young child is told that death is like sleeping, he will hear that not as a metaphor but as a reality. This child may then become fearful of falling asleep and "going away for a long, long time." The child may also believe that the death resulted from fantasy fulfillment. Bewilderment about the finality of death will probably be part of the child's thinking, and he may yearn for or try to search for the lost parent. This may cause the child to be preoccupied with memories of his parent and to idealize the lost parent. According to Raphael, when a child uses idealization as a coping strategy, the remaining parent may be seen as all bad, rejecting, punishing, controlling, and terrifying. The child may fantasize that his expressions of hostility may kill the remaining parent, or that the "bad" parent murdered the dead parent and may do away with the child (1983). If this dynamic persists, the child-parent relationship may become locked in conflict and hostility for many years.

The child's birth order in the family must also be considered. An older child may be neglected when the parent responds to a younger child's greater demands for care and attention. The surviving parent's support system is a crucial variable in mediating distress for the older child. Relatives and friends can offer the school-aged child the attention and care he needs to alleviate the rejection he feels from the grieving parent.

In school, the bereaved child may experience a sense of being "different." Withdrawal by others in the face of death is not unusual, and the child may feel helpless and stigmatized by such a response. The care-seeking behavior that the child demonstrates may bring positive response from some sympathetic adults, but it may also alienate adults and peers who respond to death silently or awkwardly.

Family assessment. Herz (1980) points out that families rarely seek treatment for the grief connected to a recent or past death. Rather, they seek treatment for a problem or dysfunction in a family member or in a relationship. Not infrequently, a school-aged child will present behavioral symptoms either in school or at home.

The Calgary Family Assessment Model (CFAM) (Wright and Leahey, 1984) provides a useful approach for work with families suffering from unresolved grief. The CFAM provides a tool for assessment of the family's developmental stage, internal and external structure, and both instrumental and expressive functioning. As Wright and Leahey (1984) point out, the nurse must determine areas of priority in the assessment process for individual families. In families where a parent has died, the nurse should obtain a presenting problem description and a brief history of the circumstances surrounding the parent's death. Based on these data, the nurse can set priorities for a more extensive assessment. In most families suffering from unresolved grief, the assessment usually focuses on: developmental stage; internal structure, especially subsystem boundaries; and expressive functioning, including emotional communication and alliances/coalitions. Finally, a more detailed account of the parent's death and of the early bereavement period will reveal the family's current level of functioning. Each area of assessment will be described in more detail with suggested questions that the nurse may wish to ask herself or the family members.

Presenting problem. The family with unresolved grief usually seeks treatment for a behavior problem manifested by a child in school, at home, or in the community. Typically, the family will seek treatment about 1½ to 2 years after the bereavement, although as many as 5 to 6 years may have elapsed since the member's death. Questions the nurse might ask are, "What things are happening in your family that you're dissatisfied with?" and "What things would you like to see changed in your family?"

Circumstances surrounding the family member's death. After determining the absent parent's death, the nurse should obtain information about the circumstances of the death. While specific questions about this period in the family's history will yield important information, equally important is the family members' behavior as they respond to the nurse's questions.

Questions to ask the family: How long ago did your spouse die? How did he/she die (cause of death)? How old were the children at that time? Who was available to help your family at that time (family resources)? What was it like for the family after he/she died (initial grieving process)?

Questions to ask yourself: Who answers the questions? What members comfort or soothe each other? If so, who does the comforting, who is the recipient? If the parent becomes distressed, do the children respond with sadness or with activity, such as teasing one another?

Developmental stage. When the grief process over a lost family member has been impeded, the children may behave inappropriately for their developmental stages. Occasionally, the school-aged child may behave precociously; far more frequently, children in families with unresolved grief behave immaturely.

Questions to ask the family: How do the children relate to each other (e.g., sibling rivalry, carrying tales, provoking arguments)? How do they relate to peers? What are their levels of achievement in school? What are their levels of productivity at home? Are they active in community or extracurricular programs? Are there behavior problems, such as bed-wetting, stealing, fire-setting, property abuse or destruction?

Parent development. The nurse should determine the stage of grieving in which the parent may be "stuck." If he or she appears depressed, she should inquire about sleeping problems, appetite disturbance, constipation, and menstrual dysfunction. Cognitive disturbances such as confusion or disorganization might also be evident. Anger at in-laws, health care providers, or school authorities may indicate unresolved grief. Finally, widows frequently experience recurring fantasies about their deceased husbands; they may hear his voice offering advice or comfort. For some women, this can be very disturbing—they may feel that they're losing their grip on reality. In the absence of other indicators of psychopathology, these women need reassurance that their experiences are a natural part of grieving.

Internal structure. Boundaries or "who participates in which subsystems and how" (Minuchin, 1974) may be diffuse or disengaged in families with unresolved grief. Diffuse boundaries may be an indication of over-concern and caretaking among members, or of ongoing conflict between two or more members. Disengagement is manifested by the parent who was oblivious to the child's school or peer-related problems until an outside agency brought it to his or her attention. Both diffuse and disengaged boundary arrangements interfere with a primary function of the family: to promote individual autonomy within a climate of interpersonal sensitivity.

Questions to ask the family: Ask the parent if there is someone he/she can talk to about adult concerns. What opportunities does he/she have to socialize without the children? What chores or responsibilities does the parent expect of the children? Ask the children who they turn to when they feel sad, angry, or upset.

Questions to ask yourself: What indications of autonomy and emotional closeness does this family convey?

Expressive functioning. In families with unresolved grief, the nurse must assess the range of emotional communication within the family. Anger, for example, may be the usual mode of expression among members. Or there may be a difference in relationships; for example, the parent may be able to express concern and caring for a younger child but finds himself/herself locked in conflict with an older child.

Questions to ask yourself: How does the family respond when talking about the deceased member? Do they respond stoically to questions about him or her? Or are they overcome with sadness? Do they seem afraid to discuss their lost member for fear of losing control? Which of the children is most sensitive to the parent's sadness, as demonstrated either through caretaking or misbehaving?

Alliances/coalitions. Wright and Leahey (1984) address the overlap of this assessment category with the structural (boundaries) and developmental categories. In assessing families with unresolved grief, a nurse should look for violations of parent-child boundaries—instances where a child functions as the parent's confidant or caretaker. The nurse should also find out if each child has direct access to the parent without going through an intermediary, such as an older sibling. Finally, there may have evolved an "unholy alliance" between parent and child: the child may have become a "problem" to mobilize the parent out of her depression.

Questions to ask yourself: Is there a child who soothes or distracts the parent when tension escalates? How does the "problem child" behave when you ask the parent questions about the deceased member? Is there an older child who consistently reprimands a younger child for misbehaving?

Planning

When a family seeks treatment for a child's behavior problem, that problem must be attended to before a working relationship between nurse and family can be established (Bowers, 1980). This is equally true for families where the child's behavior problem is linked to unresolved grief. In the author's experience, the children in these families are struggling to establish some degree of certainty in their lives—certainty that they are loved and will be cared for. In the Shannon family, Bonnie Brady's behavior problems reflected the conflict the Shannons experienced in regard to their commitment to her and Steven.

In other families, the surviving parent's own grief may interfere with his/her efforts to make the child feel secure. The systematic identification of problem behaviors and the structuring of contingencies (both limits and rewards) comprise a process that can lead parent and child to communicate more openly.

A second aspect of treatment planning involves helping the family work through its unresolved grief. As the nurse shares her thoughts with the family about the treatment process, she should tell the parent that in future sessions the family will need to talk about the deceased parent. The family will be initially reluctant, but the nurse's willingness to broach the subject reassures the family that its grief can and will be discussed openly.

The timing of sessions is an important consideration. There is support in the literature (Wright and Leahey, 1984; Selvini-Palazzoli, 1980) for spacing sessions 2 or more weeks apart. Many nurses working with families suffering from unresolved grief, however, believe the sessions should be offered weekly. The exploration of painful memories in the second phase of treatment can leave the adult member feeling emotionally "raw." The nurse's availability for weekly meetings and needed phone contact will assure the family members that they will be supported through the grieving process. During this second phase, the nurse may choose to work individually with the grieving adult for several sessions. This is not a contradiction to family intervention, merely one facet of the family intervention process. Similarly, the child himself may benefit from one or more individual sessions. The nurse thus provides a safe environment in which the child can explore frightening ideas and images.

Interventions

Specific interventions can be categorized as direct and indirect (Wright and Leahey, 1984). Direct interventions are appropriate for families who are compliant and motivated to change. Direct interventions in the behavioral domain include asking the parent to keep a record of both the child's problem behavior and the parent's responses to these behaviors to provide baseline data. The next step is to determine alternatives to these behaviors; the nurse may want the parent to try alternative responses to the child's problem behaviors.

Rehearsal within the therapy session enables the nurse to give the parent immediate feedback on necessary behavior changes. For example, after the parent has set new rules and consequences for infractions of those rules, the nurse can show her how to communicate her new expectations to the child. Coaching maneuvers should include helping the parent secure the child's attention; communicating the new guidelines, time constraints and consequences; and having the child repeat what the parent has said. If the child refuses to pay attention, or if the parent undermines her own authority by smiling or saying "Okay?" to the child, the nurse should interrupt and explain how the parent should behave to assure positive outcomes.

When the parent's responses to the child's cues are impaired, the nurse can act as a role model for the parent, demonstrating increased sensitivity and new ways of attending to the child's needs. For example, parents frequently ask their children "why" questions. The nurse can cue the parent to ask questions that the child could answer more easily (instead of, "Why don't you pay attention in class?", the nurse cues the parent to ask, "What do you think/worry about when you're in school?").

Direct cognitive interventions include providing the parent with information about normal growth and development and the ways in which children cope with stressors. This information can be provided in therapy or through recommended readings. Patterson's book, *Living with Children*, (1980), is helpful. In addition, there are several good children's books that deal with death in general and with the death of a family member. (See Grollman, 1976, for an excellent listing based on age of the child.)

In the affective domain, the family needs to talk about the deceased family members. At such moments, the nurse must be comfortable with the expression of sadness, pain, and anger that are part of the grieving process. That is, nurses who engage in this type of therapy need to be comfortable with personal loss before they can help family members deal with their pain and anger. If family members are blocked in their grieving (as indicated by denial, blunted affect, etc.), the nurse may need to focus attention on the death itself and the early bereavement period to produce movement. This should be done supportively, but with the conviction that, despite the pain, it is a necessary part of healing. During this phase of therapy, feelings and fantasies must be validated. As an example of the latter, widowed women report "hallucinating" the presence of their dead spouses (Caine, 1974). Other widows in the author's experience have described an intense sense of loyalty to their deceased spouses that may last for several years. Children report recurring fantasies that their deceased parent lives in another city, or that they are living in a "bad dream" and will "awake in the morning" to find the parent returned and life back to normal. While these are not universal experiences, grieving family members need assurances that they are experiencing normal, common feelings in response to the death of a loved one.

The nurse may wish to model for or cue the parent on how and when to support a child who is struggling with painful feelings. She can do this by helping the parent to encourage the child to talk about missing the deceased parent. For example, statements like, "It hurts to talk about Dad, doesn't it? I really miss him, too," can make the child feel less isolated. The nurse can also suggest that the family bring photographs and other mementos to the session to facilitate this process.

Indirect interventions are appropriate for families with complex problems or families that are rigid and resistive to direct interventions. Indirect interventions include requesting "...the family to do what the nurse does not want them to do" (Wright and Leahey, 1984), such as a paradoxical intervention.

Reframing and positively connoting the child's problem behavior as helpful to the parent or family is one such strategy. For example, in families with unresolved grief, the child's tantrum may distract the parent from sadness about the deceased member. The nurse might say to the parent, "Annie's tantrum is her way of caring about you. She strives to help you not be sad."

Restraining from action is another useful indirect intervention. For example, "Don't make any changes in the house before you've thought out the implications." This restraining message was used with a family where a memorial room was still intact 5 years after the father's death.

Symptom prescription is another type of indirect intervention. In one family where mother/daughter conflict was severe, both parent and child mentioned foster placement as the only solution to their dilemma. In assessing, the nurse reframed their conflict: she said that because they deeply cared for one another, each one was putting too much pressure on the other. The nurse then agreed that they both needed some space and that foster placement was probably the best solution. The mother was then instructed to begin arranging foster placement immediately. At that point in the session, both mother and daughter became confused and angry; the mother abruptly terminated the session and left without making a return appointment. She apologized for her "rude behavior" when she called the next day to schedule a return visit. At the next appointment, both mother and daughter expressed surprise that they could talk out their conflicts and were ready to move on in therapy. Foster placement was not mentioned again as a way out.

Indirect interventions such as these should be used sparingly and only after direct interventions have failed. In addition, such interventions should be well thought out in advance (Weeks and L'Abate, 1982). Inexperienced nurses should use indirect or paradoxical interventions only with the guidance of a supervisor or consultant (Wright and Leahey, 1984).

The nurse may wish to refer the family to other health care professionals or community agencies as an adjunct to the therapy process. If the parent or child appears to be clinically depressed, immediate referral to a physician for evaluation and medication prescription is appropriate. Families with limited financial resources can be referred to local welfare agencies. Where special needs exist, such as respite care for a handicapped child, the nurse may refer the family to a voluntary agency, such as the retarded citizens association, for assistance. The parent may also need help in accessing resources for the child(ren), such as Big Brother or Big Sister associations. Finally, if the nurse decides that she lacks experience in working with grieving families, she should refer the family to another therapist with the necessary skills.

Evaluation

Goldberg (1973) outlines the tasks that the family must accomplish following a member's death. These include:
• Allowing mourning to occur
• Relinquishing the memory of the deceased as a force in family activities
• Realigning intrafamily roles
• Realigning extrafamily roles

The Shannon family's progress through treatment will be used to exemplify these tasks. Both Mr. and Mrs. Shannon had progressed appropriately through the grieving process before coming into therapy. Bonnie's behavior, while problematic, was not seriously disturbed. Steven was doing reasonably well. However, their Aunt Helen's guilt over an unfulfilled promise interfered seriously with her ability to mourn the loss of her "kid sister." Thus, Helen was critical of both the Shannons' parenting skills and of the Brady children's behavior.

It was only after this facet of the mourning process was uncovered that the Shannons made significant progress in treatment. Progress for them meant a willingness, or eagerness, to commit themselves as parents to the Brady children. The adoptive procedure had been stymied for months by Mrs. Shannon's "forgetfulness" and by Mr. Shannon's serious concerns about his ability to support his family financially and emotionally. As he and his wife aligned to confront Helen about her criticism and lack of support, they discovered a new strength in their own partnership, both as spouses and as parents. Strengthened by this new alliance, they explored their options regarding the two Brady children: whether to give them up, go along as they were, or adopt them.

They agreed that the first option was no longer tenable: it would be too painful for all concerned. They decided together, without extended family pressure, that adoption was the only viable choice. Thus, they realigned both intrafamily and extrafamily roles with this decision. No longer were they merely two of several substitute parents to the orphaned children. Instead, they drew the boundary around their family unit and assigned Helen and the other relatives to their appropriate roles as extended family members. Resolution of the grieving process also focused on family rituals such as a visit to the cemetery or selection of mementos before disposing of the deceased member's possessions. The Shannon family's formal adoption of the Brady children and the family celebration to mark the event signified their movement from grieving to a higher level of adaptation.

There are a few reports in the literature on the effectiveness of family intervention for unresolved grief (Gelcer, 1983; Hare-Mustin, 1979; Herz, 1980; Krell and Rabkin, 1974; Tyrell, 1976). These clinical papers document the usefulness of family interventions in resolving what are often long-standing and complex problems. Systematic evaluation of family therapy as the intervention of choice remains to be done. Research is needed that would provide longitudinal data on family outcomes following the death of a parent. Such information would greatly facilitate primary prevention and earlier intervention with bereaved families.

CONCLUSIONS

Our culture has evolved many ways to avoid confrontation with dying and death. The conspiracy of silence and avoidance that surrounds death can prevent the bereaved family from the successful accomplishment of the grieving process, thus impeding the family's and the individual members' adaptation. School-aged children are particularly vulnerable after a parent's death. Their dependency on the surviving parent for both survival and for assistance in coping with their pain may conflict with the parent's own efforts to cope with the loss. This chapter has presented the issues that need to be considered when intervening with a family where unresolved grief is signalled by problem behavior in the school-aged child(ren). The process encompasses three phases: dealing with the problem behaviors, helping the parent to grieve, and resolving the grief process through rituals such as "saying good-bye" to the deceased member. Successful resolution of the grieving process frees the family members to move on to the next level of development.

REFERENCES

Bowers, J.E. "Planning the Therapeutic Process with the Family," in *Family-Focused Care*. Edited by Miller, J.R., and Janosik, E.H. New York: McGraw-Hill Book Co., 1980.

Caine, L. *Widow: The Personal Crisis of a Widow in America*. New York: William Morrow, 1974.

DeVaul, R.A., et al."Clinical Aspects of Grief and Bereavement," *Primary Care* 6(2):391–402, 1979.

Garmezy, N. "Stressors of Childhood," in *Stress, Coping and Development in Children*. Edited by Garmezy, N., and Rutter, M. New York: McGraw-Hill Book Co., 1983.

Gelcer, E. "Mourning is a Family Affair," *Family Process* 22:501–16, 1983.

Glicken, M.D. "The Child's View of Death," *Journal of Marriage and Family Counseling* 4(2):75–81, 1978.

Goldberg, S.B. "Family Tasks and Reactions in the Crisis of Death," *Social Casework* 54(7):398–405, 1973.

Grollman, E.A. *Talking about Death: A Dialogue Between Parent and Child*, rev. ed. Boston: Beacon Press, 1976.

Hare-Mustin, R.T. "Family Therapy Following the Death of a Child," *Journal of Marital and Family Therapy* 5:51–59, 1979.

Herz, F. "The Impact of Death and Serious Illness on the Family Life Cycle," in *The Family Life Cycle: A Framework for Family Therapy*. Edited by Carter, E.A., and McGoldrick, M. New York: Gardner Press, 1980.

Koocher, G.P. "Talking with Children about Death," *American Journal of Orthopsychiatry* 44(3):404–11, 1974.

Krell, R., and Rabkin, L. "The Effects of Sibling Death on the Surviving Child: A Family Perspective," *Family Process* 18:471–77, 1974.

Kübler-Ross, E. *On Death and Dying*. New York: Macmillan Publishing Co., 1969.

Lindemann, E. "Symptomatology and Management of Acute Grief," in *Crisis Intervention: Selected Readings*. Edited by Parad, H.J. New York: Family Service Association of America, 1965.

Minuchin, S. *Families and Family Therapy*. Cambridge, Mass.: Harvard University Press, 1974.

Patterson, G.R. *Living with Children: New Methods for Parents and Teachers*, 3rd ed. Champaign, Ill.: Research Press, 1980.

Raphael, B. *The Anatomy of Bereavement*. New York: Basic Books, 1983.

Selvini-Palazzoli, M. "Why a Long Interval Between Sessions," in *Dimensions of Family Therapy*. Edited by Andolfi, M., and Zwerling, I. New York: Guilford Press, 1980.

Tyrell, R.A. "Counseling a Child and Family Experiencing Parental Loss," *Issues in Comprehensive Pediatric Nursing* 1(4):58–66, 1976.

U.S. Bureau of the Census. *Marital Status & Living Arrangements*. Current Population Reports. Washington, D.C.: U.S. Government Printing Office, March 1983.

Weeks, G.R., and L'Abate, L. *Paradoxical Psychotherapy: Theory and Practice with Individuals, Couples and Families*. New York: Brunner-Mazel, 1982.

Wright, L.M., and Leahey, M. *Nurses and Families: A Guide to Family Assessment and Intervention*. Philadelphia: F.A. Davis Co., 1984.

12 Intervening with families of sexually abused adolescents

Glenda C. Polk, RN, DSN
Associate Dean
College of Nursing
University of North Dakota
Grand Forks, North Dakota

OVERVIEW

This chapter presents information basic to the understanding of sexually abused adolescents and their families. A case illustration presents information necessary for successful assessment, planning, intervention, and evaluation.

CASE STUDY

Alice is an attractive 13-year-old white female who has been sexually abused by her father for the past 9 months. The abuse consisted of kissing, fondling the breast and genital areas, and digital penetration of the vagina. The abuse came to the attention of health care providers when Alice was hospitalized after a suicide attempt involving an overdose of her mother's medication. The initial disclosure of the abuse was to Alice's boyfriend, who threatened to tell Alice's mother, thus precipitating the suicidal behavior. Prior to the suicide attempt, Alice had experienced nightmares and had asked not to be left alone with her father. She displayed extreme reactivity (phobic reaction) to her boyfriend's expression of sexual intimacy (kissing), experienced school problems, and was withdrawing from her friends.

Assessment

Alice is the older of two daughters; her younger sister, Amy, is 5. Alice's mother, Mary Jones, is an attractive, intelligent, articulate 34-year-old housewife who has never worked outside the home. Mary is also the older of two daughters; she describes herself as more passive than her sister and less able to express anger. Mary describes her father as a strong, dominant, authoritative man who had difficulty expressing feelings, especially warmth and caring. Mary's mother came from a wealthy family; she is described as controlling and emotionally distant, especially toward her eldest daughter. Mary recalls a developmental atmosphere without affection, warmth, or overt expressions of love. "It was like living in an emotional vacuum," she said. Mary states that the only emotional warmth she received came from her mother's brother— and that she "worshipped the ground her Uncle Bo walked on; he could do no wrong." However, when Mary was 9 years old, Uncle Bo began sexually abusing her while baby-sitting her and her 4-year-old sister. The abuse consisted of fondling of the breast and genital areas and oral sex, and continued for 5 years. After that time, Mary became concerned that Bo would abuse her sister and told her mother. According to Mary, her mother said she did not believe her. Nevertheless, the uncle was never allowed to be alone with either child again. When Mary was an adult, she learned from her sister that the uncle had abused her also, and that she had also told her mother.

John Jones is a handsome, 37-year-old chemical engineer and lay minister. An only child, he describes his father as extremely strict and authoritarian. Physicial discipline to the point of abuse was common during his childhood. John states that he was always "trying to perform perfectly in order to get (his) father's approval, however nothing was ever enough." He cannot remember his father ever expressing any overt warmth or affection toward him. John describes his mother as affectionate but passive and weak, and his early home environment as extremely "strict and religious," with a strict fundamentalist orientation.

Mary and John married when they were 24 and 21, respectively. Mary Jones was pregnant at the time. John states that he has "never been sure of her love—never sure if she would have married me if she wasn't pregnant." John admits that he always felt that he had to perform financially in order to keep her, and that he was determined to prove to his father and his wife's mother that he "could be a success." Mary describes her husband as domineering, authoritarian, and strict with both her and the children. According to Mary, he has totally controlled all aspects of family life. She characterizes him as "a monkey on a string, always doing something, always performing, but never sharing," and emotionally distant and aloof. Mary reports that she was passive within her marriage prior to Alice's abuse, that she didn't exist as a "total person." "I never had a right to my opinion—he never listened to me," she said.

Three months before Alice was first abused, Mary was diagnosed as having multiple sclerosis. At that time, Alice took on many "parental" roles, including housekeeping and baby-sitting, which were previously fulfilled by her mother; the typical triangle with a parental child emerged. Adding to the existing imbalance of husband/wife power in the marriage was Alice's assumption of the other parental role.

After Alice's suicide attempt and hospitalization, her boyfriend told her mother about the abuse. Mary confronted her husband, who did not deny the accusation. Alice confirmed the sexual abuse and the case was reported to the Department of Human Services and the police. Mr. Jones was asked to leave the home and Mrs. Jones provided support and nurturance to her daughter. A comprehensive assessment was conducted to ascertain the nature and duration of the abuse. This was essential; even though Mr. Jones had pleaded guilty to the charges, other siblings or children might have been abused. Through a criminal diversion program, Mr. Jones was ordered into treatment for an unspecified time.

Intervention

Individual therapy. Since all members of an incestuous family are needy during the crisis surrounding disclosure, individual treatment was provided for John, Mary, Alice, and Amy. Individual therapy focused on individually pertinent themes and issues. John Jones' therapy focused on his obsessive-compulsive personality and his need to control and perform. Themes included feelings of insecurity and inadequacy, fears of intimacy and rejection, and finding ways to identify and appropriately cope with stress. Mary's therapy focused on her dependent and histrionic personality, and explored her emotional reactivity and feelings of inadequacy as a person, mother, and wife. Therapy focused on empowering Mary as a person and parent by helping her confront her own victimization and the feelings of powerlessness, rage, and anger it had aroused over time. Other themes included the anger, rage, and sense of betrayal she felt toward her husband and her daughter. Her anger toward John, it was determined, stemmed directly from the abuse; in addition, Mary was angry with her daughter for not trusting her enough to ask for her help.

Alice needed to deal with anger and rage regarding the abuse and the breaking of father-daughter trust; her feelings included responsibility and guilt, confusion about sexual identity and intimacy, and anger toward her mother for lack of protection. Amy, the youngest daughter, also suffered from the incest; her father, whom she adored, was removed from the home and Alice continued to receive much special attention. Consequently, Amy needed reality testing, i.e., explanations about what was occurring and what her role in the family's recovery process was, as well as a safe place to vent her feelings of anger and jealousy toward Alice. Amy was also provided preventive educational information regarding sexual abuse. Hopefully, this last intervention would help her resist any future attempts at abuse by her father or anyone else.

Group therapy. In addition to the individual therapy, John Jones was placed in an offenders' group. Mary was placed in an adult incest survivors' group rather than a nonabusing spouse group; it was believed that she would have to deal with her own victimization before she could successfully assist in her daughter's recovery. Alice was placed in an adolescent incest group. In individual therapy, she had refused to deal with many critical emotional issues. It was hoped that a group of individuals who had experienced similar events would provide a safe environment for externalization of her feelings.

Marital therapy. Therapy involving various family subunits was also instituted. At the time of this writing, the husband/wife dyad was in treatment. The issues dealt with included mutual rage and anger about the abuse and the complete lack of trust and sexual intimacy. The lack of sexual intimacy stemmed primarily from Mary's own abuse and her paratactic projection of Bo upon John (at one point Mary called her husband Bo). The therapy also focused on Mr. Jones' anger toward his wife about her abuse, about her illness, and about his fear that she would leave him by dying. Other marital issues involved communication patterns, issues of control and power, and fears of rejection.

Parent-child therapy. Alice and Mary have been seen conjointly, primarily to resolve persistent anger. Alice remains angry about her mother's MS and afraid that Mary will die and leave her. Additional rage stems from Alice's perceptions that the MS put her in a position in which she could be abused and that her mother failed to protect her.

Mary, on the other hand, remains angry that her daughter did not trust her enough to tell her about the abuse, and therefore prevented her from stopping it. Part of Mary's anger, however, stemmed from her own victimization. By saying that it is easier for a 13-year-old than a 9-year-old to stop abusive behavior, she projected some of her own guilt and sense of responsibility for her own victimization onto her daughter. In addition, Mary is angry that Alice hasn't recognized how supportive she has been—unlike Mary's mother—and said at one point, "I wish my mother had been there for me like I have been for you."

Alice has been seen by the therapist conjointly with her father, but she could not confront him with any of her pain, rage, or resentment at being used. John has assumed full responsibility for the sexual abuse and has often attempted to ask forgiveness, only to be stopped by the nurse therapist. Asking the victim's forgiveness before she has had the opportunity to deal with all of her underlying anger and rage often points the way for revictimization. The offender is asking for something the victim is not ready or willing to give, which may trigger guilt feelings the abused client is ill-equipped to handle.

Evaluation

Within the Jones family, the marital dyad has begun to change its communication pattern. Although John and Mary are living apart, both are communicating their expectations and needs more directly and honestly. Both appear to be at a higher level of differentiation of self from family of origin, as evidenced by decreased emotional reactivity. Mary and John are aware of how Alice became triangled into marital issues and they have successfully prevented its recurrence. They have resumed sexual intercourse and Mary reports more satisfaction in their sexual relations than ever before. There has been a redistribution of power—albeit a somewhat problematic one—with Mary assuming a more powerful, assertive role as both spouse and parent. Both Alice and John have had difficulty with this redistribution. At times, John's feelings of inadequacy and powerlessness have had to be addressed by the nurse therapist, and Alice has resisted giving up some of the secondary gains of the parental child role. Mary has also been frightened by the sense of adequacy, assertiveness, and power that her new choices have given her. Mary states, "I'm just beginning to grow up and discover who I am." John and Mary are beginning to know each other as individuals and not as the roles they've played for 13 years. At this point, reconciliation is a choice that is being kept open by both.

Both Mary and Alice have just touched the surface of the feelings surrounding their victimizations. Mary has expressed and worked through many of her feelings toward the current abuse. Alice can confront her mother with her anger but not her father; her behavioral symptoms have abated. John has begun to verbalize and work through his anger towards his wife regarding her victimization and illness. However, he still has difficulty expressing feelings. It is hoped that group therapy will stimulate a move toward resolution.

In summary, this family has participated in a varied treatment program for more than 8 months. However, extensive group and family work will be needed to resolve the problems created by the sexual abuse.

NURSING PROCESS

Assessment

The health problem: Adolescent sexual abuse.
Incidence. One in four female children in the U.S. will be sexually abused before the age of 18. Estimates of the incidence of male victimization in the U.S. range from one in seven to one in four (Campbell and Humphreys, 1984); it is hypothesized that male children and adolescents, who may adhere to various male stereotypes, are less likely to report such incidents. Another difficulty in determining the

incidence of sexual abuse lies in the inconsistent definition of the term and differing mechanisms for reporting such abuse to authorities. While exact numbers are not available, it is known that most sexual offenders are family members (intrafamilial abuse) or are otherwise known to the victim (Kempe and Kempe, 1984; Campbell and Humphreys, 1984). For the purposes of this chapter, the terms intrafamilial sexual abuse and incest will be used synonymously. In addition, since most cases of sexual abuse involve family members or trusted friends, this chapter will only address those aspects of sexual abuse.

The average incest victim is first abused at age 8, and the abuse continues for an average of 5 to 7 years (Kempe and Kempe, 1984; Campbell and Humphreys, 1984; Blink, 1985; Stanford, 1985). According to Blink (1985), the average number of sexual abuse experiences per child is 530. Eight years is the *average* age of initial victimization; children as young as 6 months have been sexually abused (Kempe and Kempe, 1984). Thus, incest often begins while the child is in the developmental stage of initiative vs. guilt and continues through the stages of industry vs. inferiority and identity vs. identity confusion (Muuss, 1975).

Definitions and family dynamics. Definitions of sexual abuse include the following:
• The involvement of dependent, developmentally immature children and adolescents in sexual activities that they do not fully comprehend and to which they cannot give informed consent or that violate the social taboos of family roles (Schechter and Roberge, 1976).
• The sexual use of a child/adolescent by an adult for sexual gratification without consideration of the child's psychosocial sexual development (Mrazek and Kempe, 1981).

According to Burgess (cited in Campbell and Humphreys, 1984), critical dynamics in incestuous families are a breach of parent-child trust, power misuse, and imbalance. According to Finkelhor (1983), *all* forms of family abuse, including sexual, share common features.

Abuse of power. Abuse gravitates toward the relationships of greatest power differential (Finkelhor, 1979, 1982, 1983). In sexual abuse, the most widespread form involves male abusers who are authority figures within the family and who victimize girls in subordinate positions—abuse across unequal sexual (males victimizing females) and generational (adult-child) lines. Abuse of boys by males appears to be less common and abuse of either boys or girls by female family members is reportedly rare (Finkelhor, 1983) but is increasing.

Abuse as a response to perceived powerlessness. Offenders often abuse children sexually in an attempt to compensate for feelings of powerlessness (Finkelhor, 1983).

Effects on victims. Victims of long-term abuse report surprisingly
similar patterns: low self-esteem, self-contempt, depression, suicidal
feelings, and an inability to trust and develop intimate relationships
in later life (Herman and Hirschman, 1977). According to Finkelhor
(1983) all forms of family abuse involve the abuser's use of power
and family connection to control and manipulate victims' perceptions of
reality. Victims tend to blame themselves rather than the offender;
indeed, many maintain an incredible allegiance to the abuser. In addition, many sexual abuse victims insist that they are more angry with
their mothers for not protecting them than at the relative or friend
who abused them (Herman and Hirschman, 1977). Other common
patterns among abuse victims are extreme shame, humiliation, and the
belief that others cannot identify with or understand them. There is
also a kind of entrapment, resulting from the combination of low heir-
archical status, lack of social support, and the potent ideology of family
interdependence and loyalty, that virtually immobilizes victims.

Developmental implications. Incest disrupts the established trust-
mistrust equilibrium at the base of Erickson's first phase of development. Consequently, the very foundation of the child's ability to relate
to others is ripped away. In addition, the first level of Maslow's hier-
archy of needs is threatened—incest is an invasion of not only emotional but also physical space, undermining the victim's search for
physical safety.

The typical offender's threats of physical harm or family dissolution
should the child reveal the incest place the child-victim in a no-win
situation. Telling will harm the self or others, but keeping the secret
will lead to feelings of guilt which interfere with successful completion
of developmental tasks; the general result is difficulty with the next
developmental level, industry vs. inferiority. It is little wonder that
incest victims enter adolescence with profound role confusion and self-
doubt, low self-esteem, and reluctance to trust others and establish
relationships.

Abuse-related dysfunction. Finkelhor and Browne (1985) identify a
typology of four dysfunctional areas associated with child sexual abuse:
sexualization; stigmatization; betrayal; and powerlessness. The typology enables care providers to identify major interventional needs and
understand the dynamics and themes involved in this kind of trauma.
In addition, the typology lists behavioral manifestions (see Table 12.1)
indicative of areas of dysfunction, which are useful during the assessment phase.

Using this typology, Alice could be assessed as having:
• Dysfunction in the area of sexualization as evidenced by phobic
reactions to sexual intimacy related to sexual abuse

Table 12.1 Finkelhor and Browne's (1985) Typology of Abuse-Related Dysfunctions

Area of dysfunction	Behavioral manifestations
Sexualization	• Sexual preoccupation/compulsive sexual behaviors • Precocious/aggressive sexual behaviors • Promiscuity • Prostitution • Avoidance of/phobic reactions to sexual intimacy • Sexual dysfunction • Inappropriate sexualization of parenting
Stigmatization	• Self-isolation • Vulnerability to revictimization • Drug/alcohol abuse • Self-mutilation • Suicide (or attempt)
Betrayal	• Marital/relationship problems • Self-isolation • Suicide (or attempt) • Vulnerability to exploitation • Aggressiveness • Delinquency
Powerlessness	• Nightmares • Phobias • Somatic complaints • Eating/sleeping disorders • School problems • Delinquency • Withdrawal • Re-enaction of abuse • Later victimization

• Dysfunction in the area of betrayal as evidenced by suicide attempt and extreme difficulty in trusting authority figures as related to sexual abuse

• Dysfunction in the area of powerlessness as evidenced by nightmares, withdrawal from friends, school problems, and phobic reactions related to sexual abuse

Blink (1985) has listed seven direct clues to sexual abuse. These include:
• Verbal statement
• Observation
• Physical injury to genital area—bruising, laceration, fissures, tears
• One or more pregnancies at an early age
• Gastrointestinal complaints, burning on urination, and frequency
• Hickeys, love bites, sucker bites or marks
• Venereal disease

Campbell and Humphreys (1984) identify several factors other than direct and behavioral indicators that need to be addressed in any assessment. These include health and developmental—especially psychosexual—histories of all family members, histories of families of origin, communication patterns, and power distribution.

In addition to the previously described assessment indicators, a complete physical examination is necessary. The physical exam (a) collects evidence for possible criminal proceedings, and (b) determines if medical care (i.e., treatment of venereal infection) is needed. Despite attempts to collect physical evidence to corroborate sexual abuse charges, physical evidence is usually present in only 10% to 15% of the cases (Blink, 1985). The physical exam should include an assessment of all major systems with particular attention to the mouth, throat, genitourinary, and rectal areas.

If physical indications of sexual abuse are found, the victim should be questioned in as nonthreatening and supportive a way as possible. The nurse should allow victims to tell the facts in their own way and not pressure or coerce them to respond. She should record assessment findings in detail using the victim's exact terminology; this information will be important in any investigative and/or criminal proceedings. Regardless of whether the client confirms or denies sexual abuse, an assessment indicating its possible occurrence must be reported to the appropriate agencies for investigation, confirmation, and, if necessary, prosecution.

The abuser. Long-term intervention for the offender usually depends on whether he is incarcerated or made available for treatment. Proper assessment is needed to determine the individual's suitability for treatment. An abuser is usually considered a poor treatment risk if any or a combination of the following are present: denial of the sexual abuse; use of violence or force in the sexual abuse; history of other sexual abuse; or history of violence or other antisocial behavior.

Groth (1979) has developed a typology of pedophilia with two classifications, fixated and regressed. The fixated more closely fits the diagnostic criteria for pedophile than the regressed, since the regressed's sexual orientation is usually age-mate. Thus, for the purposes of this chapter, a continuum of sexual offenders (see Table 12.2) will be utilized with fixated at one end of the continuum and regressed at the other.

The fixated sexual offender is an extremely poor treatment risk because of his chronic, obsessive-compulsive behavior and characteristic immaturity. The fixated offender often views himself as a child and views the victim as a child. It is difficult for such an offender to recognize the imbalance of power between abuser and victim, or to understand that his actions constitute abuse.

Table 12.2   Groth's (1979) Typology of Pedophilia

Fixated	Regressed
• Orientation toward children	• Orientation toward adults
• Adolescent onset	• Adult onset
• No precipitating stress	• Precipitating stress
• Compulsive behavior	• Episodic abuse (no compulsive behavior)
• Premeditation	• No premeditation
• No age-mate sexual contact	• Age-mate sexual contact
• Male victims (usually)	• Female victims (usually)
• Maladaptive resolution of life issues	• Maladaptive attempts to cope with specific life stresses

Mr. Jones was assessed as a regressed sexual offender. His primary sexual orientation was to adults and there was a precipitating stress (Mary's MS). The offense was a substitution for the conflict-filled marital relationship and an attempt to cope with the stress. In addition, no violence or force was utilized, no history of prior abuse was noted, and Mr. Jones assumed full responsibility for the abuse and expressed regret and guilt. Consequently, Mr. Jones was assessed as a good candidate for treatment.

Planning

Planning the care of a sexual abuse victim and family usually involves multiple agencies and disciplines. The nurse therapist should confer with all those involved in the treatment to ensure comprehensive and consistent care for everyone who requires it. Involved agencies may include the school system, police, Department of Human Services, the Rape and Sexual Abuse Center, and the hospital or physician's office. Among the first steps in planning are identification of all appropriate agencies and development of a method of collaboration. Next, the nurse therapist must identify short- and long-term goals.

Intervention

Short-term interventive goals include:
• Medical care for any physical trauma
• Protection of the victim from continued abuse
• Protection of society (i.e., other children) from the unrehabilitated abuser
• Psychological support (crisis intervention) for victim, nonabusing spouse, and siblings.

In addition, the victim needs to be cultured for venereal disease and tested for possible pregnancy.

Intervention for the abused adolescent. To protect the abused youth from further victimization, (a) the offender must be removed from the home, and (b) a child ally, hopefully the mother, must be identified. Removing the offender from the home serves at least two purposes. First, it places physical distance between victim and offender, thereby decreasing the possibility of continued abuse and removing the offender's opportunity to coerce the victim into recanting or retracting charges. Secondly, removal returns the balance of power to the nonabusing parental figure and forces the victim to reestablish a relationship with the nonabusing parent.

To accomplish this second end, the nonabusing spouse must become the victim's ally. Thus, an assessment of the nonabusing spouse's ability to do so must be conducted. Assessment cues include:
• Empathy/supportiveness toward the victim
• Willingness to place responsibility on the offender
• Belief in the victim
• Externalization of anger toward the offender
• Appropriate, moderate affective response

If the nonabusing spouse exhibits anger or ambivalence towards the victim's role in the abuse, removing the victim from the house should be considered. However, such feelings are not necessarily grounds for removal; crisis intervention may help the nonabusing spouse overcome them and function successfully as an ally.

When the victim is removed from the home, the offender must also be removed. Otherwise, the victim will feel that she alone is being punished. Also, if only the victim is removed, the family will have an opportunity to reestablish its boundaries and homeostasis without her, making later reentry much more difficult.

Family intervention. Crisis intervention at the point of disclosure and initial investigation helps all family members deal with the emotional impact of disclosure. For example, the nurse therapist should encourage the victim to verbalize her hurt, anger, rage, shame, and guilt, then help her differentiate areas of responsibility for the incest. Placing responsibility for the incest on the adult helps the victim set aside internal feelings of guilt and shame. The nonabusing spouse should also verbalize negative feelings and differentiate areas of responsibility; both victim and nonabusing spouse should try to explore all available options.

The task of decision-making may seem overwhelming to the victim and the nonabusing spouse. Therefore, the nurse must instill in them a sense of competence and power—a confidence in their abilities—to cope and make decisions. This can be achieved by reinforcing decision-making and by guiding them through progressively more complex decisions.

As a rule, all members of an incestuous family are emotionally needy. Consequently, individual crisis intervention is the treatment of choice.

The most successful interventions provide emotional support and a safe environment for ventilating the strong emotions accompanying incest: anger, rage, rejection, hurt, guilt, powerlessness, and feelings of inadequacy. In addition, crisis intervention should help individuals make their own decisions. Many nonabusing spouses, for instance, have been so dependent and accustomed to the offender's authoritative rule, that they are overwhelmed by the decisions they now face.

Finkelhor (1985) describes four preconditions for sexual abuse which can complicate treatment: the motivation to sexually abuse; predisposition to overcome internal inhibitions; predisposition to overcome external inhibitors; and predisposition to overcome the adolescent's resistance.

The first precondition includes three factors that affect the motivation to sexually abuse: emotional congruence, sexual arousal, and blockage. Emotional congruence is the adult's ability to find emotional satisfaction in a relationship with a youth. The individual dynamics involved here may include arrested development, low self-esteem, and narcissistic identification with the child. Sexual arousal is the individual's ability to be aroused by fantasies of sex with children. The dynamics involved may include an arousing childhood experience, a traumatic childhood sexual experience, early modeling by others, misattribution of arousal, and biological abnormality. Some adults have experienced powerful erotic experiences in childhood which remain imprinted on their sexual arousal pattern (Groth, 1979). Men who have been sexually abused as children sometimes repeat their initial victimization in an attempt to master their own pain and powerlessness. Blockage is the individual's ability to internally control the impulse to sexually abuse children.

Factors predisposing the abuser to overcome internal inhibitors include an impulse disorder, senility, alcoholism, psychosis, and situational stress. Factors predisposing a potential offender to overcome external inhibitors include: mother absence, illness or powerlessness, a history of poor mother/child relations, paternal domination in the family of origin, social isolation, and opportunity to be alone with a child. Predisposing factors for overcoming a child's resistance include emotional insecurity, lack of knowledge, trust between child and offender, and coercion.

In a comprehensive treatment program, all four of these preconditions must be addressed. Both individual and group offender therapy must address the various motivations for sexual abuse; individual therapy, often with a behavioral approach, helps modify the sexual arousal pattern; individual, group, and family therapy all focus on helping the offender develop nonabusive internal control mechanisms for coping with stress. If they are present, drug and alcohol problems must also be treated, but always within the context of anti-abuse treatment.

Otherwise one will have nothing more than a sober sex offender. Family therapy focuses on the dynamics previously discussed, working closely with those family subunits that contribute to dysfunction within the unit.

EVALUATION

The process of evaluation is an ongoing endeavor. Treatment outcomes for the offender, victim, and nonabusing spouse are based on the previously described dynamics. Tables 12.3 through 12.7 list numerous indicators of successful treatment outcomes for the family, the couple, the offender, the victim, and the nonabusing spouse (Gentry, 1983).

Table 12.3   Indicators of Successful Treatment Outcomes for the Family of a Sexually Abused Adolescent*

- Sex abuse stops and does not recur.
- Parents learn to control their own actions and take responsibility for family functioning.
- Rules regarding privacy and sexual issues are made and followed.
- Family members can recognize the difference between privacy and secrecy concerning sexuality and other issues.
- The family can resolve problems effectively.
- The enmeshed family permits members to individuate.
- Support systems, e.g., extended family, schools, churches, social agencies, etc., are being utilized.
- The family develops, implements, and evaluates appropriate child management techniques.
- Family members can effectively communicate problems and needs among themselves.
- Role-reversal is minimized.
- Family members support the victim.
- Family members no longer deny sexual abuse.
- The family demonstrates a clear understanding of sex and sexuality.
- All members realize that sexual abuse may be harmful to their emotional health and legal status.
- The family can set and maintain limits.
- There is realization and acceptance of the damage of sexual abuse to the victims and the family—no defensive minimization.
- To the best of its ability, the family assumes financial responsibility for treatment.
- Social interaction increases.
- There is a change in the family patterns which precipitated sexual abuse.
- Family communication skills increase, i.e., conversation.
- Intrafamily competition is minimized.
- Members recognize the impact of one family member/thing/behavior on another.
- The possibility of sexual dysfunction has been explored and resolved.
- The family no longer projects blame for its problems onto the "system."
- Family members require and utilize such strengths as good health, education, job skills, and nurturing capacities.
- If alcohol has been a problem, consumption is under control, ie., temperance or abstinence.
- The family can deal with members as individuals and not internalize everyone's life situation.

*Used with permission. Charles Gentry, The Knoxville Institute for Sexual Abuse Training, Knoxville, Tennessee, June 1983.

Table 12.4   Indicators of Successful Treatment Outcomes for the Abusing and Nonabusing Spouse*

- The couple recognizes the need for consistency (i.e., in discipline, temperament) and its maintenance.
- Parents assume appropriate roles.
- Parents have taken care of "unfinished business" with (feelings about) their own parents.
- Adult partners have a satisfying or improving sexual/psychological/communicative relationship, whether they divorce or stay together.
- The parents begin to work as a team in handling family affairs.
- Both parents recognize the right to make decisions and choices in the marriage (including the decision that life with this spouse, in this particular way, is not the only choice).
- Children assume appropriate roles and are no longer parenting the parents.
- The perpetrator and spouse have learned how to ask for and obtain nurturance and support from each other.
- Parents have made reasonable progress toward individuation from their family of origin.
- The father and mother have verbally and emotionally absolved victim(s) of all blame for the abuse.

*Used with permission. Charles Gentry, The Knoxville Institute for Sexual Abuse Training, Knoxville, Tennessee, June 1983.

Table 12.5   Indicators of Successful Treatment Outcomes for the Sexually Abusive Adult*

The abuser:

- Makes restitution and apologizes to the victim(s) for the abuse.
- Accepts responsibility for own actions.
- Identifies situations which stimulate inappropriate impulses, and has mastered techniques for handling impulse aggravation and loss of control.
- Has reasonable cognitive knowledge of both male and female sexual anatomy and physiology.
- Has identified own arousal pattern, has formulated and implemented a plan to decrease and/or alter the pattern, and has had that plan evaluated.
- Accepts responsibility for own thoughts and actions and can discriminate between thoughts and actions (fantasy vs. reality).
- Is establishing appropriate relationships with adult members of the opposite sex.
- Demonstrates a healthy self-image.
- Recognizes the potential and/or actual harm caused by sexual abuse.
- Sees self as an adult—as parent to own child and not as a peer.
- Has, over an extended period of time, identified traumatic or conflict-producing developmental issues and, with help, has developed, implemented, and evaluated a treatment plan.
- Is aware of own needs and how to meet them—realizes the nature of feelings and how to express them effectively.
- Recognizes whatever sexual abuse might have occurred during own childhood and understands the resulting confusion and anger.
- Does not use "kiddie porn" to become sexually aroused.
- Has a realistic view of family life.
- Admits that sexual abuse occurred.   *(continued)*

Table 12.5 Indicators of Successful Treatment Outcomes for the Sexually Abusive Adult (continued)

The abuser:

● Submits to multidisciplinary review to determine if the inappropriate sexual arousal pattern has been altered or eliminated.

● Has identified fantasies and thoughts that have supported sexual maladjustment and, with the therapist's assistance, has developed, implemented, and evaluated a specific plan to extinguish them.

● No longer abuses any child or adolescent.

*Used with permission. Charles Gentry, The Knoxville Institute for Sexual Abuse Training, Knoxville, Tennessee, June 1983

Table 12.6 Indicators of Successful Treatment Outcomes for the Victim of Sexual Abuse*

The victim:

● Can make decisions independently and recognizes the right and reason to do so.

● Demonstrates self-enhancing, as opposed to self-destructive behaviors and choices.

● Seems to have a positive self-image.

● Can view the offender as an individual without generalizing and projecting feelings derived from the abuse to all members of that sex.

● Feels minimal guilt about the abuse.

● Realizes that she is not to blame for the sexual abuse.

● Understands that anger is acceptable.

● Displays minimal symptoms.

● Is more assertive; recognizes the right to protect herself.

● Recognizes that she has personal needs and can fulfill them in legal, adaptive, and nonharmful ways.

● Can experience meaningful, appropriate relationships with members of both sexes.

● No longer feels that victimization is inevitable.

● Has replaced fear with feelings of anger.

● Has a sense of the universality of her experience and knows that she is not the only one this has happened to.

● Attends school or has a viable life plan.

● Realizes that she has power over her body and a choice of when, where, and with whom to be sexual.

● Uses the natural and social environments to enhance survival skills (in the absence of parental help).

● Recognizes that parents have limitations.

● Recognizes and expresses feelings of anger, betrayal, and disappointment.

● Can say "no" and report reabuse.

● No longer hates her own body.

● Accepts own mistakes without being excessively self-punitive.

● Recognizes, experiences, differentiates, and identifies feelings; uses feelings as a base for understanding self and others.

*Used with permission. Charles Gentry, The Knoxville Institute for Sexual Abuse Training, Knoxville, Tennessee, June 1983.

Table 12.7   Indicators of Successful Treatment Outcomes for the Nonabusing Spouse*

The nonabusing spouse:

- Does not feel she is the "property" of the spouse, or that children are "property."
- Assumes the role of woman in the household.
- Will listen to and protect her children from further misuse.
- No longer blames the victim(s); in fact, absolves victim(s).
- Has expressed and resolved jealousy toward the child who received the sexual attention she deserved.
- Has become assertive and does not accept sexual abuse for any reason.
- Has a positive self-image, e.g., confidence about intelligence, overall skills, ability to defend beliefs, sexual desirability, interpersonal skills, etc.
- Decreases use of somatization (if present previously).
- Enjoys relationship with and being a role model for children/adolescents.
- Demonstrates good reciprocal communication with children/adolescents.
- Is supportive of victim.
- Enjoys sexual intercourse.
- Can solve problems.
- Has and uses a support system of friends and/or organizations.
- Can discipline adolescents appropriately.
- Can send and receive open, honest communication.
- Expresses and uses anger appropriately.

*Used with permission. Charles Gentry, The Knoxville Institute for Sexual Abuse Training, Knoxville, Tennessee, June 1983.

CONCLUSIONS

Incest involves the total family unit, not just the victim and the offender. All family members inevitably suffer. Treatment must be truly comprehensive, offering multiple treatment modalities.

REFERENCES

Blink, L. Presentation at the Child Welfare League of America Conference. Gatlinburg, Tenn., May 1985.

Burgess, A. "Intrafamilial Sexual Abuse," in *Nursing Care of Victims of Family Violence.* Edited by Campbell, J., and Humphreys, J., Reston, Va.: Reston Publishing Co., 1984.

Campbell, J. and Humphreys, J. *Nursing Care of Victims of Family Violence.* Reston, Va.: Reston Publishing Co., 1984.

Finkelhor, D. "Common Features of Family Abuse," in *The Dark Side of Families: Current Family Violence Research.* Edited by Finkelhor, D., et al. Beverly Hills, Calif.: Sage Publications, 1983.

Finkelhor, D. "Sexual Abuse: A Sociological Perspective," *Child Abuse and Neglect,* 6:94-102, 1982.

Finkelhor, D. *Sexually Victimized Children.* New York: Free Press, 1979.

Finkelhor, D., and Browne, A. Presentation at the Child Welfare League of America Conference. Gatlinburg, Tenn., May 1985.

Gentry, C. Workshop Information, Child and Family Services of Knox County, Inc. Knoxville, Tenn., July 1983.

Groth, N. *Men Who Rape.* New York: Plenum Press, 1979.

Herman, J., and Hirschman, L. "Father-Daughter Incest," *Signs* 2:1-22, 1977.

Kempe, R., and Kempe, H. *The Common Secret: Sexual Abuse of Children and Adolescents.* New York: W.H. Freeman Co., 1984.

Mrazek, P.B., and Kempe, C.H., eds. *Sexually Abused Children and Their Families.* New York: Pergamon Press, 1981.

Muuss, R. *Theories of Adolescence.* New York: Random House, 1975.

Schechter, M.D., and Roberge, L. "Sexual Exploitation," in *Child Abuse and Neglect: The Family and the Community.* Edited by Helter, R.E., and Kempe, C.H. Cambridge, Mass.: Ballinger, 1976.

Stanford, L. Presentation at Assessment and Treatment of Juvenile and Adult Sex Offenders Workshop. Nashville, Tenn., June 3, 1985.

13 Intervening with families of adolescents with bulimia

Jo Ann Futrell, RN, MN
Clinical Nurse Specialist
Psychiatric/ Mental Health
Baptist Medical Center
Columbia, South Carolina

Carol Romick Collison, RN, PhD, CS
Associate Professor
College of Nursing
University of South Carolina
Columbia, South Carolina

OVERVIEW

The chapter presents a case study of a family with a bulimic adolescent and compares it with findings about similar families. Conceptually based on developmental, family systems, crisis, and stress theories, the suggested therapeutic process employs both the nursing process and a family systems approach. A variety of nursing roles are suggested to prevent the disorder and to help diagnosed bulimics and their families.

CASE STUDY

The family consists of Mr. and Mrs. Milanio, both age 51, and their 18-year-old daughter, Laura. The older daughter, Wendy, age 26 and married for 4 years, lives outside the home.

Laura was brought to therapy by her mother after a suicide attempt. She ingested a bottle of Tylenol and was taken to the emergency room where her stomach was pumped. She was seen there by her family doctor, who pronounced her physically sound but suggested counseling. Laura presented with symptoms of depression and guilt, because it is against her family's religious beliefs to take one's life.

Assessment

Laura described herself as an unhappy person, dissatisfied with her life. She had graduated from high school 3 months prior to initial contact with the nurse therapist and had recently moved into a dorm to begin her freshman year at college. 40 miles from home. Her boyfriend had just left for a university 200 miles away. Laura claimed no close friends other than her boyfriend, and said she had great difficulty opening up to anyone about her feelings. She said she did not feel close to anyone in her family, especially her parents, but did feel more accepted by her sister and grandmother. Her grandmother's acceptance, however, was a double-edged sword; Laura compared herself unfavorably to her grandmother, whose psychiatric history included depression and a suicide attempt.

Laura described a pattern of several months' duration in which tension built up and led her to act impulsively when she could not find an appropriate outlet. Indeed, this pattern had led to her suicide attempt. She had been unhappy because her family and grandmother left her alone to attend a church meeting. Although she was asked to attend with them and refused, she was angry with them for leaving her.

After Laura's suicide attempt, the family insisted that she move back home temporarily because they did not want her to be alone. She had already been coming home every weekend since enrolling in college and her mother had visited her twice to shop for items for her dorm room.

After talking with Laura, the nurse arranged a session with her and her parents. Mrs. Milanio seemed concerned about her daughter. She noted that Laura kept things to herself; she also appeared resentful that she was shut out of parts of her daughter's life. However, she also had established rigid rules and regulations controlling Laura's behavior. Laura had indicated earlier that Christian beliefs and morality regulated behavior in her family, and Mrs. Milanio appeared to be the rule maker and enforcer of these beliefs. She seemed unaware of Laura's conflict regarding these beliefs; she was also unaware that, by doing as her parents dictated and playing the good child to gain her parents' approval, Laura was suppressing her own feelings.

Mr. Milanio was concerned about his daughter but he was less involved with her problems and the family itself than was his wife. In fact, he said he could not participate regularly in future family sessions because his work schedule often kept him out of town and made advance planning impossible; he agreed, however, to come when he could. Mr. Milanio seemed committed to his career and content to let his wife manage affairs at home. On the surface, he appeared to support Mrs. Milanio's handling of Laura and to accept a secondary parenting role. However, in later sessions, mental conflict and his overriding authority in the family surfaced. Ultimately, Mr. Milanio expressed regret at his distant relationship with Laura.

The therapy contract called for family sessions that would include Mrs. Milanio and Laura, and Mr. Milanio when he was in town. Also scheduled were individual sessions with Laura, which would be conducted within a family systems framework.

During an individual session, Laura's bulimia was revealed. The initial mention was casual—"I sometimes overeat and then vomit"—and came after several weeks of weekly individual sessions. Further exploration revealed that the girl had always feared becoming overweight like her sister, who was indeed obese. In fact, Laura considered herself chubby, although she did not appear to be, and wanted to lose weight. She carried a calorie counter and monitored her food intake, making a conscious effort to control her appetite. However, just before graduating from high school, she began to experience periods of binge eating in response to stress. A typical binge might include one dozen doughnuts, five candy bars, three bags of potato chips, several packages of crackers, a submarine sandwich, a banana split, and three Cokes.

It would be followed by self-induced vomiting in an attempt to maintain normal weight. These binge-purge episodes occurred in secret when Laura was lonesome, angry, or both, and were followed by periods of depression and guilt. Laura was concerned about her behavior and wanted to stop, but she could not control herself. On the average, she experienced these episodes every two weeks.

Originally, the suicide attempt and other symptoms led the nurse therapist to focus on Laura's depression. However, when the bulimia was revealed, it became the primary concern. The precipitating factors in the onset of the condition were: unhealthy family dynamics, leaving Laura with excessive dependency needs, poor individuation and low self-esteem, as well as inadequate coping mechanisms (impulse control, tension release, and conflict resolution); and her anticipated and actual movement out of the family system to college, which activated existing intrapsychic conflicts.

Enmeshment, rigidity, overprotectiveness, and inadequate conflict resolution were the family's primary systemic problems; all are typical in families of the psychosomatically ill (Minuchin et al., 1978).

The Milanio family was assessed through assembly of a family history and interviews in which each member described the family's problems from his perspective. The family and nurse therapist set mutually agreeable goals; progress toward them was continuous. The individual therapeutic course also began with the collection of a history (Laura's). Goals were set collaboratively and ongoing evaluation initiated. Therapy continued for 9 months, throughout Laura's freshman year of college.

NURSING PROCESS

Assessment

The health problem: Bulimia
Bulimia. The pursuit of thinness enthralls contemporary American society. In 45% of U.S. households, someone diets during the course of a year (Medical World News, 1984), and countless goods and products are available to those who want to reshape their bodies. Health spas, fat farms, and weight clubs such as TOPS and Weight Watchers are a dime a dozen, all offering the opportunity to create and/or maintain a slim physique. Advertisements in the media, especially TV, depict everyone as slender, glamorous, and desirable. Perfectly shaped, trim models suggest that success in life, achievement, fun, sexual desirability, and happiness all accompany thinness. Actors and actresses, newscasters, politicians, and other public figures are also typically thin, thus encouraging widespread adulation of this body type. Even news accounts are replete with human interest stories on the negative consequences of being overweight. In a typical example, a school system and its consulting physicians, except one, supported a high school curriculum committee decision to keep fat girls off the drill team unless they lost a pound a week (Associated Press, 1981). In short, U.S. culture is hooked on weight control and thinness (Medical World News, 1984).

The urge to conform to this pervasive standard of slimness drives some people to conclude that any body fat at all is undesirable.

In a culture fixed on thinness, considerable attention has naturally focused on eating disorders, specifically bulimia and anorexia nervosa. Bulimia is characterized by episodic binge eating, with rapid consumption of food in large quantities in a single period of time, followed by purging to ensure near normal weight. *The Diagnostic and Statistical Manual of Mental Disorders (DSM III*; American Psychiatric Association, 1980) describes bulimia as a disorder involving:
• Recurrent episodes of binge eating (rapid consumption of a large amount of food in a discrete time period, usually less than 2 hours)
• At least three of the following:
—Consumption of high caloric, easily ingested food during a binge
—Inconspicuous eating during a binge
—Termination of binges by abdominal pain, sleep, social interruption, or self-induced vomiting
—Repeated attempts to lose weight by severely restrictive diets, self-induced vomiting, or use of cathartics or diuretics
—Frequent weight fluctuations greater than 10 pounds due to alternating fasts and binges
• Awareness that the eating pattern is abnormal and fear that it cannot be stopped voluntarily
• Depressed mood and self-deprecating thoughts following eating binges
• The bulimic episodes are not due to anorexia nervosa or any known physical disorder.

Although bulimia is *DSM III*'s official term for this disorder, other names have been applied, including bulimia nervosa, bulimarexia, the gorge-purge syndrome, and the dietary chaos syndrome (Hart and Ollendick, 1985; Boskind-White and White, 1983; Johnson and Sinnott, 1981).

Bulimia has been classified in *DSM III* as a distinct disorder since 1980. Although it does occur separately from anorexia nervosa (Medical World News, 1984), the two aberrant eating patterns can be associated. Various studies suggest that bulimia is either a chronic stage or a distinct subtype of anorexia nervosa (Casper et al., 1980). However, it is believed that bulimia without major weight loss is a separate disorder from the bulimia in anorexia nervosa (Lacey, 1982). There have been few comparison studies of these groups to determine the justification of the diagnostic distinctions (Garner et al., 1985).

Bulimia vs. anorexia nervosa. Since bulimic symptoms frequently appear in anorexia nervosa and the disorders have common characteristics (though the *DSM III* definition of bulimia requires that it not be due to anorexia nervosa), anorexia nervosa should be defined to clarify the two diagnoses. According to *DSM III,* anorexia nervosa is a disorder involving:

• Intense fear of becoming obese, which does not diminish as weight loss progresses.

• Body image disturbance, e.g., claiming to feel fat even when emaciated.

• Loss of at least 25% of original body weight (in those under 18 years old, loss from original body weight plus weight gain expected from growth charts may be combined to calculate the 25%).

• Refusal to maintain body weight appropriate to age and height.

• No known physiological cause for weight loss (American Psychiatric Association, 1980).

Even *DSM's* detailed definitions do not allow diagnostic differentiation between anorexia nervosa and bulimia; they fail to distinguish between bulimia as a separate disorder and the bulimic symptoms associated with anorexia nervosa. The fact that at least 50% of anorectics also suffer from bulimia adds to the confusion between the two diagnostic entities (Johnson and Sinnott, 1981; Casper et al., 1980).

Tables 13.1 and 13.2 list the commonalities and differences between bulimia (alone or associated with anorexia) and anorexia nervosa established through current studies. At least one study found that women with bulimia and women with anorexia nervosa and bulimia were more similar to each other than to women who have anorexia alone (Garner et al., 1985).

Theories of causality of bulimia. The causes of bulimia are not fully understood, but there are several causal theories. One theory suggests that bulimia results from neurological dysfunction much like Parkinsonism (Johnson and Sinnott, 1981). A second theory proposes that bulimia results from a disturbance in the appetite center in the hypothalamus (Johnson and Sinnott, 1981), while a third posits that bulimia is abnormal learned behavior reinforced by stress relief (Boskind-White and White, 1983; Johnson and Sinnott, 1981; Casper et al., 1980).

A fourth idea is that bulimia results from an unsuppressed oral urge (Johnson and Sinnott, 1981) and that, in time, binging-purging becomes habitual, making precipitating factors irrelevant; the behavior then occurs at any time and under any circumstances. The pattern becomes an entrenched and crippling coping mechanism and a major part of the bulimic's lifestyle (Boskind-White and White 1983). Bulimic etiology may also stem from early disturbances in ego functioning; that is, the person develops an ineffective superego which cannot control the urge to eat. This disturbance in self control may be due to identification with parents who argue and act out (Wilson and Mintz, 1982).

Table 13.1 Characteristics Common to Bulimia and Anorexia Nervosa

- Eating disorder (American Psychiatric Association, 1980)
- Cause/causes not fully understood (Keltner, 1984)
- Almost always occurs in women (Wilson and Mintz, 1982; Halmi, 1982; Johnson and Sinnott, 1981; Garfinkel et al., 1980)
- Fear of being fat (Wilson and Mintz, 1980)
- Intrapsychic conflicts (Wilson and Mintz, 1982)
- Revulsion toward own body (Boskind-White and White, 1983)

Table 13.2 Areas in which Bulimia Differs from Anorexia Nervosa

- Results in weight fluctuation rather than weight loss (Keltner, 1984)
- Weight maintained within normal range rather than loss of up to 25% of usual body weight (Halmi, 1982; APA, 1980).
- More extroverted individuals than introverted (Casper et al., 1980)
- Older than the average anorectic (Casper et al., 1980)
- More difficulty with impulse control (i.e., sexual promiscuity, stealing, lying) (Wilson and Mintz, 1982; Halmi, 1982; Garfinkel et al., 1980)
- Higher incidence of affective disturbance (Strober et al., 1982)
- More frequent family history of psychiatric illness (Strober, 1981)
- Menstrual disturbances without amenorrhea (Wilson and Mintz, 1982; Halmi, 1982)
- Admits strong appetite rather than denies hunger (Casper et al., 1980)
- More likely to attempt suicide or mutilate self (Halmi, 1982)
- Greater tendency to abuse alcohol and street drugs (Halmi, 1982; Casper et al. 1980)
- More obvious family conflict (Strober, 1981)
- More secrecy regarding binges-purges rather than openness about weight loss attempts (Keltner, 1984; Boskind-White and White, 1983; Mitchell et al., 1981)
- Childhood defiance rather than compliance (Strober, 1981)
- Eats food belonging to others vs. attempts to get others to eat her food (Wilson and Mintz, 1982)
- More anxiety, guilt, interpersonal sensitivity, somatic complaints (Casper et al., 1980)

Still another etiologic theory argues that bulimia results from early familial interaction involving parental (especially maternal) overcontrol, overprotectiveness, and rigidity, as well as inadequate conflict management (Medical World News, 1984; Wilson and Mintz, 1982). These disturbed family dynamics leave the child with inadequate coping skills, making the normal adolescent tasks of separation and self-mastery and control major crises; bulimic symptoms develop as a form of rebellion and disobedience (Medical World News, 1984; Keltner, 1984; Wilson and Mintz, 1982).

A sixth causal theory implicates cultural obsession with thinness in bulimic pathogenesis (Medical World News, 1984); elaborations of that theory implicate various psychosociological factors as well as cultural views of thinness (Bruch, 1979).

A seventh theory holds that bulimia results from endocrine dysfunction (Medical World News, 1984).

A connection between a major affective disorder and bulimia has also been suggested (Medical World News, 1984), but the causal link is unknown.

Incidence of bulimia. Like bulimia's causes, the number of bulimics remains uncertain, for a number of reasons:
• Secrecy arising from embarrassment (Boskind-White and White, 1983; Johnson and Sinnott, 1981)
• Inadequate medical assessment of individual nutritional status and eating habits (Johnson and Sinnott, 1981)
• Misinterpretation of bulimia-related depression and self deprecation symptoms as the psychiatric problems (Johnson and Sinnott, 1981)
• The need for personal recognition and reporting of abnormal eating behavior which may be impossible if patients lack insight or deny symptoms (Johnson and Sinnott, 1981)

Estimates of the incidence of bulimia vary markedly. Several surveys suggest that 68% to 79% of all U.S. college women engage in binge eating and purging (Hart and Ollendick, 1985). Numerous authors indicate that the disorder is an epidemic in adolescent and young adult women (Hart and Ollendick, 1985; Boskind-White and White, 1983), while others suggest that the disorder is prevalent enough to be regarded as a major adolescent public health problem (Halmi, 1982). However, others report a much smaller number of actual cases of bulimia, saying that some studies fail to distinguish between binge eating and bulimia. Binge eating, they contend, is not unusual among young women, while the bulimic syndrome is much less common (Hart and Ollendick, 1985).

Although its incidence remains uncertain, one fact is clear: bulimia is a serious problem for adolescents and young adults. Moreover, the illness not only affects young individuals, but also constitutes a developmental crisis for their families.

Families with adolescents and bulimia. Families with an adolescent face the developmental tasks of launching that child into the outside world (Carter and McGoldrick, 1980; Duvall, 1971); at the same time, the adolescent is struggling to develop identity and self individuation (Erikson, 1959). Successful achievement of these parallel tasks requires that parental authority and control be balanced against the adolescent's need for self-differentiation and personal control (Ackerman, 1980).

Adolescents and parents in healthy families can negotiate a balance between dependence and independence. In the bulimic family, however, family dynamics keep the adolescent enmeshed, preventing the

development of skills necessary for individuation and healthy functioning independent of the family. Some adolescents respond with binge-
purge symptoms to cope with their emotions (Reed and Sech, 1985;
Casper et al., 1980)—fear of failure in independent activities and
interpersonal relationships, anger at being kept from independence and
individuation, and ambivalence at the double-bind message of grow
up/don't grow up. The bulimic symptoms further prevent both the
family's and the patient's completion of their developmental tasks.

The dynamics of the Milanio family are classic for families of bulimic
adolescents. Typically, the father in such a family is both controlling
and remote (Boskind-White and White, 1983; Boskind-Lodahl and
Sirlin, 1977). The mother appears dominant, particularly with the
children, but remains submissive to her husband (Boskind-White and
White, 1983). The marital dyad is characterized by conflict and anger
(Boskind-White and White, 1983); for instance, conflict between Mr.
and Mrs. Milanio arose from his unwillingness to share control and
power. The child develops strict but ineffective superego controls by
identifying with parents who argue and act out (Wilson and Mintz,
1982). Their fathers' unmodulated expression of hostility (Strober et al.,
1982) leaves many bulimic adolescents with poor impulse control and
few conflict resolution skills; they experience affective disturbances
like depression—in short, an inability to handle anger and conflict.
Depression has been found in blood relatives of bulimics (Strober, 1981;
Keltner, 1984), a finding borne out in Laura's case (her maternal
grandmother had been diagnosed with depression).

Conflict between bulimic adolescents and parents often begins with
the first childhood steps toward separation and independence. The
father in such a family reacts by encouraging the child to become
dependent and submissive like the mother; the mother participates by
requiring the child to be good, obedient, and perfect (Boskind-White
and White, 1983; Wilson and Mintz, 1982). In bulimic families, the
child's independent function is inhibited; she is not given an opportunity
to learn the skills necessary for coping with the outside world. Besides
hindering development of coping skills, this overprotectiveness and
rigid control leave the adolescent with an abnormally low self-concept
(Boskind-White and White, 1983). When the child leaves home, perhaps
to attend college, and the family fails to protect her, she is especially
vulnerable.

Certainly the bulimic's family dynamics do not help her deal effectively with interpersonal relationships. Because her family relationships
have been unpleasant, she cannot enjoy involvement with others and
may well display anhedonia in other areas, such as school, work, and
play (Boskind-White and White, 1983; Garfinkel, 1981).

Throughout childhood and into adolescence, many bulimics have stifled feelings of resentment, anger, and rebellion. Eventually, increased aggressive drive and psychic instability combine and present as bulimia. Frustrated by her ability to control parental and peer relations, the bulimic's interests at play and school focus on achieving independence, control, and self-direction through disobedience (Keltner, 1984; Medical World News, 1984; Wilson and Mintz, 1982)—disobedience manifested as binge eating and purging and in some cases, lying, sexual promiscuity, stealing, and substance abuse. This behavior appears during periods of anticipated or actual separation from the family, in response to feelings of insecurity, frustration, and increased stress (Medical World News, 1984; Fairburn, 1983; Boskind-White and White, 1983). Such occasions as graduation from high school or leaving for college are common triggering events (Medical World News, 1984; Boskind-White and White, 1983), as was the case with Laura.

Laura's binges are classic in bulimia. She consumes high caloric, easily ingested foods, particularly doughnuts, a food frequently ingested during binge episodes (Mitchell et al., 1981). She always eats more than one food per episode, which is also typical. The frequency of Laura's binges (approximately once every 2 weeks) also fits the normal bulimic profile; in some cases, however, reported frequencies have been much higher (Mitchell et al., 1981).

The bulimic binge-purge behavior reflects a lack of impulse control, a key factor in the disorder's high suicide risk (Medical World News, 1984; Halmi, 1982). Other factors contributing to a bulimic's excessive suicide potential include separation from family (and the resulting insecurity), poor interpersonal skills, ineffective means of coping with anger and conflict (and frequently, the resultant depression), along with inadequate methods for managing stress, guilt, and self-deprecation following binging.

As reported in the case example, suicidal behavior and depression were thought to be Laura's primary problems. Nondisclosure of binge-purge episodes is typical, and patients are frequently diagnosed as simply depressed (Keltner, 1984; Johnson and Sinnott, 1981); the secretive nature of bulimia mandates that nurses become more aware of the disorder's clinical manifestations (Keltner, 1984).

Theoretical approaches. The family of a bulimic adolescent can be understood using a conceptual framework combining developmental, family systems, crisis, and stress theories. The Milanio family's experiences, for instance, can be illuminated through such a multitheoretical approach.

Developmental theory. Central to developmental theory is the notion that an individual passes through various maturational stages in his lifetime, with each stage building on the previous one and requiring accomplishment of developmental tasks. Performance of each task allows the individual to move ahead; if, however, the task is not completed satisfactorily, personality deficits arise, hindering function in the next developmental stage and leaving the individual with inadequate coping skills (Stuart and Sundeen, 1979; Erikson, 1959).

Families as well as individuals pass through developmental stages, and must successfully complete their own developmental tasks (Carter and McGoldrick, 1980; Duvall, 1971).

Developmentally, adolescence is one of the most complex life stages, and the one most often characterized by the onset of major mental illness; vulnerability apparently stems from the adolescent's own biological frailty combined with decreased family involvement (Ackerman, 1980). Adolescence is also a nodal point in the family life cycle; major restructuring is necessary for successful negotiation of that stage (Ackerman, 1980).

An understanding of developmental theory is essential to understanding the problems of bulimic adolescents and their families. Knowing the maturational crises in which each person is involved will help the nurse promote successful mastery of crisis situations and apply the interventions needed to correct maladaptions.

Family systems theory. An underlying concept of family systems theory is that no single person is the sole victim of pathology or recipient of treatment; the family is treated as a unit. Family unit assessment focuses on the quality of relationship between family members and the need for improvement in interactional patterns, so that each family relationship has a mutual give and take (Ackerman, 1980). A change in one relationship produces changes in other members and in turn changes the entire system (Miller, 1971). While various theoretical approaches to family systems therapy can be used to improve the family's interactional patterns, the therapeutic focus remains the family system rather than isolated relationships (Beal, 1980). This approach keeps the nurse from focusing solely on the bulimic symptoms and symptom-bearer as the only source of pathology.

Crisis theory. Although both the adolescent's and the family's developmental crises can produce bulimia, adolescence itself is the preeminent crisis and the origin of much individual and family restructuring (Ackerman, 1980). In any crisis, established coping and adaptive mechanisms are in disarray; because it is both a disorganizing and a reorganizing process, crisis holds the potential for growth as well as dysfunction (Caplan, 1964). The use of binging and purging to resolve crises is dysfunctional and pathological, and suggests a strong need for intervention. For the bulimic family, whose enmeshment, rigidity, overprotectiveness, and lack of conflict resolution skills may already be maladaptive, successful crisis resolution without intervention is unlikely. The key to successful crisis resolution is identification and application of both established and new coping mechanisms, and bulimics and their families must learn new, appropriate coping methods.

Stress theory. Stress is a natural part of family life, especially in the face of change. It can lead to the development of coping mechanisms, but it can be damaging if it overwhelms existing coping strategies, or if the individual believes it to be overwhelming and acts as if it were (Coleman, 1976). Such life events as the departure of a child from the home are sometimes viewed in terms of life change units that reflect the amount of stress associated with the event (Holmes and Rahe, 1967). By this standard, leaving home is a significant stressor for both individuals and family systems; it taxes everyone's coping resources. The bulimic and her family are ill-prepared to cope with the stress of the child's leaving the family system for college.

Severe stress can lower efficiency, deplete adaptive resources, damage individual health, and, in extreme cases, cause disintegration and death (Coleman, 1976). When prolonged, stress can lead to either pathological insensitivity, such as a loss of hope or extreme apathy, or to pathological overresponsiveness, as illustrated by the "last straw response" (Coleman, 1976), perhaps typified by binging and purging.

Family assessment. The four theoretical components just described influence all aspects of the nursing process: assessment, planning, intervention, and evaluation. The nurse first assessed the Milanio family by collecting a three-generational family history, including the nuclear family and each parent's family of origin. This data was placed, with the family's help, on a genogram (Stuart and Sundeen, 1979). Each family member was also asked for his own perceptions of the family's problems. Laura was also assessed individually regarding her bulimia and associated physical and psychosocial problems.

By analyzing the assessment data within the multitheoretical framework, the Milanio problems were collaboratively identified. The problems thought to be associated with Laura's bulimia were: fusion/ lack of differentiation among family members; inadequate communication of feelings (especially anger) and poor conflict resolution; and ineffective resources for stress management and control. The first problem was associated with family rules fostering dependency; the parents demonstrated a tendency to focus on Laura in order to avoid dealing with more basic problems such as triangulation, rigid boundaries preventing adaptive change, conditional love based on obedience, and Laura's low self-esteem and poor self-image. The second problem, inadequate communication, had led to fighting between and the emotional divorce of the elder Milanios, triangulation of Laura, conditional love, family governance by dominance and control, unsatisfying inter-personal relationships, and, in Laura, depression and suicidal potential. The third and final problem, lack of effective coping resources, had led Mr. Milanio to recurrent, unmodulated expressions of hostility, Laura to binging/purging and attempted suicide, Wendy to obesity, Mrs. Milanio to passivity, and the entire family unit to overprotectiveness.

Planning

The nurse developed specific therapeutic goals for the Milanio family:
• Separation and individuation of family members. Related subgoals for Laura included increasing self-esteem and sense of identity.
• Development of communication skills to allow clear, open expression of feelings, effective conflict resolution, and improved relationships. Laura's subgoals included outward expression of feelings (especially anger) and appropriate management of feelings.
• Effective family stress management and control. Laura's subgoals included substituting an appropriate coping technique for binging and purging.

Interventions

Families of bulimics, like the Milanios, rarely enter therapy for any-thing other than a child-centered problem. Physical complications of the bulimia or, as in the Milanio case, a suicide attempt (Minuchin et al., 1978) are characteristic. The Milanios focused on Laura, indicating they would do anything to help her. As a rule, bulimics' parents are quite concerned about their child's well-being and will strive to help her get well (Wilson and Mintz, 1982).

For most psychosomatic families, child-centered problems are system maintaining (Jones, 1980). Therefore, within a family systems frame-work, initial nursing intervention should divert attention from the child onto the family as a whole.

Fostering individuation. In families like the Milanios, emotional reactiv-ity reflects enmeshment and a need for differentiation and individuation among family members; family loyalty and protection typically take precedence over autonomy and self realization. A child growing up in such a system learns to subordinate herself to gain approval and love, to be dependent and compliant, and experiences guilt and shame at any disobedience of family rules (Minuchin et al., 1978).

In the above sense, Laura's violation of family rules of morality—her suicide attempt—reflected a disobedient and pathological yet autono-mous act. The family's response was to reassert control. The therapist reframed these transactional patterns by pointing out that Laura's independent action had had a positive outome in bringing the family to therapy. This intervention supported the value of independent functioning and depreciated family overprotectiveness by relabeling the crisis as growth-producing. The intervention was repeated when Laura's bulimia was revealed. Each intervention was aimed at goal one: separation and individuation. In such cases, the therapist should continually and consistently communicate the message of separateness (Minuchin et al., 1978).

Rigid rules that enforce obedience, compliance, and overinvolvement within families should be challenged by the nurse, perhaps by blocking observed protective behavior and reinforcing independent action. Specifically, the nurse can question the need for the protective behavior and encourage autonomous action, thus prolonging moments of individual competence (Minuchin et al., 1978). For example, Laura had a curfew of 11 p.m. when she was at home and her mother always waited to be certain she came in on time. The nurse challenged this behavior, pointing out that Laura had set her own schedule while at college and had managed to get back to the dorm at an appropriate hour without supervision. Mrs. Milanio agreed that she had no need to wait up and that Laura could be responsible for returning home on time.

Therapists attempting to foster individuation within a family must create a climate favorable to independent action. Flexibility in conduct promotes tolerance in relationships and mutual respect. In another example, Laura was required to spend time with the family, attend church with them, and visit her grandmother when she came home on weekends, even if this kept her from more age-appropriate behavior such as seeing her boyfriend. The nurse questioned these rules on the basis of Laura's need for age-appropriate pursuits. Subsequently, Laura was allowed free use of her time while at home, as long as she went to church and spent several hours with her family.

The nurse can help families create open systems that reinforce everyone's self worth (Satir, 1972). Feelings of worth can flower only in an atmosphere where individual differences are appreciated and respected and rules are flexible (Satir, 1972).

While individuation is important, the nurse must also support family members' concern for each other; she should recognize that overprotectiveness stems from natural warmth and care (Minuchin et al., 1978). The Milanio family was encouraged to redefine their relationships so that Laura might receive the validation she needed to shape a competent separate identity, as required by her developmental level (Erikson, 1959).

Individuation depends on validation of self by the family system (Minuchin et al., 1978). For example, the Milanios' established pattern was to treat Laura as a child who needed parental attention and protection, and for Laura to respond as a dependent child. The therapist relabeled Laura as an adolescent who needed to experiment with new behavior and who could often make her own decisions with minimal parental guidance. In this way, Laura's more competent, age-appropriate identity was validated. Additionally, Mr. and Mrs. Milanio were asked to spend more time together—to nurture their relationship rather than nurturing Laura so much. At the same time, Laura was asked to experiment with meeting her own needs. These directives initiated the process of strengthening the marital dyad and of separating Laura from the undifferentiated family ego mass (Bowen, 1978).

While remaining within a family systems framework, the nurse scheduled individual sessions with Laura as a means of further validating her identity. Laura was encouraged to express herself and identify her strengths. She was told that each sessions was *her* individual time to talk about herself and her feelings, and that the nurse accepted her and would not judge her. Laura was allowed to find herself, to work on the developmental task of identity formation, and to increase her interpersonal skills and self worth. To help her accomplish this, Laura was given a copy of Satir's declaration of self-esteem which begins, "I am me" (Satir, 1972).

These sessions strengthened Laura's sense of self apart from the family. The therapist's coaching in self differentiation (Bowen, 1978) enabled Laura to express her feelings and ideas in family sessions. Her increased expressiveness facilitated development of adult to adult relationships between Laura and her parents, a hallmark of successful completion of the launching stage of the family life cycle (Carter and McGoldrick, 1980).

Fostering open communication and conflict resolution. The launching stage of the family life cycle also requires renegotiating the marital dyad (Carter and McGoldrick, 1980). The Milanios' therapist encouraged the couple to focus on each other to strengthen their marriage. When Mr. Milanio was present, the therapist asked the couple to sit together and communicate their concerns and observations directly; the therapist refused to be pulled into these discussions (Minuchin et al., 1978) but made the Milanios aware of their habitual attempts to communicate through Laura or to involve her in issues concerning the two of them. For example, Mrs. Milanio wanted to redecorate the house but Mr. Milanio resisted. He saw no need to refurbish or spend money on household items. Mrs. Milanio tried to involve Laura by asking her to agree that their furnishings needed repair or replacement. In another instance, Mrs. Milanio was afraid to tell her husband about a minor accident with the car, and used Laura as a messenger. In both cases, the therapist pointed out the Milanios' unnecessary involvement of Laura in their issues; this and subsequent interventions were used to accomplish goal two.

As Laura was allowed to separate herself from her parents' issues, Mr. and Mrs. Milanio were encouraged to express their feelings openly, honestly, and directly. When they could not communicate clearly, the therapist employed modeling, coaching, and teaching interventions (Coleman, 1976; Bowen, 1978; Satir, 1972). For example, when Mrs. Milanio felt intimidated by her husband's aggressiveness, the therapist modeled assertive behavior. She coached Mrs. Milanio in asserting herself and helped Mr. Milanio modify behaviors which inhibited his wife's communication. At times during therapy, the therapist taught both the Milanios and Laura basic assertiveness concepts (Alberti and Emmons, 1982).

As Mr. and Mrs. Milanio began to express their feelings more openly, and as Laura became more individuated and less willing to be their focus of attention or their communication link, parental conflict appeared. Deprived of their exclusive concentration on Laura, the Milanios could not deny or avoid dealing with their differences (Lieberman et al., 1974). Therefore the therapist began to teach and model appropriate conflict resolution techniques (Bach, 1968). Laura's parents were asked to "fight" in front of their daughter, in order to demonstrate the fair fight process. Laura in turn was asked to argue with each parent, practicing effective conflict resolution (Minuchin et al., 1978). Homework assignments allowed the family to practice negotiation and resolution of differences; the efforts were discussed in subsequent sessions. As a result of these interventions, family communication became increasingly open; stronger communication skills allowed family members to express their feelings on previously avoided topics. Family members also learned how to give each other appropriate feedback. The entire process helped Laura express her long-standing anger at being controlled and dominated, and to "unlearn" the pattern of swallowing her feelings which had contributed to the excessive tension that produced the suicide attempt.

Laura's suicide potential was assessed throughout the course of therapy. If she had been judged suicidal at any time, referral to her family physician for hospitalization might have been necessary (Minuchin et al., 1978). Fortunately, because Laura began to express previously suppressed feelings verbally in therapy, she could release sufficient tension to avoid further life-threatening crises. It was particularly helpful for her to express her anger in appropriate ways; previously, she had internalized it as depression.

Developing appropriate coping methods for stress.
Recognizing feelings. A relationship appears to exist between anger and binge-purge behavior. Laura, for instance, could not express anger directly in most situations. She would become frustrated or upset and attempt to "swallow" her feelings, creating enormous tension. With

the therapist's assistance, she could recognize how this had led to her bulimia; such recognition was an important first step toward modifying that behavior. This and subsequent interventions were used to accomplish goal three.

Many bulimics' binge-purge behavior is well-established, habitual, and unrelated to specific precipitating events. The triggers for Laura's pathologic behavior were primarily interpersonal; like most bulimics, she had poor interpersonal relationships. For example, Laura did not get along with a series of roommates; one was too messy, another did not respect her things, and a third did not include Laura in her activities and left her feeling lonely and rejected. Laura was often disappointed in her boyfriend because he could not meet the dependency needs expressed in her requests for letters, phone calls, visits, and exclusive attention when he was in town. Additionally, when her parents did not respond as desired to her bids for attention and support, which were disguised as requests for money or for assistance with roommate problems, Laura would feel rejected. Laura could not express her feelings appropriately in these circumstances and could not resolve the conflicts that contributed to accumulated tension and the eventual binge-purge response. Anxiety, rejection, confrontation, and disappointment are all common precursors to binge-purge episodes (Boskind-White and White, 1983).

The decision to binge-purge is often linked to bulimic women's inability to assert themselves and deal with their problems directly (Boskind-White and White, 1983). Bulimics rarely express anger because, as discussed previously, they have been socialized by their families to be agreeable and compliant. Often they are unaware of their inability to express anger, and rationalize their need to contain this emotion; for instance, they may convince themselves that their anger might hurt others or make people avoid them. Shame and guilt over the binge-purge behavior also leads the bulimic to suppress anger. Thus, the action and problem-solving that follow anger and assertion—the very things that lead to productive change—are unavailable to most bulimics.

Engaging in physical activity. Subsequent to recognition of the feelings associated with binge-purge behavior, a major therapeutic focus in bulimia is to develop alternative methods of dealing with stressful situations, particularly interpersonal ones. Specifically, the bulimic should be encouraged to substitute alternative stress response behaviors (Fairburn, 1983). In Laura's case, tension release via physical activity was explored; she found that jogging helped her during the day, but seemed unsafe to her at night.

Talking with others. Sharing feelings with others is another alternative.

While Laura had few friends, she could, with encouragement, talk to her sister. Also, with support from the therapist, she identified a potential friend in one of her classmates and attempted to confide in her. Social reopening can be a highly effective intervention for helping a person cope with stress (Aguilera and Messick, 1974). Sharing her feelings with the therapist and with the family helped Laura learn to communicate more openly instead of binging and purging. Assertiveness training also proved helpful to Laura (Boskind-White and White, 1983).

Using relaxation techniques. Relaxation techniques can also defuse tension build-up (Stuart and Sundeen, 1979); Laura found these techniques helpful during test taking.

Establishing regular eating patterns. Bulimics should develop a regular three to four meal a day pattern of eating with no snacking in between as a substitute for binging and purging. A regular eating pattern prevents the intense craving for food that perpetuates the binge-purge cycle (Reid, 1983). Such groups as Overeaters Anonymous can also provide support for modifying this addiction to food (Reid, 1983). Laura developed a regular eating pattern of three meals per day; she said that it reduced her desire for large amounts of food and enabled her to discard her calorie counter.

Learning the physical complications of binging-purging. Few bulimics fully comprehend their continuing binge-purge behavior. Such patients should be frankly informed of the hazards and complications of binging and purging (Fairburn, 1983; Lucas, 1982): enlargement of the salivary glands, erosion of dental enamel, menstrual irregularities, abrasion of and callous formation on the knuckles, changes in bowel habits, dehydration, hypokalemia, muscle weakness, possible renal and cardiovascular failure (Lucas, 1982), and gastric dilation (Mitchell et al., 1982). The nurse might also refer the bulimic to the family physician for evaluation and treatment of these problems. Due to early intervention, however, Laura showed none of these physical complications.

The development of alternative stress management methods apparently helped Laura. These and other interventions allowed her to give up her bulimic behavior 3 months prior to termination of therapy.

Exploring alternate methods of family stress management. The therapist also explored alternative stress management methods in family sessions. Family overprotectiveness inhibited the development of successful coping responses; therefore alternative ways of relating, including flexibility, experimentation, negotiation, and problem-solving, were encouraged to increase positive coping. Throughout treatment, the therapist helped the family experiment with alternative interpersonal responses until the process became family-reinforcing and members tried out new responsive behaviors automatically (Minuchin et al., 1978). Therapy showed the Milanios that the crisis produced by Laura's adolescence and her leaving home was related to the inflexibility of their established coping responses, and that Laura's suicide attempt and bulimia might have been avoided.

The therapist used crisis theory to help the Milanio family view Laura's bulimia as a cue to resolve family crises (Wilson and Mintz, 1982). She suggested positive alternatives to use in critically tense situations in the future. The family members discussed what they might do in other developmental and situational crises.

Evaluation

The final step in the therapy process, evaluation, should be the culmination of the ongoing monitoring of all stages of treatment.

The literature is inconclusive about the value of therapy for bulimics and their families. Recurrence is not uncommon and must be tolerated by the therapist until treatment approaches are further refined (Reid, 1983; Fairburn, 1983). Although various approaches have been used, no single treatment of choice has emerged (Medical World News, 1984). For Laura and her family, however, the benefits of family systems–oriented therapy were undeniable, at least in the short term.

CONCLUSIONS

Many unanswered questions linger as to the cause/causes of bulimia and the most effective treatment approaches. Nurses must keep abreast of research regarding this disorder; new information will undoubtedly improve the overall outcome and prognosis for the bulimic and her family. Nurses themselves could conduct some of that research or participate in others' research projects.

Even with current knowledge about bulimia, nurses can function in a variety of helpful roles. Preventively, they can promote physical and emotional health by teaching: good nutrition and proper diet; parenting skills based on unconditional love and fostering a positive self concept (including body image) in the adolescent; normal individual and family growth and development, successful completion of the parallel tasks of launching the adolescent from the family and (for the adolescent) achieving self-individuation. Additionally, the nurse can advocate the acceptance of more reasonable societal expectations of body shape. Whenever possible, she can neutralize the pervasive standard of thinness by challenging this artificially contrived conception with facts about the realistic variety of normal body types. In specific situations where weight is an issue, she can question its value as a criterion.

Case-finding is also a critical nursing role. Nurses, particularly school and college/university infirmary nurses, are often gatekeepers of the health care system, and their work institutions serve large numbers of at-risk adolescent and young adult women. Such nurses must know the clinical symptoms of bulimia, not only because of the disease's apparently increasing incidence and need for early intervention, but also because of the bulimic's frequent denial of the problem, even after the disorder's potentially serious physical complications are pointed out. Additionally, bulimia represents a family developmental crisis, and as such entails serious social implications. The unresolved family issues expressed by bulimia can be passed into future generations and/or externalized, creating societal instability (Beal, 1980).

Nurses can also link bulimics and their families with existing resources. They should know about appropriate treatment options and resources and should inform the families of bulimic adolescents of all the available alternatives. For example, some cities now have eating disorder clinics which offer structured bulimia treatment programs (Reid, 1983); other municipalities rely on mental health clinics or private therapists to provide treatment. Another important resource is ANAD, the National Association of Anorexia Nervosa and Associated Disorders. ANAD is a national, nonprofit educational and self-help organization dedicated to the needs of eating disorder victims and their families.

Additionally, nurses have a role in bulimia treatment. Nurses in psychiatric settings may take a therapeutic role in a structured treatment program; appropriately trained psychiatric nurses can also function as primary therapists. Finally, medical surgical nurses, who may come in contact with bulimics hospitalized for treatment of medical complications, can utilize the nurse-patient relationship as a vehicle for therapeutic interaction. For example, involving the bulimic in decision-making about her care helps her become more individuated and competent.

In short, nurses who are knowledgeable about bulimia can function in a wide variety of roles to help the bulimic and her family. Equally important is nursing's contribution to bulimia prevention, which may ultimately reduce the risk factors for adolescent young adult women and their families.

REFERENCES

Ackerman, N.J. "The Family with Adolescents," in *The Family Life Cycle: A Framework for Family Therapy.* Edited by Carter E.A., and McGoldrick, M. New York: Gardner Press, 1980.

Aguilera, D.C., and Messick, J.M. *Crisis Intervention Theory and Methodology.* St. Louis: C.V. Mosby Co, 1974.

Alberti, R.E., and Emmons, M.L. *A Guide of Assertive Living: Your Perfect Right,* 4th ed. San Luis Obispo, Calif.: Impact, 1982.

American Psychiatric Association. *Diagnostic and Statistical Manual of Mental Disorders,* 3rd ed. Washington, D.C.: American Psychiatric Association, 1980.

Associated Press. "Fat Girls Losing Out on School Drill Team," *New York Times,* 57, December 20, 1981.

Bach, G.R., and Wyden P. *The Intimate Enemy.* New York: William Morrow, 1968.

Beal, E.W. "Separation, Divorce, and Single-Parent Families," in *The Family Life Cycle: A Framework for Family Therapy.* Edited by Carter E.A., and Mc-Goldrick, M. New York: Gardner Press, 1980.

Boskind-Lodahl, M., and Sirlin, J. "The Gorging-Purging Syndrome," *Psychology Today* 50-52, 1977.

Boskind-White, M., and White, W. *Bulimarexia: The Binge/Purge Cycle.* New York: W.W. Norton & Co., 1983.

Bowen, M. *Family Therapy in Clinical Practice.* New York: Jason Aronson, 1978.

Bruch, H. *The Golden Cage: The Enigma of Anorexia Nervosa.* New York: Vintage Books, 1979.

Caplan, G. *Principles of Preventive Psychiatry.* New York: Basic Books, 1964.

Carter, E., and McGoldrick, M. "The Family Life Cycle and Family Therapy: An Overview," in *The Family Life Cycle: A Framework for Family Therapy.* Edited by Carter E., and McGoldrick, M. New York: Gardner Press, 1980.

Casper. R.C., et al. "Bulimia. Its Incidence and Clinical Importance in Patients with Anorexia Nervosa," *Archives of General Psychiatry* 37:1030-35, 1980.

Coleman, J.C. *Abnormal Psychology and Modern Life,* 5th ed. Greenview, Ill.: Scott, Foresman Co., 1976.

Duvall, E. *Family Development.* Philadelphia: J.B. Lippincott Co., 1971.

"Eating Disorders: The Price of a Society's Desire to Be Thin," *Medical World News,* 38-52, 1984.

Erikson, E. *Identity and the Life Cycle.* New York: International Universities, 1959.

Fairburn, C.G. "Bulimia: Its Epidemiology and Management." *Psychiatric Annals* 13(12):953-60, 1983.

Garfinkle, P.E. "Some Recent Observations on the Pathogenesis of Anorexia Nervosa," *Canadian Journal of Psychiatry* 26:218-23, 1981.

Garfinkle, P.E., et al. "The Heterogeneity of Anorexia Nervosa," *Archives of General Psychiatry* 37:1036-40, 1980.

Garner, D.M., et al."The Validity of the Distinction Between Bulimia With and Without Anorexia Nervosa," *American Journal of Psychiatry* 142(5):581-87, 1985.

Halmi, K.A. "Pragmatic Information on the Eating Disorders," *Psychiatric Clinics of North America* 5(2):371-77, 1982.

Hart, K.L., and Ollendick, T.H. "Prevalence of Bulimia in Working and University Women," *American Journal of Psychiatry* 142(7):851-54, 1985.

Holmes, T., and Rahe, R. "The Social Readjustment Rating Scale," *Journal of Psychosomatic Research* 11(2):213-18, 1967.

Johnson, R.E., and Sinnott, S. "Bulimia," *American Family Physician* 23:141-43, 1981.

Jones, S.L. *Family Therapy: A Comparison of Approaches.* Bowie, Md.: Robert J. Brady, 1980.

Keltner, N.L. "Bulimia: Controlling Compulsive Eating," *Journal of Psychosocial Nursing and Mental Health Services* 22(8):24-29, 1984.

Lacey, J.H. "The Bulimia Syndrome at Normal Body Weight: Reflections on Pathogenesis and Clinical Features," *International Journal of Eating Disorders* 2:59-66, 1982.

Lieberman, R., et al. "An Integrated Treatment Program for Anorexia Nervosa," *American Journal of Psychiatry* 131(4):432-36, 1974.

Lucas, A. "Pigging Out," *Journal of the American Medical Association* 247(1):82, 1982.

Miller, J.C. "Systems Theory and Family Psychotherapy," *Nursing Clinics of North America* 6(3):395-406, 1971.

Minuchin, S., et al.*Psychosomatic Families: Anorexia Nervosa in Context.* Cambridge, Mass.: Harvard University Press, 1978.

Mitchell, J.E., et al. "Frequency and Duration of Binge-Eating Episodes in Patients with Bulimia," *American Journal of Psychiatry,* 138(6):835-37, 1981.

Mitchell, J.E., et al. "Gastric Dilation as a Complication of Bulimia," *Psychosomatics* 23(1):96-97, 1982.

Reed, G., and Sech, E.P. "Bulimia: A Conceptual Model for Group Treatment," *Journal of Psychosocial Nursing and Mental Health Services* 23(5):16-22, 1985.

Reid, W.H. *Treatment of the DSM-III Psychiatric Disorders.* New York: Brunner-Mazel, 1983.

Satir, V. *Peoplemaking.* Palo Alto, Calif.: Science and Behavior Books, 1972.

Strober, M. "The Significance of Bulimia in Juvenile Anorexia Nervosa: An Exploration of Possible Etiologic Factors," *International Journal of Eating Disorders* 1:28-43, 1981.

Strober, M., et al. "Validity of the Bulimia-Restricter Distinction in Anorexia Nervosa: Parental Personality Characteristics and Family Psychiatric Morbidity," *Journal of Nervous and Mental Disorders* 170:345-51, 1982.

Stuart, B.W., and Sundeen, S.L. *Principles and Practice of Psychiatric Nursing.* St. Louis: C.V. Mosby Co., 1979.

Wilson, P.C., and Mintz, I. "Abstaining and Bulimic Anorexics: Two Sides of the Same Coin," *Primary Care* 9(3):517-31, 1982.

14 Intervening with families and teen pregnancy

Beth Vaughan-Cole, RN, PhD
Associate Professor
Division of Psychosocial Nursing
College of Nursing
University of Utah
Salt Lake City, Utah

Bonnie C. Clayton, RN, PhD
Associate Professor
Division of Psychosocial Nursing
College of Nursing
University of Utah
Salt Lake City, Utah

OVERVIEW

Today, teen pregnancy poses a problem of such magnitude that it can potentially undermine the fabric of our society. The implications for the health care professions, and for nursing in particular, are significant. In response to this challenge, this chapter proposes a theoretical framework that draws upon developmental, self-help, decision-making, interpersonal, and family theories to help nurses care for pregnant teenagers and their families, including the teenaged fathers and grandparents. Several nursing assessment variables, including the pregnant teen's health status, age, race, social and family characteristics, are discussed. A decision-making model is proposed, followed by a presentation regarding the nursing plan and intervention strategy. The conflict between professional and personal values experienced by nurses practicing in this problem area is also discussed.

CASE STUDY

Jenny Clark was a 34-year-old single woman and mother of a 15-year-old daughter, Penny. She was hospitalized with schizophrenia, paranoid type, when Penny was an infant and had been a client of the community mental health system since then; Ms. Jones, a nurse clinician, had been her primary therapist for 3 years. Jenny was scheduled for weekly socialization group therapy, but her attendance was poor. She met with Ms. Jones as needed to manage day-to-day situations, and her medications were monitored at a mental health clinic. The family had no relatives in the state and depended on welfare and Aid to Families and Dependent Children (AFDC).

Jenny called Ms. Jones in a highly agitated state; she said Penny was pregnant and she threatened to kill herself and Penny.

Her daughter's announcement of the 2-month pregnancy had resulted in a screaming argument. When Penny threatened to run away with an 18-year-old boy, Jenny became hysterical and threatened to kill her daughter and herself.

Ms. Jones met with the two women individually and together to identify key issues prior to planning, executing, and evaluating interventions. Jenny was stabilized on medication and subsequently participated, as actively as she could, in discussions directed toward resolving the crisis.

Jenny described Penny as the dominant figure in family decision-making on financial, social, and religious issues, including the timing and location of their frequent moves from one inexpensive apartment to another. She was afraid of her daughter's anger and aggression, and of her own inability to curb the girl's delinquency and association with a "wild crowd." Jenny denied knowing that Penny was sexually active; she hinted that rape was involved in the pregnancy. She would not discuss adoption of the expected baby; she equated offering the infant to someone else with giving away "a puppy you really like." She became detached at the mention of abortion, saying that was "Penny's business." She was ambivalent about Penny keeping the baby, however, and complained about money, time, her own illness, and fear of being "stuck as a baby-sitter."

Assessment

Jenny. Ms. Jones concluded Jenny's fragile adjustment was jeopardized by the current crisis, which clearly threatened the family's interpersonal structure. Jenny's dependent, near-symbiotic relationship with her daughter was not ideal, but it was all she had.

Penny. Penny was attempting to complete the normal developmental tasks of early adolescence, particularly separation/individuation. Ms. Jones concluded that Penny was a typical adolescent who needed direct assistance in coping with her ill mother and in evaluating and managing the stresses of school, peer relationships, and her own sexuality. Penny regarded the pregnancy as evidence of her rotten luck. She had not told her boyfriend, and talking with her girlfriends only left her more confused and frightened.

Family intervention

Ms. Jones's interventions focused on the issues of teenage sexuality, pregnancy, and plans beyond the immediate crisis point. The nurse augmented Jenny's preexisting therapeutic programs and counseled the women individually and as a family.

Penny was referred to a women's health center for additional counseling; she elected to have an abortion. Further plans emphasized continued support of the family. Ms. Jones arranged transportation for Jenny to her weekly group therapy sessions and planned to be more available to her on an individual basis. Counseling to help Penny complete her developmental tasks was provided.

THE NURSING PROCESS

Assessment

The health problem: Teen pregnancy. Teen pregnancy represents the most obvious, and, in most cases, least welcome outcome of teenage sexual activity.

Because most of the American population lives according to the Judeo-Christian legal/ethical system, sexual activity is traditionally condoned only within a marital relationship. If the pregnant teenager marries, the pregnancy is sanctioned by society and no social dilemma exists. Whether the pregnancy was wanted, whether it jeopardizes the young mother's health, or whether the marriage was "forced," are not questions of general concern.

In contrast, the pregnant but unmarried teenager becomes party to one of the major social problems of our day. According to Furstenberg (1981), sexual activity among unmarried teens has increased dramatically over the last two decades, and begins at ever lower ages. Statistics indicate significant differences in sexual activity between black and white adolescents. O'Connell and Moore (1981) noted that between 1939 and 1954 the rate of first births resulting from premarital conception remained constant at 25% for white women and 60% for black women. Not all of these pregnancies, of course, resulted in out-of-wedlock births: during the same period only 10% of all first births to white women and 40% of those to black women were out of wedlock. From 1955 to 1973 the percentage of first births due to premarital conceptions increased to 63% for white women and 90% for black women. The proportion was higher for 15-to-17-year-olds than for the 18-to-19-year-old women.

Premarital activity among teenagers has been an increasing health care concern. Tough questions must be answered, including:
• Was there mutual consent, or was incest or other sexual abuse involved?
• Is venereal disease present?
• Are there maternal and child health and welfare concerns?
• Was lack of contraceptive education or availability of contraceptives a problem?
• What are the psychosocial implications?
Many state and national legal agencies and funded programs exist to meet the needs of teenaged mothers, regardless of societal responses to their condition.

Since the 1970s, national attention has focused on providing prenatal health care to pregnant teenagers to minimize complications in pregnancy. Typically, teenagers have little contact with health care services; therefore encouraging pregnant teens, married or unmarried, to utilize available services early in their pregnancies is a major concern of health care professionals.

Age range of pregnant teenagers. The age of the pregnant mother matters a great deal to health care providers. While the "teens" are defined generally as the adolescent years of 13 to 19, the ramifications of a 13-year-old girl's pregnancy are profoundly more complex than those of a 19-year-old woman's. The basic factors may be the same, but younger girls are more vulnerable in all respects. The mother, the pregnancy, and the baby are all at higher risk.

The age of menstrual onset has changed markedly over the last 40 years (Tanner, 1968). Menses among American and European girls today begins just before age 13; 40 years ago that age was 15 years. The combination of earlier reproductive ability and a higher incidence of youth sexual activity has contributed to a substantial increase in pregnancy among girls in the younger teen years.

On the one hand, children who are 18 to 21 years old, depending on their place of residence, have achieved legal majority. They can enter contracts and are generally treated as adults. On the other hand, younger teens' legal status is often ambiguous. In some states, a girl who has given birth is considered an adult or an emancipated minor no matter what her age.

According to Carey and colleagues (1983), pregnancy in the early teens correlates with higher maternal death rates and higher rates of the serious pre- and postnatal complications, such as pregnancy-induced hypertension, cephalopelvic disproportion, iron deficiency anemia, low birth weight, and prematurity. In contrast, Hollingsworth and colleagues (1983) stated that such findings are due not to age alone but also to the mother's socioeconomic status (SES) and to lack of prenatal medical care. For instance, a major prenatal hazard associated with low SES is poor adolescent nutrition. Carey and colleagues (1983) cited other intervening health problems including alcohol, tobacco, or street drug use, and a high incidence of sexually transmitted diseases. When SES and medical care are controlled, age is not the critical determinant of these complications. There is some evidence that pregnancy before age 14 may carry more risk of health-related complications, but there are to date few reported studies on this age group.

Social consequences of teenage pregnancy. Teen pregnancy has a number of major social consequences, not the least of which relate to education-career and economics. Until the last decade, the usual scenario for the pregnant teenager was to withdraw immediately from public school;

she rarely completed her education and thus remained limited for life to low-paying jobs and poor career options (Furstenberg, 1981; Menkin, 1981; McCarthy and Radish, 1983). In the last decade, federally-funded programs for pregnant girls have attempted to interrupt this negative cycle; several such interventions have succeeded by providing the pregnant girl or young mother with educational preparation to meet her new responsibilities (Jekel and Klerman, 1983).

Another social consequence of teen pregnancy is the overall higher fertility rate of women who deliver their first child during their teens. Teenaged mothers subsequently bear more children over less time than women who do not have children until after age 20. In addition to the obvious socioeconomic implications, there is a strong association between problem pregnancies and closely spaced births. A major focus of teen programs is encouraging young mothers to space their children, for their own and their children's health.

Teen pregnancy also has a major psychosocial impact on most adolescent fathers. While there have been numerous studies of sexual behavior and contraceptive use by adolescent males, there have been few examinations of the psychological and social consequences of teen pregnancy on the fathers. Elster and Panzarine (1983) summarized some of the limited findings, noting that, psychologically, most teenaged fathers are struggling with masculine identity formation; they generally obtain less formal education and subsequently move into lower paying jobs than average males who do not father a child during adolescence.

As expected, many adolescent fathers marry the pregnant girl (Felton and Siegel, 1980). Robbins and colleagues (1985) speculated, however, that many young men are probably unaware that they impregnated their sexual partners. In any case, denial is easy because Western society seldom holds young fathers accountable. The Robbins and colleagues' (1985) study of 994 young adults revealed that by age 21, 26% of girls, but only 15% of boys, reported involvement in an adolescent pregnancy.

The Ford Foundation and the Bank Street College of Education collaborated in an eight-site program called The Teen Father Collaboration, with findings similar to those reported by Robbins and colleagues. Two-thirds of the teen fathers were unemployed and had low self-esteem. However, most had a 2 to 3 year relationship with the mother of the child, and strong intentions of continuing to father the child (Klinman et al., 1986).

Adolescent couples' divorce rate is more than two to four times that of adult couples. While teenaged fathers encounter many of the same problems that older adult males face, they are less mature and have had less time to adjust to such unfamiliar social roles as provider, father, and husband (Russell, 1980).

All of these social consequences have implications for nurses and other health professionals as well as for those involved in shaping social policy.

Theoretical Approaches to Family Assessment. There is, of course, no "typical family profile" descriptive of teen pregnancy or of any other complex family problem. Rather than looking for typical features, the most effective nurse will rely on a firm understanding of family dynamics and application of that understanding within a theoretical framework. That framework is a base for the nursing process.

Selecting an assessment framework. The choice of a theoretical framework is highly individualized; however, perhaps because of their profession's persistent emphasis on holistic health, most nurses will prefer an eclectic approach, with broad conceptualization of the individual within a multidimensional context. In addition, basic nursing education is itself eclectic, and draws from a rich panoply of arts and sciences.

Most clinical nursing approaches, however, balance this eclecticism with sound preparation in developmental, self-help/decision, interpersonal, and family systems theories. All four of these theoretical premises are, of course, relevant to problems related to teen pregnancy.

Developmental theory. In the case study of Jenny and her daughter Penny, developmental theory provided the basis for Ms. Jones' evaluation of both women's relative maturity. The nurse facing such a situation might well consider the pregnant girl's progress in achieving the major developmental goal of adolescence: separation/individuation; that is, becoming her own person socially, intellectually, psychosexually, and emotionally. The mother's readiness to assume the additional responsibilities of a new infant in an already unstable household can also be evaluated using developmental theory. In the Clark case, Jenny's rivalry with her daughter, her ambivalence toward her own therapists, and her own interpersonal instability are best understood when viewed in a developmental context.

Additionally, nurses counseling teenagers should be aware of the unborn child's needs, not only as the object of the pregnancy but as an individual who will make demands after birth and who will become another individual, either in the family of origin or in another family constellation (Luthman and Kirschenbaum, 1974; Wright and Leahey, 1984).

Self-help and decision theories. A nurse who is convinced that a particular teenaged girl is not ready developmentally for pregnancy and motherhood, can avoid imposing her own external value system on the client and her family by relying on self-help theories. In such a situation, the nurse should provide information, pose alternative choices for consideration, and support clients as they struggle to make their own decision (Orem, 1980). Figure 14.1 summarizes critical decision points in teen pregnancy. Nurses may interact with patients at one or more of these points.

Interpersonal theory. The traditional nurse-patient relationship rests on principles of interpersonal theory. The nurse helps the client make decisions within an interpersonal context of positive regard, empathy, humanistic values, and understanding of dynamic processes (Wilson and Kneisl, 1983).

Family systems theory. A teenager's pregnancy always impacts upon the family system, regardless of the family's geographic and socioeconomic circumstances. The concept of the interactive family system therefore facilitates nursing care planning and intervention. The family systems perspective broadens the clinical focus beyond the "problem" member and, if successful, will mobilize support for the pregnant girl. Because it is more complex than unilateral techniques such as individual counseling, a family approach often leads to constructive, long-range problem-solving and mobilization of multiple kinship resources. This is perhaps the most complicated aspect of nursing assessment, because the family system's drive toward homeostasis often continues at the expense of individual members. The nurse must be aware of family tendencies to withdraw and exclude strangers. Effective care requires interpersonal skills and an understanding of coping mechanisms for emotional pain.

This case example illustrates a style of nursing that focuses on the family as the client. Nurses in such situations must recognize the danger of focusing only on the pregnant teenager to resolve "the problem." Circumstances, including therapy, that threaten family equilibrium can cause systemic anxiety and resistance; therefore, the family systems nurse monitors each member's stress levels. The Clark case shows how family energies, if well-directed, can help restore order. This family's fragile homeostasis was restored by Penny's abortion. On a long-term basis, the nurse should anticipate further upheaval as the adolescent girl tries again—as she must—to achieve independence from her mother (Miller and Janosik, 1980; Wright and Leahey, 1984).

Family assessment. There is danger of oversimplifying family assessment into a linear sequence of events; in real life the steps are interactive in several directions. Assessment must precede planning and intervention, but the process can—and should—be repeated as new information is introduced. In an event as complicated as teen pregnancy, certain high stress points at which intervention can be effective can

Figure 14.1   Process Chart for Teenage Pregnancy

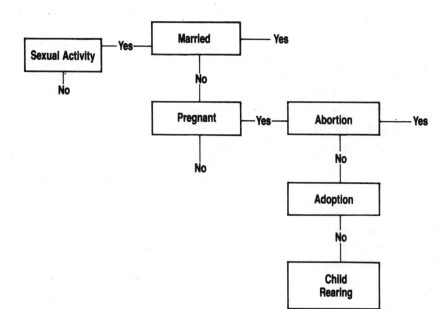

be identified. These decision points will determine the family's future welfare.

Figure 14.1 structures the teen pregnancy issue around a matrix of six decision points, any or all of which may need nursing attention and assessment. Understanding this total picture will help the nurse plan goals, interventions, and evaluation within a sound humanistic and scientific framework.

Planning

The options open to a pregnant teen are often controversial. Therefore, nurses who work with such clients must recognize that their own values and beliefs may agree or conflict with those held by everyone involved, including the employing agency or institution. These beliefs should be shared with the client, so the client is aware of the professional's frame of reference for counseling.

Planning revolves around establishing goals, although an immediate individual or family crisis may temporarily take priority over long-term planning. The threatened suicide in the Clark family, for example, determined the focus of the initial nursing assessment. Ms. Jones, the nurse, evaluated Jenny's and Penny's conflicting reports of the incident and intervened to stablize Jenny with medication and provide emotional support. After the immediate crisis passed, planning longer-term interventions to help the family deal with Penny's pregnancy became possible.

Intervention

Decisions about the outcome of a pregnancy often overwhelm a teenaged girl and her family; professional assistance should intercede at critical points (Presser, 1980). Recent data indicate that most girls who decide to complete their pregnancy keep their babies. Early in the pregnancy, however, struggling with decisions may create serious family conflict. In such situations, the nurse's steadying influence can be invaluable.

Decisions about abortion. In many communities, the pregnant teen can choose legal or illegal abortion. There are no accurate statistics, but sociologists estimate that 1.3 million abortions are performed per year (Olson, 1980), many of them for teenagers. The decision to abort is a significant one for any teenager; many make that choice with family support. Some legal, moral, and religious institutions, however, hold opposing views and can generate conflict. The influence of all these forces must be considered by the intervening nurse.

Some nurses attempt to sway teenagers and their families on the issue of abortion. Little literature exists on the effects of abortion on adolescent adjustment, but the nature of the act itself and its status as a crisis event, demands significant pre- and postabortion counseling. The nurse could, for instance, give the teenager accurate and sensitive information about abortion, the physiological responses to each kind of abortion, the procedures involved, and risks and benefits. However, forced counseling, which is neither successful nor desirable, should never be required.

Decisions about adoption. One option for the unmarried teenaged mother is giving the infant up for adoption. There have never been enough children to meet the demands of would-be, often infertile, adoptive parents, and many of these couples must wait long periods, often many years. In fact, the number of adoptable children has decreased in recent years, largely because of increased abortion rates, although no studies confirm that relationship. Other trends may be of equal significance: the tendency, for example, of young unmarried women to keep their babies. Adoption services traditionally report higher demand for Caucasian infants, but today's trend is toward adoptions of children of other races.

Baldwin (1983) noted that black children born out of wedlock are usually raised by their mothers or their mother's families. Presently, 93% of all out-of-wedlock infants born to teenagers are raised under these circumstances.

Decisions about childrearing. Children raising children has concerned many child development scholars (Baldwin, 1983; Kinard and Klerman, 1980). Early studies noted that children of teenaged parents had lower intelligence scores than other children their age. However, Kinard and Klerman concluded that the age of the young parent or parents was not the primary factor; rather, socioeconomic status and family structure had the most influence on cognitive development. Mothers under age 18 tended to live with extended family members, whereas older teenage mothers tended to live alone or with a partner. The additional stimulation provided by extended family members can offset the adolescent parent's immaturity (Kinard and Klerman, 1980).

Maternal nurturance or support has also concerned child development experts. Numerous authors have investigated maternal bonding or attachment among very young mothers and their babies. McAnarney and colleagues (1979) and Wise and Grossman (1980) concluded that infants at the greatest developmental risk were those born and raised by the youngest mothers and those with the least adequate family support systems. According to McAnarney and colleagues (1979), younger mothers are less apt to hug their infants or talk to them. Mothers under age 15 interact with less synchrony, verbal communication, and closeness with their infants.

Issues of maternal nurturance or support have long-term developmental implications because a strong link exists between nurturance and high self-esteem, academic success, and creativity. The long-term effects of deficits in mothering have not been studied. Again, mothering behaviors seem to be modified by socioeconomic level and family structure. Combined with age, these seem to be important determinants of the success of teenage mothers' child rearing practices.

When a teenager decides to keep her child, the nurse should carefully assess the young mother's resources for neonatal care and management. Evaluation of the teen's knowledge of growth and development, as well as her child care management skills, might prompt a referral to courses, classes, or to a public health nurse for further instruction. The nurse may also, along with state or county health departments, monitor how the teenaged mother meets the infant's basic needs.

Evaluation

In evaluating their work with pregnant teenagers and their families, nurses should ask themselves:
- To what extent did I influence the teenager's decision about the pregnancy?
- How effectively did I handle my own beliefs about what should or should not have been done regarding the outcome of the pregnancy?
- What could I do differently the next time I help this or a similar family make decisions about sexual activity, marriage, pregnancy, abortion, adoption, and child rearing?

The nurse can also evaluate the success of interventions by asking:
• Who in the family is *most* satisfied with the decision about the pregnancy? Who is *least* satisfied?
• How will you deal with conflict about the decision-making process and its outcome?
• In 3 months' time, how will the decision about the pregnancy have changed your family?

CONCLUSIONS

Teenage pregnancy is a complex problem marked by a series of decision points, at which the adolescent may interact with nurses and other health care professionals. Recognition of these key points in the pregnancy cycle can help the nurse provide the best care.

Because a major factor in adjustment of the adolescent parent and her infant is their support system, the nursing assessment must be family-centered, and should include the pregnant teenager's family of origin; it may instead (or also) include the new family or the new mother, infant, and father. A wider focus will enhance the likelihood of a healthy outcome for all.

REFERENCES

Baldwin, W. "Trends in Adolescent Contraception, Pregnancy, and Childbearing," in *Premature Adolescent Pregnancy and Parenthood*. Edited by McAnarney, E. New York: Grune & Stratton, 1983.

Bedger, J.E. *Teenage Pregnancy: Research Related to Clients and Service*. Chicago: Charles C. Thomas, 1980

Burchind, L.G. "Trends and Prospects for Young Marriages in the United States," *Journal of Marriage and the Family* 27:243–54, 1965.

Caldwell, S.B. "Life Course Perspectives on Adolescent Parenthood Research," *Journal of Social Issues* 36(1):130–46, 1980.

Carey, W.B., et al. "Adolescent Age and Obstetric Risk," in *Premature Adolescent Pregnancy and Parenthood*. Edited by McAnarney, E. New York: Grune & Stratton, 1983.

Elster, A., and Panzarine, S. "Adolescent Fathers," in *Premature Adolescent Pregnancy and Parenthood*. Edited by McAnarney, E. New York: Grune & Stratton, 1983.

Felton, E., and Siegel, B. "Precocious Fathers," *American Journal of Orthopsychiatry* 50(3):469–80, 1980.

Friedman, S.B., and Phillips, S. "Psychosocial Risk to Mother and Child as a Consequence of Adolescent Pregnancy," in *Premature Adolescent Pregnancy and Parenthood*. Edited by McAnarney, E. New York: Grune & Stratton, 1983.

Furstenberg, F.F., Jr. "Burdens and Benefits: The Impact of Early Childbearing on the Family," *Journal of Social Issues* 36(1):64–87, 1980.

Furstenberg, F.F., Jr. "The Social Consequences of Teenage Parenthood," in *Teenage Sexuality, Pregnancy, and Childbearing*. Edited by Furstenberg, F.F., Jr., et al. Philadelphia: University of Pennsylvania Press, 1981.

Hales, D., and Bergen, M. "Maternal Behavior at First Contact with Her Infant: A Comparison of Adolescents and Adults," *Pediatric Research* 13:327, 1979.

Hollingsworth, D.R., et al. "Impact of Gynecologic Age on Outcome of Adolescent Pregnancy," in *Premature Adolescent Pregnancy and Parenthood*. Edited by McAnarney, E. New York: Grune & Stratton, 1983.

Jekel, J.F., and Klerman, L.V. "Comprehensive Service Programs for Pregnant and Parenting Adolescents," in *Premature Adolescent Pregnancy and Parenthood*. Edited by McAnarney, E. New York: Grune & Stratton, 1983.

Kinard, E.M., and Klerman, L.V. "Teenage Parenting and Child Abuse," *American Journal of Orthopsychiatry* 50(3):481–88, 1980.

Klinman, D.G., et al. "The Teen Father Collaboration: A Demonstration and Research Model," in *Adolescent Fatherhood*. Edited by Lamb, M., and Elster, A. Hillsdale, N.J.: Lawrence Erlbaum Assoc., 1986.

Kreipe, R.E. "Prevention of Adolescent Pregnancy: A Developmental Approach," in *Premature Adolescent Pregnancy and Parenthood*. Edited by McAnarney, E. New York: Grune & Stratton, 1983.

Luthman, S.G., and Kirschenbaum, M. *The Dynamic Family*. Palo Alto, Calif.: Science & Behavior Books, 1974.

McAnarney, E.R., et al. "Premature Parenthood: A Preliminary Report of Adolescent Mother-Infant Interaction," *Pediatric Research* 13:328, 1979.

McCarthy, J., and Menkin, J. "Marriage, Remarriage: Marital Description and Age at First Birth," in *Teenage Sexuality, Pregnancy, and Childbearing*. Edited by Furstenberg, F.F., Jr., et al. Philadelphia: University of Pennsylvania Press, 1981.

McCarthy, J., and Radish, E.S. "Education and Childbearing Among Teenagers," in *Premature Adolescent Pregnancy and Parenthood*. Edited by McAnarney, E. New York: Grune & Stratton, 1983.

Menkin, J. "The Health and Social Consequences of Teenage Childbearing," in *Teenage Sexuality, Pregnancy, and Childbearing*. Edited by Furstenberg, F.F., Jr., et al. Philadelphia: University of Pennsylvania Press, 1981.

Miller, J.R., and Janosik, E.H. *Family–Focused Care*. New York: McGraw-Hill Book Co., 1980.

O'Connell, M., and Moore, M.J. "The Legitimacy Status of First Births to U.S. Women Aged 15–24, 1939–1978," in *Teenage Sexuality, Pregnancy and Childbearing*. Edited by Furstenberg, F.F., Jr., et al. Philadelphia: University of Pennsylvania Press. 1981.

Olson, L. "Social and Psychological Correlates of Pregnancy Resolution Among Adolescent Women: A Review," *American Journal of Orthopsychiatry* 50(3):432–45, 1980.

Orem, D.E. *Nursing: Concepts and Practice*, 2nd ed. New York: McGraw–Hill Book Co., 1980.

Osofsky, H., and Osofsky, J. "Adolescent Adaptation to Pregnancy and Parenthood," in *Premature Adolescent Pregnancy and Parenthood*. Edited by McAnarney, E. New York: Grune & Stratton, 1983.

Presser, H.B. "Sally's Corner: Coping with Unmarried Motherhood," *Journal of Social Issues* 36(1):107–29, 1980.

Robbins, C., et al. "Antecedents of Pregnancy Among Unmarried Adolescents," *Journal of Marriage and the Family* 47(3):567–84, 1985.

Russell, C.S. "Unscheduled Parenthood: Transition to 'Parent' for the Teenager," *Journal of Social Issues* 36(1):445–63, 1980.

Sklar, J., and Berkov, B. "Teenage Family Formation in Post-War America," in *Teenage Sexuality, Pregnancy, and Childbearing*. Edited by Furstenberg, F.F., Jr., et al. Philadelphia: University of Pennsylvania Press, 1981.

Tanner, J.M. "Earlier Maturation," *Scientific American* 218:21-27, 1968.

Wilson, H.S., and Kneisl, C.R. *Psychiatric Nursing*, 2nd ed. Menlo Park, Calif.: Addison-Wesley Publishing Co., 1983.

Wise, S., and Grossman, F.K. "Adolescent Mothers and Their Infants: Psychological Factors in Early Attachment and Interaction," *American Journal of Orthopsychiatry* 50(3):454–68, 1980.

Wright, L.M., and Leahey, M. *Nurses and Families: A Guide to Family Assessment and Intervention*. Philadelphia: F.A. Davis Co., 1984.

15 Intervening with launching-stage families and spouse abuse

Mary Jane Amundson, RN, PhD
Associate Professor
School of Nursing
University of Hawaii
Honolulu, Hawaii

OVERVIEW

Abuse of female partners is a complex social and health problem, caused and reinforced by no single factor. Nurses have a unique opportunity to control and reduce the impact of the battered woman syndrome on individuals, families, and society. Frameworks advanced to explain the causes and dynamics of abuse encompass individual, cultural, and social organizational factors; these have included personality characteristics, stress, poor impulse control, conflict, an intergenerational cycle of violence, and male domination within a relationship.

Although wife abuse generally appears first in younger families, it is not unusual in the launching phase. This chapter's case study illuminates the dynamics of, causes of, and typical interventions in one selected abuse situation. The inclusion in treatment of the battering spouse is *not* always feasible or desired, but, as the case illustrates, it can stimulate both spouses to grow, as individuals and as a couple.

Taking a systems approach, couples therapy focuses on reorganizing the patterns of the woman-man relationship; reality therapy is suggested as a model for creating behavioral change within families with wife abuse.

While this chapter focuses on secondary and tertiary treatment techniques, there is a documented need for more systematic confrontation of wife abuse on the primary prevention level.

CASE STUDY

Maile Cooper, a 38-year-old high school administrator of Japanese ancestry, was referred to a family therapy institute by a family stress information and referral service. During her husband's most recent incidence of physical violence, she had been pushed down a flight of stairs. Her husband, Matt, a

39-year-old Hawaiian policeman, had been drinking with his coworkers before the abusive incident. Emergency room examination revealed severe bruises with no apparent fractures or other injuries.

At the time of referral, Maile had moved out of her house and was staying with her sister. Matt had agreed to seek marital counseling as a condition for her return home. Their only child, Jan, an 18-year-old daughter, was attending an Eastern university and was not home at the time.

The couple was first interviewed separately, to reduce resistance and increase the opportunity for communication. The nurse acknowledged the clients' feelings of embarrassment, fear, and anger, and obtained a brief family history, constructing a genogram and gathering data on the duration and severity of battering, as well as the circumstances and consequences surrounding the last acute incident.

The nurse also explained Walker's (1979) three-stage cycle of violence in light of the Coopers' case. The *first stage* is the initial or build-up phase, characterized by relatively minor violent incidents. These gradually escalate in severity, culminating in a *stage two* (acute battering) incident. Stage one might last only a short time or it might continue for months; stage two usually lasts no more than 24 hours, but involves a harmful or acute escalation of the level and intensity of the violence. The ensuing "honeymoon," or *stage three,* is characterized by cessation of violence and remorse on the part of the abuser, who promises not to be violent again and offers affection and intimacy. This period varies in length. As the cycle repeats itself, stages one and three may be abbreviated. When the cycle is repetitive, the relationship is labeled a "battering relationship."

During the first session, Maile declared that "anything can set Matt off. He has a lightning-fast and ferocious temper. Over the last 15 years he has shoved me or hit me with his hand on my face or arms; sometimes he has hit me with his fist." She reported injuries including black eyes, bloody noses, swollen lips, body bruises, and a broken arm.

Assessment

Guidelines. Assessment began during the separate interviews with Maile and Matt and continued through the first joint session and the remainder of therapy.

The best means of obtaining information on wife abuse is to encourage the woman to talk about the problem from her perspective (Kinlein, 1977), and to listen empathetically without interruption and to clarify what she says. A nurse should explore the woman's feelings about the beatings and reassure her that strong and undesirable emotions are normal in her situation. To facilitate this expression of feelings, the nurse might explain that abused women often feel angry, trapped, and hopeless, and at times fearful of love. They may also lack confidence that the violence is finally over.

Identifying the pattern of abuse is central to total assessment. This identification must address the degree of danger, escalation of frequency and severity, and violence duration and type. Assessment can also focus on stressors within the relationship and displayed types of controlling behavior, such as jealousy and isolation. Exploring these factors with the abused woman shows her where her feelings of low self-esteem, dependence, and depression may originate.

The nurse should also assess each member of a family with domestic violence, since child abuse is frequently found in such homes (Straus et al., 1980; Rosenbaum and O'Leary, 1981). Sexual abuse and discomfort in the sexual relationship should also be assessed, since either may exacerbate existing family conflict.

Models. Two useful assessment documents are Area of Assessment with At-Risk Responses and Indicators of Potential of Actual Wife Abuse from History and Physical Examinations, both of which are described in Campbell (1984a).

The nurse helped Maile plan protective measures for her return home, providing assistance in identifying cues to potential battering situations, deciding who to call and where to go in case of violence, and identifying community support services.

In his initial session, Matt was encouraged to talk about his relationship with Maile. Several predominant themes emerged: anger and loss of control, conflict over role expectations, and feelings of inadequacy.

The nurse openly supported the strength and courage Matt displayed by agreeing to meet with her, and reassured him that he could learn to control his own temper rather than have his behavior "controlled by someone else." Matt was urged to eliminate violence from his relationship with Maile; the therapist helped him recognize cues to uncontrollable anger build-up. Matt identified physical signs (shortness of breath and clenched fists) that usually occurred after a tiring day at work or an evening of "drinking with the guys." Alternatives to battering—relaxation, signals to Maile, physical exercise, and "time out"— were stressed. Matt also was encouraged to seek out others at times of potential crisis. He agreed to a contract for nonviolence, acknowledging that "it's causing me too much trouble."

Assessment yielded a nursing diagnosis of physical abuse related to conjugal violence (Table 15.1). The separate session identified a mutual desire to work on the marital relationship and confirmed that a recurrent cycle of violence was in place.

Planning

Care planning for Matt and Maile began with the initial contact; within Maile's first therapeutic session, goals and interventions were developed. Observable, measurable goals for short-term achievement would reinforce problem-solving and decision-making behaviors. Maile's primary goal was to involve her husband in the counseling process; she was afraid, however, that he would be angry about her seeking help and would refuse to participate. The therapist helped her explore alternatives and suggested options; Matt agreed by phone to attend an individual session and a second meeting with Maile to discuss their situation. Both hoped to continue the marriage.

Both short- and long-term goals were spelled out in an 8-week contract for couples therapy (with individual sessions as necessary). Support and alternative plans were offered freely. Maile and Matt were encouraged to discuss the risks and benefits of exploring their relationship.

Contracting. The first of the couple's 16 therapeutic sessions focused on establishing a contract. Negotiations defined the boundaries of the therapeutic situation, set up a framework of guidelines and expectations, and created a psychologically safe treatment environment.

Maile and Matt's contract included:
• 1.5-hour meetings each week for 8 weeks, followed by progress evaluation and assessment.
• A flexible format allowing both couple and individual counseling as indicated.
• Participation in therapy: Acknowledgement of responsibility for individual behavior and a focus on the present, without violence.
• Behavior between sessions would include no retaliation for feelings or ideas shared in the sessions and no violence.
• Strict therapist confidentiality.
• Work toward mutually negotiated goals.

The goals were based on the belief that violence is a learned behavior—an acquired expression of frustration, anger, hostility, dominance, and aggression—and can be changed. The act of violence was not viewed as the product of a single factor but as a combination of intra- and interpersonal, environmental, social, biological, and situational forces (Drake, 1984).

Matt and Maile's contracted goals were:
• Increased understanding of self, partner, and the dynamics of the relationship.
• Enhanced feelings of self-worth.
• Improved management of stress-producing factors.
• Recognition of anger in oneself and others; development of alternatives to violence.
• Flexibility in sex role expectations.
• Improved problem-solving skills.
• Expanded social and support networks.

Intervention

Intervention for Maile and Matt focused on cognitive-behavioral and communication techniques, especially on the cognitive, problem-solving approach of reality therapy, a series of theoretical principles developed by Dr. William Glasser (1979). Focusing on the present and on behavior,

Table 15.1   Nursing Diagnosis: Physical Abuse Related to Conjugal Violence

Characteristics	Result	Intervention	Outcome (in the Cooper case)
Low self-esteem	• Lack of coping and problem-solving skills • Impaired stress management	• Identify stressful and anxiety-producing situations • Role play problem-solving in identified situations • Rehearse relaxation	• Reduced number of stress-producing factors • Established effective problem-solving process
Dysfunctional communication	• Inability to communicate needs • Increased frustration and anger	• Initiate communicating activities —listening —paraphrasing —feedback —"I" messages • Provide information on cycle of anger • Encourage behavioral rehearsal of angry situations	• Paraphases message to partner's satisfaction • Uses "I" messages to communicate needs • Receives negative feedback without anger
Social isolation	• Lack of support system in crisis • Dependence on mate	• Establish support systems —schedule visits with a family member —join women's and men's support groups	• Seeks out family member for support and comfort • Attends battered women's/men's group on weekly basis for 12 sessions
Unrealistic role expectations	• Increased feelings of anger and sadness • Punishment of mate	• List each partner's expectations • Use paradigm for conflict negotiation	• Wife enrolls in school part-time with mutual agreement • Family schedule viewed as more flexible • Conflict resolution used to negotiate differences
Low impulse control	• Striking out in anger • Verbal disparagement	• List alternatives to hitting —hierarchy of responses —time out —signaling when tension rises —writing about angry feelings • Encourage reduced alcohol intake	• No physical violence in relationship • Drinking no more than three beers, once a week, with co-workers

Table 15.2 Steps in Reality Therapy

Step	Nursing Intervention	Goal
Involvement	• Encourage the use of personal pronouns • Take a genuine interest in the clients' situation; an understanding approach • Reassure clients that they can be happier and are capable of more responsible behavior	• Keep the relationship within the bounds of reality
Focus on behavior	• Relate clients' discussions of feelings to current behavior • Focus on behavior that can be changed, as well as on positive behaviors • Refer to the past only in terms of character-building experiences and finding constructive alternatives to past problems	• Help clients recognize their own roles in determining what happens to them
Self-examination	• Ask clients to judge their own behavior—was it responsible, good for the individual/relationship? • Encourage clients during self-evaluation • Do not make value judgments for clients	• Clients should make value judgments about their own behavior
Planning for behavioral change	• Help clients list alternative behaviors • Guide clients toward the most reasonable, responsible, and effective alternative(s)	• Make specific plans for changing failure behavior to success behavior
Commitment to the plan for change	• Encourage clients to take specific action toward behavioral change	• Enhance clients' feelings of self-worth and maturity through formulation and execution of a realistic behavioral plan
Follow-up	• Make it clear that excuses for failed plans are unacceptable • If clients cannot fulfill the plan, try to make alterations or redesign the program • Do not use punishment—it reinforces the failure identity and harms the nurse-client relationship (note that natural consequences of irresponsible behavior are not considered punishment)	• Establish clients' success identities

the therapist using Glasser's approach guides individuals toward accurate perceptions of themselves and each other; acceptance of reality and fulfillment of individual needs without harm to self or others are highly valued. The crux of this theory is personal responsibility for behavior. Reality therapy assumes that everyone needs a distinct individual identity, that a meaningful identity is essential for full mental health, and that one inevitably sees oneself as having either a successful or failed identity.

The principles of reality therapy provide six major guidelines for directing clients toward more responsible behavior and better feelings about themselves (Table 15.2).

Briefly, reality therapy guides clients to examine their behavior and be critical of it, and then to organize a plan for change, if necessary. Therapy focuses on clients' strengths, successes, and potentials as it helps them lead responsible lives.

In couples counseling, the nurse should clarify mutual goals by asking such questions as, "Have you decided that you definitely want this marriage to work?" The therapist must ask a variety of questions to decipher marital and interpersonal patterns.

In reality therapy, the nurse-therapist builds a relationship based on trust and understanding, provides information, corrects misconceptions, introduces community resources, and supports clients in the decisions they make.

Several general areas should be discussed:
• Responsibility. The wife may feel responsible for her husband's behavior; reinforce that the husband is responsible for his own actions.
• Isolation. Some couples believe that marital violence is happening only to them, and are therefore afraid to discuss it.
• General occurrence. The couple may believe that all marriages are like theirs, so there is no way to solve or eliminate the problem.
• Progress. The couple may feel that the abuse patterns will change spontaneously. Only an end of the violence testifies to actual and lasting change.
• Relationship. The couple may still love each other; help them examine their relationship's strengths and detriments.

Evaluation

After eight sessions, the Coopers and the nurse-therapist agreed that progress in anger identification and management had resulted in the cessation of physical violence and improved communication. Maile and Matt requested an eight-session contract renewal to continue work in these and other areas of difficulty.

At termination, the couple and therapist concurred that behavioral changes had helped resolve problems of low self-esteem, dysfunctional communication, social isolation, unrealistic role expectations, and low impulse control. The Coopers had attended battered women's/men's groups and benefitted from the experience.

Follow-up arrangements were made. Maile and Matt agreed to return for eight additional monthly sessions; the duration of their violent relationship contributed to this decision.

NURSING PROCESS

Assessment

The health problem: Wife abuse. Battering of female partners has recently been recognized in the literature as a significant social problem. According to Walker (1979), a battered woman "is a woman who is repeatedly subjected to any forceful or psychological behavior by a man in order to cause her to do something he wants her to do without any concern for her rights." Physical violence generally refers to hitting, punching, or shoving; common forms of nonphysical abuse include verbal degradation, social isolation, economic deprivation, and home imprisonment (Germain, 1984). The battered woman is the victim of intentional acts of physical violence during the course of an intimate interpersonal relationship with a spouse or male partner. The woman is generally afraid of the man's superior strength and combative ability and has no way of effectively defending herself or stopping him. She has not agreed to the behavior and has no option for reversal, postponement, discussion, or escape. The abusive male intends to cause injury and pain and does not expect retaliation (Davidson, 1978).

At the completion of the first couples therapy session and throughout treatment, the therapist should assess her own feelings and attitudes. A nurse's self-assessment tool for helping families cope (Drake, 1973) applies to this situation:
- To what extent am I meeting my own needs rather than those of my clients?
- Are some of my feelings, such as pity, fear, or helplessness, inappropriate?
- Am I attempting to cope with my feelings about the couple's progress by withdrawing, blaming them prematurely, confronting them, or pressuring them to make a decision?
- Do I believe that the couple has the resources, strengths, interests, and abilities necessary to cope constructively with their difficulties?

Significance of the problem. Time magazine recently reported the following statistics:
- Nearly six million women are abused by their partners each year.
- An estimated 50% to 60% of all women are abused at some time during their marriage.

- Nationwide, police spend one third of their time responding to domestic violence calls.
- Battery is the leading cause of injury to women over 18 years of age.
- In 1981, at least one third of female homicide victims in the United States were killed by a current or estranged husband or boyfriend.
- In 13% of all wife abuse cases, children are also assaulted.
- From 1978 through 1980, the YWCA sheltered 46,100 women and children and counseled 50,000 abused women (only 20% of whom sought assistance) (O'Reilly, 1983).

A Domestic Violence Fact Sheet prepared by the California Commission on the Status of Women (1978) included other information:
- 25% of all murders in the United States occur within the family; 50% are husband-wife killings.
- In California in 1971, one of every three female homicide victims was killed by a mate.
- 25% of all abused women are beaten while pregnant.
- 40% of all police injuries and 20% of all police deaths occur in domestic violence situations.
- Only 2% of all men who beat their female partners are ever prosecuted.

Abuse of female partners is a significant and complex health problem (Campbell, 1984b). Nurses in emergency rooms (Greany, 1984; Stark et al., 1979), community health (Germain, 1984), and maternity settings (Sammons, 1981) must all identify and assess abused women. Greany (1984) states that:
- 21% of all women who use emergency room services are battered.
- Battering precipitates one in every four female suicide attempts.
- 50% of all rapes of women over 30 are part of the battering process.

Psychiatric-mental health nurses counsel women, men, and couples who are both perpetrators and victims of abuse. These nurse-therapists use various theoretical models and frameworks, such as the existential (Weingourt, 1985), family systems (Gemmil, 1982), and grief (Lieberknecht, 1978; Weingourt, 1979) frameworks.

During assessment of potential or identified abused women, nurses must examine their own values, beliefs, and attitudes about the problem. Myths related to female abuse can impede both identification and intervention. Hofeller (1983) describes the most prevalent of these misconceptions and related research findings (Table 15.3).

The assessing nurse must also remain aware of the numerous characteristics shared by most couples experiencing marital violence (Finley, 1981; Loraine, 1981; Pahl, 1985):
- A higher incidence of alcohol abuse
- Absent or weak religious affiliation

- Recurrent verbal disputes
- Low socioeconomic and educational status
- Prior exposure to family violence
—abused as children
—watched one parent batter another
- Adherence to rigid, traditional sex roles.

However, the nurse-therapist must also recognize that an exclusive focus on these characteristics is too narrow and limits data collection.

Violence in the launching-stage family. Although family violence occurs predominantly in young families, the launching-stage family (Wright and Leahey, 1984) is subject to the stressors associated with transition and disruption, which might exacerbate an abuse situation. Even characteristic developmental tasks can provoke battering behavior.

Establishment of independent identities for parents and child(ren). The launching-stage family must relinquish established parent/child roles and negotiate new relationships.

Table 15.3   Myths Surrounding Marital Abuse

Myth	Relevant Research/Findings
Wife abuse occurs only in lower socioeconomic groups	• Domestic violence occurs in all economic, racial, religious, occupational, and age groups • Lower socioeconomic classes are often over-represented in abuse statistics because middle- and upper-class victims have more resources and might be reluctant to report battering
Battered women enjoy abuse (otherwise they would leave)	• Women remain in abusive relationships for many reasons, including: —indoctrination into standard sex roles (learned helplessness, passivity, subservience to the husband, dedication to motherhood) and fear of failing in their role —fear of physical harm —affection for the husband —lack of resources (social and material) —family; friends; medical, legal, and social agencies; shelter; money (Lichtenstein, 1981) —lack of self-esteem
Battered women provoke abuse	• Stated reasons for abuse are usually trivial, e.g. "The food wasn't warm enough," "I didn't like the way she looked at me"
If the abuse complaint were serious, the victim could have her husband arrested	• In some states, police must witness the beating • Many women fear retaliation

In Maile and Matt's case, this adaptation had increased existing disequilibrium. Although violence had occurred consistently over the 15 years while their daughter was living at home, its intensity and frequency increased with her departure. Maile sought assistance after "my only support and reason for staying" disappeared. Her decreased investment in child caretaking also forced her to examine the other meaningful commitments in her life.

Renegotiation of the marital relationship. The launching stage frequently entails an alteration of the basic tenets of the marital relationship.

With child caretaking behind her and an increased need for self-esteem, Maile considered a return to graduate school. Matt, who had completed 3 years of college, viewed this action as a threat to his dominance. For a family already experiencing difficulties in communication, self-esteem, role expectations, and conflict negotiation, the additional stress exceeded the Coopers' limited coping abilities.

Theoretical frameworks. The literature on the causes of wife abuse indicates psychological, sociological, and biological determinants (Dobash and Dobash, 1979; Hilberman, 1980). Feminist literature views woman abuse as a historical expression of male domination manifested within the family and reinforced by current institutions, economic arrangements, and sexist division of labor (Breines and Gordon, 1983; Schechter, 1982). Other authors make commendable attempts to integrate these causes (Giles-Sims, 1983; Rounsaville, 1978).

The roles of intrapsychic factors, alcohol, stress, socialization to abuse, and cultural support have all helped explain woman abuse. Wife abuse has also been placed in the wider perspective of violence against women. The concept of machismo (Campbell, 1984a) proposes that patriarchal social organizations and cultural support for wife abuse set the stage for stress-precipitating violence against wives in men who have learned abusive behavior.

Family systems theories have also emerged as frameworks for understanding marital relationships characterized by chronic physical violence (Bograd, 1984). Wright and Leahey's (1984) family functional assessment (CFAM) considers the details of partners' individual behavior relative to one another, and assesses two basic aspects of family functioning:

The *instrumental* aspect, which refers to such routine daily living activities as eating and sleeping, and includes recognizing the significance of the everyday physical environment in human experience and behavior.

For Maile, the home is not a safe place to vent frustration and hostility, or to express deep feelings. It does not foster emotional security or open communication.

The *expressive* aspect, which centers on the here-and-now, guides data collection in the characteristic subcategories:

• *Emotional communication.* Maile and Matt cannot express the full emotional spectrum; Maile is submissive and overly compliant while Matt has difficulty sharing any but angry feelings.
• *Verbal communication.* Focuses primarily on the couple's relationship as expressed through meaning of words. In the Cooper family, needs and wants were not expressed in words but indirectly, masked by actions.
• *Nonverbal communication.* Both Maile's attempt to avoid Matt's physical space and her constant visual tracking of his movements indicates her constant state of alert.
• *Circular communication.* Refers to reciprocal interpersonal communication and the repetitive sequences noted within relationships. For the Coopers, this communicative pattern is characterized by the battering cycle.
• *Problem solving.* Initially, Matt did not label his battering as a problem. Although Maile wanted to discuss the chronic problem with someone, she felt ashamed and fearful that "it would get back to Matt." This long-term pattern of unresolved conflict increased the stress that already interfered with family problem-solving. The last acutely violent incident, after their daughter had left for college, required medical attention and motivated Maile to call a community assistance agency she had seen advertised in the newspaper.
• *Roles.* The established patterns of behavior for individual family members. Although Maile works full time, she believes that she must fulfill all traditional female roles; Matt views himself in the machismo role described by Campbell (1984a). Since neither partner's expectations are flexible, role conflict is inevitable. Cultural heritage must also be considered since such behaviors as physical control are typical in families of Hawaiian ethnicity.
• *Control.* Methods of influencing another's behavior. Matt exerts psychological control through demeaning and deprecating statements; after physical abuse, he usually apologizes and seeks approval. The use of physical control is usually unpredictable to both partners, although at times violence occurs because Matt wants Maile to do something she does not want to do or disapproves of something she has done. Maile consistently speaks of her lack of power in the relationship and her inability to influence the situation.
• *Beliefs.* Expectations and attitudes. Both Maile and Matt value marriage and closeness with their extended families, but conflicts arise over their differing attitudes toward work and education. Maile gains satisfaction in her employment and seeks higher education to improve her career potential. She states a desire for Matt to further his education also, so that he can achieve a more satisfying position. Matt, however, seems content with his job and values his leisure and recreational activities.
• *Alliances/Coalitions.* The direction, balance, and intensity of intrafamily relationships. Bowen (1976) explains that a three-person relationship is more stable and flexible than a dyad, and is characterized by higher anxiety tolerance and more effective handling of life stresses. In the Cooper family, Maile received nurturing and a sense of togetherness with their daughter, Jan. Jan's departure for college added stress to Maile's relationship with Matt. With more contact with and emphasis on the spouse, the Coopers' incidence and intensity of violent acts increased.

Planning

After the nurse has identified and listed the client family's strengths and problems and summarized the assessment, the couple must help specify target problems, set priorities, and develop goals and interventions that seem workable to them both. Short-term goals should be kept simple and concrete, with efforts aimed at areas where change will produce maximum benefit. Achievement of these early goals shows the couple that their problems have solutions, that they can make changes, and that working toward long-term goals is feasible. Because the couple may feel powerless to alter their present situation, they may react passively to this goal-setting process. The nurse must recognize this and actively help them establish objectives; she should offer support and suggest alternatives as indicated. At this stage, the nurse must also recognize signs of helplessness, frustration, and anger within the couple, as well as rescue fantasies, which may affect care planning.

Goal setting and treatment planning should address the nursing diagnosis of physical abuse related to conjugal violence and should take into account the intensity and form of the violence and the couple's receptiveness to therapy. In abuse therapy, repeated violence must be considered a possibility, and efforts should be made to remove the conditions contributing to the battering. The treatment contract should specify initial, safety-related management decisions, treatment options, and support systems.

Intervention

A review of the past decade's literature on wife abuse reveals a variety of views on dynamics, causation (Roy, 1977; Walker, 1979), perpetration of abusive relationships (Iyer, 1980), and characteristics of male batterers and female victims (Fitch and Papantonio, 1983; Straus, 1976). Treatment of this widespread problem has received less attention; clinical theory and therapeutic models are in the beginning stages of development.

The earliest steps toward treating abused women have been taken by women, some of whom have themselves been battered. There is now a fairly widespread network of shelter homes, support groups, and other services (Cook, 1984; Finley, 1981; Germain, 1984). A second phase in battering intervention involves treating the male abuser. Such programs as Minneapolis' Domestic Abuse Project (Cook and Frantz-Cook, 1984) offer comprehensive individual, group, couples, and family therapy for both men and women involved in violent relationships.

Group therapy, for female victims, male abusers, and couples with violent relationships, alone or in combination with other forms of therapy, is gaining momentum as the treatment of choice (Ponzetti et al., 1982; Rounsaville et al., 1979; Weingourt, 1985). Treatment groups have definite advantages, allowing individuals to:
• Appreciate similarities between concerns and problems.
• Obtain support and feedback on adaptive and maladaptive behaviors.

- Practice new behaviors.
- Improve self-esteem (Mahon, 1981).

A more systemic approach to treatment is also being developed. Nurses must become aware of the diverse factors associated with marital battering and the necessity for treating each partner separately in the initial phases. Bograd (1984) suggests that family systems approaches to wife battering are weakened by inherent biases against women. Her perspective stresses a basic tenet of many feminist theories: that male-female relationships are structured by an unequal, gender-based power structure, and that violence is the most overt and visible form of class control wielded by men over women. Systemic approaches to battering therefore might inadvertently sanction violence against women, or deflect attention from the social conditions that engender battering.

Couples and marital therapies are popular treatment modalities (Cook and Frantz-Cook, 1984; Saunders, 1977). Couples therapy is indicated when the victim is protected from further violence and/or the husband is motivated to seek help, a situation that is more likely when the batterer no longer has access to the victim (Gemmil, 1982). Couples therapy is an appropriate treatment because both batterer and victim play active roles in the dynamics of the relationship. Therapy allows them to learn more about themselves within the marriage framework. Also, it may be easier to acknowledge shared (marital) rather than individual problems, at least initially. Factors influencing the abuser's behavior, such as blaming, communicative dysfunction, and power conflict may also become more apparent through interaction with the victim.

The nurse-therapist must remain alert to certain inherent dangers in couples therapy with batterers and their victims. If the couple does not understand the dynamics of the abuse, unchecked negative feelings following a session can enhance the potential for violence at home. Therapeutic strategies effective for couples with other problems may not be appropriate in violence cases. These couples do not need to learn how to fight fair; the batterer must learn to control his anger and exercise nonfighting techniques.

The primary therapeutic goal in marital abuse is not the survival of the relationship. After the cessation of physical violence, the overall goal is to strengthen the individuals so they can build a new, healthier relationship based on mutual interdependence.

Although no empirical studies compare the outcomes of the various treatment modalities in battering cases, a growing consensus holds that violence will resist change without the treatment or modification of external circumstances, and that couples can be taught to control their violent interactions (Cook and Frantz-Cook, 1984). The specific dynamics of husband-wife violence and their effect on treatment should be the nurse-therapist's focus; four factors should be emphasized (Bograd, 1984):

Nature of the therapeutic alliance. Couples therapy assumes that a mutual treatment alliance has been established between the battered woman and the abusive man. An abusive man may attempt to control therapy; the woman may risk retaliation from her husband after a treatment session. Therefore, a strict no-violence contract must be established at the initial session, mandating that couples therapy will continue only if no violence exists.

Violence as the primary treatment issue. Because family systems therapists often attribute battering to underlying systemic dysfunction, violence can be minimized as the central therapeutic issue in couples therapy. Nevertheless, the life-threatening potential of wife battering must be addressed; complete cessation of violence might be established as the primary goal of intervention. Such issues as unequal power distribution, dysfunctional communication, distorted expectations, and poor problem-solving abilities are potential secondary goals.

Clarification of traditional sex roles. It is axiomatic of some family therapy models that the system can be modified through intervention with the most responsive member. In couples therapy for marital abuse, this member is almost always the wife.

Subtly, the woman may be guided to exert control over her husband's violence by strengthening her female role. However, suggestions that a wife modify her behavior to protect herself against her husband's violence must not imply that the woman initiates abuse.

Some therapists ally themselves with the abusive husband to keep him in therapy. Ideally, he should be considered responsible for his inappropriate expressions of anger. This does not preclude examination of the stressful situations that may create a setting for violence. But the focus must remain on the husband; he is the one who must learn to control his anger. Therapists can address these stresses defined as violence-related without diminishing the wife's power. Until the innate inequality of the marriage is addressed, the likelihood of male domination remains.

Exploration of the marriage. Couples therapy for marital violence should change the context of violent behavior. An abused wife may choose other alternatives, such as moving to a shelter or obtaining a legal order temporarily barring her husband from their home. She may need time to sort through ambivalent thoughts about leaving the relationship. Therefore, structured separation may be included in the initial therapeutic stage (Cook and Frantz-Cook, 1984), with contact restricted to the telephone and therapy sessions.

Feminist theorists hold the man fully responsible for battering, but take the systemic view that the couple is locked into—and perpetuates—a vicious cycle. This view is not incompatible with couples therapy.

Weitzman and Dreen (1982) take an explicitly systemic view of couples therapy in wife beating. They maintain that when a couple is locked into a rigid unilateral control system and the man has learned to be violent in response to stress, battering may become the couple's "resolution" of conflict. Violence erupts from a struggle for control over the relationship's functional rules, rather than from specific problems in the relationship.

Supporting the systems view, Hoffman (1981) cites Berman and colleagues' unpublished suggestion that the cycle of marital violence is characterized by abuse of an "overadequate" spouse by an "underadequate" one. In other words, status inconsistency and incompatibility between partners increase the risk of spouse abuse.

Saunders (1977) reviews social learning models and other theoretical approaches to couples therapy. These interventions, which include communication training, are largely behavioral and encourage problem-solving; their primary aim is elimination of violence through behavioral self-control by both spouses. His model uses cognitive-behavioral strategies.

Table 15.4 summarizes the basic themes emerging from the family abuse literature:

Table 15.4   General Characteristics of Marital Violence

- Violence is cyclical and resists change unless interrupted by treatment or circumstances.
- Violence and the victim's response(s) to it are, at least partially, learned.
- Abusive spouses can be taught to control their violent behavior.
- Couples can be taught to reduce and control dysfunctional anger and violence in their relationship.
- Major systemic problems perpetuate cycles of marital violence, among them:
    —status incompatibility (overadequate wife/underadequate husband)
    —regulation of distance and intimacy
    —jealousy/loyalty
    —control/power/powerlessness.

Evaluation

Nursing evaluation is based upon goal achievement, as perceived by the clients and indicated by established criteria. These questions assist

the evaluation by the nurse-therapists:
- Were goals accomplished? At what level?
- What did the partners learn about themselves? Each other? Their relationship?
- What behaviors have changed?
- Which strategies were successful/helpful and which were not?

Although it is essential to measure results during and after treatment, the success of couples counseling can be truly measured only by the permanence of change. Follow-up sessions increase the likelihood of a positive outcome.

CONCLUSIONS

Physical abuse of females by males is well documented. The proposed causes of wife beating combine theories of personality characteristics, stress, poor impulse control, conflict, intergenerational cycles of violence, and inequitable power distribution. Psychopathology, childhood exposure to family violence, economic stress, cultural sexual norms, isolation from the extended family, and discrepancy between the wife's and husband's achievements also contribute. Often, alcohol use is associated with these conditions, but it is not considered a causal factor in spouse abuse (Gemmill, 1982). Rather, any explanation needs to be located in a broader social context, particularly the context of the structural and ideological forces shaping male/female relationships in marriage and within the wider society.

A systemic approach to treatment of wife battering must consider the relationships between the clinician, the clients (individually and as a couple), and society at large. By neglecting any of these interrelated systems, couples therapists might unintentionally sanction violence against women, construct formulations that hold the wife accountable for the violence, or employ interventions that support a return to traditional gender-based roles.

Psychoanalytic and similar "insight" therapies have dominated marital counseling for battering; they have accomplished little beyond diverting attention from more crucial "here and now" issues. Such approaches reinforce society's tendency to blame the victim, to perpetuate myths of female masochism, and subtly to encourage traditional passive/accepting female roles. On the contrary, reality therapy employed within a systems framework helps eliminate the processes and structures that maintain men's cultural power over women.

In marital abuse, couples therapy has advantages and disadvantages. The woman may not progress toward independence as rapidly as she would in individual or group therapy, but she will probably conquer her acute, immobilizing anxiety and learn to manage anger more constructively. The man will learn to be more appropriately assertive, asking directly for what he wants without threatening and hitting the woman if she fails to satisfy him. Individuals in couples therapy also learn to cope with their periodic depressions and to change their relationship by negotiating as equals, improving communication skills, recognizing each other's anger cues, and adopting alternatives to violence. The therapist concentrates on enabling them to define and clarify their relationship, distinguish between thinking and feeling, learn to take "I" stands, and apply conflict resolution skills.

For meeting needs that fall beyond the scope of professional nursing, the nurse-therapist functions as facilitator, enlisting colleagues in other disciplines. By making such referrals, the nurse also functions as the client's advocate within the health care team (Drake, 1984).

Recognition, analysis, and treatment of violence between intimates is still in its early stages. Understanding a violent act involves integrating psychological and cultural analysis into behavioral descriptions of intimate relationships. No act of violence is simply the pitting of one individual against another; violence contains deep cultural, psychological, and social meanings. At the same time, violent assaults do not merely express a social or cultural problem, such as poverty, unemployment, or male dominance. Each assault is also the personal act of a unique individual. Prevention of wife battering involves changing the overall social structure, as well as changing the rules and values that guide an individual member's behavior and interactions.

REFERENCES

Bograd, M. "Family Systems Approaches to Wife Battering: A Feminist Critique," *American Journal of Orthopsychiatry* 54(4):558–68, 1984.

Bowen, M. "Theory in the Practice of Psychotherapy," in *Family Therapy: Theory and Practice.* Edited by Guerin, P. New York: Garden Press, 1976.

Breines, W., and Gordon, L. "The New Scholarship on Family Violence," *Signs—Journal of Women in Culture and Society* 8(3):490–531, 1983.

California Commission on the Status of Women. *Domestic Violence Fact Sheet.* Sacramento, Calif., 1978.

Campbell, J. "Abuse of Female Partners," in *Nursing Care of Victims of Family Violence.* Edited by Campbell, J., and Humphreys, J. Reston, Va.: Reston Publishing Co., 1984a.

Campbell, J. "Nursing Care of Abused Women," in *Nursing Care of Victims of Family Violence.* Edited by Campbell, J., and Humphreys, J. Reston, Va.: Reston Publishing Co., 1984b.

Cook, D.R., and Frantz-Cook, A. "A Systematic Approach to Wife Battering," *Journal of Marriage and Family Therapy* 10(1):83–93, 1984.

Davidson, J. *Conjugal Crime.* New York: Hawthorn Books, 1978.

Dobash, R.E., and Dobash, R. *Violence Against Wives.* New York: Free Press, 1979.

Drake, R. "Guidelines for Helping Patients and Families Cope with Traumatic Illness," in *Family Centered Community Nursing.* Edited by Reinhart, A.M., and Quinn, M.D. St. Louis: C.V. Mosby Co., 1973.

Drake, V.K. "Battered Women: A Health Care Problem in Disguise," *Image* 14(2):40–48, 1982.

Drake, V.K. "Therapy with Victims of Abuse," in *Mental Health–Psychiatric Nursing.* Edited by Beck, C., et al. St. Louis: C.V. Mosby Co., 1984.

Finley, B. "Nursing Process with the Battered Woman," *Nurse Practitioner* 6(4):11–13, 29, 1981.

Fitch, F.J., and Papantonio, A. "Men Who Batter: Some Pertinent Characteristics," *Journal of Nervous and Mental Disorders* 171(3):190–92, 1983.

Gemmil, F.B. "A Family Approach to the Battered Woman," *Journal of Psychosocial Nursing and Mental Health Services* 20(9):22–39, 1982.

Germain, C.P. "Sheltering Abused Women: A Nursing Perspective," *Journal of Psychosocial Nursing and Mental Health Services* 22(9):24–31, 1984.

Giles-Sims, J. *Wife Battering: A Systems Theory Approach.* New York: Guilford Press, 1983.

Glasser, W., and Zunin, L.M. "Reality Therapy," in *Current Psychotherapies,* 2nd ed. Edited by Corsini, R.J., et al. Itasca, Ill.: F.E. Peacock Publishers, 1979.

Greany, G.D. "Is She a Battered Woman? A Guide for Emergency Response," *American Journal of Nursing* 84(6):724–27, 1984.

Hilberman, E. "Overview: The Wife Beater's Wife: Reconsidered," *American Journal of Psychiatry* 137(11):1336–47, 1980.

Hofeller, K. *Battered Women, Battered Lives.* Palo Alto, Calif.: R&E Research Associates, 1983.

Hoffman, L. *Foundations of Family Therapy.* New York: Basic Books, 1981.

Iyer, P. "The Battered Wife," *Nursing80* 1:53–55, 1980.

Kinlein, M.L. *Independent Nursing Practice with Clients.* Philadelphia: J.B. Lippincott Co., 1977.

Lichtenstein, V.R. "The Battered Woman: Guidelines for Effective Nursing Intervention," *Issues in Mental Health Nursing* 3:237–50, 1981.

Lieberknecht, K. "Helping the Battered Wife," *American Journal of Nursing* 78(4):654–56, 1978.

Loraine, K. "Battered Women: The Ways You Can Help," *RN* 44(10):22–28, 102, 1981.

Mahon, L. "Common Characteristics of Abused Women," *Issues in Mental Health Nursing* 3:137–57, 1981.

Martin, D. *Battered Wives.* San Francisco: Glide Publications, 1976.

O'Reilly, J. "Wife Beating: The Silent Crime," *Time* 122(10):23–26, 1983.

Pahl, J., ed. *Private Violence and Public Policy.* London: Routledge and Kegan Paul, 1985.

Ponzetti, J., Jr., et al. "Violence Between Couples: Profiling the Male Abuser," *Personnel and Guidance Journal:* 222–24, December 1982.

Rosenbaum, A., and O'Leary, D. "Children: The Unintended Victims of Marital Violence," *American Journal of Orthopsychiatry* 51(4):692–99, 1981.

Rounsaville, B.J. "Theories in Marital Violence: Evidence from a Study of Battered Women," *Victimology* 3(1–2):11–31, 1978.

Rounsaville, B., et al. "The Natural History of a Psychotherapy Group for Battered Women," *Psychiatry* 42:63–78, 1979.

Roy, M., ed. *Battered Women: A Psychosociological Study of Domestic Violence.* New York: Van Nostrand Reinhold Co., 1977.

Sammons, L.N. "Battered and Pregnant," *Maternal-Child Nursing* 6(4):246–50, 1981.

Saunders, D. "Marital Violence: Dimensions of the Problem and Modes of Intervention," *Journal of Marriage and Family Counseling* 3:43–52, 1977.

Schechter, S. *Women and Male Violence.* Boston: South End Press, 1982.

Stark, E., et al. "Medicine and Patriarchal Violence: The Social Construction of a 'Private' Event," *International Journal of Health Services* 9(3):461–93, 1979.

Straus, M.A. "Sexual Inequality, Cultural Norms, and Wife Beating," *Victimology* 1(1):63–66, 1976.

Straus, M.A. "A Sociological Perspective on the Prevention and Treatment of Wife Beating," in *Battered Women: A Psychosociological Study of Domestic Violence.* Edited by Roy, M. New York: Van Nostrand Reinhold Co., 1977.

Straus, M., et al. *Behind Closed Doors: Violence in the American Family.* Garden City, N.Y.: Anchor Books, 1980.

Walker, L.E. *The Battered Woman.* New York: Harper & Row, 1979.

Walker, L.E. "Battered Women, Psychology, and Public Policy," *American Psychologist* 39(10):1178–82, 1984.

Weingourt, R. "Battered Women: The Grieving Process," *Journal of Psychiatric Nursing* 17(4):40–47, 1979.

Weingourt, R. "Never to Be Alone: Existential Therapy with Battered Women," *Journal of Psychosocial Nursing and Mental Health Services* 23(3):24–29, 1985.

Weitzman, J., and Dreen, K. "Wife Beating: A View of the Marital Dyad," *Social Casework* 63:259–65, 1982.

Wright, L.M., and Leahey, M. *Nurses and Families: A Guide to Family Assessment and Intervention.* Philadelphia: F.A. Davis Co., 1984.

16

Intervening with middle-aged families and post-traumatic stress disorder

Loretta Macon Birckhead, RN, EdD
Assistant Professor
School of Nursing
Center for the Health Sciences
University of California, Los Angeles
Los Angeles, California

OVERVIEW

The diagnosis posttraumatic stress disorder (PTSD) comes from a somewhat unconventional aspect of psychosocial theory. By definition, it is a result not so much of pretraumatic psychological factors as of the trauma itself—in short, it asserts that *anyone* would have difficulty coping with such a trauma. PTSD-producing traumas have included incest and serving in the Vietnam war. Although the PTSD diagnosis applies to individuals, it is best treated by considering *both* the individual client *and* that client's family.

The nurse can expect to find that the PTSD client's alienation, sleep disturbances, inappropriate reactions to safe posttraumatic circumstances, rage, and lack of concentration have had a profound effect on the family. Combined cognitive and direct problem-centered techniques are useful in work with such families.

CASE STUDY

During individual psychotherapy, Pamela Triffen expressed increasing distress at the state of her marriage. She did not know what to do with her husband Stan, whom she described as unpredictably enraged and unresponsive to her. Though in emotional pain and depressed, Pamela described her difficulties easily. After two sessions with his wife, the nurse-therapist decided to ask Stan to participate in a couples session with Pamela.

Assessment

Stan is 45 years old, Pamela 43. They have two children, Ethel (11) and Mac (13). The family lives in an upper-middle-class neighborhood and the children attend a private school. Both children's behaviors are age-appropriate, despite Pamela and Stan's rigid and overzealous nurturance and discipline, respectively. The spouses state that they "care very much for each other, but find it difficult to make things go smoothly now."

Pamela is the identified patient. She reacts with crying and silence to what she perceives as slights from other family members. Both Stan and the children treat her as weak. In the assessment of Pamela's background it was revealed that, although she grew up with many material possessions, she had no expectations placed upon her for development of her own identity. What was expected of her was to marry and have a man "take care of her," the same role her mother played with her father.

The assessment of Stan's background revealed that he was a military veteran of Vietnam; he described this experience as a "horrible one." Stan never discussed this period with his wife since "she wouldn't want to hear about it," but during the past several years he has relived the experience through nightmares. He explains these dreams to Pamela as "concerns about the business." Upon further assessment Stan was diagnosed as having posttraumatic stress disorder. (PTSD).

Planning

In planning the Triffens' family treatment it was decided that Stan and Pamela would undergo 12 sessions of couple's therapy, one every 2 weeks. They would also be seen individually every other week. Parents and children would be seen together once every 2 months.

Intervention

The nurse-therapist helped Pamela explore whether or not she wished to change her life's direction, that is, to assume different family and societal roles. This was accomplished by guiding her in discussions of the positive and negative aspects of her current identity, as well as by encouraging her to test new roles.

Stan was helped to explore his Vietnam experience and how it had affected him and his marriage. He was asked to review difficult wartime experiences and monitor his stress reactions. He was also asked to identify ways in which he could continue to work through his Vietnam experience after family therapy ended.

Ethel and Mac were encouraged to discuss with their parents specific events in their lives, emphasizing whatever benefit they derived from that activity. They were also asked to react to their parents' description of what was occurring in their own lives.

At the conclusion of therapy Stan had shared his Vietnam experience with Pamela, and expressed a sense of unburdening as a result. There was a sense of genuine caring as Pamela and Stan reviewed Stan's Vietnam tour. Pamela enrolled in nutrition classes, though it was unclear what goal they would ultimately serve. She also became less dependent on the family in structuring her life. The children readily learned how to share their own thoughts and experiences, and frequently gave useful feedback when their parents did not communicate effectively.

Evaluation

One central therapeutic goal, however, was not achieved: perceived momentum toward family growth. Both Pamela and Stan needed to break individual barriers to self-actualization; each made significant progress in that area, but their relationship did not gain a sense of cohesiveness. Perhaps time would allow each spouse's intrinsic growth orientation to come to the fore as individual pain and trauma subsided. The termination process included the development of a plan to involve Pamela and Stan individually in a nonfamily support network, which could introduce additional ideas and energy for further growth.

NURSING PROCESS

Assessment

The health problem: Posttraumatic stress disorder (PTSD). PTSD can involve any of a number of severe emotional reactions to experienced trauma—trauma to which it would be difficult for anyone to adjust. These reactions may occur shortly after the traumatic event(s) or years later. War, incest, concentration camps, captivity, and natural disasters have all been known to produce PTSD.

The Diagnostic and Statistical Manual of Mental Disorders III or DSM III (American Psychiatric Association, 1980) establishes the following diagnostic criteria for PTSD:
• An identifiable stressor.
• Reactions (i.e., memories, dreams, "flashbacks," or behaving as if the traumatic event were recurring) *after* the occurrence of a traumatic event.
• Decreased interaction with the world (blunted emotions, withdrawal, alienation).
• At least two of the following symptoms that were not present before the traumatic event:
—Hyperalertness.
—Sleep disturbance.
—Survival guilt or guilt about actions necessary for survival.
—Lack of concentration.
—Retreat from experiences reminiscent of the trauma.
—Exaggerated symptoms when events similar to the traumatic event(s) occur.

PTSD was a new listing in DSM III. DSM II contained no listing for Traumatic Neurosis; even DSM I's diagnostic categories related to war neurosis had been removed.

Currently, there are no clear indications of the number of trauma victims in the general population. During the Vietnam war years, 2.5 to 4 million soldiers served (Berman et al., 1982), and 17% of those now experience combat-related flashbacks (Hendin et al., 1984). Even these figures are incomplete, however. Indeed, many incest victims and veterans suffering repercussions of their experience are just now coming to the attention of health care providers.

Middle-aged families. Stan and Pamela Triffen are a middle-aged couple.

exploited as a result of the war experience, but he did not understand these emotions and could not explain them to others. He believed people would "think less of him" if he talked about his Vietnam experience.

Recommitting energy formerly devoted to child care to new pursuits. Since returning from Vietnam, Stan had pursued no new interests. He was deeply ashamed of what his country had done in Vietnam and did not know how to make sense of the war. He had developed a business selling outdoor equipment, but airplane travel associated with the business reminded him of helicopter flying in the Vietnam jungles, and caused more intense nightmares. The horror of Vietnam sapped his energy; work, family, and other pursuits seemed unimportant.

Reestablishing the basis of relationships as roles and interests change. Intimacy in general was a family concern. Stan had been close to the friends who had died in Vietnam. Since that time he had sealed himself off from others; being close meant the pain of tragic loss. He refused to attend group meetings with other Vietnam veterans where he might have begun to share his experiences and learn to be close again.

Using developed competencies to expand or deepen interests. America's army in Vietnam had been the youngest in the nation's history—the average age was 18 (Berman et al., 1982). After his military service, Stan was uncertain about a career, although he had been employed since high school. College did not interest him. His father had died while Stan was in his teens, leaving the boy to support the family. Stan went from working during and after school to the Army, and back to working, eventually setting up his own business. He had never had Erickson's "psychological moratorium" (Berman et al., 1982)—that is, a time in late adolescence to postpone lifetime commitments in favor of exploring options and developing an enduring sense of identity. Instead, Stan's military experience had left him with a sense of meaningless-ness that threatened his marriage.

Adapting to events of the latter part of middle age. In general, Stan was not dealing with his age group's developmental issues. It was as if the events of middle age were there, but he was too numb to experience them. His continued involvement with the war kept Stan from being aware of present events.

Theoretical approaches. A number of theories or models can guide the nurse-clinician working with PTSD families. Potentially, important assessment elements are:

Family structural assessment: Internal boundaries. At initial assessment, the Triffen family had rigid boundaries: spouses disengaged from each other, Stan disengaged from his children. There were also diffuse boundaries in Pamela's enmeshment with her children.

Family developmental assessment: Maladaptive attachments. No close emotional ties existed between Stan and Pamela or between Stan and his children.

Family functional assessment: Expressive emotional communication and roles. Stan could not express emotions to his family; Pamela expressed emotion but only sadness. Control was a central role problem: Stan controlled other family members by his distance and dictatorial nature, while Pamela controlled the others by crying and withdrawal (pouting).

Figley (1978) and Egendorf and colleagues (1981) have described the nature of the Vietnam veteran and the veteran's family in terms of their potential problems. Williams (1980) has written on the particular needs of women partners of the Vietnam veteran.

From an assessment standpoint, it is best to include questions about war or other traumatic experiences on assessment forms. Doing so will make it harder for the *clinician* to evade difficult topics. Laufer and colleagues (1984) provide a scale for measuring the extent of combat (as the extent to which the person's life was threatened or participation in/witnessing abusive violence). The nurse can use such a scale to determine the nature of the veteran's war experience if the veteran states he did serve in the military and denies having the PTSD symptoms listed in DSM III. Herman and Hirschman (1981) have described similar ways to elicit information about incest—e.g., paternal violence, a disabled mother, or an "acting-out" adolescent girl.

In sum, Stan was not working to accomplish age-appropriate developmental tasks. His difficult Vietnam experience and resulting PTSD is likely to hinder growth within his family until it is worked through.

Stan's family was not productively working on its developmental tasks, because the energy needed for growth was being expended on individual issues. Pamela, with her poor sense of identity, waited for Stan to provide one for her. Stan, in impossible fashion, was waiting for a chance to repeat—and alter his role in—the Vietnam war.

Planning

Effective planning for nurses working with middle-aged families with war-related PTSD depends upon:
• Familiarity with the nature of potential problems faced by the (Vietnam) veteran. The nurse will not find this information easy to obtain since systematic, scholarly studies of Vietnam veterans are scant (Egendorf, 1982).
• Familiarity with the potential problems faced by *families* of the (Vietnam) veteran.
• Readiness to deal with personal reactions to client descriptions of war-related experiences (Haley, 1985).

• Skill in dealing with reality-oriented issues in a manner that does not alienate the veteran/client.

• A positive outlook. Given the "tightrope" that the middle-aged family may walk between giving in to normal personal losses and maintaining the energy necessary for revitalizing life at a new developmental stage, the nurse must believe that there are still worthwhile goals to complete in middle age and beyond.

Intervention

Two-pronged therapy—family and individual—is indicated for Vietnam veterans with PTSD. Individual therapy helps the veteran work through residual feelings from the combat experience, feelings that are blocking further growth. The conflict arising from the war service must be resolved if growth is to proceed.

(With incest survivors, the nurse should work first with the victim individually before involving the family of origin, in order to strengthen the client for discussions with a family that is itself trauma-causing. In the case of the Vietnam veteran it is the war, not the family, that "causes" the trauma.)

In some cases, the PTSD veteran can integrate satisfying relationships, but others in his environment perpetuate difficulties rather than assist in their resolution. Family therapy can serve as a bridge for fully integrating the individual veteran and the family.

Family therapy would be contraindicated, however, for the psychotic PTSD victim. Such clients should be treated individually until they can cope with the affects and issues that would be discussed in family therapy. Similarly, the nurse should not pursue the discussion of traumatic events with the client until the client can cope with the related anxiety. The unique etiology of PTSD requires that the caregiver be able to withstand the horror, fear, or other extreme emotion(s) resulting from hearing about the traumatic experience (Haley, 1985).

In many PTSD treatment situations, it may be harder for the caregiver to withstand the difficult emotions associated with discussions of severe trauma than it is for the client. This can result in the nurse's directly or indirectly encouraging the client not to talk about the trauma. In such cases, the client may be directed to talk about something that the clinician *can* stand to hear—depression, passivity, and so on. This can delay the recovery process in a devastating way; it may replicate in the clinical situation a major symptom of the illness itself— silence. Often the Vietnam veteran, for instance, cannot talk about war-related trauma, feels guilty about what happened in Vietnam, and does not think anything can be done to ease the negative feelings.

Types of intervention. The interventions used in the Triffens' case were direct, meaning that the family was requested to do or not do some cognitive, affective, and/or behavioral task(s) (Wright and Leahey, 1984). Direct interventions were chosen because the family was compliant; members wanted change but lacked the experience and behavioral/ affective repertoire of conducting their life together differently.

Several *general* principles should be remembered when working with the Vietnam veteran:
• No one in the family should be made to feel ashamed. Both Stan and Pamela were vulnerable to this emotion: Pamela for not developing her own identity, and Stan for not coming to terms with his Vietnam experience.
• The caregiver should be nonjudgmental. A veteran, for example, might have been personally involved in atrocities, or the therapist might disagree with the United States' presence in Vietnam, but such phenomena should not affect the health professional's behavior toward the client.
• The nurse-therapist should decide how to answer the client's claim that only someone who has experienced the same trauma can understand.
• The nurse-clinician in the community is in an ideal position to treat the PTSD victim in the family context. The nurse's education has included preparation in crisis theory and the working nurse should be familiar with community support resources. Also, the nurse has expertise in identifying client needs and making referrals to the appropriate professionals. For instance, the veteran may need psychiatric hospitalization or medication such as antidepressants or propranolol (Berman et al., 1982).

The nurse treating a PTSD family—particularly the family of a Vietnam veteran—might also use the following *specific* interventions:

Cognitive. Provide information to the family about:
• The nature of the Vietnam war, particularly from the soldier's standpoint, which may be different from the standpoint in previous wars. Provide this information while obtaining validation from the client.
• How the war affected the soldier (including tendencies toward abuse and behavioral/emotional problems, or antisocial behavior).
• The meaning of PTSD.

After approximately four or five sessions with the couple and with the spouses individually, discuss with the entire family how the PTSD affects the victim and the family. Help family members describe the chain reaction of events in their family—what triggers PTSD behaviors and what adaptive functions they serve. Defining PTSD's *adaptive* function is especially important if relatives are to understand that the victim's behavior had some purpose beyond simply hurting the family.

In the Triffen family, Stan would "order" the children to do things, in the belief that he was letting the children know what was expected. Pamela viewed such behavior as cold. The nurse-therapist defined the behavior as "Stan's building a sense of security for the children, though each one in the family viewed such behavior in Stan differently." Casting the behavior in a positive, supportive light helped ease the surrounding tension, which enabled members to comment on it casually when it occurred. Over time Stan's conduct lost its hurtful connotations.

Affective. The nurse-therapist should also, through a positive, supportive attitude, encourage disclosure, foster family support, and encourage family controls on extreme negative emotions (such as Stan's or Pamela's irritability and withdrawal, or Pamela's sadness).

Behavioral. The nurse can assign "homework" for the spouses. Pamela, for example, was to read and report on selected literature describing the Vietnam veteran's experience before, during, and after the war; Stan wrote an essay from Pamela's standpoint entitled, "This is me." Both spouses needed to practice communicating, and to plan and implement alternative behaviors. Each practiced using humor, described family happenings as "simply" another aspect of reality (thereby removing some of the emotional charge), talked "as if" the particular spouse were his or her "old self" during a happier period of their life, and played out potentially difficult scripts in the relatively nonpressured environment of the couple's session.

Evaluation

The evaluation process consists of assessing whether or not the nurse and family have attained the goals they established for themselves at the start (Wright and Leahey, 1984). A useful goal for a family in treatment is achieving awareness of the need for the coexistence of oneself and others in the family system. This awareness should occur in the context of a renewed sense of well-being both within the individuals and within the family as a unit (Birckhead, 1984).

As stated earlier, Stan and Pamela's family did not attain a sense of *family* momentum for growth, though each parent made individual strides. There was still no joy in togetherness. It was difficult for Stan to demonstrate such feelings to Pamela. He maintained strong bonds with the servicemen with whom he had endured hardship and trauma. In Vietnam, for instance, Stan had carried items from fellow soldiers, obtaining from them a sense of protection. How could Pamela provoke such a bonding reaction when her upbringing had encouraged her to look to her husband for stimuli and direction?

Generally, when evaluating progress in the PTSD client, the nurse should look for:
- The client's ability to recognize his self- and other-directed emotions.
- Reorganized perceptions of the traumatic experience—a broader and more balanced view.
- Tolerance of strong emotions, especially grief and rage.
- The ability to communicate needs and experiences.
- The ability to care for others.

It was the latter goal, the ability to care for others, that Stan and Pamela could not meet. Such a goal could be worked on in a Vietnam veterans' support group or couples therapy. Stan stated that he did not want to be around other veterans "who are depressed" but said he would seek some other type of group support. Stan and the therapist agreed to disagree about the usefulness of his joining a group of other Vietnam veterans.

CONCLUSIONS

Posttraumatic stress disorder is a new diagnosis for a problem that has existed for many years. Incest, for instance, has occurred for centuries, yet only recently have psychiatric researchers and clinicians focused on the trauma itself as a clinical event, rather than on such secondary problems as depression and anxiety. The Vietnam war has produced in many veterans such delayed stress reactions.

Family therapy is central to any effective PTSD treatment. Brett and Ostroff (1985) stated numerous reasons why PTSD is *not* identified by clinicians, including the fact that it is often misdiagnosed as another illness (i.e., schizophrenia) and the fact that clients are frequently silent about traumatic events.

The nurse can be a pivotal figure in identifying PTSD cases, as well as in referring and treating them. For various reasons, society continues to be silent and uncomfortable about PTSD-producing traumas, including combat experiences and incest. The nurse cannot afford to observe these taboos.

PTSD has as one of its symptoms impaired relationships with others; this impairment is best dealt with in therapy with the family members themselves. If family therapy is not feasible, the nurse may work with individuals. Bowen (1978, p. 342) has said that the person in individual psychotherapy can affect the family; that is, if the therapist "can manage a viable and moderately intense therapeutic relationship with the (individual) patient, and the patient remains in viable contact with the family, it can calm and modify relationships within the family." However, much more "reality" can be dealt with if the clinician can work with the family itself, since it is with family members that clients actually live their lives. No quantitative research exists to compare the effectiveness of the various combinations of family, group, and individual psychotherapy in PTSD treatment.

REFERENCES

American Psychiatric Association. *Diagnostic and Statistical Manual of Mental Disorders,* 3rd ed. Washington, D.C.: American Psychiatric Association, 1980.

Berman, S., et al. "An Inpatient Program for Vietnam Combat Veterans in a Veterans Administration Hospital," *Hospital and Community Psychiatry* 33:919-22, 1982.

Birckhead, Loretta."The Self/Other Dialectic Model: A Conceptual Framework for Psychiatric/Mental Health Nursing," Manuscript submitted for publication, 1984.

Bowen, Murray. *Family Therapy in Clinical Practice.* New York: Jason Aronson, 1978.

Brett, E., and Ostroff, R. "Imagery and Posttraumatic Stress Disorder: An Overview," *American Journal of Psychiatry* 142:417-24, 1985.

Egendorf, A. "The Postwar Healing of Vietnam Veterans: Recent Research," *Hospital and Community Psychiatry* 33:901-08, 1982.

Egendorf, A., et al. *Legacies of Vietnam: Comparative Adjustment of Veterans and Their Peers.* Washington, D.C.: Veterans Administration, 1981.

Figley, C., ed. *Stress Disorders among Vietnam Veterans.* New York: Brunner-Mazel, 1978.

Haley, S. "Some of My Best Friends Are Dead: Treatment of the Posttraumatic Stress Disorder Patient and Family," *Family Systems Medicine* 3:17-26, 1985.

Hendin, H., et al. "The Reliving Experience in Vietnam Veterans with Posttraumatic Stress Disorder," *Comprehensive Psychiatry* 25:165-73, 1984.

Herman, J., and Hirschman, L. "Families at Risk for Father-Daughter Incest," *American Journal of Psychiatry* 138:967-70, 1981.

Laufer, R., et al. "Posttraumatic Stress Disorder (PTSD) Reconsidered: PTSD Among Vietnam Veterans," in *Posttraumatic Stress Disorder—Psychological and Biological Sequelae.* Edited by Van Der Kolb, B. Washington, D.C.: American Psychiatric Association, 1984.

Lidz, T. "Phases of Adult Life: An Overview," in *Mid-Life: Developmental and Clinical Issues.* Edited by Daton, N. New York: Brunner-Mazel, 1980.

McCullough, P. "Launching Children and Moving On," in *The Family Life Cycle: A Framework for Family Therapy.* Edited by Carter, E., and McGoldrick, M. New York: Gardner Press, 1980.

Murray, R.B., and Zentner, J.P. *Nursing Assessment and Health Promotion Through the Life Span.* Englewood Cliffs, N.J.: Prentice-Hall, 1979.

Williams, C. "The Veteran System with a Focus on Women Partners: Theoretical Considerations, Problems, and Treatment Strategies," in *Post-Traumatic Stress Disorders of the Vietnam Veteran: Observations and Recommendations for the Psychological Treatment of the Veteran and His Family.* Edited by Williams, T. Cincinnati: Disabled American Veterans, 1980.

Wright, L., and Leahey, M. *Nurses and Families: A Guide to Family Assessment and Intervention.* Philadelphia: F.A. Davis Co., 1984.

17 Intervening with aging families and depression

Kathleen S. King, RN, MS
Clinical Assistant Professor
College of Nursing
University of Utah
Salt Lake City, Utah

OVERVIEW

Using a case study as illustration, the author presents a family therapy model, Functional Family Therapy (FFT), and its application to depression in aging families. This model combines systems and behavioral perspectives for family assessment and intervention in a brief, problem-focused treatment context. FFT-based assessment, including interpretation of family dynamics, and FFT-based therapy are described, and advantages and disadvantages of the model for aging families are discussed. The case study centers on assessment of family dynamics to determine whether an older woman suffered from dementia or depression.

CASE STUDY

Doris and John Blake were referred for marital therapy because Doris had increasing difficulty functioning at home. The couple moved to a mobile home 3 months previously, after returning from a foreign country where they had chaperoned young missionaries from their church. According to John, Doris was forgetful. He complained that she burned meals on the stove, could not find items she had put away, and had difficulty remembering commitments. She knew she was forgetful and believed she was ill, but she complained only of fatigue and sadness. Doris was evaluated for Alzheimer's disease at a university medical center; the physician referred the couple for counseling because he was not certain whether she suffered from dementia or depression.

Family values and ties were very important to this couple. Their two adult children lived nearby. Their son, Sam, was divorced but planned to remarry soon. Their daughter, Janet, was married to Bob; they were experiencing financial and marital difficulties. Their children's difficulties disheartened the Blakes, because such things conflicted with the family's religious values. Doris worried constantly about her children, yet resented what she perceived as Janet's disrespect toward her. Relations were strained and uncomfortable.

This family was seen by a nurse at the geriatric clinic where Doris was evaluated. The chosen treatment method, Functional Family Therapy (FFT), was developed by James Alexander. It is a short-term, problem-focused approach to resolving family difficulties (Alexander and Parsons, 1982), based on the view that behavior is neither healthy nor unhealthy. Instead, the key factor—and that which the nurse must assess—is the degree to which family members meet their interpersonal needs. The most powerful intervention used is reattribution or relabeling to create a positive, blameless context for resolution of differences.

The Blake family was seen for eight sessions. During the first, John and Doris talked about themselves and their concerns. John repeatedly and negatively labeled Doris as "sick, forgetful," and a "worrier." In a typical interaction, John identified something Doris forgot and pointed it out to her; Doris then complained of feeling "put down" and withdrew. John tried to hug her and get closer, but she became angry and pushed him away. Obviously, their interpersonal needs were mismatched at this time: Doris was creating distance while her husband was trying to get closer.

Changing the perceived meaning of Doris' behavior to minimize blaming and maximize positive understanding was an important intervention. In this case, her forgetfulness was relabeled "preoccupation"—a consequence of their recent move and their children's difficulties. This suited John's belief that "all that's wrong with Doris is she worries too much," and thus provided an alternate (to dementia) and more acceptable explanation for her behavior. Doris was glad to be called preoccupied; she agreed that, given their recent return to the United States, their move to a mobile home, and the family discord, she *did* have a lot on her mind and that it was no wonder she forgot things from time to time.

John's complaints to and about Doris were relabeled as "conscientious" and "concerned" instead of critical. The couple's unsynchronous interaction patterns were relabeled as poor timing, so that Doris would not be identified as "cold" or John as "insensitive." In addition, the nurse focused on the *relationship* between Doris and John rather than on Doris' competence or lack thereof.

Doris and John had asked for assistance in working through some of the issues with their adult children, so the nurse saw the entire family in the later sessions, hoping that this would shed further light on family interactional patterns. Janet and Bob attended four sessions; Sam attended three. Janet fit the pattern described by Kuypers and Bengtson (1983): she felt overly responsible for her mother's care and predicted continual decline for her. Sam, on the other hand, played down the family's troubles and said everything was fine. Then Janet and Sam would fight about who was right! Bob supported Doris but remained disengaged from conflicts.

Toward the end of therapy, when the adult children no longer attended, a precipitating factor to Doris' mental deficits emerged: Bob had stolen his in-laws' credit cards and run up huge bills. No one mentioned that, perhaps for fear that the nurse would insist he be prosecuted. In light of this fact, the family relationships made more sense—Janet felt guilty and burdened with responsibility for her husband's act. By choosing to protect Bob despite their unhappiness with their losses, the Blakes increased the existing strain. As Herr (1984) noted, how could such a group deal with their hurt and anger and still remain a family?

Because she knew nothing about the theft until late in the course of therapy, the nurse had based her relabeling of the family difficulties on the changes that inevitably come with age, instead of on Doris' "sickness." This aspect of therapy legitimized some of the boundaries between the Blakes and their children, which helped unify Doris and John as a couple. Their mutual support became the foundation from which they survived the crisis caused by Bob's theft and exploitation.

Trust between the Blakes and their nurse developed slowly, which was a drawback in such a time-limited therapeutic context. Short-term and immediate issues were addressed, but long-range concerns were not.

NURSING PROCESS

Assessment

The health problem: Depression. Depression is the most prevalent mental disorder among older adults in both inpatient settings and communities (Butler and Lewis, 1982). Gurland and colleagues' (1980) epidemiological study of depression revealed that approximately 13% of elders meet the criteria for a major affective disorder; another 9% meet most of them. In this age group, distinction between symptoms of depression and those of dementia is crucial. Depression is treatable and reversible; dementia is not.

Clinically, the depressed elder is less likely than a younger adult to present with dysphoria (Zarit, 1980). The older adult more often complains of memory loss, thus leading the clinician to look for organic brain disease. In addition, depressed elders often exhibit psychomotor retardation, fatigue, and loss of interest in pleasurable activities (Zarit, 1980). These symptoms, in conjunction with complaints about memory loss, can confound accurate diagnosis. Interestingly, Zarit (1984) claims that none of his elderly clients with dementia has ever presented with complaints of memory loss; family members usually report this problem.

Alzheimer's disease has, over the past few years, become the subject of intensive international research and debate. Zarit (1984) claims an "epidemic" of dementia has emerged, with laymen and scientists alike trying to recognize and diagnose the illness. Because identification of dementing illness is frequently imprecise, behavior related to other difficulties may be atttributed to Alzheimer's or a related disorder. In the worst case, an elder can be mistakenly diagnosed and labeled as "demented," resulting in a self-fulfilling prophecy (McKay, 1975). Such individuals are treated *as if* they are demented and they eventually begin to act that way (Alexander and Parsons, 1982; Tudor, 1952; Zarit, 1980). Thus, assessment must be accurate. Kahn (1975) suggests that clinicians should err on the side of *not* diagnosing dementia when it might be present. Given time, a demented person's function will decline, and the dementia will get worse, making itself known.

Elderly families. The family with aging members faces special tasks and issues. Kuypers and Bengtson (1983) describe four predictable transitions or crises that influence well-being in old age. These include child launching, retirement, widowhood, and physical decline. Although the impact of these will differ with the individual family, "each of these events involves other family members as willing or unwilling participants in the negotiation of change" (p. 214). Any one of these developmental crises, especially when combined with other situational demands, can upset the balance of family life.

Subjective interpretations of crisis influence the perceived severity of stress and consequently the choice of coping responses. Kuypers and Bengtson (1983) suggest that when an elderly parent becomes the source of stress, the meaning that adult children attach to that transition may magnify its intensity and increase the extent of systemic disruption. These assigned meanings may arise from cultural stereotypes of aging, which include inevitable, irreversible decline and increasing dependence. Middle-aged children may feel threatened—squeezed for time, energy, and resources to meet the demands of both elderly parents and their own children. As a result, they may deny the significance of a parent's problem and delay action, or they may overreact, trying to do everything for the elder and taking away independence.

Unresolved family conflicts can also complicate identification of, and effective intervention for, the depressed elder. Kuypers and Bengtson (1983, p. 225) note:

> Issues of dependency, individuation, and survival are never resolved. By virtue of abated yet lingering tensions, older families exist in a state of potential disruption, with yesterday's issues likely to reemerge as family intensity is increased in efforts to work together on a developing crisis.

In summary, predictable transitions occurring in a context of unresolved conflict can make the aging family more vulnerable and less able to manage crises. Obviously, not all older families break down in the face of a crisis, but clinicians should recognize that the potential for disintegration exists and must be assessed along with the presenting problem.

Theoretical models: Individual-oriented approaches. Nurses frequently assess and intervene by focusing on the individual client. Yet family dynamics plays an important role in the development and management of all individual health difficulties. Models for understanding dementia and depression in old age are, for the most part, individually oriented (Gallagher and Thompson, 1983; Zarit, 1980). Although families are considered important sources of information and support, their dynamics are seldom considered in explaining an elder's behavior.

Several techniques have proven successful in nursing depressed older adults. Gallagher and Thompson's (1983) investigation of the clinical management of depression showed that brief, individual psychotherapy—behavioral, cognitive, or psychodynamic—was effective. Chaisson and colleagues (1984) also claim that individual cognitive therapy helped their small sample of depressed older people.

Although he has not investigated treatment approaches empirically, Zarit (1980, 1984) believes that his adaptation of Beck's cognitive therapy of depression suits older adults. He suggests starting with individual therapy, then recommending family or group intervention as needed.

Family approaches: FFT. No individually-oriented approach incorporates assessment of family dynamics, despite the fact that individual and family competencies are linked (Kuypers and Bengtson, 1983). Herr and Weakland (1979) were the first to promote a specific model of family intervention for the elderly. They noted that "all behavioral problems, no matter how great or small, have an interactional element to them" (p. 184). They take a brief, problem-focused approach to family difficulties, directing their energy toward resolution of specific issues rather than wholesale "growth" or family reorganization. Depression and confusion were among the family problems covered by their model.

Under the FFT model, the clinician's first critical question is: How does each person's behavior contribute to the fulfillment of relationship needs? Assessment, therefore, focuses on the emotional, cognitive, and relational outcomes of family interactions. FFT differs from some other family therapy models in the sense that no ideal notion of healthy family life guides the therapist (Barton and Alexander, 1981). A family member's behavior is viewed as neither "good" nor "bad." Instead, the nurse determines how effectively that behavior meets the family's interpersonal needs. Viewed on a continuum, need-satisfaction ranges from contact/closeness to distance/independence. Nurturing another is an example of contact; having many outside activities is an example of distancing. Depression contributes neither to closeness or distance because the depressed person sends simultaneous "come here/go away" messages. In the Blake case, the initial FFT assessment found that Doris' past illnesses had elicited attention and support from her children. Indeed, illness became a technique for initiating contact with her children.

Interventions—the techniques that create hope and promote positive images of oneself and others—are the meat of FFT. A major therapeutic goal is to help family members see each other in new and benign ways (Alexander and Parsons, 1982). The nurse's first objectives are to divert blame from the identified patient and to show families that problems arise not from a single person but from the group's inability to resolve its differences acceptably. Intervention goals include focusing on relationships, not the "problem" person, and changing the meanings that family members attach to their interactions with each other.

The last phase of treatment is education: teaching family members how to maintain their changed perceptions of the problem and its solutions. Many strategies, including communication effectiveness, message centers, token economies, behavior management, contingency contracting, and relaxation techniques, can be applied.

Like most family therapy models, FFT works best when all family members are involved in treatment from the beginning. Preliminary mental health evaluation of the "problem" client alone can reinforce the "sick" label.

Coyne (1976) and Watzlawick and Coyne (1980) favor systemic family assessment in depression. Interaction between the family and its depressed member can become a vicious cycle: the depressed person complains of feeling blue or down; family and loved ones respond, understandably, with messages to "cheer up," "just get busy and you'll feel better," and "try taking a more positive attitude;" such responses can make the depressed person *more* anxious and sad. In extreme cases, depressed clients may consider suicide to convince their families that their difficulties are genuine and serious. As loved ones consciously try to appear cheerful, the depressed person sinks lower, and the cycle continues. Although medication can help elevate mood in depressed elders in the short term (Herr, 1984), long-term improvement requires an understanding of the systemic interactions surrounding the depressive behavior (Barton and Alexander, 1981).

Considered in isolation from her family, Doris' problems could not be identified clearly as either depression or dementia. While meeting with the client's daughter and son-in-law, however, the nurse observed patterns of interaction similar to those described by Coyne (1976). Janet spoke with dramatic flair about the enormous burden she carried to keep the family going. Her mother and father were falling apart and she believed that all responsibility fell on her shoulders. Her brother, Sam, would not help. And although Janet believed that she was like her father, she complained about the way he "browbeat" her mother and made her feel sad and weak. Janet insisted that if her mother would "assert herself" with John, everything would be just fine. Doris countered with a list of reasons why she could not do that; she was "too sick" and she did not think it would help anyway. Doris' illnesses and dependence on her family, particularly on Janet, lay at the heart of several old conflicts.

Planning

According to Alexander and Parsons (1982), out-of-session reviewing and planning is as important as in-session work. FFT assessment focuses specifically on family interaction patterns and their interpersonal outcomes. Between-session planning may involve identifying family dyads and their functions and developing a set of nonjudgmental relabels to use in future sessions. In this case, John sought greater closeness with Doris, who sought both contact and privacy—in other words, her behavior seemed to be mid-pointing with John's. Midpointing is the interpersonal function that results from a blend of intimacy and distance.

FFT emphasizes understanding of dyads because mismatched functions between two people often produce interpersonal conflict (Barton and Alexander, 1981). The operation of an entire family cannot be understood until all the involved pairs have been assessed and their interpersonal outcomes identified. For instance, increased contact with one family member may increase distance from another. When Doris called Janet to discuss her conflicts with John, she at once became closer to her daughter and more distant from her husband. Even when given only sketchy clues, an observant nurse can arrive at a plausible explanation for a family's seemingly senseless and painful, yet repetitive, interactions.

The nurse should review her assessment data about each family member. If it turns out that little information was obtained about one or more person(s), the nurse should try to determine why that happened and develop further assessment goals for the next session. Letting any participant remain in the background can result in incomplete information about the relational impact of behavior, lack of focus on the interdependent nature of family life, and a lack of commitment to the therapy process. In other words, the absence of even one family member will undermine the process of change for everyone else.

Intervention

Successful interventions require careful between-session planning (Alexander and Parsons, 1982). Initially, the nurse's goal is to enter the family conveying confidence, hope, and caring. She should use a nonjudgmental stance and positive relabeling to instill hope. It is during the planning stage that interpersonal functions, the personal meanings of behavior, and informational gaps are identified and potential relabels developed. Tables 17.1 through 17.4 present the Blakes' nurse's speculations about those areas for each family member.

To avoid alienating any individual, the nurse must understand what it is like to be this person in this family. The meaning of each member's behavior and concerns must be clarified. Clients will make statements that seem innocuous enough, but which may be quite idiosyncratic in meaning. For instance, Janet said at one point, "I'm a lot like my Dad." That statement might indicate pride, shame, or nothing at all, but unless the nurse probed the meaning it had for her and for the other family members, wrong assumptions could easily be made. Regarding that issue, when the nurse asked Bob what Janet meant when she said she resembled her father, he replied that "he's too domineering." The meanings each family member expressed about various issues are listed in Table 17.1.

Besides exploring personal meanings for behavior, the nurse should illuminate through questions and comments the interdependent nature of family life. She might ask the others to comment about one family member's statements, as in the example above, or she might have the family describe sequences of behavior. Instead of letting one person describe an entire sequence, the nurse should switch from one member to another, thus vividly demonstrating how one person's behavior affects another's. For instance, when Doris complained that John criticized her for forgetting things, the nurse asked Janet, "How did you get involved in this?" Startled, Janet said that her mother would call her and complain; then Janet would go to her father and demand that he "lay off." Predictably, *they* would get into an argument. At this point,

Table 17.1 Clarifying Meaning of Thoughts and Behavior

Mother	Sickness and timidity seemed to be ways of getting attention and perhaps avoiding responsibility; she is also an emotional center for the family and her pain is felt by all.
Father	Came to therapy to make things right with his family again even though he did not believe it was proper to go to outsiders for help; talked with little emotion, perhaps to maintain image of being in control.
Daughter	Came across as pushy and domineering, which she believed was necessary to get something done for her parents, who she thought were doing very poorly; when she described herself as being like her father, she meant she felt as if she were too domineering.
Son-in-law	In charge, in his nuclear family; told his wife to sign permission to videotape form and she did; stayed out of family disputes but was very supportive of his mother-in-law (it was not clear why).
Son	Assumed his parents were doing well and would manage; valued his own and his family's independence and did not want to interfere in his parents' lives.

the nurse pointed out that Doris' "forgetting" gave Janet and John a chance to talk. Arguing was a definite, if not overly pleasant, way of making contact. Comments and interpretations like these can be used to identify the kinds of interpersonal outcomes family members seek and how effectively they are achieving them. Table 17.2 lists strategies used to establish a relational focus for each family member.

The nurse must also create an environment of hope. A nonjudgmental context and behavior relabeling can accomplish that end. Relabels should simultaneously describe interpersonal functions and recast them in a more positive light (Barton and Alexander, 1981). This technique avoids negation; the words used should elicit understanding and positive feelings (King et al., 1983). "As descriptions of the sequences, feelings, cognitions, and attributes are repeated, the therapist through relabeling begins to challenge the family's reality, creating a new one that describes each family member in different and nonblaming terms" (Alexander and Parsons, 1982, p. 112).

To minimize blaming, a nurse can point out similarities between family members (Alexander and Parsons, 1982). Another's behavior is understandable the more it is "like" one's own. The author relabeled Janet as being a lot like her mother, a tactic that surprised and pleased both. Relabeling can also offer a plausible, more positive explanation

Table 17.2 Interventions to Establish a Relationship Focus

	Assessed Problem	Intervention
Mother		• Suggested that similarities between her and her daughter that made the mother seem strong • Emphasized the biological link between them
Father	Strongly value-based responses pushed others away	• Suggested that his complaints were demonstrations of concern and caring
Daughter	Was not proud of herself as being like her father	• Suggested that intense feelings showed how much she cared for her parents
Son-in-law	Unclear relationship with his wife (unstated family issue)	• Suggested that concern for his mother-in-law was his way of becoming involved with the family
Son	Sister complained that his lack of involvement left her with full responsibility of care for her parents	• Suggested his distance was a form of respect for his parents' ability to solve problems on their own

of behavior. When Sam joined the family sessions, he was on the defensive because his sister had labeled him as uncaring and uninvolved. The nurse suggested that Sam's "hands off" policy regarding his parents demonstrated his faith in their ability to manage their own problems. This placed Sam in a positive light and protected his interpersonal function of maintaining distance. Other relabels used with each family member are listed in Table 17.3.

Another effective relabeling technique is to cast the whole family as victims of their problems. For instance, the nurse portrayed the Blake family as victims of change. Successful relabeling reduces family defensiveness and resistance, and enables members to change their concept of the problem and of the problem person.

The last important area the nurse should explore is the functional importance of interpersonal behavior (see Table 17.4). First, the nurse determines the outcomes of interactional sequences. As noted earlier, John sought contact with his wife, who pushed him away when she felt hurt and angry. He sought intimacy; she sought midpointing—closeness tempered by independence. These mismatched functions pitted the Blakes against each other at a time when they wanted to be united. The goal of FFT is to *not* change those functions, i.e., to get John to retreat or Doris to get closer, but rather to legitimize each person's perspective and interpersonal goals. In this case, the nurse focused on the timing of John's requests for intimacy. He was not *unreasonable* in his wishes, but he could more be *effective* in his choice of when to approach Doris. Similarly, Doris was told that her independence was important, but for it to work, she needed to give John clearer messages as to when she was available to him.

Table 17.3   Relabels

Mother	Relabeled forgetfulness as "preoccupation," which seemed to make sense to her and her husband.
Father	Relabeled his complaining as protection and his worry as a "burden of responsibility" to keep the family going.
Daughter	Relabeled as individually like her mother (had family, raised children, center of family life), relabeled her criticism as "honest feedback" (even though it might hurt, she was truthful).
Son-in-law	Relabeled his disagreements with his wife as concern for his mother-in-law.
Son	Relabeled his lack of involvement with his parents as his way of showing them his faith in their ability to handle whatever comes along and being protective of his and others' independence.

Relabeling individual and family behavior is an indirect strategy designed to "confuse" family members. Alexander and Parsons (1982) assume that families come in with a clear definition of their troubles; usually they blame one member (or more), the scapegoat, and claim that if this person were more cooperative or more open, everyone would be satisfied. The relabeling process involves attributing benign or positive intentions to the problem behavior, which confuses the other family members and forces them to look at the situation in new and hopeful ways. This strategy also yields important assessment information—it reveals who accepts or rejects the new labels and who becomes enthusiastic about communicating.

The nurse can begin relabeling during the initial assessment, even before she knows the family well. This allows positive interventions early on and keeps the family from becoming discouraged. Other models call for more extensive data gathering prior to relabeling (for example, Herr and Weakland, 1979) because inaccurate relabels might inhibit family members' willingness to raise issues. For instance, the Blakes' nurse relabeled Doris' complaints about her husband as "honest" early in the first session, and effectively stopped John from talking about other concerns. Therapists need to time their relabels carefully and keep them tentative so that clients can challenge those that do not fit. Supervision is a critical component of FFT.

The education phase of FFT is a direct intervention. As noted earlier, education involves teaching family members skills and providing experiences that shore up their new positive perceptions of themselves

Table 17.4   Functions of Interpersonal Behavior

Mother	Her needs brought everyone together; she seemed to be asking for more independence but not to be cut off from family; seemed to be midpointing with John.
Father	Wanted more contact with his wife, but his "shoulds" put her (and others) off; was seeking contact but did not know how to establish it.
Daughter	Could feel her and her parents' pain deeply and intensely; pushed people away with her anger; the nurse wondered if she wanted contact with parents without having to deal with her or their problems.
Son-in-law	Sought contact with Doris by supporting her; overall, seemed to be hanging uninvolved in the background; perhaps was midpointing—not involved and not completely independent.
Son	Seemed to be seeking independence from parents and sister; placed high value on making it on his own.

and their problems. The therapy phase involves "unfreezing" rigid behavioral, cognitive, and emotional patterns within the family. Education solidifies new response patterns that more efficiently and effectively fulfill interpersonal functions. In this case, education centered on legitimizing the need for distance between the elder couple and their adult children. In addition, John worked on the timing of his approaches to Doris for intimacy.

Evaluation

FFT is a time-limited approach and the nurse is encouraged to avoid long-term issues unless specifically asked to deal with them by the family. Termination criteria include greater observable spontaneity in family discussions and problem solving. Some families will begin to do their own positive relabeling; others will simply announce that they have gotten what they wanted and are ready to end the sessions. Alexander and Parsons (1982) encourage clinicians to make termination open-ended, reminding families that they can come back if they wish.

After a few FFT sessions, Doris' problems disappeared. She had less trouble with her memory and began to limit Janet's involvement in her relationship with John. John made special dates with her, which met some of his needs for contact. Once the elder Blakes were united, they no longer wanted counseling.

A pitfall of short-term therapy for older adults is that trust may take a long time to develop, and the nurse might not learn about important issues until it is time to terminate. Doris and John, for instance, waited until the end of the FFT sessions to divulge the fact Bob had stolen their credit card. Doris may indeed have developed memory problems in order to forget the emotional and financial loss. Although they had not learned how to manage their feelings and still remain a family (Herr, 1984), the Blakes left therapy once again on the same "team." It was hoped that the positive relabels of each other that they now carried would allow them to continue working through their loss.

Investigating the effects of FFT with families of juvenile delinquents, Klein and colleagues (1976) found that this model ameliorated the problem adolescent's behavior and prevented younger siblings from committing delinquent acts. Unfortunately, no empirical study of this model's application to the problems of aging yet exists. As in many areas of mental health and aging, little clinical research has been done with older people (Zarit, 1984). The limited clinical evidence available suggests that FFT can improve the elder member's efficacy. Pragmatic older adults seem to appreciate the direct, brief, focused treatment that FFT provides. The pitfalls are that trust may develop too slowly and that the nurse must act on limited information. If, however, small changes can be made in the ways family members perceive each other, they are in a better place to continue their own problem solving.

CONCLUSIONS

Older adults seek counseling for many of the same reasons people of any age group do, as well as for issues peculiar to aging (Zarit, 1980). Thus, a spectrum of therapeutic offerings will be necessary to meet diverse demands. Brief therapies offer families an opportunity to focus on specific, troublesome aspects of their lives and make initial changes to get back on the "right track." When the presenting complaint is relieved (Weakland and Fisch, 1984), termination is indicated, whether or not the nurse had dealt with ongoing family themes and issues.

In the case study, Doris and John's presenting complaint was not clear until family dynamics were assessed. It was helpful to know that, historically, Doris had had contact with her children, especially Janet, when she was ill. When means other than illness were developed for her to communicate with family members, her forgetfulness decreased. Through relabeling, John and Doris learned to side with each other instead of blaming each other, which helped them resolve their anger and hurt. Janet and Bob were encouraged to manage their marital and financial difficulties independently; contact with John and Doris was to be structured around family gatherings. Successful relabels defined Doris as "preoccupied" instead of "sick," and John as "conscientious" instead of "meddling."

Doris and John decided to protect Bob from criminal prosecution, and were reluctant to discuss his theft until they were sure that the nurse would listen without compelling them to press charges. Although this was not suggested to Doris and John, they were, in fact, "protective to a fault." Doris had chosen to appear demented rather than expose her son-in-law's crime. Assessment and intervention with the family revealed that Doris was not demented, and these efforts prevented further mislabeling. The gains in therapy enabled Doris and John to become united again and face their ongoing concerns as a couple.

REFERENCES

Alexander, J., and Parsons, B. *Functional Family Therapy.* Monterey, Calif.: Brooks/Cole Publishing Co., 1982.

Barton, C., and Alexander, J. "Functional Family Therapy," in *Handbook of Family Therapy.* Edited by Gurman, A., and Kniskern, D. New York: Brunner-Mazel, 1981.

Butler, R., and Lewis, M. *Aging and Mental Health: Positive Psychosocial and Biomedical Approaches,* 3rd ed. St. Louis: C.V. Mosby Co., 1982.

Chaisson, M., et al. "Treating the Depressed Elderly," *Journal of Psychosocial Nursing* 22:25–30, 1984.

Cohler, B. "Autonomy and Interdependence in the Family of Adulthood: A Psychological Perspective," *Gerontologist* 23:33–39, 1983.

Coyne, J. "Toward an Interactional Description of Depression," *Psychiatry* 39:28–39, 1976.

Gallagher, D., and Thompson, L. "Effectiveness of Psychotherapy for Both Endogenous and Nonendogenous Depression in Older Adult Outpatients," *Journal of Gerontology* 38:707–12, 1983.

Gurland, B., et al. "The Epidemiology of Depression and Dementia in the Elderly: The Use of Multiple Indicators of These Conditions," in *Psychopathology in the Aged.* Edited by Cole, J., and Barret, J. New York: Raven Press, 1980.

Herr, J. "Aging Families," *MRI Summer Series.* Palo Alto, Calif., 1984.

Herr, J., and Weakland, J. *Counseling Elders and Their Families: Practical Techniques for Applied Gerontology.* New York: Springer Publishing Co., 1979.

Kahn, P. "The Mental Health System and the Future Aged," *Gerontologist* 15:24-31, 1975.

King, K., and Haas, L. "Brain Pathology or Family Dysfunction: Application of a Family Therapy Model to Issues of Aging." (in press.)

King, M., et al. *Irresistible Communication: Positive Skill for the Health Professional.* Philadelphia: W.B. Saunders Co., 1983.

Klein, N., et al. "Impact of Family Systems Intervention on Recidivism and Sibling Delinquency: A Model of a Primary Prevention Program Evaluation," *Journal of Clinical and Consulting Psychology* 45:469–72, 1976.

Kuypers, J., and Bengtson, V. "Toward Competence in the Older Family," in *Family Relationships in Later Life.* Edited by Brubaker, T. Beverly Hills, Calif.: Sage Publications, 1983.

McKay, J. "The Label That Disables," in *The Psychiatric Nurse as a Family Therapist.* Edited by Smoyak, S. New York: John Wiley & Sons, 1975.

Tudor, G. "A Sociopsychiatric Nursing Approach to Intervention in a Problem of Mutual Withdrawal on a Mental Hospital Ward," *Psychiatry* 15:174–216, 1952.

Watzlawick, P., and Coyne, J. "Depression Following Stroke: Brief, Problem-Focused Family Treatment," *Family Process* 19:13–18, 1980.

Weakland, J., and Fisch, R. "Cases That 'Don't Make Sense': Strategic Treatment in Medical Practice," *Family Systems Medicine* 2:125–36, 1984.

Zarit, S. *Aging and Mental Disorders: Psychological Approaches to Assessment and Treatment.* New York: Free Press, 1980.

Zarit, S. Personal communication, January 27, 1984.

18 Intervening with single-parent families with children having school problems

Evan Imber-Black, PhD
Coordinator, Psychosocial Training
Social Medicine Residency Program
Montefiore Medical Center
Albert Einstein College of Medicine
New York, New York

OVERVIEW

This chapter addresses the school-related problems of children in single-parent families from the perspective that the family-school system interaction is the most salient issue. After reviewing relevant statistics on single-parent families, the chapter will focus on the life cycle, highlighting the diverse problems of single-parent families. A multicontextual assessment model is presented, identifying family and school as the essential systems in a child's life. Nursing roles and responsibilities, particularly in school and community health settings, are discussed, with a focus on the ways nurses can foster more positive attitudes toward single-parent families. An intervention evaluation continuum, illustrated by case material, concludes the chapter.

CASE STUDY

At the start of the school year, two fifth-grade boys, Bill Zuker and Alan Majeski, began appearing regularly in the nurse's office complaining of illness and asking to go home. Medical examinations revealed no organic causes for their complaints. Both were bright boys with no history of problems.

Bill, age 11, lives with his mother and father. When an appointment was made by the school principal, both parents attended, impressing school personnel with their commitment to their child's well-being. Together, the teacher, principal, school nurse, and parents devised a simple behavioral plan to keep Bill at school and help him overcome his initial difficulties. The parents cooperated and Bill's problems abated.

Alan, also 11, lives with his mother. His parents had divorced 2 years before and his father moved away; Alan saw him infrequently. Nevertheless, Alan had made a fairly good adjustment to his changed family situation until the present school year, when he found his new teacher to be harsh and intimidating. School personnel knew Alan and his mother, and treated the family in special ways, expecting less from both child *and* parent than they did from other families. Rather than inviting Alan's mother in for a conference, school personnel decided that Alan "lacked a male role model" and told her that he needed a "Big Brother." Alan's mother, who already felt guilty about the boy's situation, began to feel even worse. Alan, noticing her increased sadness, began wanting to stay home and comfort her, and began developing more in-school stomach aches.

At that point, the school decided that Alan's mother was needy and referred her for therapy, suggesting that she request a male counselor. Alan, too, was referred for therapy, separately from his mother. By December, Alan and his mother had three professional helpers in their lives (a "Big Brother" and two therapists), and the school telephoned Alan's mother weekly. Alan, noticing that his mother was at least busier and somewhat less lonely, continued to have intermittent problems; school personnel had begun to accept them as an unresolvable "part of Alan's situation." Alan's mother felt far less competent than she had 4 months earlier, and was convinced it was all "because she was a single parent."

NURSING PROCESS

Assessment

The single parent family
Statistical overview. Twenty-three percent of all children under 17 in the United States live with a single adult who is either a parent, another relative, or a nonrelative (Hacker, 1983). Twenty percent of all school-aged children live in single-parent families, and 90% of those single parents are women (Morawetz and Walker, 1984). The median family income for such female-headed single-parent families is less than half that of other families (Francke, 1983). According to the United States National Advisory Council on Economic Opportunity, single women and their children will comprise all of the nation's poor by the year 2000 (1983). Fifty-nine percent of single-parent women are awarded child support. Thirty-five percent of this group actually receive such support (Morawetz and Walker, 1984).

Many single parents require education and job training to adequately care for their families. Often, they find themselves in the impossible situation of being encouraged to seek training without adequate funds to do so, and of being told to seek work while simultaneously being criticized for not remaining at home with their children (Imber-Black, 1985). Since the work day is usually longer than the school day, the single parent requires adequate and reasonable day care, which is sorely lacking. Only 100 school districts in the United States provide the before and after school programs needed by single and working parents (Francke, 1983).

While these statistics present a grim view of the hardships faced by many single-parent families, awareness of the diversity of single-parent families is crucial; neither the family form nor its functioning should be stereotyped. Too often, the single-parent family is studied and examined for what is missing, rather than for its inherent strengths (Imber-Black, in press). Negative definition of the single-parent family often becomes a self-fulfilling prophecy.

Life cycle tasks. Professional helpers working with single-parent families can often normalize, rather than pathologize, family difficulties. Here, a family life cycle perspective is extremely useful. A nurse needs answers to the following questions:

How long has the family head been a single parent? Any family that has lost a member, whether through separation, divorce, hospitalization, imprisonment, or death, requires time to reorganize, redistribute roles, and accommodate individual members' responses to loss and change. Thus, a recently formed single-parent family is often dealing with stresses not experienced by similar families of longer duration. Such stresses may run the gamut from social-emotional turmoil to pragmatic issues of finances and child care.

What circumstances surrounded the organization of the single-parent family? A family rebuilding after a recent divorce faces social and emotional issues unlike those faced by a family dealing with a parent's death. By the same token, a single-parent family in which there never was a marriage and from which the father has always been absent is different from one where the parents have separated after 15 years of cooperative child-rearing. Social attitudes vary greatly toward these differing circumstances; the child and widowed parent are more likely to receive sympathy and understanding, while the divorced family may be viewed as riddled with incompetence and failure. Even with changing attitudes, the never-married parent is often viewed as morally suspect. Society sends powerful messages to the single-parent family about itself; these attitudes and judgments are often most apparent to children in school settings, where they are reflected in the behavior of other children and in teacher/administration expectations.

What visiting arrangements exist for the noncustodial parent? A nurse must discover if visiting patterns are comfortable for all concerned, or if they are difficult or are being contested. Children who are the object of custody or visitation struggles often find themselves in a fierce loyalty bind where to love and enjoy one parent means siding against the other. Vigorous questioning by parents regarding the absent spouse's visitations and behavior may make the child an unwilling go-between for two warring adults. Such children are frequently at risk for developing symptoms as an effort to escape their impossible situation.

What family and social support systems exist for the single-parent family?
A nurse should discern whether the single-parent family exists within a
larger support network of relatives and friends or is cut off and isolated. As new single-parent families consolidate their organization,
friends and extended family often feel compelled to take sides. Friends
of the former couple, usually couples themselves, may withdraw because of their own discomfort with separation and divorce. The extended
family may view the single parent herself as a child, as one who cannot
head a household. On the other hand, a single-parent family may have
many relatives and friends, and may use such supports to enhance
its functioning.

Obviously, before offering services to single-parent families, a nurse
must assess and use existing supports. In Alan's case, he spent much
valuable time with an uncle; school authorities ignored this when they
advocated referral for a "Big Brother."

What other life cycle tasks is the family facing? A single-parent family
deals with many of the same developmental tasks as any other family,
e.g., children beginning school, adolescent struggles for independence,
children leaving home, providing support for aging and often ill grandparents—tasks that may not be acknowledged or accomplished if "single
parent" status becomes the overriding preoccupation.

One critical life cycle issue for single-parent families is remarriage of
the divorced spouse, which requires yet another reworking of every
established relationship. Previously agreeable visitation and financial
support patterns may be called into question, and children will have to
adjust to myriad new stepparent and sibling relationships.

A second critical developmental issue is a child's "leaving home."
This transition, which is difficult for most families, can be especially
problematic for the single-parent family; the child leaving home may
have been a "parental" child who assisted with younger children, served
as the parent's confidant or main source of emotional support, or acted
as the go-between for warring parents. As young adults, these children
may face difficulties leaving home, and find many reasons for postpon-
ing emancipation (Whiting, 1980).

A careful assessment of a single-parent family with school-age children requires sensitivity to both the unique life cycle issues inherent in
such organizations and the generic developmental tasks that all families face. If the initial life cycle task facing single-parent families—that
of consolidating a functional family unit that differs from, but is not
inherently less viable than, a two-parent family—is not accomplished,
all subsequent problem-solving and development may be handicapped.

The single-parent family and the school system. The two most important systems in the life of a developing child are the family system and the school system. When one encounters school-related problems in a child from a single-parent family, the nurse must examine both systems and their interaction before intervening. Too often, only the family system is assessed, and the school system and its idiosyncratic interface with the single-parent family is ignored. The following areas of contextual assessment command attention.

Dyadic cycles. The single-parent family and the school form an interacting pair, or dyad. As such, predictable interaction cycles may develop. Such cycles may be *complementary* or *symmetrical.* In a complementary cycle, for instance, the school might offer specific help that the single mother accepts. In such a relationship, school and parent exchange behaviors that mirror each other, e.g., the role of help-giver versus help-receiver. However, in a problematic interaction, the school labels the single parent as "incompetent" or "helpless" and offers too much or inappropriate assistance. The single parent may respond with increased "helplessness," thus leading the school to refer her to experts who, again, label her as "incompetent."

This pattern of *escalating complementarity* can be seen in Alan's case. Without carefully assessing the family's circumstances, the school system offered an abundance of "help," all of which exacerbated Alan's mother's senses of guilt and failure. With more and more "help," she became increasingly "helpless." Actions by one system escalated responses in the other.

In a *symmetrical* cycle, school and family exhibit similar behaviors. Thus, the school may advise the family and the family may advise the school regarding the shared member, the child. School systems, in their interactions with two-parent, middle-class families whose norms and perceived morals match the school's, often form comfortable symmetrical relationships marked by mutual respect. However, families, including single-parent families, that do not meet the school system's expectations of "normal" may get into *symmetrically escalating* struggles marked by competition over "who knows what's best" for the child. The school may insist on one course of action, the family on another. Cooperation disappears, and often the child's problems continue or worsen.

Since single-parent families are often viewed as inherently deficient by society at large—which the school system represents—and since many single parents accept this view of themselves, escalating complementary cycles are the most common problematic patterns encountered between single-parent families and school systems.

Problematic triads. The single parent, school personnel, and the child may interact in ways that promote the formation of dysfunctional triads. In situations of marked and intense divergence between home and school, the child may be caught in a loyalty bind (similar to that between divorced parents and a child) that handicaps adequate functioning (Coppersmith [Imber-Black], 1982). A child caught between two parents *and* between home and school might suffer serious developmental and coping problems, and might become a person who feels he can never do anything right, and for whom taking a stand is dangerous, since it implies breaking relationships.

Such triadic patterns between single-parent families and schools can become increasingly complex as other professionals or the noncustodial parent manipulates the relationship through unplanned alliances and splits.

Brief example. Karen, 13, was the only child of a single mother, Ms. Cane, who had never married and who had given birth to Karen at age 17. At age 30, Ms. Cane was poor and possessed no job skills. She and Karen shared a close and loving relationship when Karen was small, but this deteriorated as Karen entered adolescence.

When she had become pregnant with Karen, Ms. Cane was treated badly by her own school system and was forced to leave. She acquired resentment toward public schools, and felt schools did not protect one's best interests. At Karen's school, a guidance counselor took a special interest in her, subtly suggesting that she could provide better nurturing for Karen than Ms. Cane could. The more Karen and her mother argued, the more the counselor took Karen's side, inadvertently preventing the two from solving their own problem together. Ms. Cane felt more and more threatened by her daughter's relationship with the counselor; Karen felt torn; it seemed impossible to love and care for her mother and to receive the counselor's support. When Karen began reporting to the school nurse's office complaining of headaches, the school nurse, after ruling out organic causes, sided with the counselor against Ms. Cane. Feeling more and more blamed for her daughter's problems, as well as overwhelmed and unsupported, Ms. Cane agreed to foster care placement for Karen. Karen interpreted her mother's decision as rejection, and her well-being deteriorated further as more and more professionals became involved.

A more efficacious approach would have been for the counselor to join firmly with Ms. Cane, affirming her role as Karen's mother and helping her negotiate solutions. Or the nurse could have remained neutral in the struggle between Ms. Cane and the counselor, and facilitated problem-solving from a nonallied position.

Boundaries. The single-parent family and school systems exist on opposite sides of a boundary that regulates the flow and nature of information exchange, and which organizes participants' decision-making and problem-solving for a developing child. Minuchin (1974) describes a continuum of boundaries from "enmeshment" (diffuse) to "disengagement" (rigid). When the boundaries between the single-parent family and the school are diffuse, the school may intrude into a widening circle of family concerns that are beyond its appropriate educational mandate (Coppersmith [Imber-Black], 1983a). Such intrusion may handicap parental functioning, as it did in Karen's case. On the other hand, a single parent who is isolated and lacks an adequate support network might invite enmeshment with school personnel; indeed, she may come to rely on teachers or counselors in lieu of friends. To maintain such close involvement between school personnel and a single parent, a child may display problematic behavior (Imber-Black, 1985). Enmeshment between home and school may also be characterized by "gossip" among school personnel about the single parent's circumstances.

When the boundaries between the single-parent family and the school are too rigid, the exchange of appropriate information becomes difficult. Relationships are marked by mutual distancing and mistrust, and each system develops distorted views of the other that are not correctable by feedback. Here, the child's needs may suffer, because neither of these two salient systems can create meaning for the other.

Attitudes and beliefs. The school system's attitudes toward single-parent families, and a particular single-parent family's attitudes towards both schools *and* single-parent families, will shape and underpin many of the interactions between the two systems.

If the school system, as a representative of society, adopts the negative viewpoint generally taken toward single-parent families, it will overlook the families' strengths and resources and magnify their flaws and weaknesses. Children from single-parent homes will be treated differently than children from two-parent families, in ways that are subtle and unspoken. Academic expectations will be lower; problems (e.g., handicaps, learning disabilities, behavioral problems involving peers, etc.) that are, in fact, unrelated to the family's single-parent status will be attributed to it, and solutions will be sought within the wrong context (e.g., in the family, rather than in the school, or between family and school).

On the family side, one must look at two areas. The single-parent family, due to unpleasant past experiences with schools, might hold negative attitudes toward the education system; this can handicap problem-solving. Conversely, single parents who hold the school in extraordinary esteem may forget their own ability to contribute to their child(ren)'s development, and grow even more timid in the face of authority.

Finally, the single parent's attitudes toward single-parent families must be addressed. A single parent who has accepted the cultural myth of deficits and weaknesses will assume more responsibility than is appropriate for a child's problems, and will be unable to hold the school system accountable for providing adequate services. If both school and family share the deficit view of single parents, then the suprasystem formed by school and family will grow more rigid and inflexible due to a lack of new information or alternative viewpoints.

Planning

The school or community health nurse may function as a front-line professional, one who first encounters children from single-parent homes who have school-related problems. Further, the nurse may belong to an interdisciplinary team of specialists and teachers who assist children with special learning needs. From these positions, the nurse can often contribute to overall assessment, specific care planning, and appropriate referral. Armed with adequate knowledge of the complex family-school interplay, the nurse may be a mitigating influence in the face of stereotyping and blame-placing.

The nurse carrying out these functions must first clarify her own values and attitudes toward single-parent families, especially poor, female-headed families. She must then avoid unplanned alliances and splits. By itself, the single-parent family may already present complicated triadic patterns among parents, stepparents, and extended family. When the school and medical systems enter the family sphere, the possibilities for triangulation expand geometrically. The nurse must carefully avoid inadvertent side-taking and be able to examine the macrosystem of existing triads.

A third responsibility involves defining the nature of the problem and the appropriate locus of intervention. In the case of Alan and his mother, the school system defined Alan's problem as stemming from family relationships, and intervened accordingly. At no time was Alan's difficulty with his new teacher examined; had the school encouraged Alan's mother's input into problem solving, as they did with the two-parent family, she could have told them this. The nurse who appreciates the multidisciplinary nature of children's psychosocial problems and the need for intervention in the child's key contexts (e.g., home and school) can avoid individual and family-blame oriented problem definitions, while broadening the range of intervention possibilities.

Interventions

Interventions for single-parent families with school-related problems run the gamut from preventive-educational measures addressing the whole school community to specific, family-school focused interventions, and finally to referrals for special services (e.g., therapy). Unfortunately, most school systems rely exclusively on the last category, ignoring conceptualizations that would include the school as the locus of intervention.

Effective interventions exist on a continuum from less to more intrusion in family life; some interventions advocate family-school partnerships, while others define the family or the family *and* school as clients. Interventions that are less intrusive and are partnership-forming should always be implemented first.

Preventive-educational interventions. In this category one finds macro-systemic interventions; they are intended to alter negative attitudes toward single-parent families via in-service training for teachers and other school personnel. The school nurse should encourage a broader focus on children's psychosocial problems, perhaps by providing or facilitating access to consciousness-raising material. Crucial to such efforts are value-clarification exercises regarding single-parent families, and education about the broad diversity of single-parent family forms. If Alan's school had undergone such an educational effort, Alan's mother would probably have been treated as a capable adult, able to function on her son's behalf.

Other preventive programs addressing the needs of single-parent families are those that expand the availability of day-care programs, which can alleviate stress on working single mothers. The school nurse could also establish a breakfast program for children from single- or working-parent homes.

Family-school interventions. The problems (e.g., learning, behavioral, psychosomatic) that children of single-parent families show *in* school are best tackled initially by responsible adults in both school *and* family systems. Rather than defining the family as a school "client," the nurse should try to form subsystems (Bloomfield et al., 1984) in which "partnerships" make decisions on behalf of the child. The facilitator of such a network must affirm the special and distinct knowledge about the child that both the parent and the school personnel bring to the problem-solving process, and to circumscribe the areas for intervention to protect family privacy.

One decisional subsystem in Alan's case would have consisted of his mother, the school nurse, Alan's teacher, the school counselor, and the administrator. With the help of an unbiased facilitator, one who could mobilize each participant's resources, a plan might have been established to help Alan manage the stresses that prompted his frequent visits to the nurse's office. Such a decisional subsystem would dissolve following the resolution of Alan's problem and would not delve into other family-related issues.

Referrals to special services. In some cases, family-school decisional subsystems cannot resolve children's problems, because of complications arising within the single-parent family or because the family-school relationship has disintegrated, or because family-school relationships have been disrupted by multiple triads.

Referral of the single-parent family for therapeutic services must be made carefully. If, for instance, family problems appear to stem from ongoing arguments over custody, access, or visitation, and if such arguments are affecting the child's school adjustment, the referral of *both* parents for mediation may be appropriate. If, however, a child's problems seem related to, for instance, worries about a parent, then family therapy may be more appropriate. In either case, referral should be undertaken with sensitivity, without implying blame or heightening guilt, as happened in the case of Alan and his mother. If the school nurse is the referral source, she should:
• Raise the possibility of family therapy *without* insisting that this is the only correct course of action.
• Discern if the parent is receptive or if therapy would be too foreign to the family's values.
• Offer explanations that demystify the therapeutic process, and only make referrals to professionals with proven expertise in counseling single-parent families.

Following referral, school personnel should retreat and respect the family's privacy, unless they are requested to attend sessions or are given information by the family.

When family-school relationships have deteriorated as much as they had in Karen's case, or where professional intervention may complicate the network without achieving any positive result (e.g., Alan's case), the intervention of choice is for family and school to seek an independent consultant to sort out relationships and facilitate a fresh start (Coppersmith [Imber-Black], 1983b). The school nurse should remain alert to such situations and perhaps suggest ways to obtain such assistance.

In the case of Alan and his mother, a consultant was sought. She brought together the family, outside professionals, and interested school personnel, and exposed the pattern in which more and more "help" was leading to more and more "helplessness" for Alan's mother. While validating each involved party's concern, she nevertheless proposed a new definition of the problem focusing on Alan's wish to have his mother help him with his school-related difficulties. Alan's mother could do that, and the school increased its regard for her parenting skills, thereby initiating a cycle marked by strength and capacity rather than incompetence. Alan's trips to the nurse's office ceased.

Evaluation

All of the intervention categories described must, of course, be evaluated for their efficacy. In evaluating her work, the nurse could ask the following questions:

- How frequently do our school personnel refer children from single-parent families for special services (e.g., counseling)?
- Do we tend to empower single-parent mothers or "take over" for them?
- In our case conferences, do we promote stereotypes about single-parent family functioning?
- How useful has the family found our interventions? What was *most* helpful? *Least* helpful?

CONCLUSIONS

Human systems are natural ecologies. As such, the single-parent family system demonstrates great diversity. It should always be examined for its strengths, and not for the deficits that might make it "less than" a two-parent family. The single-parent family system and the school system can form complex interactional patterns that will either create/exacerbate a child's problems or facilitate their resolution. Using her knowledge and influence, the nurse may be in a position to establish positive interactions between the school and the single parent for the benefit of their shared concern, the developing child.

REFERENCES

Bloomfield, S., et al. "Retarded Adults, Their Families and Larger Systems: A New Role for the Family Therapist," in *Families with Handicapped Members.* Edited by Coppersmith, E. Rockville, Md.: Aspen Systems Corp., 1984.

Coppersmith, E. (Imber-Black). "The Family and Public Service Systems: An Assessment Model," in *Diagnosis and Assessment in Family Therapy.* Edited by Keeney, B. Rockville, Md.: Aspen Systems Corp., 1983a.

Coppersmith, E. (Imber-Black). "The Family and Public Sector Systems: Interviewing and Interventions," in *Journal of Strategic and Systemic Therapies:* Fall, 1983b.

Coppersmith, E. (Imber-Black). "Family Therapy and Public Schools" in *Questions and Answers in the Practice of Family Therapy.* Edited by Gurman, A. New York: Brunner-Mazel, 1982.

Francke, L.B. *Growing Up Divorced.* New York: Linden Press, 1983.

Hacker, A., ed. *U/S: A Statistical Portrait of the American People.* New York: Viking Press, 1983.

Imber-Black, E. "Towards A Resource Model in Systemic Family Therapy," in *Family Resources.* Edited by Karpel, M. New York: Guilford Press, in press.

Imber-Black, E. "Women, Families and Larger Systems" in *Women's Issues in Family Therapy.* Edited by Riche, M. Rockville, Md.: Aspen Systems Copr., 1985.

Minuchin, S. *Families and Family Therapy.* Cambridge, Mass.: Harvard University Press, 1974.

Morawetz, A. and Walker, G. *Brief Therapy with Single Parent Families.* New York: Brunner-Mazel, 1984.

National Advisory Council on Economic Opportunity. "No, Poverty Has Not Disappeared," *Social Policy* 25–28, January/February, 1983.

Whiting, R. *First Semester Freshman College Dropouts: A Family System Perspective,"* Unpublished dissertation. Amherst, Mass.: University of Massachusetts, 1980.

19 Intervening with single-parent families and depression

Carol Romick Collison, RN, PhD, CS
Associate Professor
College of Nursing
University of South Carolina
Columbia, South Carolina

Jo Ann Futrell, RN, MN
Clinical Nurse Specialist
Psychiatric/Mental Health
Baptist Medical Center
Columbia, South Carolina

OVERVIEW

The newly-formed single-parent family faces a difficult adjustment to divorce and a major life-style transition. This chapter illustrates the benefits of family therapy in such cases. It presents a case study, and points out the problems commonly associated with divorce and life-style change. A depression cycle, which is one response to these circumstances, is discussed. A therapeutic process that uses the nursing process as well as concepts from family systems, loss, crisis, and stress theories is highlighted and offered as a model for nurses working with single-parent families experiencing psychosocial problems.

CASE STUDY

The Boroski family consists of Mr. and Mrs. Boroski, both age 43, and two teenaged daughters, Sue, 16, and Dawn, 14. After a 19-year marriage characterized by emotional distance and conflict, Mr. Boroski left the family home to live with his girlfriend. Mrs. Boroski filed charges of adultery.

When Mr. Boroski left, the children found themselves torn between warring, angry parents. Each parent interrogated the children for information that could be used against the other in court. Each parent selected one child as a confidant and ally. The children responded initially by taking sides, one with the mother and one with the father. As the parents' legal confrontations continued, the father withdrew more and more from his children; at one point, he refused all contact with them until the divorce decree was final.

When the divorce was granted, Mrs. Boroski was awarded custody and minimal child support. Mr. Boroski was given visitation rights every other weekend. No alimony was granted. Mrs. Boroski was forced to seek a job; she put the house up for sale and prepared to move to more modest quarters.

Mrs. Boroski and the children expected that their move would make it difficult to maintain neighborhood friendships. For Mrs. Boroski, however, that distancing process began soon after the separation, with the withdrawal of her married friends; she was left virtually without a close friend or confidant during the divorce itself. While the children retained their school friends, they feared at first that the divorce would jeopardize their friendships as it had their mother's.

Mrs. Boroski's and the children's relationships with family members and extended kin changed almost immediately after the separation. She and the girls were ostracized from Mr. Boroski's family; even Sue and Dawn's calls to their paternal grandparents were rebuffed. Mrs. Boroski's parents were in ill health and could not help their daughter or grandchildren.

Mrs. Boroski and the girls reacted with hurt and depression to these real and anticipated losses of significant relationships.

Mr. Boroski, on the other hand, made plans to leave the area with his girlfriend and accepted a job out of state. He implied that child support might end when he leaves, knowing that Mrs. Boroski would have difficulty collecting payments outside the state's jurisdiction. The children were hurt, confused, and depressed about this apparent rejection by their father. Their mother's hostility and bitterness toward her ex-husband continued to escalate, as did her depression over the losses associated with the divorce. Periodically, she projected these feelings onto the children—particularly Sue, who initially sided with the father and retains the closest emotional tie to him. Mrs. Boroski's alignment with Dawn made Dawn less of a target for her mother's frustrations, but further estranged her from Mr. Boroski. The children have responded with anger, rebellion, and depression in their attempts to cope with the changes in their mother's and father's parenting behavior. Other responses have included regressive behavior, precocious sexual acting out, withdrawal from peers, insecurity, and difficulty in school.

Mrs. Boroski made the initial request for therapy. She was in crisis over the loss of her marital relationship; she experienced intense anger and a desire to retaliate against her ex-husband. She was also overwhelmed by her role as a single parent of two teenagers. After 2 months of individual weekly therapy, she regained some control over her feelings and increased her confidence about parenting. During that time, the children were included in several sessions focusing on parent-child roles. It quickly became apparent that the girls were experiencing difficulties of their own in adjusting to the divorce and the single-parent life-style. Family therapy was eventually initiated. Mr. Boroski was asked to participate in some sessions to help resolve issues concerning Sue and Dawn; he refused. Family therapy has been ongoing for approximately a year and a half.

Depression and coping with loss were identified as the family's primary health problems. However, the crisis of divorce and forced socialization to a single-parent family life-style precipitated symptom development. Assessment involved taking a family history and asking each family member to describe her perceptions of the family's problems. Goals were set collaboratively with family members; the direction of therapy is evaluated continuously. Family therapy with a systems focus remains the primary intervention.

NURSING PROCESS

Assessment

Single-parent families. Family demographics in our society are changing. Rapidly fading in predominance is the idyllic scenario of mother, father, and two children that remains familiar only through TV reruns of *Ozzie and Harriet* and *Leave It to Beaver.* Statistically, this nuclear family constellation is fast being replaced by other modes of family living, especially the single-parent, female-headed family.

Substantiating the above statements are U.S. Bureau of the Census data showing that in 1960, 7.4% of all families with one or more children—approximately one in 14 families overall—were single-parent families headed by a woman. In 1982, this figure increased to 18.9%, or approximately one of five families (U.S. Bureau of the Census, 1984). In 1984, 22.9% or close to one in four families were single-parent families headed by a woman (Associated Press, 1985a).

In 1970, 11.2% of children 17 years of age and younger resided in single-parent families headed by the mother. By 1980, this figure increased to 28.4% (U.S. Bureau of the Census, 1984). That means that well over one fourth of all minor children are currently being reared by their mother in a nontraditional family mode. In 1984, President Reagan, recognizing the increasing numbers of single parents, projected that one half of our nation's children will have lived part of their lives with a single parent before they reach the age of 18; in 90% of these cases, that parent will be the mother (Barnes, 1984).

The widespread social phenomenon of separation and divorce is a major cause of this incredible increase in single-parent families. In 1960, 18% of families were headed by a divorced woman, a percentage that more than doubled by 1982 to 42.9% (U.S. Bureau of the Census, 1984). It is not unreasonable to say that more than half of all recent marriages will end in divorce (Bumpass and Rindfuss, 1979). At the same time, the proportion of divorces involving children has escalated, so that three out of four divorces now occur in families with children living at home (Westman, 1972).

Emotional issues. The Boroskis' experience was typical of families going through divorce. It is usually the father who leaves the family home (Westman, 1972). The movement of either parent from the home produces a sense of insecurity and feelings of abandonment and lost love in the children (Miller, 1974). The parental separation also produces a need to seek protection and security by aligning with the remaining parent, and can leave lingering fears of abandonment by the custodial parent as well (Wallerstein and Kelly, 1974).

Children's fears are fueled by the often real withdrawal of parental interest at the time of divorce. Both parents—understandably—become preoccupied with their own needs, and their emotional availability, attention span, and even time spent with the children is markedly reduced (Wallerstein and Kelly, 1976). Children may react to these circumstances with regressive dependence or precocious sexuality in search of love (Wallerstein and Kelly, 1974). The latter typically occurs in adolescents like Sue Boroski. Her sister Dawn responded with dependent behavior.

Separation and divorce also involves the loss of the love that existed between the spouses. While divorce may be consciously perceived as rejection, it requires "letting go" by both spouses. Divorce does not automatically end a marital relationship; years of emotional and sexual closeness, mutual dependence, and ingrained habits of living and loving create bonds too strong for a legal decree to sever immediately. Conventional wisdom permits only the abandoned spouse to yearn for the lost marriage, but in truth no divorced man or woman is instantly free of past emotional ties (Krantzler, 1975). Mrs. Boroski, for instance, experienced acute feelings of loss despite the often stormy nature of her marriage.

Many divorcing couples pull children into their conflicts (Spanier and Casto, 1979). Even parents who consciously seek to avoid using their children in this way often do so in some subtle way (Kressel and Deutsch, 1977). Research indicates that, because of this process, most children cannot maintain a good relationship with both parents following divorce (Wallerstein and Kelly, 1976).

Most devastating to children can be the emotional and legal guerilla warfare between parents, during which many children become the primary weapons—as was the case for the Boroskis. The fighting may go on for years as the wife brings the husband back into court for additional child support or for a counteraction, and the children pay a terrible price. Mrs. Boroski is already anticipating such action before Mr. Boroski leaves the state. Unfortunately, it is more socially acceptable to attack the spouse in his or her parental role, through the children, than in the unflattering capacity of rejected husband or wife (Kressel and Deutsch, 1977). And current social and legal structures provide too little of the right kind of support, meaning that children often suffer more from divorce than their parents. Society continues to ignore the need for laws protecting both custodial and noncustodial parents' rights without compromising the children. Such laws would keep children from being brought into conflicts between the parents and would focus attention where it belongs, on the couple's problems.

Even an amicable dissolution of a marriage and conversion to a single-parent family exacts some cost from everyone involved (Collison and Futrell, 1982). The literature supports the idea that divorce *per se* is not necessarily detrimental (Rubin and Price, 1979), but that the sequelae often make it a wrenching, bitter, and devastating experience for parents and their children (Kressel and Deutsch, 1977). Divorce has been compared to death in its impact, yet it may be more traumatic when there are children involved because the separation is never final (Collison and Futrell, 1982). Many single parents view their children as remnants of the marriage, permanent reminders of a painful relationship (Gordon, 1979). Also, for the sake of the children, divorced couples must often maintain contact. Additionally, divorce allows children to view the departed parent as an object of intense longing and/or living out of conflict (Wallerstein and Kelly, 1977).

Financial issues. Since the father is typically the one to leave the household, most children remain in the home with the mother. However, the mother is often forced by financial need to sell that home, or otherwise modify residential arrangements to lower the standard of living. Nine of 10 single mothers lose 50% of their income after divorce (Barnes, 1984).

For many divorced women with minor children, the economic problems surrounding divorce affect their entire adjustment (Spanier and Casto, 1979). In 1980, 40% of female-headed single-parent families were defined as poor; in 1983, that figure had risen to 47% (Nuta, 1984). Children living with their mother alone are now considered the poorest in the country; in 1983, for instance, 55.4% or 6.7 million children of single mothers were living in poverty (Nuta, 1984). Even for those divorced mothers and children who are not poor, data suggest that the family life-style differs markedly from that preceding the divorce (Bumpass and Rindfuss, 1979).

One cause of this economic hardship is the father's failure to pay child support on time—or to pay it at all. Mr. Boroski is tardy with his payments, but thus far has not neglected to pay the court-ordered amount. Actually, many such families are worse off than the Boroskis. In 1984 President Reagan, in a dialogue with presidential candidate Walter Mondale, indicated that in 1981 only 47% of custodial parents received full court-ordered child support payments; 28% received nothing at all. It is not unusual for a husband to leave the state—as Mr. Boroski has threatened to do—in an attempt to avoid child support payments, and in many cases the mother is left with inadequate legal resources to collect what is due.

The U.S. child support system has been called a "national disgrace... fostering parental irresponsibility and impoverishing children" (Armbrister, 1985). In 1984, labeling some parents' failure to support their children as a "blemish on America," President Reagan signed a tough new federal child support enforcement law. It bodes hope for the future but has yet to be implemented in most states (Armbrister, 1985).

Economic discrimination against divorced women compounds their financial hardship. Credit institutions sometimes refuse credit to divorced women, or grant it only in the ex-husband's name. Banks frequently deny mortgages or other loans to divorced women without a responsible male cosigner (Gordon, 1979; Brandwein et al., 1976).

Ultimately, many single-parent families headed by divorced women suffer financially because the parent least able to support the family has been left with the major economic responsibility (Brandwein et al., 1976). Typically, the divorced mother is forced to work to make ends meet, often without the benefit of marketable job skills. On the average, these women earn only a little more than half what men earn (Porterfield, 1984). In Mrs. Boroski's case the discrepancy is even greater. Many single mothers report discrimination in hiring practices as well as pay rates (Spanier and Casto, 1979).

Single parents also suffer more intensely the hazards of being a parent and a worker. They must struggle to fit child-care costs into their paycheck and reconcile work schedules with school calendars and parental responsibilities (Nuta, 1984). "Single... mothers in our society are expected to handle child-care chores unassisted, work outside the home for one half of what a man would make in the same position,... and accept their lot with equanimity" (Hormann, 1984). On the other hand, some divorced mothers put additional pressure on themselves to be supermom or superwoman to compensate for guilt over the divorce (Kaseman, 1975). This juggling act is difficult for Mrs. Boroski.

Role issues. Specific family functions are still generally assumed to be the proper role of one sex or the other. The roles of breadwinner and disciplinarian are frequently ascribed to men, nurturer and homemaker to women (Brandwein et al., 1976). Single parents like Mrs. Boroski find it difficult to perform all these functions, and suffer from role overload because of the lack of relief (Collison and Futrell, 1982). Also, there are few social supports or positively accepted role models. Mrs. Boroski continually complains of overload and resents her ex-husband for contributing so little to the family. She also resents his plying the children with gifts and acting like the good guy, while she must discipline them, say no to their requests, and deal with the negative fallout. An additional dynamic is Mrs. Boroski's inability to follow through when the girls fail to complete their share of family responsibilities.

Network issues. Because marriage remains the social norm, divorced individuals are often estranged from their predivorce friendships. Often in divorce, friends know how to relate only to the couple, and cannot adjust to the reality of two individual relationships (Bozarth-Campbell, 1982). Those friends who do remain in contact, however well meaning, can rarely be objective and often end up taking sides with one spouse or the other (Kaseman, 1975). Even old friends may become distant and superficial, perhaps due to difficulty focusing on the loss, fear of divorce itself, or inability to adjust to the divorced friend's new life-style. Therefore many women, at a time when they feel a great need for companionship as they cope with a marital breakup, end up feeling isolated and lonely—as did Mrs. Boroski (Kaseman, 1975). Children often feel ashamed and humiliated about the divorce and conceal it from friends because they fear rejection or negative reactions. Adolescents are particularly sensitive to the social repercussions of divorce, as evidenced by Sue and Dawn Boroski (Westman, 1972).

Research confirms that divorce also alters kinship relationships (Anspach, 1976). The father's absence can mean an end to social relationships with his relatives, as was the case with the Boroskis. Mr. Boroski's departure broke the pivotal link between his nuclear family and kin who had always been positive and supportive. This cutoff created an asymmetrical kinship system for Mrs. Boroski and her children.

Of all outside parties, the spouses' own parents are the greatest complicating factor in separation and divorce. Actual meddlesomeness is rarely the primary difficulty; instead, it is the anticipation of how parents will react to the divorce (Kressel and Deutsch, 1977). Some divorcing couples refuse even to tell their parents for fear of rejection. While Mrs. Boroski did not react this way, her parents' ill health prevented them from offering her much assistance or support.

Health care issues. Divorce has also been recognized as a predisposing factor for both physical and psychological illness (Kitsen and Raschke, 1981). Indeed, it is second only to death in its potential for producing secondary illness throughout a family unit (Cadoret et al., 1972), and it has been clearly identified as a factor in depression (Stuart and Sundeen, 1979).

The health problem: Depression. Considerable evidence supports the fact that depression is associated with the kind of real or threatened personal losses that occur in divorce; divorced and separated persons are listed among the high-risk groups for depression (Associated Press, 1985b). Depression results when an individual fails to manage loss properly by completing stages of the grieving process (Kaseman, 1975).

From a family systems perspective, such psychiatric symptoms as depression occur when the naturally unfolding family life cycle is disrupted (Gordon, 1979). The dissolution of a marriage and transition to the single-parent life-style constitute a disruption of crisis proportions. Depressive symptoms signal that the family has problems dealing with its new roles and relationships. No member of the family system is thoroughly immune to the depression that another member experiences; therefore, one could say that depression within a family system is contagious (Swanson, 1975).

Depression is the United States' number one mental health problem—it is the common cold of mental diseases (Trafford, 1983). It affects millions of Americans annually; actual statistics on depression as a response to such personal loss as divorce are difficult to obtain because of its multisymptomatic nature.

Depression is primarily characterized by mood disturbance, including sadness, hopelessness, and discouragement; the depressive loses interest in all usually pleasurable activities and pastimes. Depression is also associated with other symptoms, such as appetite disturbance, weight change, sleep disturbance, psychomotor agitation or retardation, decreased energy, feelings of worthlessness or guilt, difficulty concentrating, thoughts of death or suicide, and suicide attempts (American Psychiatric Association, 1980).

Depression is a predictable response to a phase of life problem, and it is considered a normal *short-term* response to divorce (American Psychiatric Association, 1980).

The increasing frequency of divorce in American society emphasizes the need to develop better means of handling the transition to a single-parent life-style. Unlike other major variations on traditional family composition, the single-parent family has yet to be socially recognized as a positive family form (Gerwig, 1984), a stigma that complicates transition.

There are virtually no rituals or rites of passage to help families resolve this life event. It has even been said that divorce adds a whole stage to the family life cycle (Beal, 1980)—a stage unrecognized by society at large.

The affected family must grope its way through divorce, struggling to survive without social support or understanding. Furthermore, society's willingness to accept responsibility for resolving family problems often hinders the family's ability to handle problems from within, leaving unresolved difficulties to be passed on to children and/or externalized. The less resolution within divorcing families, the more instability within society (Beal, 1980).

It has been suggested that a formal "uncoupling" ritual be developed for spouses undergoing divorce. If both spouses choose to participate, they and their respect support networks might commemorate the end of the marriage and incorporate that loss into a positive wish for separate futures. If they have children, public confirmation of love and commitment to them would be an important part of the ritual (Bozarth-Campbell, 1982).

Marital breakup and transition to a single-parent family mode involve two separate but overlapping tasks: first, adjustment to the dissolution of the marriage, and, second, adjustment to a new life-style. The first task concerns mourning the loss of the predivorce family and renunciation of the aspirations attached to it. This process also involves coping with the emotional effects of dissolution: feelings about the former spouse/parent—for instance, love, hate, bitterness, guilt, envy, concern, and attachment; feelings about the marriage—e.g., regret, disappointment, bitterness, sadness, and failure; personal feelings—especially failure, depression, euphoria, relief, guilt, decreased self-esteem, and confidence (Spanier and Casto, 1979; Wallerstein and Kelly, 1977). This task also requires legal settlement of property and child custody claims. For the children, these arrangements mean accepting a newly circumscribed relationship with the noncustodial parent and adjusting to a revised custodial parent relationship. Finally, this initial task requires informing the social network—business acquaintances, friends, immediate family, and extended kin—about the divorce, and resolving any ensuing interpersonal repercussions (Spanier and Casto, 1979).

The second task, the creation of a new life-style, can include moving to a new residence, living on less money, and getting a job or applying for welfare; it also means adjusting to single parenthood, redefining one's social network, forming new friendships, and accommodating altered relationships with family, friends, and kin. Accommodation will probably include establishing new heterosexual relationships for the parent. Additionally, this task may require emotional adjustment to fear, frustration, loneliness, shame, embarrassment, inadequacy, and related feelings elicited by the change to a single-parent family life-style (Spanier and Casto, 1979).

Depression blocks the accomplishment of these two tasks; it triggers a counterproductive cycle that the single-parent family will have difficulty modifying. The divorced parent feels an overwhelming need to complete the developmental sequelae of separation; failure to do so generates stress, which feeds depression, which continues to block complete resolution.

Theoretical approaches. The newly divorced family can be assessed through a conceptual framework based on family systems, loss, crisis, and stress theories. The Boroski family's experiences underscore the value of a multitheoretical approach in such cases.

A fundamental tenet of family systems is that no single, identified patient should be the focus of pathology and treatment. The family is treated as a whole unit. Assessment of that unit, therefore, focuses on the quality of relationships among family members and the need for improved interaction. Because any change in one family member relationship produces necessary changes in other members and affects the entire system (Sedgewick, 1974; Miller, 1971), an exclusive therapeutic focus on vested individual interests or even a single relationship overlooks important systemic aspects (Beal, 1980). Therefore, family systems therapy emphasizes family interactional patterns. Since divorce is a family matter (Westman, 1972), family systems theory is especially useful; it is an obvious method of helping families cope with that experience.

Loss theory describes the process of grief work, which encompasses such stages as denial, anger, bargaining, depression, and acceptance (Kübler-Ross, 1969). These stages can be assessed through behaviors characteristic of each. Uncomplicated grief work progresses through each stage without interruption; in other words, feelings run a natural course toward resolution. In pathological grief, the various stages are delayed, avoided, or distorted (Bassett, 1985). One of these distortions can be severe depression. The purpose of intervention is to reactivate the grief process, to set it in motion again, so that it can reach resolution. As stated earlier, the divorced parent needs to resolve his or her personal losses through the normal grieving process (Beal, 1980).

Divorce constitutes a time-limited crisis where customary coping and adaptive mechanisms are in disarray. As a crisis, it is a disorganizing and reorganizing process that can produce growth as well as dysfunction; mastery of the crisis may add an effective new method of coping to a person's repertoire, while the inability to deal adequately with the problem may impair future coping because failure is expected (Caplan, 1964).

The lack of prescribed guidelines for negotiating a successful divorce makes positive resolution of this crisis a particular challenge (Porterfield, 1984). For this reason, crisis intervention can prevent dysfunctional adaptation (Coleman, 1976). Successful crisis resolution requires identification and application of both previously used and new coping mechanisms in order to facilitate adaptive function. Identification and expression of feelings associated with the crisis is a first step in this process.

Stress is a natural part of family life; it increases in response to change. Life events such as divorce produce "life change units," which reflect the amount of associated stress (Holmes and Rahe, 1967). As indicated by life change unit points, divorce places both individuals and family systems under severe or excessive stress. Stress is a means by which life's coping mechanisms are set in motion; however, stress can be damaging if it overwhelms a person's coping resources or if that person believes it will and acts accordingly (Coleman, 1976).

Severe stress can exact a high cost in terms of lowered efficiency, depletion of adaptive resources, wear and tear on the physical systems, and in extreme cases, disintegration and death (Coleman, 1976). Prolonged stress may lead to either pathological overresponsiveness (for instance, the "last straw" response) or pathological insensitivity (as in loss of hope or extreme apathy) (Coleman, 1976); both symptoms are characteristic of depression.

Two to three years of stressful disequilibrium is not unusual for divorcing families (Rubin and Price, 1979). This period may not seem significant in the overall adult life span, but it may come at a particularly formative part of a child's lifetime. Regardless of the individual's age, it can be a taxing time. Assessment of stress levels and adaptive response mechanisms forms the basis of intervention for stress reduction.

Family assessment. The four theories in the previously described theoretical framework determine the processes of nursing assessment, planning, intervention, and evaluation. The Boroski family was assessed by collecting a three-generation family history that included the nuclear family and each parent's family of origin. The genogram was dated and family participation noted (Stuart and Sundeen, 1979). Following this activity, each family member was asked to describe the family's problems.

Planning

Using the conceptual framework and data from this initial assessment, with input from Mrs. Boroski and her daughters, the Boroskis' problems were identified and goals of family therapy developed conjointly with Mrs. Boroski and the two girls (Table 19.1).

Intervention

Because Mr. Boroski had moved out prior to the nurse's contact with the family, the first intervention was to assist the family with the grieving process. Using Kübler-Ross' framework, the nurse helped the family deal with feelings about their loss of Mr. Boroski as a husband and readily accessible father. Each person was encouraged to face the loss and to express feelings, thus facilitating the gradual release of intense emotional ties to the lost object (Bassett, 1985). Throughout, attention was paid to the fact that each was moving through the grieving process at her own rate, as is typical (Aguilera and Messick, 1974). For example, the girls were afraid that they would hurt their

Table 19.1 Divorce-Related Problems and Therapeutic Goals: The Boroski Family

Problems	Goals
• Loss of Mr. Boroski as husband and readily accessible father (conceptualized as loss of love)	• Complete the grief process. Subgoals: —(Mrs. Boroski) accept redefined relationship with ex-husband —(children) create new, separate postdivorce relationship with father
• Financial difficulty necessitating lifestyle change	• Understand new financial circumstances and develop joint decision-making processes
• Parenting difficulties: —discipline —different parenting styles —use of children as weapons in parental conflict	• Strengthen Mrs. Boroski's disciplinary function/role • Help children develop appropriate responses to differing parental styles • Disengage girls from parental disputes
• Role overload (Mrs. Boroski) and underinvolvement by the children	• Identify and equitably distribute new family role responsibilities
• Lack of support systems (Mrs. Boroski)	• Encourage development of alternative support systems
• Changes in the family kinship network	• Facilitate adjustment to kinship realignment
• Depression (response to divorce and lifestyle change)	• Relieve depression/improve functioning

mother if they expressed sadness over Mr. Boroski's leaving while she was still angry and bitter toward him. However, anger over being abandoned was, at least intermittently, an issue for all of them. Denial surfaced periodically when Mrs. Boroski and her daughters indulged in a wishful fantasy that Mr. Boroski would return. Ultimately, they became depressed over the loss and remained so for an extended period. Perhaps the most common effect of denied anger is depression, which ties up emotional energy (Krantzler, 1975).

People can become mired in the grieving process or they can persevere and become victors instead of victims (Bozarth-Campbell, 1982). Support of the Boroskis in each grief stage—denial, anger, bargaining, and depression—and active listening to their feelings about the divorce led them to accept the permanence of the loss.

Family members were encouraged to restructure their relationships with Mr. Boroski; Sue and Dawn were encouraged to adjust their relationship with their mother. Mrs. Boroski chose to denigrate Mr.

Boroski as part of her grieving process, which made it difficult for Dawn to reestablish a positive relationship with him. Sue's response, on the other hand, was to defend him and resent her mother. The importance of developing a new relationship with their father was explained to the girls, with emphasis on the need to feel OK about loving him and accepting his love, as well as their mother's. Dawn was specifically encouraged to develop a closer relationship with her father and to reduce overinvolvement with her mother, while Sue was encouraged to do the reverse—to move closer to her mother and decrease her involvement with her father. The aim was for the two girls to create separate, objective, and equitable relationships with each parent. An additional purpose of restructuring Sue's relationship with her father was to limit his opportunities to discuss his sexual liaison. One of the most difficult tasks for a divorcing parent of adolescents is to avoid flooding the child with revelations about the parent's sex life. Such a parent is no longer viewed as a safe object, and a breakdown of healthy generational boundaries may occur (Krantzler, 1975).

As a first step in restructuring family relationships, Mrs. Boroski was encouraged to resolve her bitterness toward her ex-husband; this was a necessary prelude to helping the children redefine their relationships with both parents (Barnes, 1984). Examining and understanding her feelings of anger assisted in that process.

Another significant step was the implicit giving of permission for individual feelings and an individual relationship for the daughters with their father and for Mrs. Boroski with Mr. Boroski. This step encouraged the process of self-differentiation for each family member (Bowen, 1978). The single most helpful step in resolving the multiple problems of the single-parent family is recognizing that family members are separate yet interdependent individuals (Krantzler, 1975).

Since financial difficulties caused stress for the family even before therapy, the second intervention confronted these difficulties. This discussion focused on identifying sources of income, balancing the needs of the individuals against the welfare of the family, and developing a budget. This discussion allowed the family to feel greater control over their financial situation.

Also, a framework incorporating Haley's belief that members must find gain in proposed goals (1976), Jackson's quid pro quo (1965), and Padberg's bargaining process (1975) provided a mechanism for joint decision-making to handle necessary life-style events. The family decided to have periodic meetings to implement this mechanism. For example, when Sue wanted a special dress for her school's homecoming, family negotiations took place. Mrs. Boroski agreed to the purchase if

Sue contributed to the cost by babysitting and mowing the lawn, a task they normally paid a neighborhood boy to do.

A third intervention was to strengthen Mrs. Boroski's role as disciplinarian. Her previously inconsistent and ineffective efforts often caused power struggles between herself and her daughters, especially Sue. When a single parent chooses to apply punishment inconsistently, children learn that they are dealing with the parent's whims and that enough argument may cause the parent to change her mind (Barnes, 1984). When a parent takes the time to enforce rules consistently, children learn to accept responsibility for their behavior and feel the emotional security that comes with effective discipline (Mumford, 1976).

The nurse validated Mrs. Boroski's right to discipline Sue and Dawn. For example, the nurse-therapist said to them: "This is your mother. She is responsible for disciplining you." Mrs. Boroski was also encouraged to set appropriate and consistent limits and consequences for misbehavior. As she grew more confident and consistent, she handled discipline more effectively.

Contrasting parenting styles remained a source of family difficulty. While Mrs. Boroski learned to be more firm with Sue and Dawn, her ex-husband remained extremely permissive. Initially the children took advantage of these differences by engaging in behavior when with Mr. Boroski that was off limits at home with their mother. For example, they went to R- and X-rated movies when with their father; their mother forbade the practice. Mr. Boroski did not appear to undermine Mrs. Boroski's rules purposely so much as he abdicated his traditional parental role for one of a pal or even a peer, apparently to gain his daughters' affection. In another example, Mrs. Boroski, particularly during the process of the divorce, played the role of "poor me" with her children, apparently to elicit their pity and support. Sometimes they responded by supporting her, but more often her behavior encouraged manipulations, which undermined her parental role. Parents should not fear admitting vulnerability and uncertainty to their children; to imply, however, that the parent is so helpless that she can no longer make proper parenting decisions demoralizes the children and erodes the adult's self-esteem (Krantzler, 1975). When divorce destroys the comfortable roles that provided emotional stability for both parents and children, families can fall into destructive game-playing to reestablish a sense of control and permanence (Krantzler, 1975). Adolescents are especially vulnerable; they need reasonable limits to protect them from their frightening new impulses and to show them that they are still loved (Krantzler, 1975).

The children were urged to avoid these games and to relate to their mother and father as parents. Mrs. Boroski was encouraged to stop her destructive game playing. Since Mrs. Boroski was the custodial parent and since Mr. Boroski refused to participate in therapy or to behave like a parent, the girls were urged to accept Mrs. Boroski's rules as their behavioral standards and to ask that Mr. Boroski support those rules. The family learned to develop reasonable rules, and the girls were taught responsibility for their own behavior. To validate this process, a written contract was negotiated for each girl and was signed by her and Mrs. Boroski. This intervention provided stable and consistent boundaries for behavior even when one or both parents could not do so.

Another parenting issue was the critical need not to use the children as weapons in parental conflict—to detriangle them, so to speak. Triangling occurs when one or both members of a dyad, such as a married couple, becomes upset or anxious and involves a vulnerable third party to dilute the anxiety. The pair may reach out and pull in the other person, the emotion may overflow to the third person, or the third person may be emotionally programmed to initiate involvement (Goldberg and Goldberg, 1980; Bowen, 1978).

For example, Mrs. Boroski used one or both daughters as an audience for extended tirades against Mr. Boroski. In another instance, Mrs. Boroski overreacted to a lie told by Sue, accused her of being just like her father, and punished her excessively. Mrs. Boroski was clearly ventilating anger toward her ex-husband. On a third occasion, Mrs. Boroski reacted to Mr. Boroski's lateness with child-support payments by chastising him in front of his daughters, which angered Dawn so much that she refused further contact with him. In essence, Mrs. Boroski had programmed Dawn to express her (Mrs. Boroski's) anger and to fight her battles.

As this triangulation was pointed out to Mrs. Boroski and her daughters, each became aware of the negative effects of bringing a third party into a conflict. Although the process did not cease, their behavior changed considerably. The ultimate goal was for each family member to handle conflict directly and not to triangulate. Even though direct resolution was not always possible for Mr. and Mrs. Boroski (he often refused to talk with her), she learned to discuss her feelings with the nurse-therapist rather than triangle the children.

A fourth intervention centered on identifying each family member's role and clarifying the expectations that each had of the others. Discussion focused on the most problematic roles in this family's functioning: breadwinner, disciplinarian, nurturer, and homemaker. Through dialogue, Mrs. Boroski's efforts to fulfill all four of these role functions were recognized, as was the need for a more equitable balance of role functions among all three family members.

A major problem for all single parents is task overload (Beal, 1980). Many single parents subconsciously encourage their children's dependence in an effort to feel needed (Barnes, 1984) or out of guilt over the divorce (Kaseman, 1975). In Mrs. Boroski's case, this interactional pattern backfired, creating irresponsible children and an overwhelmed parent.

Reasonable role expectations were discussed and functions reassigned according to their appropriateness to family members' time and abilities. For example, the girls picked up homemaking tasks while breadwinning remained one of Mrs. Boroski's primary functions. Nurturing was identified as a role all could share; each child negotiated her own time with her mother and learned to give Mrs. Boroski time to nurture herself or to spend with her peers. The girls also acknowledged their ability to nurture each other. The restructuring of the breadwinner and disciplinarian roles have already been discussed (see interventions two and three, respectively).

A fifth intervention concerned the development of a postdivorce support system for Mrs. Boroski and her daughters. Mrs. Boroski was troubled by loneliness in the wake of desertion by many of her predivorce friends. This feeling is typical (Barnes, 1984). She was encouraged to make new contacts and identify compatible individuals who might become friends. The nurse suggested groups where such contacts could be made; for instance, a "single again" Sunday school class and a local unit of Parents Without Partners. Such social support systems as church groups, clubs, and community organizations were also proposed as healthy and realistic alternatives for meeting social needs (Kaseman, 1975). Like Mrs. Boroski, most divorced women belong to fewer organizations and have fewer friends than their married counterparts do (Spicer and Hampe, 1975), even though studies have shown that social participation is correlated with lower distress, better adjustment, and personal growth (Weiss, 1975).

Mrs. Boroski's efforts to reach out were hampered by feelings of inadequacy, fears of rejection, and depression; thus the creation of an adequate support system was slow. The nurse-therapist/client relationship provided needed support while Mrs. Boroski developed new friendships and a new social life. Also crucial to the therapeutic relationship was an understanding of the varying tempo of change for different individuals. Thus, Mrs. Boroski was given permission for strategic withdrawal (Krantzler, 1975), and when necessary, interpretation of her avoidance of relationships (usually from resistance or depression).

Sue and Dawn also needed the nurse-therapist's support. A consistent, caring adult who could listen to their feelings and help them cope with the divorce and transition to a single-parent life-style was invaluable in their overall adjustment. In a sense, there was a transference to the therapist as an idealized extended family member. Advocacy of the children gives the therapist working with divorcing families both leverage and moral authority—in effect, a parental role (Wallerstein and Kelly, 1977). This empathetic relationship oftens fills a void strongly felt by children of divorce (Wallerstein and Kelly, 1977). The therapist should realize the value of individual sessions with each child, as long as the therapist does not violate the family systems framework. Also, the opportunity to spend time with a concerned adult has significance to such children apart from any content discussed (Wallerstein and Kelly, 1976).

Both girls displayed a continuing fear of losing friendships as a consequence of the divorce. Dawn coped with such feelings by withdrawing from her friends, which decreased their ability to support her. Sue, on the other hand, turned to her friends for support and soon became aware that many of her friends were facing similar circumstances of separation and divorce.

The nurse-therapist encouraged discussion of the girls' fears of rejection. Dawn's reclusive response was examined and she was prompted to reach out to selected friends and to spend more time with her peers. Sue acknowledged sharing every detail of the divorce with her friends as a means of coping with her feelings. She was encouraged to use this network but also to consider the impact on her friends and family of discussing every incident. Finally, Mrs. Boroski was asked to fulfill reasonable requests to link the girls with their friends—for instance, by providing transportation or allowing invitations to the family home. Although one cannot say that good friendships always ease the impact of divorce, the lack of supportive friends appears to thwart children's development (Wallerstein and Kelly, 1977). The urgency of developing and strengthening the Boroski children's friendship network was made obvious by their positive response.

Some children find support in school. Their attitudes and performance can earn them sufficient gratification from teachers to sustain them in the face of divorce stress (Kelly and Wallerstein, 1977). Dawn found support in that setting, but poor grades kept Sue from finding similar satisfaction. Discussion centered on ways to improve Sue's school performance, with the goal of decreasing stress and increasing her opportunities for support in this area. Sue improved her grades, earning praise from her teachers.

A sixth intervention helped the family adapt to changed kinship relations. Emotional withdrawal by Mr. Boroski's parents resulted in a loss of both support and material resources. Family assistance during divorce is known to be related to approval of the action itself (Kitsen and Raschke, 1981). Mr. Boroski's parents obviously disapproved of Mrs. Boroski's decision to initiate divorce proceedings against their son.

The family was encouraged, within a framework of loss theory, to identify and ventilate feelings. Mrs. Boroski and her daughters were shown that their emotional predicament was typical of divorcing families, and that they were not alone in being cut off. The family gradually worked through their feelings and accepted the reality of these circumstances, but they continued to reach out to Mr. Boroski's parents in hopes that the response might change.

The seventh and final intervention focused on relieving depressive symptoms. The normality of depression as a postdivorce grief stage was explained, as was its generally transient nature.

In any case of divorce, the nurse-therapist must assess for pathological depression and intervene to restart the grieving process if necessary; at the time of intervention, none of the Boroski's had shown indications of being unable to progress appropriately through grief stages. Because each person is unique, it is impossible to impose a timetable on grieving. One significant sign of completion is a strong sense of survival, of being able to make it alone, a sense that despite surges of nostalgia or resentment, the past no longer dominates the present (Krantzler, 1975). Lifting of depression is an additional sign that individual family members have progressed to the final state of resolution.

During grief, and especially during depression, the nurse should help the family recuperate from the stress caused by the loss and return to an optimal level of functioning. Stress relief can be hastened by good nutrition, adequate rest, and daily exercise (Schultz and Dark, 1982). Referral to a wellness program is an adjunct for accomplishing this goal as well as for meeting needs for contact with others (see intervention five). Mrs. Boroski joined a health spa and has enjoyed it immensely.

As an additional step, the nurse should urge family members to identify and nurture individual strengths to help offset their emotional pain (Schultz and Dark, 1982). Members of single-parent families often suffer from lowered self-esteem because of the rejection involved in divorce, which also fuels depression (Herman, 1975). A focus on strengths helps relatives feel better about themselves and increases their resistance to contagious depression. The Boroskis felt more positive as they began to recognize their plusses.

The cycle of depression within single-parent families must be interrupted to restore family equilibrium. Complex tasks should be broken down into realistic, achievable components that, when accomplished individually, will generate positive feedback to family members. Establishing priorities, solving problems, and the experience of success can reestablish a sense of control over the crisis (Krantzler, 1975). Successful interruption of the depression cycle, and therefore enhanced feelings of control, remains an ultimate goal for the Boroskis.

Because emotional pain absorbs a great deal of thought and energy, tunnel vision may result; this makes it more difficult for the family to progress (Krantzler, 1975). A sense of helplessness during depression can lead family members to contemplate suicide as the only alternative for relief from the cycle. Therefore, the nurse-therapist must watch for signs of self-destructive potential until control is reestablished. Both Sue and Mrs. Boroski expressed suicidal thoughts during the divorce and were helped to explore alternatives for dealing with anger and other negative feelings. If this intervention had not been helpful, it may have been necessary to refer one or both for inpatient psychiatric treatment and/or medication until they were no longer a threat to themselves.

Evaluation

The final step in the therapy process is evaluation. Evaluation must be an ongoing aspect of therapy and, therefore, has been discussed with respect to each goal and intervention in this chapter. The importance of family therapy in divorce has been well documented in the literature (Westman, 1972), and the efficacy of this approach was proven in the Boroskis' transition through divorce to a single-parent life-style.

Therapy is valuable at any point during the 2 to 3 years of instability that follow divorce; for some families, however, intervention may be needed only during the immediate crisis. In any case, termination of therapy should be a joint decision between the nurse-therapist and the family. Termination is indicated when the family can adapt to the divorce and to a single-parent life-style—that is, when its members reestablish a sense of control over their lives.

CONCLUSIONS

If society begins to legitimize the single-parent family life-style and can provide more understanding and support for divorcing families during their rituals and rites of passage, this traumatic life event may be resolved with less need for therapeutic intervention. Schools, churches, and other social institutions that touch the lives of single parents and their children must also assume a greater role in supporting these families.

Professional intervention, including nursing intervention, should always be an available alternative, however. The nurse's role with these families can be a preventive one; it can increase social awareness of their needs, create appropriate social support systems, and link family members to existing resources. The nursing function can also involve early case finding and therapy with these families as well as assistance in working through pathological grief reactions. Therefore, nurses must be increasingly aware of this growing at-risk population and of the interventions that can improve family functioning (Collison and Futrell, 1982).

REFERENCES

Aguilera, D., and Messick, J. *Crisis Intervention: Theory and Methodology,* 2nd ed. St. Louis: C.V. Mosby Co., 1974.

American Psychiatric Association. *Diagnostic and Statistical Manual of Mental Disorders,* 3rd ed. Washington, D.C.: American Psychiatric Association, 1980.

Anspach, D.F. "Kinship and Divorce," *Journal of Marriage and the Family* 38(2):323–30, 1976.

Armbrister, T. "Crackdown on Deadbeat Dads," *Readers Digest:* July 1985.

Associated Press. "Single-Parent Families," *The State Newspaper.* Columbia, S.C.: Columbia Newspapers, May 15, 1985a.

Associated Press. "Cutting the Cost of Depression," *The Record.* Columbia, S.C.: Columbia Newspapers, May 23, 1985b.

Barnes, R.G., Jr. *Single Parenting: A Wilderness Journey.* Wheaton, Ill.: Tyndale House, 1984.

Bassett, B.D. "The Nature of Grief," *Emory Magazine:* March 1985.

Beal, E.W. "Separation, Divorce, and Single-Parent Families," in *The Family Life Cycle: A Framework for Family Therapy.* Edited by Carter, E.A., and McGoldrick, M. New York: Gardner Press, 1980.

Bowen, M. *Family Therapy in Clinical Practice.* New York: Jason Aronson, 1978.

Bozarth-Campbell, A. *Life Is Goodbye, Life Is Hello: Grieving Well Through All Kinds of Loss.* Minneapolis: Comp Care, 1982.

Brandwein, R., et al. "Women and Children Last: Divorced Mothers and Their Families," *Nursing Digest* 4(1):39–43, 1976.

Bumpass, L., and Rindfuss, R.R. "Children's Experience of Marital Disruption," *American Journal of Sociology* 85(1):49–64, 1979.

Cadoret, R., et al. "Depressive Disease, Life Events, and Onset of Illness," *Archives of General Psychiatry* 26(2):133–36, 1972.

Caplan, G. *Principles of Preventive Psychiatry.* New York: Basic Books, 1964.

Coleman, J.C. *Abnormal Psychology and Modern Life,* 5th ed. Greenview, Ill.: Scott, Foresman, 1976.

Collison, C.R., and Futrell, J.A. "Family Therapy for the Single Parent Family System," *Journal of Psychosocial Nursing and Mental Health Services* 20(7):16–20, 1982.

Gerwig, K. "Congressman Robert Torricelli: Champion of Single Parents," *Single Parent* 27(4):26, 1984.

Goldberg, I., and Goldberg, H. *Family Therapy: An Overview.* Monterey, Calif.: Brooks/Cole Publishing Co., 1980.

Gordon, V. "Women and Divorce: Implications for Nursing Care," in *Women in Stress: A Nursing Perspective.* Edited by Jervik, D., and Martinson, I. East Norwalk, Conn.: Appleton-Century-Crofts, 1979.

Haley, J. *Problem Solving Therapy.* San Francisco: Jossey Bass, 1976.

Herman, S. "Divorce, a Grief Process," *Perspectives in Psychiatric Care* 12(3):108–12, 1975.

Holmes, T., and Rahe, R. "The Social Readjustment Rating Scale," *Journal of Psychosomatic Research* 11(2):213–81, 1967.

Hormann, E. "Rebuilding Your Life in the Aftermath of Divorce," *Single Parent* 27(9):9–10, 1984.

Jackson, D.D. "The Family Rules: The Marital Quid Pro Quo," *Archives of General Psychiatry* 12:589–94, 1965.

Kaseman, D. "The Single-Parent Family," *Perspectives in Psychiatric Care* 12(3):113–18, 1975.

Kelly, J., and Wallerstein, J. "Brief Intervention with Children in Divorcing Families," *American Journal of Orthopsychiatry* 47(1):23–39, 1977.

Kitsen, G.C., and Raschke, H.J. "Divorce Research: What We Know, What We Need to Know," *Journal of Divorce* 4(3):1–33, 1981.

Krantzler, M. *Creative Divorce.* New York: New American Library, 1975.

Kressel, K., and Deutsch, M. "Divorce Therapy: An In-depth Survey of Therapists' Views," *Family Process* 16(4):413–43, 1977.

Kübler-Ross, E. *On Death and Dying.* New York: Macmillan Publishing Co., 1969.

Miller, D. *Adolescence: Psychology, Psychopathy, and Psychotherapy.* New York: Aronson Press, 1974.

Miller, J.C. "Systems Theory and Family Psychotherapy," *Nursing Clinics of North America* 6(3):395–406, 1971.

Mumford, A.R. *By Death or Divorce...It Hurts to Lose.* Denver: Accent Books, 1976.

Nuta, V.R. "Single Mothers Hard Hit Financially in Last Four Years," *Single Parent* 27(9):7–8, 1984.

Padberg, J. "Bargaining to Improve Communications in Conjoint Family Therapy," *Perspectives in Psychiatric Care* 13(2):68–72, 1975.

Porterfield, K.M. "Single Parent Housing: Warren Village," *Single Parent* 27(6):16–18, 1984.

Reagan, R. "A Presidential Proclamation for National Single Parent Day," *Single Parent* 27(4):24, 1984.

Reagan, R., and Mondale, W. "Where the Candidates Stand on Single Parent Issues," *Single Parent* 27(9):12–13, 17, 1984.

Rubin, L., and Price, J. "Divorce and Its Effects on Children," *Journal of School Health* 49(10):552–56, 1979.

Schultz, J.M., and Dark, S.L. *Manual of Psychiatric Nursing Care Plans.* Boston: Little, Brown & Co., 1982.

Sedgewick, R. "The Family as a System: A Network of Relationships," *Journal of Psychiatric Nursing and Mental Health Services* 12(2):17–20, 1974.

Spanier, G.B., and Casto, R.F. "Adjustment to Separation and Divorce: An Analysis of 50 Case Studies," *Journal of Divorce* 2(3):241–53, 1979.

Spicer, J.W., and Hampe, G.D. "Kinship Interaction after Divorce," *Journal of Marriage and the Family* 37(1):113–19, 1975.

Stuart, G.W., and Sundeen, S.J. *Principles and Practice of Psychiatric Nursing.* St. Louis: C.V. Mosby Co., 1979.

Swanson, A.R. "Communicating with Depressed Persons," *Perspectives in Psychiatric Care* 13(2):63–67, 1975.

Trafford, A. "New Hope for the Depressed," *U.S. News and World Report* 39–42, 1983.

U.S. Bureau of the Census. *National Data Book and Guide to Sources,* 104th ed. Washington, D.C.: U.S. Department of Commerce, 1984.

Wallerstein, J.S., and Kelly, J.B. "Divorce Counseling: A Community Service for Families in the Midst of Divorce," *American Journal of Orthopsychiatry* 47(1):4–22, 1977.

Wallerstein, J.S., and Kelly, J.B. "The Effects of Parental Divorce: The Adolescent Experience," in *The Child in His Family, Vol 3.* Edited by Anthony, E.J., and Koupernick, C. New York: John Wiley & Sons, 1974.

Wallerstein, J.S., and Kelly, J.B. "The Effects of Parental Divorce: Experiences of the Child in Later Latency," *American Journal of Orthopsychiatry* 46(2):256–69, 1976.

Weiss, R.S. *Marital Separation.* New York: Basic Books, 1975.

Westman, J.C. "Effect of Divorce on a Child's Personality Development," *Medical Aspects of Human Sexuality* 6(1):38–53, 1972.

20 Intervening with stepfamilies and the problem of functional encopresis

Mary Anne Stanitis, RN, CS, EdD
Assistant Professor, Division of Nursing

William J. Matthews, PhD
Assistant Professor, Counseling Psychology
  Program

Judith Davis, MEd
Director, Office of Human Relations
University of Massachusetts
Amherst, Massachusetts

OVERVIEW

Functional encopresis reflects serious relational dysfunction and loyalty conflicts within a family. Its occurrence within a stepfamily is difficult to treat due to the increased number of interacting family members. Management of encopresis often requires the cooperation of many helpers, including the family physician and other medical specialists, the school nurse, pediatric nurse practitioner, guidance counselors, and teachers. This chapter describes the multidisciplinary treatment of functional encopresis in a 10-year-old boy from a stepfamily. Four and one-half months of family systems treatment, culminating in a strategic embedded metaphor, reduced the encopretic behavior significantly. The construction of that embedded metaphor is described and illustrated.

CASE STUDY

The therapy team

The therapy team included a psychiatric nurse clinical specialist, clinical psychologist, and three mental health therapists, all in private practice. All were educated in structural and strategic family systems therapy and in the use of therapeutic metaphor and Ericksonian hypnotic techniques. The team's collaborative strategy designated one member as family therapist, with the others evaluating sessions from behind a one-way mirror.

The presenting problem

The team received a call from a woman requesting help for her 10-year-old grandson who was "messing in his pants every day." When asked why the child's mother had not called, the grandmother said that the mother could not handle the situation and was depressed. The grandmother wanted the problem taken care of immediately since the child was growing older and would be interacting more with peers; she feared that his maturation would be inhibited if the soiling problem persisted. An appointment was arranged with the team, which asked to meet all family members, since the problem affected each of them.

Family composition and history

The Mikelchuk family consisted of a divorced mother; her two children, John, age 10 (the identified patient) and Robert, age 6; and the mother's boyfriend of 2 years, who lived in the home. The children's father and maternal grandparents lived close by, and both boys spent time in all three adult households.

Ten sessions of individual therapy had produced no change in John's encopretic behavior. The problem reportedly developed at the time of his parent's divorce, 3 years before. Both boys had been toilet-trained by age 3½, with no reported difficulties. A thorough medical exam revealed no physiologic basis for the behavior, which typically occurred either on the bus home from school or in the home. John was encopretic in all three of the adults' homes, but more often at his mother's and grandmother's house, where he spent the most time.

John defecated in his pants unnoticed; he hid his soiled clothes and denied the encopretic behavior. If his mother or grandmother suspected that he had soiled himself, they would examine and clean him. Both women responded to John's behavior with anger, raised voices, attempts to make him admit the truth, and seldom-enforced threats of behavioral restriction. John's mother and grandmother declared that they had "tried everything" to solve the problem. They sought out and tried to enforce reward systems, punishments, incentives, retoileting schedules, and lubricants, all to no avail. The family's explanation for John's encopresis was that he was "lazy." They felt that if he did not need to be yelled at for messing in his pants, he would need to be yelled at for something else.

Case analysis

The Mikelchuk family apparently had confused generational boundaries and was developmentally blocked. The grandmother was over-involved and had never completed the developmental tasks appropriate to grandparenthood; John's grandfather was disengaged. Mrs. Mikelchuk had not yet separated successfully from her parental home, adapted to her role as a mother, or created functional couple and parental subsystems with her boyfriend. John was hostile to his mother's boyfriend and constantly compared him to his father. John's encopresis stimulated his mother and grandmother (both of whom he called "Ma") to provide care more appropriate to a much younger child. In addition, none of the adults in the family—grandparents, divorced parents, and boyfriend—could agree how to deal with John's problem.

Initial hypotheses

The team hypothesized that John's symptoms reflected the regulation of closeness and distance between his mother and grandmother. The encopresis apparently served to distract John's mother from her depression by having her focus on his immediate problem behavior. The team concluded that family patterns subtly reinforcing the encopresis also prevented everyone from advancing to the next developmental stage.

Based on these initial hypotheses, treatment goals were established to encourage appropriate developmental progress and generational boundaries; i.e., John's mother and her boyfriend would be in charge of her children, and the grandmother would relinquish her direct parenting responsibilities. The team assumed that more effective boundaries within the family system would help John curb his encopretic behavior.

THE NURSING PROCESS

Assessment

The health problem: Functional encopresis. Functional encopresis is chronic, inappropriate fecal soiling. The American Psychiatric Association's (1980) Diagnostic and Statistical Manual of Mental Disorders, 3rd edition (DSM III) defines the disorder as repeated voluntary or involuntary passage of feces of normal or near-normal consistency into places that are not appropriate for that purpose in the individual's own sociocultural setting; it is functional when not due to any physical disorder.

Little has been written on encopresis, perhaps reflecting a negative attitude on the part of health professionals toward this problem (Fritz and Armbrust, 1982). An estimated 1.5% of the general population is affected (Wright et al., 1979); this estimate might be low, however, since lack of information and embarrassment may make families reluctant to report cases (Margolies and Gilstein, 1983-84).

Encopresis is four to five times more common in males than in females; most victims are males between the ages of 4 and 16. Incidence decreases in later adolescence (Fritz and Armbrust, 1982, p. 291; Margolies and Gilstein, 1983-84, p. 141). Bellman (1966, p. 1) suggested possible familial tendencies toward encopresis, reporting that 15% of patients' fathers and 1.3% of their mothers had a history of encopresis between the ages of 7 and 14.

Encopresis is not an uncommon problem; it accounts for up to 20% of all pediatric gastroenterology referrals. Differential diagnosis involves distinguishing between functional encopresis and organic fecal incontinence secondary to such disorders as Hirschsprung's disease, anorectal stenosis or fissure, intestinal smooth muscle disease, pseudoobstruction syndrome, hypothyroidism, or hypercalcemia; it may stem from chronic codeine or phenothiazine use, or from problems that cause fecal soiling without retention, such as central nervous system or diarrheal disorders, and sensory or motor defects in the anorectum or pelvic floor muscle (Fleischer, 1976, p. 710–11).

Functional encopresis is categorized by two factors: toilet training age and conditions, and whether the disorder is "retentive" or "nonretentive."

Encopresis is labeled primary or "continuous" when appropriate toileting habits were never established; when the disorder constitutes a regression to pre-toilet training behavior, it is called secondary or "discontinuous." This distinction, however, is of limited use, since no significant differences in training methods, personality, family dynamics, or prognosis between the two categories has been documented (Margolies and Gilstein, 1983-84, p. 142).

Although degree of retention is an accepted standard for classifying encopresis, almost all encopretic children exhibit both retention and nonretention of stools throughout the course of this problem (Margolies and Gilstein, 1983-84, p. 142). It is therefore more useful to determine the overall pattern of the encopretic behavior rather than to assign a rigid classification.

Johns (1985, p. 155) describes the classic encopretic behaviors and physical symptoms:

> Parents often describe a cyclical pattern of longer periods of fecal retention with abdominal distention and pain, moodiness, reduced appetite, and increased soiling... The child is often unaware of his own soiling—a situation that causes constant conflict with parents as well as peers.

Fritz and Armbrust (1982, p. 291) describe the typical "secrecy" surrounding encopretic soiling:

> The encopretic child typically passes a small amount of solid or liquid feces into his clothes in secret... The soiled clothing is often hidden about the house and discovered only accidentally by the parent.

Other common physical manifestations of encopresis are abdominal pain relieved by an adequate, often voluminous bowel movement; posturing or "doing a little dance," "stiffening," "crawling," or other symptoms of suppression of colonic signals to defecate. Chronic constipation, stools with the consistency of peanut butter, and moderate abdominal distension frequently accompany encopresis. Fecal smearing is rare among encopretics. Approximately 30% of encopretic children are also enuretic or urine-incontinent during the day (Silverman and Roy, 1983), although only 8% of enuretic children also exhibit encopresis (Fritz and Anders, 1979). Fisher (1979) reported other behavioral problems in encopretic children: eating and sleeping disturbances, headaches, tics, nailbiting, poor academic performance, truancy, stealing, and temper tantrums.

Family dynamics and functional encopresis. In 1925, Pototsky coined the term encopresis and described it as a child's punitive response to the parents. Bellman (1966) observed a correlation between the onset of encopresis and incidents threatening the child's closeness with his parents: the start of school, separation from the mother, marital breakup, and birth of a sibling. After a study of 40 encopretic children, Baird (1974) described four family transactional patterns organized around the symptom: withholding, infantilization, mishandled anger, and miscommunication. Bemporad and colleagues (1978) associated family conflict, among other factors, with encopresis.

Fritz and Armbrust (1982) commented on the complexity of the problem of functional encopresis and the difficulty in clarifying its etiology. They assert that psychosocial and physiologic elements interact to develop and maintain the problem, and observe that the degree to which encopresis can itself lead to psychopathology, rather than result from it, is poorly understood.

There are myriad treatment recommendations for managing encopresis. Medical approaches include vigorous bowel catharsis and long-term administration of lubricants; psychiatric approaches include individual psychotherapy and play therapy for the child; and behavioral approaches are directed toward establishing parental administration of a toileting routine. Indications for choice of treatment strategies remain unclear, however, and the success rates reported for different types of interventions vary and are difficult to explain. Emphasis on individual pathology and historical antecedents rather than on transactional family processes that reinforce the symptom further hinders understanding of the encopretic behavior and appropriate intervention indications.

Margolies and Gilstein (1983-84) also addressed the extreme complexity of encopresis, characterizing it as a process rather than as a static, symptomatic disorder. They focused on the significance of family transactional patterns in symptom maintenance. They believed that each case of encopresis is affected by so many significant factors that it must be considered as a unique situation; this led them to devise a multimodal treatment approach grounded in family systems theory. When 3½ months of family therapy resulted in the elimination of encopretic behavior in a 14-year-old boy, they concluded that traditional linear thinking about pathological cause and effect were generally unhelpful to practitioners managing encopresis. They wrote that:

> Encopresis, like many other functional disorders, consistently reveals itself to be a non-static process with varying personal and interpersonal manifestations... Efforts need to be directed toward identifying the family contexts in which

encopresis occurs rather than trying to identify unidirectional influences (p. 151).

Stepfamily dynamics. A stepfamily is defined as a family suprasystem of more than one adult-led households who are involved with each other in sharing the care of children. Katz and Stein (1983) identified two crucial areas of stepfamily assessment: how the "power" or executive subsystems renegotiate transactions, and how they interact across multihousehold boundaries. The Mikelchuks, as described in the case study, consisted of three households that shared responsibility for two children. The family demonstrated disruption of both key transactional factors: effective adult cooperation and boundary reorganization.

The Mikelchuks' situation illustrates the developmental arrest typical of many blended family systems. Intense grandparental involvement in child care during the Mikelchuks' divorce and periodic instability between the children's mother and her boyfriend strengthened the affectionate bond between grandparents and grandchildren; a bond that, as noted by Sager and colleagues (1983), is hard to attenuate and that may make it harder for grandparents to accept a lesser, yet more appropriate, role with the children. Such shifts in intimacy bonds increase the complexity of the boundary reorganization necessary when another adult enters the parental/spousal subsystem; it places children under the pressure of divided loyalties. John's hostility to his mother's boyfriend and negative comparisons of this man to his father indicated the same loyalty conflicts expressed by John's encopresis. As McGoldrick and Carter (1980) observed, parenting functions that overlap across households blur children's perception of boundaries and can intensify loyalty conflicts.

Assessment of a family. Assessment of functional encopresis must include a complete physical examination to rule out any possible physiologic causes, and a thorough history of current family systems (Table 20.1) to help identify the meaning of the child's behavior in the family system.

Table 20.1 Family Systems Assessment in Functional Encopresis: Areas of Assessment

- History of the problem
- Patterns of encopretic behavior
- Each family member's response to the child's soiling
- Attempted solutions to the soiling behavior and their relative success
- Each involved household's approach to the problem, and whether those approaches are similar or dissimilar, agreed upon or individually pursued, etc.
- Other problem(s) the family might be concerned about if the soiling were not the major issue

While interacting with the family and observing members' interactions, the nurse should attend to verbal and nonverbal cues identifying sub-system boundaries and alliances. Such information is useful in understanding the blended family's developmental progress and uniqueness. Elkaim (1985) has suggested that the assessment interview itself can benefit the family by reassuring them that the nurse understands their situation and by encouraging them to think about their problem together in a new way.

Planning

When the nurse understands the functions of encopresis in a family and the transactional patterns that maintain the symptoms, she can plan effectively. Intervention begins in the initial assessment interview, however, since the nurse's questions and facilitation of family interaction about the problem help the family members to rethink their difficulties. Interventions must address the individual family's interactional patterns and attempted problem resolution. However, the following general guidelines may be helpful:

• Avoid suggesting solutions that have already been tried and have failed.
• If a homework task is indicated, tailor the assignment to the family's strengths, capabilities, and living conditions. Be sure that all family members understand their assignments; ask them to explain their tasks before they leave the session. A written task summary might also be useful. Make the task realistic; avoid overwhelming the family with a task that is too "big" or complex. Ask the family what might cause the homework assignment to fail, and ask members' help in modifying the assignment if indicated.
• Remind the family that a change in the soiling behavior might be slow. This allows them to take charge of the pace of change and neutralizes possible systemic resistance to the nurse's directives.
• Use other systems-oriented interventions, such as positive connotation (Selvini-Palazzoli et al., 1980), developmental reframing (Imber-Coppersmith, 1981), and symptom prescription (Weeks and Abate, 1982), to help the family experience, in new and more flexible ways, the relational and responsive patterns surrounding the soiling behavior.

Intervention

The Mikelchuk family was seen for eight sessions over a period of 4½ months. The first seven sessions involved a wide range of structural and strategic interventions—positive connotation, developmental reframing, restraint from change, symptom prescription, homework assignments, team splits, and formal letters from the team—designed to achieve the treatment goals. These interventions were based on the work of Haley (1980); Selvini-Palazzoli et al. (1980); Imber-Coppersmith

(1981); and Watzlawick et al., (1974). For example, the soiling was *connoted positively* as an "invitation to parenting" and was set in a *developmental reframe* that cast the identified patient as "not bad, not mad, just young" (Imber-Coppersmith, 1981).

Through *paradoxical interventions* (Weeks and Abate, 1982) the family was invited to change while remaining unchanged. *Symptom prescription* was used in this context; in addition, the family was *restrained from change,* and was counseled to "change slowly" and "not change too soon" at selected points in the therapy to mobilize systemic change. *Team splits* were used for their paradoxical effect of offering the family suggestions for change in the guise of "illusion of alternatives." For example, the family was exposed to carefully planned differences of opinion between the therapists and the team, which empowered them to choose between appropriate therapeutic alternatives. Team splits also enabled the team to influence the family's relational balance, maintain systemic neutrality, and symbolically comment on family dynamics.

In spite of the structural and strategic work of the first seven sessions, John's soiling problem persisted without much improvement. In addition, the family lost interest in therapy and wanted to terminate.

For the eighth session the team decided to shift its focus to John's symptoms, hoping to improve his quality of life even though the family system might remain unchanged. The team decided to use a multiple embedded metaphor because this approach was indirect and matched isomorphically the family style of interaction (DeShazer, 1982) and provided an opportunity to identify the resources necessary for John to control his behavior (Lankton and Lankton, 1983).

The metaphor session

As had occurred in most of the previous meetings, session eight involved John, his grandmother, his mother, and his brother. After a brief discussion of the week's events since the last session and the reaffirmation of rapport with all family members, the therapist told John that she wanted to tell him a story, one that might contain some lessons for all his family members. The therapist used intonation, strategic eye contact, dramatic pacing, and planned pauses to hold the family's attention through the following story:

I. Once upon a time there was a little prince who was bright, sensitive, and handsome. This prince was born to a king and a queen whose families came from two different kingdoms which had chosen to unite for the sake of the marriage and the baby. When the prince was still very young, war broke out in this kingdom. There was a terrible battle. As a result of this battle, everyone moved apart. The king moved to a kingdom on one side of the forest, the queen moved to a kingdom on the other side of the forest, and the parents of the king and queen moved to a kingdom in yet another part of the forest. The little prince was very sad. He remembered what it was like when everyone was together, safe behind the castle walls; no knights could attack; no monsters could come in. The moat kept all dragons away. The little prince was sad. Everyone was sad. The little prince was sad and confused. He wanted everyone to be together again and happy. He hadn't wanted this battle. He didn't want everyone to be divided and unhappy. He wanted to be with all members of his family and for everyone to be happy.

As he got a little older, the young prince began to travel back and forth between the different kingdoms. He would put on his mantle and put on his spurs. He saddled up his horse and rode across the forest from one kingdom to another. But the trouble was, he could never arrive quite on time at any of the kingdoms. He was late for everything: late for breakfast, for lunch, and for dinner; he was late for hunting trips and even for jousting matches. He was always late and always confused, always off-schedule and always uneasy. Somehow his mind never seemed to focus on what he was doing or what he needed to do. Somehow he was always thinking about the kingdom where he wasn't. When he was at the king's castle, he thought about the queen's castle. When he was at the queen's castle, he thought of the king's castle. When he was at the queen mother's castle... and so forth. He was never *doing the job he needed to be doing at the right time.* Even in the special school for princes, he never did his job. He often forgot to bring his sword, and he fell behind in jousting class. His mantle was rarely polished properly. He did poorly in knightsmanship, and his boots were always messy. It got so bad that all of the other little princes were beginning to treat him not like a blue-blooded prince, but like a peasant. He *knew* that *he was a prince*—he just looked like a peasant. Everyone was worried about him and irritated by him. Everyone—his sister, his brother, his uncle, his jousting teacher, the court jester, and even the little animals in the forest—were always reminding him of *the job he had to do,* and *when he had to do it.* The more confused the little prince became, the more worried and angry everyone else became. The more worried and angry they became, the more confused and unhappy the little prince became. This went on and on. Everyone reminded him of what came first, what came next, what came before that, and what came after the thing that just came.

One of the little prince's biggest problems was that each kingdom followed a different schedule. In one kingdom, the court jester was summoned a half hour before the evening meal. In the other castle, the horses were groomed 2 hours before the noon meal, and in the other the meals were served 3 hours after the horses were groomed. In one kingdom, the entertainment began a half hour after the last meal. In another, it ended a half hour after the second meal.

Adding to the little prince's difficulty was the fact that he had never learned how to tell time. Ordinarily, this would be easy for such a bright and growing boy, but with all of his traveling between kingdoms and all of his worrying, he couldn't *concentrate on timing.* Even worse, there was a different kind of sundial in each of the kingdoms. In one kingdom the sundial had notches but no clear numbers; it was kind of secret. In the second kingdom, the sundial was elaborate, and fancy—so fancy that the little prince could not make out the numbers. In the third kingdom, the sundial kept changing; as soon as he thought he could make out the time, the shadow changed and once again the little prince couldn't figure it out. This little prince was in a terrible fix.

II. There was so much the little prince had to learn. As you know, John, you've learned lots of things in your life. As a baby, your mother fed you. As you got a little older, she let you feed yourself. At times you would spill your milk and slop up the cereal, but gradually you learned to do more for yourself.

How proud you were when you could eat by yourself! Do you remember that feeling? When you were a baby, your mother would dress you, put on your jacket, and tie your shoes. How *proud you were* when you could get dressed by yourself! You can *remember how proud you were,* and how good it felt when you could stay outside all by yourself. You can *remember how proud you were* when you learned how to ride a bike by yourself. At first the grownups who loved you did everything for you, but gradually you could *do so much by yourself.* They had the wisdom to learn from each other and from you, and they *let you make mistakes* and *learn to do things on your own.*

And, of course, you know how you learned to tell time. First you learned to count—one finger, two fingers—count with me; good. Then you learned how to tell one number from another. Number one looked different from number two... number eight from number nine... number eleven from number twelve. Slowly you learned the idea of time. When it was dark, you would sleep, and when it was light, you would wake up, and when your tummy was empty it was time to eat. As a baby, your mother told you when to wake up and when to sleep, when to eat and when to drink, but as you got older you began to understand about *time and what your body was telling you.* You knew when you were hot, when you were cold, when you were full, when you were empty. At first your mother covered you with a blanket, but soon you learned to listen to your body, and you learned that everyone's body is different. One person might drink a half an hour after waking up, while another might wait an hour. One person might eat exactly at noon, while another might rest at noon and eat in the afternoon. Some people might need a snack as soon as they come home from school. *Each person has different timing,* and *every person is the boss of his own time and his own body.* And even a young boy, John, can look back at the end of a day and *take pleasure in knowing that he knows his body and is the boss of his body. Wise parents* know about timing too. They know all the complicated things a parent needs to learn, from each of their children, and from each of *their* parents.

III. This reminds me of another child I saw recently. He was about your age, and he was losing some of his baby teeth. Well, one of his teeth was loose for the *longest* time. Everyone thought it should have come out long ago. But that baby tooth was hanging on. It wouldn't budge. His mother tried wiggling it, his father tried shaking it, his grandfather said he would tie a string to it. But I told him, *"You know when that baby tooth will be ready to come out.* You know and no one else knows. That baby tooth will fall out just when it's ready, just when the grownup tooth starts coming out." I told him, *"You know when it's going to come out and that's between you* and the tooth fairy. *No one else needs to know.* But when it happens, won't everyone be surprised and won't they be pleased?"

IV. Speaking of being pleased, let me tell you what happened to that little prince. Just like you, the little prince—with help from the queen, king, queen mother, teachers, and sometimes even the forest animals—began to learn about time. He learned slowly at first, with lots of mistakes and lots of accidents. But, slowly, he began to understand the different sundials, the notches, and the fancy markings on the one that kept changing. He began also to *listen to his own body* and to understand *what jobs he had to do and when he had to do them.* Gradually, he began to be *his own boss, in his own time.* He knew that when he woke up at daybreak and his mouth was dry, he needed to go to the water bucket and fill up the water ladle. He could feel that when his stomach rumbled he needed to find the cook and get some venison. He knew that when he was tired from jousting lessons he had to go to his tent and rest. He knew that when he entered a race he had to concentrate. Gradually, he began to *know what he needed to do to get his jobs done.* No matter what kingdom he was in, he *knew what he needed* and *what he had to do.* He was taking *charge of his own body by himself.* He was growing up, and becoming less and less confused. As he grew less confused, everyone around him grew less confused and less worried. It became clearer and clearer that indeed this was a royal prince and not a messy little peasant.

V. As he grew and matured, *everyone knew that more growth and more changes would be coming.* There would be new confusions, and new developments. Even in his sleep he knew he was growing. The little prince was happy about the changes, as were all of the other people in all of the kingdoms and all of the little animals in the forest, and he looked forward to even more. The royal family took pride in his changes and how he grew in his own time.

VI. And speaking of time...

John, you can continue to think about this story; you can take your time and learn from it for as long as you want. You know a lot already and you have lots still to learn. *All* of us *learn what we can from stories like these.* Because time is important for everyone.

And the time *now* is getting late. What time does that clock say, John? You have school tomorrow. We can stop now and let you continue to grow at *your* own pace, even while you are sleeping in your own bed.

Discussion of the metaphorical intervention. A fairy tale was created to parallel the therapist's focus on the child's problem; such stories have a universal appeal and usefulness in revealing new meanings for life. Bettelheim (1977) asserted that fairy tales enrich inner life by speaking of severe inner pressures in subtle, nonthreatening ways and by offering temporary and permanent solutions to pressing difficulties. John's therapeutic story offered a metaphorical representation of his family's life to promote unconscious identification with the characters and events, as well as with the tale's implied resolution. This is the therapeutic effect of using metaphor in therapy (Gordon, 1978; Welch, 1984).

Construction of an embedded metaphor

An "embedded metaphor" is a therapeutic metaphor tailored to a client's unique situation and intended to enhance the client's choices for change. This intervention was developed by Lankton and Lankton (1983) based on Milton Erickson's strategic hypnotic work. Embedded metaphor development is a seven-stage process:

Inducing trance. Use principles of hypnotic trance induction to maintain the client's attention and create an atmosphere conducive to learning. The therapist engaged John and his family's attention by stating that she was going to tell them a story; it was a new and unexpected announcement that took the family by surprise. The therapist's dramatic yet playful storytelling, combined with strategic eye contact, nonverbal joining, lively intonation, and planned pauses kept the family "entranced" throughout the delivery of the metaphor. The family's attentiveness made them more receptive to the messages in the therapeutic metaphor.

Matching the metaphor. Construct the initial dramatic metaphor to parallel the problem situation, and leave the story unresolved. Part I of the sample story sought to isomorphically match John's presenting problem and life situation.

Retrieving resources. Use elements in the story to highlight client strengths and resources. In Part II of the story the therapist describes developmental accomplishments John had mastered earlier in his life, and upon which his resources are based. Embedded messages (italicized phrases) are also interspersed throughout and vocally emphasized by the therapist's tone shift. This section of the metaphor emphasizes John's need to listen to messages from his body and concentrate on appropriate timing.

Directing work. Address the most serious aspect(s) of the client's difficulty rather than the most obvious conscious concerns. "This is the phase where the therapy works to resolve unconscious emotional conflicts and, metaphorically speaking, to free bound energy that needs to be directed more constructively in the client's life" (Lankton and Lankton, 1983, p. 122). Part II introduces the concept of differentiation: "Each person has different timing, and every person is the boss of his own time and his own body." The notion of differentiation is reframed within the notion of appropriate intergenerational relatedness: "And wise parents know about timing. They know all the complicated things a parent needs to learn, from each of their children, and from each of their parents." This portion of the metaphor facilitates restructuring of intergenerational boundaries.

Linking resources. Resolve tangential metaphors by including images of the future that will help the client discover resources useful in situations to come. Part III of John's metaphor emphasizes development— growing and maturing over time and giving up infantile activities in favor of more age-appropriate behaviors. This part also contains a tangential but related story that was inserted into the fairy tale to emphasize the direct work and connect self-knowledge about developmental readiness with successful "knowing" in the future.

Ending the matching metaphor. End the metaphor by modeling desirable outcomes. In John's case, Part V of the story contains messages for the mother and grandmother about normal developmental changes. Part VI also gives John suggestions for future applications of the lessons in the story.

Reorientation. Suggest ways for the family to apply lessons from the story to their daily lives, and refer to present events. John's family had remained absolutely quiet, attentive, and motionless throughout the story. After reorienting them to the room, the therapist inquired about the next session; she did not return to the story. The family said that they might not return to therapy.

Case analysis

The Mikelchuk family did not return to treatment. John's mother remained depressed and had difficulties with her boyfriend; the children spent more time with their grandparents. The grandmother reported that John's encopretic behavior was significantly reduced—to once or twice a week—and that she was pleased.

The decision to terminate seemed directly related to John's improvement. The initial request had been for assistance in ending John's encopresis. When this goal was achieved, the family's desire for further treatment ceased. Within the context of the family's original request, the treatment was successful. The team sent a termination letter to both homes expressing respect for the family's decision to end therapy; a 6-month follow-up indicated that John's encopresis had stopped almost completely, although the family situation was unchanged.

Evaluation of the embedded metaphor strategy reveals that symptomatic relief was accomplished, and the grandmother reported no replacement behaviors in either John or his brother. John's improvement may have been related to the metaphor in combination with other factors, not the least of which was the increased stability in the grandparents' home.

Evaluation

Evaluation of intervention effectiveness in families with the problem of functional encopresis is straightforward. If the soiling behavior stops, the therapy has achieved its goal. However, this problem is a complex and difficult one, and usually reflects severe and/or long-term family dysfunction. The family is the best evaluator of therapeutic progress, and the nurse should inquire how much and what kind of change the family hopes to gain from therapy. Interventions that do not produce the change the family requests are best discarded for solutions more congruent with the family's world view or transactional style.

While the use of therapeutic metaphor successfully helped John adopt a new behavior pattern, such an approach cannot be done by formula. Rather, the use of metaphor needs to grow directly from the defined treatment goals, which are set by a useful nursing diagnosis (Lankton and Lankton, 1983). Every therapeutic interaction must reflect feedback from the client system so that new information can be made available to the family system. Therefore, the effective use of therapeutic metaphor results from a carefully organized process that tailors the intervention to the individual and/or family system.

CONCLUSIONS

Functional encopresis is a serious problem that reflects disruption in both individual and family development. Collaborative, interdisciplinary therapy, in which the nurse plays a key role, can be a useful treatment model. Intervention must be based on an understanding of the problem's complexity and an appreciation of the affected family's unique world view, symptom function, and potential for change and growth.

REFERENCES

American Psychiatric Association. *Diagnostic and Statistical Manual of Mental Disorders,* 3rd ed. Washington, D.C.: American Psychiatric Association, 1980.

Baird, M. "Characteristic Interaction Patterns in Families of Encopretic Children," *Bulletin of the Menninger Clinic* 39:144–53, 1974.

Bellman, M. "Studies on Encopresis," *Acta Pediatrica Scandinavia* 170(Supp.):1–151, 1966.

Bemporad, J., et al. "Neurotic Encopresis as a Paradigm of a Multifactorial Psychiatric Disorder," *Journal of Nervous and Mental Diseases* 166:472–79, 1978.

Bettelheim, B. *The Use of Enchantment: The Meaning and Importance of Fairy Tales.* New York: Knopf, 1977.

Clements, I.W., and Roberts, F.D. *Family Health: A Theoretical Approach to Nursing Care.* New York: John Wiley & Sons, 1983.

DeShazer, S. *Brief Family Treatment.* New York: Guilford Press, 1982.

Elkaim, M. "New Approaches to Family Systems Therapy," *Master Therapists Conference.* Farmington, Conn.: University of Connecticut Health Center, 1985.

Fisher, S.M. "Encopresis," in *Basic Handbook of Child Psychiatry.* Edited by Noshpitz, J. New York: Basic Books, 1979.

Fleischer, D. "Diagnosis and Treatment of Disorders of Defecation in Children," *Pediatric Annals* 5:72, 1976.

Fritz, G.K., and Anders, T.P. "Enuresis: The Clinical Application of an Etiologically Based Classification System," *Child Psychiatry and Human Development* 10:103–13, 1979.

Fritz, G.K., and Armbrust, J. "Enuresis and Encopresis," *Psychiatric Clinics of North America* 5(2):283-96, 1982.

Glick, P.C., and Norton, A.J. "Marrying, Divorcing and Living Together in the U.S. Today," *Population Bulletin* 32:5-28, 1977.

Gordon, D. *Therapeutic Metaphors.* Cupertino, Calif.: Meta, 1978.

Haley, J. *Leaving Home: The Therapy of Disturbed Young People.* New York: McGraw-Hill Book Co., 1980.

Hoffman, L. "The Family Life Cycle and Discontinuous Change," in *The Family Life Cycle: A Framework for Family Therapy.* Edited by Carter, E. A., and McGoldrick, M. New York: Gardner Press, 1980.

Hoffman, L. *Foundations of Family Therapy.* New York: Basic Books, 1979.

Imber-Coppersmith, E. "Developmental Reframing," *Journal of Strategic and Systemic Therapy* 1(1):1–8, 1981.

Johns, C. "Encopresis," *American Journal of Nursing* 3:153–56, 1985.

Katz, L., and Stein, S. "Treating Step-Families," in *Handbook of Family and Marital Therapy.* Edited by Wolman, B.B, and Stricker, G. New York: Plenum Pubs., 1983.

Lankton, S., and Lankton, C. *The Answer Within: A Clinical Framework for Ericksonian Hypnotherapy.* New York: Brunner-Mazel, 1983.

Levine, M. "The School Child with Encopresis," *Pediatrics in Review* 2(9):285–89, 1981.

Margolies, R., and Gilstein, K.W. "A Systems Approach to the Treatment of Chronic Encopresis," *International Journal of Psychiatry in Medicine* 13(2):141–52, 1983-84.

McGoldrick, M., and Carter, E.A. "Forming a Remarried Family," in *The Family Life Cycle: A Framework for Family Therapy.* Edited by Carter, E.A., and McGoldrick, M. New York: Gardner Press, 1980.

Minuchin, S. *Families and Family Therapy.* Cambridge, Mass.: Harvard University Press, 1974.

Pototsky, C. "Die Encopresis," in *Psychotherapie Korperlicher Symptome.* Edited by Schwartz, O. Berlin: Springer Publishing Co., 1925.

Sager, C.J., et al. *Treating the Remarried Family.* New York: Brunner-Mazel, 1983.

Sedgwick, R. *Family Mental Health: Therapy and Practice.* St. Louis: C.V. Mosby Co., 1981.

Selvini-Palazzoli, M., et al. *Paradox and Counterparadox: A New Model in the Therapy of the Family in Schizophrenic Transaction.* New York: Jason Aronson, 1980.

Silverman, A., and Roy, C.C. *Pediatric Clinical Gastroenterology,* 3rd ed. St. Louis: C.V. Mosby Co., 1983.

Watzlawick, P., et al. *Change: Problem Formation and Problem Resolution.* New York: W.W. Norton & Co., 1974.

Weeks, G.R., and Abate, L. *Paradoxical Psychotherapy: Theory and Practice with Individuals, Couples, and Families.* New York: Brunner-Mazel, 1982.

Welch, M.J. "Using Metaphor in Psychotherapy," *Journal of Psychosocial Nursing and Mental Health Services* 22(11):13–18, 1984.

Wright, L., et al. *Encyclopedia of Pediatric Psychology.* Baltimore: University Park Press, 1979.

21 Intervening with remarried families and alcoholism

Nancy B. Fisk, RN, MS
Lecturer and RN Coordinator
Division of Nursing
School of Health Sciences
University of Massachusetts
Amherst, Massachusetts

OVERVIEW

This chapter focuses on interventions that nurses in any setting might use when they encounter alcoholic clients and their families. A family systems perspective is employed and illustrated through a case study emphasizing a remarried family. Throughout the chapter, theoretical and philosophical issues are integrated as a basis for suggested interventions. Areas for further development in nursing care for these families are also described.

CASE STUDY

Lydia, age 36, and Wally, age 34, have been married for 2 years and have one daughter, Nancy (now 10 months). Lydia had three children when she married Wally: Laurel, 16, born out of wedlock, Lynn, 10, and Mike Jr., 7, all products of a 12-year marriage to a violent and abusive spouse. Lydia began divorce proceedings shortly after Mike Jr.'s birth, because she learned that her husband had made sexual overtures to Laurel. (Refer to the genogram, Figure 21.1, for further information about family history.)

Assessment

The Lipsky family was known to the visiting nurse agency, which first assisted Lydia several years before in the home of her mother Ann, who is severely disabled by arthritis. The same agency later made prenatal and postpartum visits to Lydia's home. A trusting relationship had developed between the Lipskys and the nurse who helped them solve the many problems associated with Ann's home care.

Laurel wants to become a nurse, and has been taught the details of her grandmother's medical and home care regime. Recently she has provided the bulk of Ann's in-home assistance before and after school, since Lydia is pregnant (much to everyone's dismay).

When the visiting nurse arrived for a prenatal visit she found Lydia angry and tearful. Wally was in the hospital with a broken leg, cracked ribs, and cuts and bruises from a driving while intoxicated (DWI) accident. She told the nurse that Wally had always been a heavy drinker but that, since Nancy's birth, his drinking had become excessive to the point that he missed several work-days. Even before the accident, his job was in jeopardy. "Now he won't be able to work for weeks and we are so behind in our bills. We fight about it all the time and the kids are a wreck just like I am. He spends about $80.00 a week drinking at the bar after work."

During this visit the nurse obtained, through skillful use of open and closed questions as well as basic attentive listening, further data about Wally's alco-holism. Two more visits were made soon after to counsel Lydia and further assess her needs and coping skills. The nurse brought some pamphlets written for families of problem drinkers and assessed more carefully Lydia's knowl-edge about alcoholism. The following nursing diagnoses were derived:

- Knowledge deficits *re* alcoholism facts and family effects.
- Ineffective family coping related to alcoholism in a family member.
- Alteration in family process related to immediate situational crisis of spousal drinking-driving accident.
- Potential alteration in parenting style related to stress of current crisis.

Planning and Intervention

The nurse planned and carried out an individualized educational program as well as a referral plan for definitive alcoholism treatment for Wally and ongoing self-help group involvement for the entire family. Visiting Wally in the hospital, the nurse could act on all five categories of the NNSA (National Nurses Society on Alcoholism) 1978 *Position Statement on the Role of the Nurse in Alcoholism:*

- Identifying the problem with alcohol.
- Communicating about the problem with alcohol.
- Educating about alcohol use, abuse, and alcoholism.
- Counseling the alcoholic individual, family, and significant others about alcoholism and its secondary problems.
- Referring for further definitive alcoholism treatment and/or aftercare.

Evaluation

A follow-up visit revealed that in the Lipskys' case the therapeutic goals were met as well as could be expected within the established time frame (2 weeks). Wally was in residential alcoholism treatment after experiencing mod-erate (responsive to medication) withdrawal symptoms during his post-accident hospitalization. Lydia enrolled in family outpatient counseling and attended one Al-Anon meeting; she persuaded Laurel to attend an Alateen meeting. Because of the family's health situation, the nurse maintained contact and continued to evaluate the family's progress in dealing with Wally's alcoholism.

NURSING PROCESS

Assessment

The health problem: Alcoholism. Despite continuing interdisciplinary disagreement about some aspects of alcoholism definition and etiology, there is agreement on key elements of its management. Thus, there is a growing informational base for assessment and intervention. One definition of alcoholism that nurses might find useful is offered in Appendix A.

Figure 21.1 Genogram—The Lipsky Family

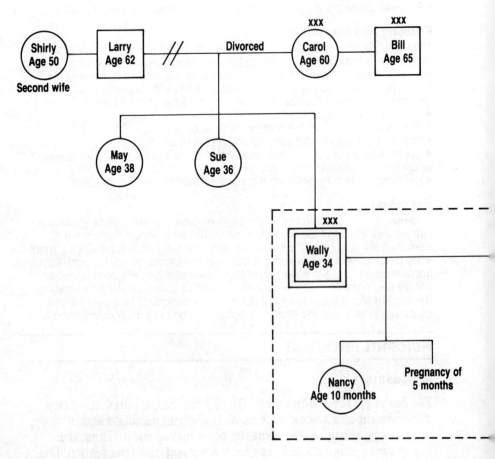

Key: xxx = Alcoholism

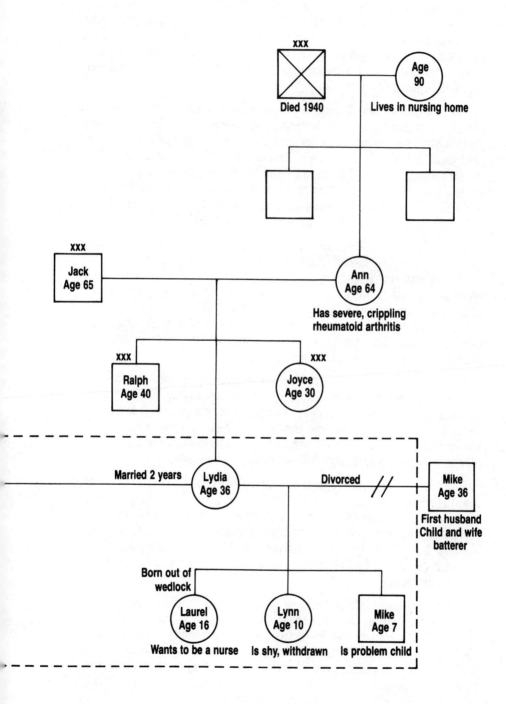

The present discussion will bypass controversial theoretical areas to focus on the practical issues that should guide nursing approaches to alcoholic families. The following material represents the author's own synthesis of key theoretical points with the working definitions, assumptions, and biases she developed during 15 years of specialized alcoholism nursing.

Most of the nursing literature on alcoholism focuses on the individual problem drinker. Typically, there is a discussion of the disease concept and its stages of progression as first described by Jellinek (1960), as well as of the diagnostic criteria developed by the National Council on Alcoholism (1972). Heinemann and Estes (1976), Reed (1976), and Estes et al. (1980), for instance, have provided assessment models and tools for individual alcoholics. Practical information on assessing the alcoholic's family unit is not as readily available.

Remarried families. The rate of remarriage after a first divorce is approximately 75% in the United States (McGoldrick and Carter, 1980). Given the extremely high number of divorces and an additional though smaller number of remarriages after widowhood, a large proportion of families fall under the heading of "blended" or "remarried" (with or without civil or religious formality). The process of forming and maintaining a remarried family is not well defined or explored in either the family study or nursing literature.

Remarried individuals carry at least three types of "emotional baggage" or entanglements: from the family of origin; from the first marriage; and from the process of separation, divorce, and the period between marriages. All three areas are infinitely more complex when one or both of the remarried spouses is an alcoholic, comes from an alcoholic family, and/or has had an alcoholic spouse.

The Lipsky family is typical in that both Lydia and Wally come from families with histories of alcoholism. Since Wally had never before married, the pattern on his side is slightly less complicated. If, for example, he had been older and previously married with children, each of his two families might be at different developmental stages, with different problems, facing issues and tasks that would compound their present situation.

Triangling can pose a problem in remarried families. The most apparent triangle in the case study formed between Lydia, Wally, and Mike Jr. Lydia protects Mike Jr. from Wally's attempts to discipline him; she explains that Wally hates Mike Jr. because he hated Mike Sr., and that his drunken ravings reveal unfounded jealous paranoia toward Lydia's ex-husband. This type of triangle is the most common found in remarried households (McGoldrick and Carter, 1980).

Developmental tasks for remarried families have been described by McGoldrick and Carter (1980). Table 21.1 is the author's own adaptation of their description.

Table 21.1 Developmental Tasks of Remarried Families

- Resolve attachment(s) or "emotional divorce" from previous marriage(s).
- Accept the need for time and patience during the adjustment to a complex and ambiguous new situation.
- Maintain cooperative coparental relationship with ex-spouse.
- Help children deal with fears, loyalty conflicts, and membership in two-family systems.
- Realign extended family relationships to include new spouse and children.
- Help children maintain connections with previous extended family.
- Restructure family boundaries to include new spouse/stepparent.
- Realign relationships throughout subsystems to permit interweaving of several systems.

Source: Adapted from McGoldrick and Carter, 1980.

The Lipsky family clearly fell short of completing some of these tasks or resolving key issues. For instance:
- The ex-spouse is not in the same state; in fact, his whereabouts are unknown. In any case, the relationship is characterized by extreme conflict.
- Neither extended family was happy about the remarriage. Wally's mother considers Lydia a loose woman, and there has been emotional cutoff from Wally's family. Lydia's family tolerates Wally, barely.
- Wally is not functioning as a parent to the older children, and only somewhat fulfills a parental role with the baby. He adores the infant but would rather not have the older children around.
- It is impossible to sort out the impact of alcoholism on family development and vice versa, except to affirm that severe effects may be attributed to multigenerational alcoholism on both sides of the family as well as to the currently alcoholic household.

Theoretical approaches. The work of family researchers outside nursing (especially family therapists) offers useful perspectives for assessing alcoholism in families. Bateson (1972) and Steinglass (1976) were among the first to study alcoholism from a systems viewpoint. Professionals in the alcoholism field have begun to incorporate aspects of systemic thinking into the way they conceptualize the problem. Though the approach is still controversial, some prominent alcoholism treatment programs have adapted family therapy models for their recovery programs.

The family systems perspective yields several parameters for both assessment of and intervention for alcohol abuse. First, it calls for treatment of the entire family system as a unit, and seeks to change the family's systemic structure and/or dynamics so the members can cease to foster pathologic drinking. Although family systems therapy often employs joint meetings with all family members, its aims may also be accomplished with only one person present (Berenson, 1976) or with a couple alone (Bowen, 1973). In any case, the family context and systems thinking must provide the foundation of the session. This is important in alcoholism treatment, since working with an actively drinking alcoholic can be impractical. In such cases, initial access to the family system should be obtained through the nonalcoholic spouse, who might function at a higher level.

Family systems thinking emphasizes circular or mutual, rather than linear, causality. In alcoholism, where negative stereotypes and non-sympathetic attitudes prevail even (or especially) among the helping professions, family systems counselors should be (theoretically) more nonjudgmental and accepting of family problems and concerns. The "family illness" perspective of Alcoholics Anonymous and Al-Anon (1972) similarly helps absolve blame and guilt. This assertion is confirmed by the fact that AA has helped alcoholics achieve sobriety at rates probably higher than those of any other single form of treatment.

Philosophical agreement between those who provide counseling at different stages of alcoholic recovery would provide greater continuity and less confusion for the patient.

Wegscheider (1981), a prominent family therapist specializing in alcoholism treatment, stresses that the counselor must view alcoholism as a blameless disease. Shifting blame from the patient to the spouse to the family by negative labeling only perpetuates blaming. Coppersmith (1982) states that:

> A systemic perspective on human problem formation and human problem resolution is holistic, collaborative, dialectical, process-oriented, and circular, and as such represents a major paradigm shift from the traditional Western linear perspective, which is individualistic, reductionistic, mechanistic, content-oriented, and unidirectional.

Keeping a systemic perspective is an ongoing challenge for those who wish to work effectively with alcoholic families.

Paolino and McCrady (1977) reviewed studies of the wives of alcoholics and found no evidence of a stereotypic alcoholic personality; this result contradicts previous negative portraits derived from studies done between 1937 and 1969. Negative, blaming, and judgmental attitudes toward alcoholics will only intensify the denial that alcoholics and their families typically display, which constitutes the most serious obstacle to alcoholic self-help. Jackson (1954) was the first to delineate the stages of family adjustment to alcoholism, demonstrating that not until the family reaches a state of chaos and disorganization do its members begin to recognize that alcohol lies at the root of the problem.

The nurse should therefore not expect the family to volunteer data about the alcoholic member's drinking, but should rely more on indirect clues. Later, in stage four (of seven stages), the nonalcoholic spouse (female in the Jackson research) will stop hiding the drinking: at this point older children may also acknowledge their parent's alcoholism. The coping roles played by each member of an alcoholic family system have been described by Booz-Allen and Hamilton (1974), Wegscheider (1981), and Black (1981).

More recently, others have written about the children of alcoholics, shedding new light on the dynamics of the early years of life with alcoholic parent(s) (Deutsch, 1982) and the impact of that experience on the fully grown adult child of alcoholic parent(s) (Woititz, 1983). Nurses have also looked at family dynamics in alcohol and other substance abuse; readers may refer to Hanson and Estes (1977), Blades (1979), and Finley (1983).

The literature frequently indicates that interaction patterns in alcoholics' families impose a rigid posture or role that persists in all future relationships. Thus, alcoholic parents can have a negative effect on the mate attraction, career choice, and social behavior of their own children and succeeding generations.

The Lipsky children had clearly assumed survival roles: Laurel, the "family hero" (Wegscheider, 1981)—a "super coper" (Booz-Allen and Hamilton, 1974) or "responsible one" (Black, 1981)—wanted to be a nurse and act as Mom's and Grandmom's helper; Lynn, the "lost child" ("flighter" or "adjuster"), was quiet, shy, and withdrew to her room; Mike, the "scapegoat" or "fighter", was the problem child whose behavior was irritating to the entire family, but especially to Wally. From this pattern, one might predict that Nancy would soon become the "family mascot", the "perfect child" or "placator." Wally would take on the role of "victim" and Lydia the role of "chief enabler," according to the Survival Role schema devised by Wegscheider (heavily influenced by Bandler et al., 1976).

Planning

Having assessed the family, the nurse should set priorities and write long- and short-term goals. These goals should consider the family's capabilities and limitations, as well as the nurse's own skill and experience. Progressive client-centered objectives for meeting the short-term goals can then be written; they must be agreed upon by both nurse and family. The nurse must also be realistic about the amount of time she can devote to the family.

Mutual goal-setting is problematic in alcoholic families because of the nature of the disease and the denial that often characterizes it. The nurse must be keenly aware of each family member's level of denial, and should try to resolve the problem based on her knowledge about alcoholism. This is where the nurse must rely upon professional experience, judgment, and timing.

Each alcoholic family is different, in terms of both individual disease progression and family adjustment. Usually, the nonalcoholic spouse and/or other nonalcoholic family members will abandon their denial before the alcoholic member does. Therefore, the nurse should work primarily with the nonalcoholic member(s) at first.

In the Lipsky case, the alcoholic member (Wally) was absent when the nurse first visited the home, due to his hospitalization for alcohol-related injuries. Such an alcohol-related situational crisis as this offers a golden opportunity for intervention because it makes denial more difficult. Faced with the real consequences of Wally's drinking, Lydia communicated openly with the nurse about it.

Each of the four identified nursing diagnoses was evaluated and prioritized; each had its own degree of urgency and requirements for further assessment. By the end of the first visit, the nurse identified a need to reinforce information about alcoholism and to supplement what Lydia had read on her own. The nurse also determined that the young children's physical and safety needs were met by Lydia and Laurel, who had stayed home from school that day because of the family crisis. The immediate situational crisis was being handled fairly well; Wally would be in the hospital for at least 5 days and the nurse would visit him there and talk with his primary nurse about discharge plans. The most critical nursing diagnosis focused on family coping and alcoholism. Lydia and the nurse agreed that the family needed help managing its current situation, and the following long-term goals were established:

• The family will recognize its need for and seek outside help specific to alcoholism.
• Each family member will understand alcoholism on an age-appropriate level and accept it as a family disease.
• The family will begin the recovery process and continue toward permanent sobriety as well as personal growth and productivity for each member.
• The family will recognize the need for and seek family therapy during recovery.

Intervention

In alcoholism, nursing intervention is vital to real recovery. Nurses in all settings have access to hundreds of affected families; by virtue of their sheer numbers, diversity of practice settings, and their family orientation toward health care, nurses can contribute enormously to alcoholism prevention and treatment.

Alcoholism *is* treatable. Many families have recovered completely. AA alone reports at least one million sober alcoholics. A greater problem is how to initiate treatment; many alcoholic families never enter AA or other treatment.

Using the Position Statement developed by the National Nurses Society on Alcoholism (1978) as a springboard, both basic and higher level interventions can be specified. The assessment section of this chapter dealt with Category 1, identification of the alcohol problem. The following excerpts from the remaining four categories give clear mandates for nursing action:

Category 2—Communicating about the problem with alcohol.

NNSA believes nursing intervention should facilitate communication about the alcohol problem with the patient, the family or significant others, and the appropriate members of the interdisciplinary health team. Such communication should be consistent, nonjudgmental, and based on a body of knowledge and philosophy conducive to recovery.

Category 3—Education about alcohol use, abuse, and alcoholism.

NNSA believes that every nurse is responsible for educating patients, families, and significant others about alcohol use, abuse, and alcoholism. Nurses with special alcoholism-related skills should educate other members of the interdisciplinary health care team, as well as community groups.

Category 4—Counseling the alcoholic individual, family, and significant others about alcoholism and its resulting problems.

NNSA takes the position that nurses in all settings should acquire enough basic knowledge and skill to provide alcoholism counseling. The use of denial as a defense mechanism by alcoholic individuals, families, and significant others is a major deterrent to recovery. Because inadvertent nursing reinforcement of that denial can be detrimental, nurses must intervene to identify and confront the reaction. In alcohol-specific settings, nurses should also have direct counseling functions (including individual and group therapy) and they must be active members of the treatment team.

Category 5—Referring for further definitive alcoholism treatment and/or aftercare.

NNSA believes that all nurses, regardless of setting, should know enough about available resources to make a treatment referral for the alcoholic patient and/or significant others who express a desire for help. The importance of timing such referrals cannot be overemphasized.

Nurses who practice in alcohol-specific settings should acquire additional resource knowledge to individually match agent/agency to the need(s) of the patient, family, and/or significant other. Successful recovery may depend upon the appropriateness of the treatment or aftercare referral. Continuity in care and follow-up are essential nursing responsibilities in all settings.

Definitive nursing interventions. When treating a disorder as complex as alcoholism, it is tempting to initiate a comprehensive nursing care plan with interventions aimed at the full spectrum of associated physical, mental, psychoemotional, social, cultural, and spiritual complications. Such elaborate interventions, however, would be contrary to the purpose of this chapter and would mask or submerge the real issue: the alcoholism itself. The author suspects that, in nursing practice, this is often what happens: the alcohol problem is overlooked or buried under volumes of nursing process rhetoric. Therefore, the first steps in definitive nursing intervention are recognizing and counteracting denial in health professionals themselves—including nurses— with respect to alcoholism. The nurse should follow the NNSA's lead by addressing only definitive nursing actions, that is, "only those functions of the nurse which directly and specifically define the role of the nurse in relation to the problem with alcohol" (NNSA, 1978).

The nursing interventions in families where alcoholism is still actively progressing (that is, where the drinking has not yet ceased) are quite direct and have the single goal of helping the family coerce the alcoholic into treatment. This entails consideration of the alcoholic's physiologic status, the family's financial situation (including health insurance coverage), and miscellaneous factors such as geographic location or family preference. It may seem backward to discuss discharge planning with the family and arrange referral at this time, but the nurse must have the mechanisms in place so that everyone can act immediately upon the alcoholic member's agreement to accept treatment.

Johnson (1973) points out, as do many others in the alcoholism field, two important intervention considerations: that crises related to alcohol become the nodal points at which the alcoholic will "hit bottom," and that a multidisciplinary team approach is the most effective treatment. Wegscheider (1981) gives a step-by-step formulation of an early intervention strategy that was originated by the Johnson Institute and is now widely used in alcoholism treatment. This approach is based on the therapeutic use of alcohol-related crises by family, friends, employers, and health team members and centers around confrontation; it has proven effective in coercing alcoholics into treatment.

Nurses can facilitate such intervention and apply some of the method's principles individually in their work with alcoholic clients and families. Using the crisis of illness, injury, and/or hospitalization constructively will help the alcoholic connect drinking and its awesome consequences. This involves what some have called "tough love": a steadfast refusal to cover, smooth over, minimize, or in any way rescue the alcoholic from the impact and emotional pain of the current crisis. Since nursing care is the first service many clients will receive, the nurse's role in such situations is pivotal. No other health professional has quite the same access.

The nurse in the case study initiated this confrontation of denial with Wally. When she visited him in the hospital, Wally joked about his broken leg and made light of the drinking that had caused the accident. He laughed and talked in a loud voice so his hospital roommates would notice his "machismo." Timing her response carefully, the nurse did not laugh, smile, or in any way reward or reinforce his comments. In a sincere and concerned tone she said, "Wally, I'm really worried about you and your family; I've noticed that lately you've had a lot of serious troubles in your life (naming a few). In each case it was clear that heavy drinking was involved. Now, I've thought of you as a responsible and caring husband and father; it doesn't seem like you to do things that damage your relationship with your family. I'd like to talk to you about getting some help for this problem."

Obviously, a positive nurse-patient relationship underpins such intervention. Wally knew, trusted, and respected the visiting nurse, so he could hear and accept her confrontational comments. He knew that they arose from her sincere interest in and concern for the whole family— that she was not taking sides or blaming him. She had always taken a neutral position in family controversy and provided advice aimed at holistic family health.

The principles set forth in Table 21.2 might help general practice nurses who hope to work more effectively with alcoholic families. Such principles apply to family members as well as to alcoholic clients. In many cases, the *don'ts* are more significant than the *do's*.

Specialist nurses with master's degrees and/or nurse/family therapists might also use such strategic techniques as paradoxical intervention, circular interviewing, and rituals in work with alcoholic families. To explore additional techniques in the realm of family therapy would go beyond the scope of this chapter. Wright and Leahey (1984) carefully delineate the differences between family interviewing and family therapy; they distinguish between the kinds of problems that are appropriate for generalist intervention and the kinds requiring specific interventions at the two levels of practice. These distinctions limit generalists to work only on normative and certain paranormative family events and to provide only direct, straightforward interventions.

Table 21.2 Guidelines for Nursing the Alcoholic Family

Don't:

- Argue, discuss or reason with someone who is at the moment drunk or drinking and/or abusing mood-altering substances.
- "Buy into" a client/family delusional system (especially the denial of alcohol as a problem or of its consequences). Alcoholics will blame every trouble in their lives—family, work, school, etc.—for their drinking. They must be helped to see that these problems are more likely results than causes of their alcohol abuse.
- Abdicate to other health team members, expecting that they will automatically deal with the alcoholism because of their better training or education in the field. Specialized knowledge, which most professional schools do not provide, is needed in such areas.
- Punish, blame, scold, label, or gossip about the family to other nurses or health team members.
- Ask the client/family "why does s/he drink?"
- Participate in jokes about or make light of drinking or drunkenness.
- Continue the client/family's conspiracy of silence about the alcohol problem.
- Accept the illusion of normalcy that the nonalcoholic spouse and children strive to present to the outside world.

Do:

- Maintain a high index of suspicion for alcoholism.
- Strive to change negative basic attitudes toward a more hopeful outlook for recovery.
- Become more knowledgeable about the family dynamics of alcoholism.
- Use accurate, straightforward language; that is, avoid the many euphemisms for drunkenness, drinking, and alcoholic/alcoholism.
- Objectively and nonjudgmentally interview families about alcohol use and problems.
- Understand that denial is widespread and the health care team is particularly prone to it.
- Counsel the client/family, helping them make the correct connections between drinking and its harmful or negative consequences.
- Confront misconceptions and incongruities (the "death traps" or "I can't be an alcoholic because..."), for example: "I only drink beer"; "I never drink in the morning"; "I only drink on weekends"; "I rarely have more than three or four"; "I never had any problems from alcohol."
- Teach the facts about alcoholism as a disease and alcohol pharmacology (long- and short-term).

Alcoholic families usually exist within "rigid," "resistant," or "defiance-based" systems, and therefore call for greater use of indirect techniques. Nurses inexperienced in family therapy techniques should not attempt such interventions without understanding their underlying theoretical concepts. Even more importantly, nurses without specialized knowledge of alcoholism and/or other addictive processes should not attempt family treatment of alcoholic family systems. The optimal therapeutic combination for this population would be intervention by a specialist in both alcoholic nursing and family therapy. The latter training would provide the theoretical background and systems view of alcoholism and the family dynamics that maintain or perpetuate (not cause) the problem.

Evaluation

Evaluation is a challenging issue in work with any type of family health problem; it is especially difficult in alcoholism because of this syndrome's complexity and chronicity, as well as its multigenerational projection. Let us look at the goals and objectives of alcoholism interventions.

If permanent abstinence from alcohol is the long-term goal of alcoholism intervention (and most treatment personnel would agree that it is), then the primary measure of outcome would be alcohol consumption. However, the chronically relapsive nature of the disease can confuse results—today's sobriety might have vanished by the time of the 6-month follow-up evaluation. On the other hand, initial failure to achieve sobriety does not mean that intervention has failed. Additionally, "drying out" without behavioral improvement and social adjustments may not improve overall family dynamics.

Nurses can look to the short-term goals identified in NNSA's five categories as standards for evaluating their interventions. Was the family's alcohol problem identified? Was communication about the problem established with the appropriate family and health team members? Did the nurse provide information at a level appropriate for understanding alcoholism and its family disease aspects? Did the nurse counsel family members concerning their own roles and deal with denial and other defenses in a caring, effective way? Were appropriate referrals made based on adequate knowledge of available resources and careful matching of treatment modality to family needs?

If the family does enter alcoholism-specific treatment, then the nurse can consider the intervention successful. In the case study, the Lipskys' nurse achieved these goals. The family became involved in professional treatment and in AA, Al-Anon, and Alateen. Not every case will be as immediately successful.

The nurse should remember, however, that change is not always dramatic or visible. Interventions often resonate slowly through the family system; they may only gradually resolve problem-maintaining interactions among nonalcoholic family members. When no immediate results appear, the alcoholic member may perceive that outside help (AA or other treatment) is the only alternative. The nurse may never know the long-term "ripple effects" of her interventions. In the case study, the nurse had an ongoing involvement with the Lipsky family, and thus had an opportunity for ongoing evaluation. She was quite gratified by the long-term successful outcome.

CONCLUSIONS

There are enormous opportunities for nursing intervention with alcoholic families. This chapter, which merely scratches the surface, deals with a particular stage in alcoholism progression and with a particular type of family. There are no stereotypes in this disease nor any immune personality types. Alcoholism affects every race, ethnic group, socio-economic group, and family configuration at every life cycle stage. Despite its commonalities, the disease will affect each family system uniquely, depending on the system's resources and limitations.

Much work remains to be done by the nursing profession in the area of alcoholism prevention and health promotion. Anticipatory guidance for parents of very young children might focus on ways that parents, by their attitudes and examples, influence their children's attitudes toward alcohol and other abusive substances.

As recovery from alcoholism becomes more of a reality, nursing intervention can help families rebuild their resources and manage stress, thus making relapse less likely. Working with AA and Al-Anon, nurses can play an important role in helping families avoid the pitfalls of an alcoholic-oriented world on the one hand and a medication-oriented health care system on the other.

REFERENCES

Al-Anon. *Alcoholism: The Family Disease.* New York: Al-Anon Family Group, 1972.

Bandler, R., et al. *Changing with Families.* Palo Alto, Calif.: Science and Behavior Books, 1976.

Bateson, G. "The Cybernetics of 'Self': A Theory of Alcoholism," in *Steps to an Ecology of Mind.* Edited by Bateson, G. New York: Chandler, 1972.

Berenson, D. "Alcohol and the Family System," in *Family Therapy, Theory and Practice.* Edited by Gueris, P. New York: Gardner Press, 1976.

Black, C. *It Will Never Happen to Me.* Denver: M.A.C. (1850 High St.), 1981.

Blades, S. "Alcoholism as a Family Problem," in *Family Health Care, Vol. II: Developmental and Situational Crises.* Edited by Hymovich, D.P., and Barnard, M. New York: McGraw-Hill Book Co., 1979.

Booz-Allen and Hamilton, Inc. *An Assessment of the Needs and Resources for Children of Alcoholic Parents.* Rockville, Md.: National Institute on Alcohol Abuse and Alcoholism, 1974.

Bowen, M. "Alcoholism and the Family System," *Family: Journal of the Center for Family Learning* 20–25, 1973.

Coppersmith, E. I. "The Place of Family Therapy in the Homeostasis of Larger Systems," in *Group and Family Therapy.* Edited by Aronson, M., and Wolberg, R. New York: Brunner-Mazel, 1982.

Deutsch, C. *Broken Bottles, Broken Dreams: Understanding and Helping the Children of Alcoholics.* New York: Teachers' College Press of Columbia University, 1982.

Estes, N.J., et al. *Nursing Diagnosis of the Alcoholic Person.* St. Louis: C.V. Mosby Co., 1980.

Finley, B.G. "The Family and Substance Abuse," in *Substance Abuse: Pharmacologic, Developmental, and Clinical Perspectives.* Edited by Bennett, G., et al. New York: John Wiley & Sons, 1983.

Hanson, K. J., and Estes, N.J. "Dynamics of Alcoholic Families," in *Alcoholism: Development, Consequences, and Interventions.* Edited by Estes, N.J., and Heinemann, M.E. St. Louis: C.V. Mosby Co., 1977.

Heinemann, E., and Estes, N. "Assessing Alcoholic Patients," *American Journal of Nursing* 76(5):786–89, 1976.

Jackson, J. K. "The Adjustment of the Family to the Crisis of Alcoholism," *Quarterly Journal of Studies on Alcohol* 15:562–86, 1954.

Jellinek, E. M. *Disease Concept of Alcoholism.* New Haven, Conn.: United Printing Service, 1960.

Johnson, V. E. *I'll Quit Tomorrow.* New York: Harper & Row, 1973.

McGoldrick, M., and Carter, E. A. "Forming a Remarried Family," in *The Family Life Cycle: A Framework for Family Therapy.* Edited by Carter, E.A., and McGoldrick, M. New York: Gardner Press, 1980.

Miller, S. R., and Winstead-Fry, P. *Family Systems Theory in Nursing Practice,* Reston, Va.: Reston Publishing Co., 1982.

National Council on Alcoholism. "Criteria for the Diagnosis of Alcoholism," *Annals of Internal Medicine* 77:249, *American Journal of Psychiatry* 129:127–35, 1972.

National Nurses' Society on Alcoholism. *The Role of the Nurse in Alcoholism.* New York: National Council on Alcoholism, 1978.

Paolino, T. J., and McCrady, B. S. *The Alcoholic Marriage: Alternative Perspectives.* New York: Grune & Stratton, 1977.

Reed, S.W. "Assessing the Patient with an Alcohol Problem," *Nursing Clinics of North America* 11(3):483–92, 1976.

Steinglass, P. "Experimenting With Family Treatment Approaches, 1950–1975: A Review," *Family Process* 15:97–123, 1976.

Wallace, J. "A Careful Look at Families in Pain and in Recovery," *Human Ecology Forum* 9(3):12–15, 1978.

Wegscheider, S. *Another Chance: Hope and Health for the Alcoholic Family.* Palo Alto, Calif.: Science & Behavior Books, 1981.

Woititz, J. G. *Adult Children of Alcoholics.* Hollywood, Fla.: Health Communications, 1983.

Wright, L.M., and Leahey, M. *Nurses and Families: A Guide to Family Assessment and Intervention.* Philadelphia: F.A. Davis Co., 1984.

APPENDIX A

Definition of Alcoholism

Alcoholism is a chronic, progressive, and potentially fatal disease. It is characterized by tolerance and physical dependency or pathologic organ changes, or both—all the direct or indirect consequences of the alcohol ingested.

• "Chronic and progressive" means that the physical, emotional, and social changes that develop are cumulative and progress as drinking continues.

• "Tolerance" means brain adaptation to the presence of high concentrations of alcohol.

• "Physical dependency" means that withdrawal symptoms occur from decreasing or ceasing consumption of alcohol.

• The person with alcoholism cannot consistently predict on any drinking occasion the duration of the episode or the quantity that will be consumed.

• Pathologic organ changes can be found in almost any organ, but most often involve the liver, brain, peripheral nervous system, and the gastrointestinal tract.

• The drinking pattern is generally continuous but may be intermittent, with periods of abstinence between drinking episodes.

• The social, emotional, and behavioral symptoms and consequences of alcoholism result from the effect of alcohol on the function of the brain. The degree to which these symptoms and signs are considered deviant will depend upon the cultural norms of the society or group in which the person lives.

This definition was prepared by the National Council on Alcoholism/American Medical Society on Alcoholism Committee on Definitions, approved by the National Council on Alcoholism Public Policy Committee on May 10, 1976 and approved by the Executive Committee of the National Council on Alcoholism Board of Directors on June 10, 1976.

Frank A. Seixas, MD, Convenor; Sheila Blume, MD; Luther A. Cloud, MD; Charles S. Lieber, MD; and R. Keith Simpson, DO, DPH; National Council on Alcoholism/American Medical Society on Alcoholism Committee on Definitions

INDEX